INTRODUCING

CHRISTIAN EDUCATION

INTRODUCING

CHRISTIAN EDUCATION

Foundations for the Twenty-first Century

MICHAEL J. ANTHONY

GENERAL EDITOR

Baker Academic
A Division of Baker Book House Co
Grand Rapids, Michigan 49516

Published by Baker Academic
a division of Baker Book House Company
P.O. Box 6287, Grand Rapids, MI 49516-6287

Printed in the United States of America

Library of Congress Cataloging-in-Publication Data

Introducing Christian education : foundations for the twenty-first century / Michael J.
Anthony, general editor.
     p.   cm.
Includes bibliographical references and index.
ISBN 0-8010-2275-4 (cloth)
1. Christian education. I. Anthony, Michael J.
BV1471.3 .I58 2001
268—dc21

00-066737

For information about academic books, resources for Christian leaders, and all new releases available from
Baker, visit our web site:
                              http://www.bakerbooks.com

CONTENTS

Contents

CONTRIBUTORS

Michael J. Anthony is professor of Christian education at Biola University's Talbot School of Theology. He has authored and edited numerous books in the field of Christian education, including *Single Adult Passages: Uncharted Territories*. A former singles pastor, he has spoken to single adult groups at numerous colleges, camps, and Christian conference centers.

Michelle Anthony has served in a variety of ministry positions. She is currently the children's pastor at Coast Hills Community Church in Aliso Viejo, California. She has written extensively for children's ministries, including materials for creative teaching techniques, games, curriculum, and topical studies. She is also a frequent seminar teacher at camps and conferences.

Wesley Black is a professor of youth/student ministries at Southwestern Baptist Theological Seminary in Fort Worth, Texas. In addition to his teaching responsibilities in youth ministry, Wes enjoys playing trombone in his church orchestra, camping out with his family, spending too much time on the Internet, and leading conferences with his wife. He and Sandi have been married over thirty-four years and have two grown children, Clay and Melissa.

Warren S. Benson is emeritus professor of Christian education at Trinity Evangelical Divinity School and also senior professor of Christian education and leadership at The Southern Baptist Theological Seminary. He travels across North America lecturing in the field of Christian education.

Lillian Breckenridge is associate professor of Christian education at Oral Roberts University. She specializes in areas of human growth and family development. She and her husband authored the text *What Color Is Your God?* which explores multicultural issues for ministry leaders.

Mark W. Cannister is associate professor of youth ministries and Christian education at Gordon College in Wenham, Massachusetts. He serves as chair of the Youth Ministries and Missions program as well as chair of the Division of the Humanities. Mark is a veteran of twenty-five years in youth ministry, serving in both church and parachurch organizations. Mark is a frequent consultant to a variety of churches and ministry organizations and is often engaged as a speaker/teacher at camps, conferences, and seminars.

Shelly Cunningham is associate professor of Christian education at Biola University's Talbot School of Theology. She has served in church ministry in a variety of staff positions. She conducts teacher training workshops and speaks for women's groups all across North America. Due to her dynamic and creative presentation skills, she is a speaker in great demand.

James A. Davies is the Cal Pac Eligibility Chair and professor of practical theology and

Christian education at Simpson College and Graduate School in Redding, California.

Dennis Dirks is professor of Christian education and dean of Biola University's Talbot School of Theology. He has held numerous church ministry positions and has spoken on Christian education topics in several foreign countries.

James Riley Estep Jr. is the senior vice president/provost and professor of Christian education at Kentucky Christian College.

James E. Gaffney is the pastor of recovery ministries at Mariners Church in Irvine, California. As a pioneer in the field of church-based recovery ministry, he has served on staff in several churches for over twenty years. While training to become a hospital pharmacist, he became addicted to drugs and alcohol. God delivered him from these addictions, and he has dedicated his life to helping others overcome the effects of abuse and dependency. Jim speaks at seminars and conferences across North America, teaching others how to develop recovery ministries in the local church.

Ken Garland is associate professor of Christian education at Biola University's Talbot School of Theology. He has served as a youth pastor for over twenty years. He is also the founder/president of the Institute for Volunteer Youthworkers (IVY). He serves as a seminar speaker, consultant, and author of numerous journal articles in the area of youth ministry. He also serves on the board of directors for the Center for Conflict Resolution, a nonprofit organization offering legal advice and counsel to churches in Southern California.

Julie Gorman is associate professor of Christian education and spiritual formation at Fuller Theological Seminary. She has authored numerous books on Christian education, including *Community That Is Christian: A Handbook on Small Groups.*

Klaus Issler is professor of Christian education and theology at Biola University's Talbot School of Theology, teaching primarily in the Ph.D. program in educational studies. He is also an adjunct faculty member in the Institute of Spiritual Formation at Biola. He holds degrees in education, theology, and philosophy, specializing in the philosophical and theological foundations of Christian education in Christian spirituality and character formation.

Alvin W. Kuest is professor of practical ministries and chair of the Practical Ministries Division at Great Lakes Christian College in Lansing, Michigan .

Kevin E. Lawson is professor of Christian education and director of the Ph.D. program in educational studies at Biola University's Talbot School of Theology.

Marlene LeFever is the director of ministry resources for Cook Communications. She is one of America's experts in the field of learning styles and their application to instructional methodology in the local church. She has an extensive travel schedule as a conference speaker, consultant, and guest lecturer in colleges and seminaries across North America.

Mary Letterman is the principal of Mariners Christian School in Costa Mesa, California. She is a frequent seminar speaker on the topics of Christian schools, public schools, and homeschooling. She has served on numerous accreditation review committees for the Association of Christian Schools International.

Richard Leyda is associate professor and chair of the Department of Christian Education at Biola University's Talbot School of Theology. He is an avid fisherman and camper as well as a deacon at his church, First Presbyterian Church of Hollywood, California.

Gary Newton is the associate dean of the Graduate School of Christian Ministries and professor of educational ministries at Huntington College. He has taught for over sixteen years at various schools, including Taylor University, Denver Seminary, and Huntington College. In addition to his teaching experience, he has also served a total of twenty years in the local church in various full- and part-time positions, including youth pastor, Christian education pastor, and senior pastor. Presently, Dr. Newton is establishing a Kid's Club ministry to unchurched children in cooperation with about twelve churches in Huntington, Indiana.

Robert W. Pazmiño is the Valeria Stone Professor of Christian Education at Andover Newton Theological School in Newton Centre, Massachusetts.

Ellery Pullman is professor of Christian education at Briercrest Family of Schools in Caronport, Saskatchewan, Canada. In addition to his teaching, Dr. Pullman has also served at Briercrest as the registrar, dean of faculty, and vice president of institutional development. He also serves on the local school board and is a consultant to public school boards in Saskatchewan.

Dave Rahn is professor of educational ministries and director of Huntington College's Link Institute for faithful and effective youth ministry. Before going to Huntington College in 1985, he served in various capacities with Youth for Christ (YFC) for thirteen years. He still volunteers in the local YFC outreach, is senior teaching minister at a Huntington church, and has two high school children of his own.

Jerry Root is associate professor of educational ministries at Wheaton College. He travels across North America as a frequent conference speaker and lecturer, specializing in the life and works of C. S. Lewis.

Mark Edward Simpson is associate dean and Gaines S. Dobbins Associate Professor of Christian Education and Leadership in the School of Christian Education and Leadership at The Southern Baptist Theological Seminary.

Nick Taylor is the pastor of spiritual formation at Coast Hills Community Church in Aliso Viejo, California and lives with his wife, Tana, and their daughter, Madison in Laguna Hills. He has a graduate degree in Christian formation and discipleship from Fuller Theological Seminary. He has served in various pastoral positions since 1982 and has been a national trainer/speaker for Cloud-Townsend Resources since 1997.

Judy Ten Elshof is associate professor of Christian ministry and leadership and the director of the Intentional Character Development program at Biola University's Talbot School of Theology. Her expertise as a teacher and conference speaker is in helping individuals and families in ministry grow in relationship to God and others. She is a staff therapist at the Biola Counseling Center and has also established and directed counseling centers in churches and Christian schools. She is founder and vice president of Hilltop Renewal Center for Christian leaders.

Jonathan N. Thigpen was former president of the Evangelical Training Association in Wheaton, Illinois.

Ted Ward is professor emeritus of educational research and international studies at Michigan State University, and also professor emeritus of Christian education and international studies at Trinity Evangelical Divinity School.

Donald W. Welch is a licensed marriage and family therapist and professor of Christian education and family studies at Mid-America Nazarene University.

Dennis Williams is professor of Christian education and leadership and the dean of the School of Christian Education and Leadership at The Southern Baptist Theological Seminary in Louisville, Kentucky. Before going to Southern Seminary, Dr. Williams was professor of Christian education at Denver Seminary. He is also the executive administrator for the North American Professors of Christian Education.

William "Rick" Yount is professor and department/division chair of Foundations of Education, School of Educational Ministries, at Southwestern Baptist Theological Seminary in Fort Worth, Texas, where he has taught for nineteen years. He is author of *Created to Learn: A Christian Teacher's Introduction to Educational Psychology* (1996) and *Called to Teach: An Introduction to the Ministry of Teaching* (1999).

FOREWORD

We are now entering the new millennium, the twenty-first century, with its many unknowns. Christian education has been at its best when it creatively faced the challenge of unknowns and empowered the church with resources that matched the needs of growing Christians as well as those outside of the faith community.

In the past, Christian education served the mission of the local church, and healthy growth ensued. Let us take a look at just a few historical snapshots as we view the significant contributions of Christian education.

At the close of the eighteenth century, the Sunday school movement emerged. The first Sunday schools began by meeting outside the local churches to focus on the children of the Industrial Revolution and then eventually gave attention to the growing needs of children inside the church. The nineteenth-century cry for meeting the impact of a culture change was answered by the American Sunday School Union. In time, Christian educators proved a valuable resource for not only the church but also public schools.

In the latter part of the 1800s, the development of liberal theology and the questioning of biblical authority again called Christian education workers to mission. Now it was not only the local church that needed to be strengthened but also the leadership in churches. The Bible institutes founded in the late 1800s birthed publishing houses that provided resources to the local leadership in the church, as well as professors in the Bible colleges. The outcome was evangelical Christian education literature that focused on sound spiritual formation and discipleship.

The twentieth century dawned, and societal values were changing. Questions on biblical authority were making inroads in the changing culture as a whole, and character formation needs could no longer be expected to keep in check the devaluation of the Christian message.

Christian educators knew there had to be broadening of partnerships to make a difference. In God's sovereignty, new resources for children and young people were developed to meet this challenge. New publishing houses were born, and they partnered with local churches, Bible colleges, Christian liberal arts colleges, and evangelical seminaries in both the East and the West. As a result, Christian education expanded its vision to the whole of human growth and development. In the 1940s teenagers came into focus. Parachurch organizations partnering with local churches brought creativity to the Christian education of adolescents and young adults.

By the 1970s the Sunday school was revitalized, and a family nurturing strategy emerged to match the human stage of development with a faith complement that strengthened our spiritual formation and development commitment. A new wind of change was blowing, new age designations emerged for young people—Busters, Generation X, Digital Generation—and with them a new attitude. Skepticism has given way to an openness to authenticity. Spiritual issues are now an option, and the "Hope Generation" has come of age with a new opportunity for Christian education in the new millennium.

In this volume my colleague, Dr. Michael Anthony, along with a team of gifted contributors, has responded to new challenges in Christian education with vision and skill. Their passion for a clearly defined spiritual formation strategy is evident throughout. I believe this volume will become a major resource text for church leaders, as well as Christian education leaders who are professors of Christian education. It will be a valuable resource in my personal library. The desired outcome will be Psalm 78:72: "He cared for them with a true heart and led them with skillful hands" (NLT).

Lester C. Blank Jr.

INTRODUCTION

Many new students enter Christian colleges and seminaries, look at the course offerings, and ask, "Just what is Christian education?" Christian education is steeped in misunderstanding and misconception. Part of the reason for this is the multidisciplinary nature of the field. Its foundation is biblical studies and theology but it seeks to integrate them with knowledge that is gleaned from the social sciences: education, sociology, and psychology. Studying Christian education gives us a biblical perspective on how God created us to learn and interact together. With these insights we are able to more strategically fulfill the Great Commission. Some students have asked, "Is Christian education what happens in private Christian schools?" "Is it what happens at church on Sunday mornings?" "Is it what occurs at camp during the summer?" The answer to each of these questions is yes . . . and a lot more.

Christian education is the process by which those who have experienced a personal spiritual rebirth in their relationship with God partner with the indwelling Holy Spirit to grow in the image of Christ. Spiritual formation takes place as individuals study the Word of God and apply what they learn to daily living. It requires lifelong learning and is best accomplished in the context of a caring community that meets periodically in both small groups and large assembly. Small group activities allow for personal accountability whereas larger assemblies facilitate corporate worship, fellowship, prayer, and exercise of spiritual gifts. Once established, the corporate body sends its members out to the local community and to the larger world for the purpose of sharing the gospel with others.

Christian education has its roots firmly planted in the teaching and traditions of the Old Testament. Likewise, the church reveres the sacred Scriptures, esteems the family as a divine institution, and celebrates special days of religious significance. It also seeks to radically alter the path of fallen humanity and reconcile humankind to the Creator.

Christ Jesus himself gave the church its commission to make disciples until the day of his return. Those who have taken up the charge over the past two thousand years have done so with spiritual enthusiasm and Spirit-driven creativity. Some have sought to spread the gospel by traveling to distant lands while others have chosen to remain behind and support their efforts. Those who do the Master's work take his commands seriously by planting new churches, establishing training schools (e.g., catechetical schools, Bible colleges, Christian universities, seminaries) and by looking for creative alternative means to communicate the gospel message (e.g., camps, radio and television programs, Internet sites, publishing companies).

Recently, a plethora of parachurch organizations have sprung up for the purpose of supporting the church by conducting evangelism and discipleship directed at selected age and people groups (e.g., Child Evangelism Fellowship, Youth for Christ, Campus Crusade, Promise Keepers, Concerned Women of America). Recognizing the need for strategic involvement in an increasingly postmodern culture, Christians have engaged in political activities through the development of additional organizations such as the Christian Legal Society and CitizenLink. Christian education has been at the heart of these organizations as they develop intentional strategies for fulfilling the Great Commission.

The twenty-first century is characterized by increased communication, rapid international markets, a global economy, free trade, and multinational relations. These innovations have had a profound impact on the lives of a new generation, but few observers would disagree that they have come with a substantial moral and ethical price tag.

Multiculturalism, naturalism, and relativism have eroded our once moral and ethical system of laws and public education. The challenges facing Christian education in the twenty-first century are to withstand the onslaught of these humanistic philosophies and to educate believers with the absolute truth found only in the Bible. The epistemological basis of our current social values system has eroded the fabric of our society. In the words of the apostle Peter, we must be willing to provide a defense for the hope that lies within us (1 Pet. 3:15).

If Christian education is to withstand the pressures of an ever-increasing secular society, we must stand firm on unwavering biblical truth (Is. 40:8) and teach a postliterate generation what it means to be reconciled to a loving heavenly Father. We must not succumb to the temptation to argue over minor details of methodology but rather keep our eyes focused on the goal of presenting every person complete in Christ (Col. 1:28).

Introducing Christian Education is designed with this purpose in mind. It begins with a broad foundation of theological, historical, and philosophical bases for Christian ministry. From there it considers the contributions within various social sciences such as sociology, anthropology, psychology, and education. Each of these areas is explored through the primary lens of biblical teaching before integrating various secular theories. Not everything that is presented in a secular theory is acceptable to the discerning Christian. However, it is possible to use some of the insights that these fields of empirical research have discovered.

Beyond these chapters is a section dedicated to the organization and administration of ministry within current practice. These principles are certainly not new, nor were they discovered in secular business schools. In fact, once Christian educators explore the teachings of Exodus, Nehemiah, Proverbs, the Gospels, and the Epistles, it becomes abundantly clear that many secular management principles that are touted in MBA programs today actually have their origin in the Bible.

The final two sections of the book deal with applying Christian education theory in the context of various age groups and specialized areas of our population. With this understanding, it is my desire to help ministry leaders design programs that integrate the changing needs of contemporary society with the unchanging truth of God's Word. Truly this is no small challenge.

Introducing Christian Education represents a significant shift in focus from its predecessor, *Foundations of Ministry: An Introduction to Christian Education for a New Generation*. Beyond the obvious need for revision and updating of content, I have also included several chapters that are relevant to our time. Churches today are struggling to find answers for issues related to differences within our generations (chapter 25), singles ministry (chapter 27), recovery ministries (chapter 29), the exploding phenomenon of Christian schools (chapter 30), and contemporary parachurch agencies (chapter 31).

I would like to express my gratitude to those who have helped make this new volume a reality. I have the privilege of calling the majority of the contributors close personal friends. They have given sacrificially of their time to write their respective chapters because they, too, believe in the academic discipline of Christian education. They are giving their lives as professors and practitioners in the field and desire to see others follow knowledgeably in their footsteps.

We would like to dedicate this volume to our many colleagues in the North American Professors of Christian Education. This association, which meets each year, serves as a catalyst for sharing and debating views within our field. Most of the contributors are long-time members of this organization. We look forward to continued fellowship and scholarly interaction in the years ahead.

Michael J. Anthony

PART ONE

Foundations
of Christian Education

HISTORICAL FOUNDATIONS
OF CHRISTIAN EDUCATION   1

Kevin E. Lawson

Christian education can be viewed as an effort to encourage people to gain an authentic relationship with God. A variety of approaches to achieve this end have been employed throughout time. Beginning with the Old Testament, this chapter traces the various formal and informal means developed by God's people to encourage others to grow in their relationship with him. Reading this historical overview will provide the reader with an appreciation for what others have done to facilitate the spiritual formation of God's people.

TEACHING AND LEARNING
IN THE OLD AND NEW TESTAMENTS

Jewish Education before the Exile

Throughout the early history of Israel, the family was the chief educational institution of society. Children learned through informal participation in family life and by parental example. Fathers were to teach their children God's law and a trade to earn a living. Deuteronomy 6:4–9, the *Shema,* presents both the goal and process of education. The people were called to acknowledge and love the one true God and to teach his Word to their children in the daily activities of life. There were no formal schools for the children to attend, but as parents grew in their knowledge of God's law, they

were to teach it to their children and reinforce it through their own example and conversation.

The Levites served as priests for the people, representing them before God in acts of worship and prayer, and as teachers, instructing them in the observance of God's laws. They led the nation in celebrating the various rites, feasts, and festivals that God had decreed. These ceremonies helped the people remember what God had done in the past and provoked curiosity in the children so that they would ask questions and be instructed by their parents. The Feast of Weeks, Feast of Trumpets, Day of Atonement, and other festivals were times for remembering and instructing (Exod. 12:25–27; Lev. 23). For example, the special foods and preparation that preceded Passover served to mark that night as different from all others throughout the year. The children noticed these differences, and their questioning became the opportunity for parents to tell how God had delivered Israel out of Egypt.

Jewish Education after the Exile

Because of Israel's disobedience and unfaithfulness to him, God used the expanding Babylonian empire to send Israel into captivity. Separated from their homeland, the people came to understand the importance of God's law, the *Torah,* and their need to know and obey it. The written Torah included the Law (the Pentateuch), the Prophets (historical and prophetic books), and the Holy

17

Writings (Psalms and wisdom literature). Oral interpretations of the written Torah, the *Mishnah,* were also passed down through the generations.[1]

The scribes were religious leaders who studied and interpreted the law and taught it to the people. Following the exile, synagogues where the Scriptures could be read and explained to the people were established in every village in Palestine. On the Sabbath, the people gathered for the recitation of the Shema, prayer, the reading of the Torah and Prophets, and the blessing. These times of instruction were geared for adults, who in turn were expected to instruct their own children.[2]

With the importance attached to knowing and understanding God's Word, education was highly valued, and the teacher, or *rabbi,* was held in highest esteem within Jewish culture. Education was viewed as a precious privilege because it allowed one to know God better and understand how to live in obedience to him. Over time, people like the Pharisees carefully studied both Scripture and the Mishnah and established rules that served as a hedge to help people keep from violating God's laws. These traditions came to be as binding on the people as Scripture itself.

Teaching and Learning in the New Testament

Compared with the scribes and Pharisees of his day, Jesus' teaching ministry was unique in many ways. First, Jesus taught as one with authority. When he taught Scripture, he gave his own interpretation, not one memorized from the Mishnah or presented on the authority of tradition (Mark 1:22). Second, he taught many people on whom the teachers of his day would not have wasted their time—women, Gentiles, and "sinners." He welcomed children and did not send them away. Third, he taught wherever he went—in the synagogue, in homes, by the sea, on hillsides, wherever the people were. Fourth, he used a wide variety of teaching methods. Object lessons, parables, dialogue, and puns helped people remember what he taught while hiding the truth from those who did not want to understand and respond to it. Finally, Jesus perfectly lived out what he taught, thus providing a model for understanding what it means to love God and our neighbors in our everyday lives. Jesus' ministry of teaching helped prepare his followers to understand the meaning of his life, death, and resurrection (Matt. 28:18–20).

The Book of Acts shows how Christ's disciples began to live out the Great Commission (Acts 2:42; 5:42; 6:2). Almost immediately we see them preaching and teaching concerning Christ's death and resurrection, exhorting people to place their faith in him and receive eternal life. The apostles gave themselves to the task of teaching those who responded to the gospel. Their teaching focused on five areas: (1) the good news of the gospel of Christ; (2) the interpretation of the Hebrew Scriptures in light of Christ's life, death, and resurrection; (3) the confession of faith held by Christians; (4) the teachings of Jesus; and (5) how to live in response to God's love and saving work.[3] Their investment in teaching others helped the church to grow and to become strong, equipped to stand against the persecution that soon came.

So important was this teaching task to the church that the ability to teach was one of the criteria in the selection of church leaders (1 Tim. 3:2). Paul taught that the Holy Spirit gave the gift of teaching to select members of the church in order that they might use this gift to build up the body of Christ (1 Cor. 12; Eph. 4:11–16). This ministry of teaching was not to be taken lightly due to the heavy responsibility of leading others into the truth (James 3:1).

LAYING FOUNDATIONS FOR FAITHFUL LIVING: EDUCATIONAL MINISTRY IN THE EARLY CHURCH

As the church transitioned from the leadership and teaching of the apostles to those who would serve future generations of believers, their educational efforts began to take new forms. What had been a predominantly Jewish movement became increasingly Gentile. Many people became Christians as adults and needed basic instruction in the faith, especially to strengthen and guide them in times of intense persecution.

In the first few centuries after Christ's birth, there was debate and confusion over diverse teachings as doctrinal issues began to be more carefully examined. Apologists were church leaders who wrote in response to persecution and to counter false accusations regarding Christian beliefs. Their works were originally addressed to the Roman emperor but were widely read by church leaders and used to instruct others concerning the faith. Bishops began to teach with doctrinal authority, using their positions to identify and counter heretical teachings. A bishop held the teaching chair or *cathedra* in the major church of a region. He was responsible for educating new converts and instructing and supervising other church leaders.[4]

Catechumenal schools were developed to prepare new converts for baptism. Candidates spent two to three years listening to sermons and being instructed in basic interpretation of Bible doctrine and prayer. The *catechumenoi* ended their training by being baptized.

By the late second century, some of the catechumenal schools began to expand their curriculum to include higher theological training as well as philosophy, logic, and rhetoric. One goal of these *catechetical* or *cathedral schools* was to refute heresy that had crept into the church after the death of the apostles. In A.D. 179 Pantaenus became head of the school in Alexandria, Egypt. To the religious instruction already in place, he added Greco-Roman philosophy and classic literature as well as other academic disciplines. The goal was to equip Christians of all ages and both genders to converse with educated nonbelievers and share the gospel with them. This growing movement exemplified the views of Justin Martyr, a teacher and church leader of the early to mid-second century, who wrote, "Whatever has been uttered aright by any man in any place belongs to us Christians; for, next to God, we worship and love the Logos which is from the unbegotten and ineffable God."[5] Catechetical schools remained a strong influence in Christian education until the fourth century.

In general, Christian educational institutions grew and gained governmental support. Through the fourth and fifth centuries, many church leaders began to consider the kind of education Christians should receive and how it should be carried out. For Gregory of Nyssa, because people were created as rational beings, education was necessary to bring the image of God in humanity to full bloom. John Chrysostom of Constantinople, a renowned preacher, wrote extensively on the responsibilities of parents, especially fathers, to instruct their children in the Christian faith and encourage proper moral conduct.[6] Cyril of Jerusalem developed the curriculum for teaching new converts. His writings in this area were widely circulated and used at other schools throughout the

last half of the fourth century.[7] Augustine of Hippo, a major leader in the early church, wrote on how to teach those coming for catechetical instruction, emphasizing the need for patience, adapting instruction to student needs, and involving the student in the learning process through dialogue.[8] Augustine is also noted for his ideas about the relationship between faith and reason in the Christian life. He believed that reason is a God-given tool to draw people to him but that faith takes precedence when reason struggles to comprehend God's truth. Centuries later, his educational theories and practices became the root for both Lutheran and Counter-Reformation catechetical instruction.[9]

Overall, the educational movement within Christianity continued to grow and flourish through the fourth and into the fifth century, with the catechumenal approach dominating instruction of the laity. However, in the midst of tensions over doctrinal orthodoxy, catechetical schools gained reputations as seedbeds for heresy and came under closer scrutiny. Most dwindled in size and influence during the fifth century, reducing the availability of formal education for prospective clergy. Many clergy members of the late fifth century and following were illiterate, having come into their positions through an apprenticeship model of leadership development without the benefit of formal instruction. Loyalty to the church and its doctrines became more important than extensive education, even in the study of Scripture. Obedience to church hierarchy and tradition characterized the growing institutionalism of the church and the weakening of its educational institutions.[10]

EDUCATION AND THE DESIRE FOR GOD: EDUCATIONAL MINISTRY IN THE MEDIEVAL CHURCH

For many historians, the year 476 marks the end of the old Roman Empire in the West and the beginning of the Middle Ages. For the next thousand years, as various empires and countries rose and fell, the church became the dominant force in Western culture. Most educational efforts of the early church continued but underwent changes in how they were implemented. Society came to rely more heavily on the church for initiative, leadership, and resources for formal education, and it was shaped more thoroughly by the informal educational influences of life under the church's control.

Medieval society was divided into three "estates"—the clergy (priests, monks), who were to pray for all people; the nobility (nobles, knights), who were to govern and protect them; and the commoners (merchants, peasants, laborers), who were to feed them. Formal educational efforts were tailored to the demands of each estate.

Typically, commoners received little formal education. Catechumenal instruction prior to baptism of adult converts was reduced to a ceremonial ritual enacted on behalf of infants at their baptism. In some parish schools, which were descendants of the earlier catechumenal schools, basic instruction was given to commoners in the Ten Commandments, the Seven Deadly Sins, the Seven Cardinal Virtues, the Apostles' Creed, and the Lord's Prayer. Instruction consisted of rote memorization with little opportunity for discussion or asking questions. These were determined to be the basic religious education needs of those in the third estate.[11]

As the power and position of the nobility increased, the education of their young men focused on military skills and tactics, governance, religion, basic reading and writing, sports, proper etiquette, and Latin. In some cases there were further academic studies, but these were generally quite limited. Nobles needed to learn how to govern and fight, so this was the focus of training for those in the second estate. The religious instruction of the nobility addressed many of the same areas as were taught to commoners, but more time was spent in reading and interpreting Scripture. Allegory was the prevailing interpretive concept, with Old Testament stories generally seen as symbolic of New Testament events.[12]

The clergy, both parish and cloistered, made up the third estate. As catechetical schools declined and the monastic movement flourished, education became a major feature of monastic life. Initially, monks were solitary, but communities of learners grew up around respected desert fathers, forming the beginning of communal monastic life. Many of the novices who came to join these cloisters were illiterate and untaught in the basics of Christian faith and practice. Monasteries established schools where those who wanted to join (*interni*) and those from the sur-

rounding community (*externi*) could come and learn reading, writing, arithmetic, prayers, and the Scriptures. This education was designed for those who would serve the church but often benefited others in the community, especially those in the growing merchant class. The quality of instruction varied greatly over the centuries, and many who served the church as parish priests did not receive this kind of preparation.[13]

A major development in the eleventh and twelfth centuries was the growth of cathedral schools and their development into universities. In the universities the curriculum broadened to incorporate the seven liberal arts (*trivium:* grammar, rhetoric, dialectic; *quadrivium:* arithmetic, geometry, music, astronomy), philosophy, canon and civil law, theology, and medicine. These schools served the needs of the church but also the needs of the state and society in the fields of medicine and law.

Where the university system was operating well, there was an increased interest in the use of Aristotelian logic to better support and understand church doctrine. Philosophy was wed to theology, with theology taking precedence and setting the agenda for philosophical inquiry. Teachers such as Anselm (1033–1109), Peter Abelard (1079–1142), Peter Lombard (1095–1160), and Thomas Aquinas (1225–1274) led in this effort, and their approaches and conclusions have continued to exert a powerful influence on studies in philosophy of religion and apologetics.

In the later Middle Ages, some began to challenge this approach, believing that God could be known only by faith, not by logical deduction. To William of Ockham and other nominalists, God was beyond all knowledge. Sensory experience and reason led to knowledge, but God was not accessible to the senses and therefore must be apprehended by faith. Inductive reasoning, rather than deductive, characterized the nominalist movement.[14]

EDUCATION FOR ALL: EDUCATIONAL MINISTRY IN THE REFORMATION AND RENAISSANCE

As the sixteenth century began, radical changes were taking place in Western European society. Politically, there was a growing sense of nationalism and less willingness to submit to the direction of a distant ruler, including the pope. Intellectually, there was a revival in learning from ancient Greek and Roman literature and art, challenging the accepted views of human nature, learning, and theology. Religiously, the corruption of the church and renewed study of Scripture in the original languages provoked calls for reform and a desire to return to a purer faith. Technologically, the invention of the printing press by Johannes Gutenberg in 1450 revolutionized the ability to communicate and aided the dissemination of differing ideas. The privileged position of the church in society, which had lasted one thousand years, was challenged, resulting in both reformation and renewal in Christian education. What follows is a sketch of some of the major movements, leaders, and educational changes of this era.

The Reformers and Christian Education

The Protestant Reformation had a major impact on both formal and nonformal Christian education. Martin Luther, a leader of the Reformation movement in Germany, saw the need for universal mandatory education for all children, not just the rich or those preparing to serve the church. Luther's ideas of the priesthood of the laity and the authority of Scripture called for all people being able to read and study the Bible, not only in the vernacular but also in the original languages.

Luther contributed to nonformal religious education by developing catechisms for instruction of the laity and the clergy, by writing hymns for congregational singing that were instructive in the basics of the Christian faith, and by translating the Bible into German so that the laity could study it. He promoted the development of libraries in schools and the recovery of parental responsibility to train their children in the Christian faith and not leave it to the church.

Other reformers, such as Zwingli (1484–1531) and Calvin (1509–1564) in Switzerland and John Knox (1505–1572) in Scotland, also organized schools and developed catechisms to aid the instruction of children in the faith. Knox also promoted the minister's role as a teacher of children in the Christian faith. Sunday afternoons were to be used for instruction in the catechism by the minister.[15]

There were other Reformation groups, collectively known as Anabaptists, who practiced congregational church polity and rejected infant baptism in favor of believer baptism. This movement included Hutterites, Mennonites, Baptists, Amish, and some Puritans. Because of the severe persecution they received at the hands of Catholics, Lutherans, and Calvinists, their educational efforts and times of corporate worship were based in the home. They also were more open than other groups to women serving as teachers.[16]

The Jesuits and the Counter-Reformation

One response within the Roman Catholic Church to the "Protestant rebellion" was to reexamine and improve their own educational efforts. Ignatius of Loyola (1491–1556) is known both for his influence on the spiritual direction movement and for founding the Jesuits, or Society of Jesus. Ignatius developed a leader's manual for those seeking to guide others in reflective exercises that would help them open up to God's cleansing and refining work. His *Spiritual Exercises* were to be carried out over a period of thirty days, involving times of solitude and conversation with the spiritual director.

In an effort to help with the reform of the church and the education of youth in the Roman Catholic faith, Ignatius established the Jesuits as a missionary and educational arm of the church. It was designed along a militaristic structure and offered some of the best education available at the time. Jesuit leaders studied the craft of teaching and utilized proven educational methods, regardless of where they came from. A major strength of this movement was the attention paid to the development of the teachers; new teachers required one year of internship and two more years of supervised teaching. Jesuit teachers were skilled in the use and supervision of dialog, debate, speeches, and games. Students ages ten to eighteen spent five hours a day in academic study and two hours in games and physical exercises. Jesuit colleges and universities were established all over the world and continue to the present day.[17]

Comenius and the New Educational Movement

One of the major educational leaders of this time was Jon Amos Comenius (1592–1670), a Moravian bishop and teacher. Comenius spent most of his life as a refugee from his homeland due to persecution by the Roman Catholic Church. He established and ran schools in Poland, Sweden, and Hungary, wrote about sound educational practice, and developed curricular materials. He sought to use education to shape and nurture the human soul and help it find solutions to the world's ills. His educational theories and methods were well received, and his influence on education extended throughout Europe and to the American colonies. He is rightly called the Father of Modern Education.

Other educators such as Francis Bacon and Étienne Bonnot de Condillac helped to promote the inductive learning approach and developed the scientific method. In the eighteenth century, educators such as Pestalozzi, Herbart, Froebel, and Rousseau took Comenius's optimistic view of human nature a step further. They denied any limiting factors due to original sin and saw education as the means by which the innate goodness of human nature might be encouraged and nurtured, countering the damaging influence of a corrupt human society. Their goal in education was not the acquisition of information but growth in character and the ability to use knowledge toward moral and ethical ends.[18]

In all, this period saw the recovery of the study of the Bible and submission to its authority in faith and practice, a growth in public education and literacy among both genders, an increase in availability of books and other literature, the development of catechisms for instructing children and adult converts, and a renewed emphasis on the role of parents to instruct and nurture their children in the Christian faith.

PIETISM AND THE GROWTH OF PARACHURCH AGENCIES: MODERN EDUCATIONAL MINISTRY

Even as universal education began to be promoted throughout Europe, there were other movements that influenced the nature of Christian education during the early modern era (eighteenth and nineteenth centuries). The growth of the German Pietist movement, the Industrial Revolution, revivalism, the parachurch movement, and a renewed understanding of the influence of parental modeling all contributed to the changing scene.

Pietism and Revivalism

The Anabaptist traditions continued to encourage growth in nonformal religious instruction through small group Bible study and by incorporating spiritual development into the goals of academic instruction. Philipp Jacob Spener (1635–1705), a German Pietist, emphasized both devotion and doctrine in his educational efforts. He helped revitalize catechetical instruction to focus on genuine spiritual experience and not just memorization of a creed. He also promoted small group Bible study led by clergy and laity alike. One of his students, August Herman Francke (1663–1737), also promoted small group Bible study and developed schools for orphans and poor children where both their minds and hearts could be cultivated.[19]

Nikolaus Ludwig Zinzendorf (1700–1760), the founder of the Moravians, attended Francke's school. In later years, Zinzendorf provided sanctuary to the Moravians from Bohemia, established schools similar to Francke's, and promoted education for all, even parents. Primary to Zinzendorf was the development of a student's walk with Christ, a genuine faith experience that gave life to the doctrine that was taught. Memorization of content was discouraged in favor of a personalized understanding and appropriation of what was being learned.

John Wesley (1703–1791) was influenced by the Moravians. He too focused much of his early educational efforts on children and helped establish schools where parents were expected to give spiritual instruction at home and support the school's efforts as well. As Wesley began to do evangelistic preaching, he promoted the development of small groups to encourage spiritual growth and provide accountability, encouraging participants to share their spiritual struggles and victories and to spur one another on to greater holiness.[20]

Industrialization, Revivalism, and the Parachurch Movement

Industrialization during the seventeenth and eighteenth centuries had a tremendous impact on society. Young people flocked to the cities for jobs. In so doing, they left behind the influence of home and church. With six-day workweeks and child labor a common practice, many poor children had little opportunity for education, and young men had little time for church involvement. Concern for their spiritual and moral state among business leaders and pastors soon grew.

As early as 1632, merchants in London formed associations composed of apprentices who met early on Sunday mornings for "prayer and religious conversation." By the early 1700s, many religious societies for young men were springing up in urban areas of England for prayer, Scripture reading, and encouragement in righteous living. These kinds of religious societies also developed in university settings. John Wesley was part of such a group at Oxford in 1729.[21]

Beginning about 1720, the Great Awakening, a series of spiritual revivals, spread through England and America. This movement emphasized a religious conversion experience and a call to holy living. As people responded, educational ministry efforts benefited in two ways. First, there were more people looking for opportunities to join with others in Bible study, fellowship, and mutual encouragement. Second, there were more people recognizing a call to serve others, to teach and preach the gospel, and to encourage the spiritual growth of converts. Leaders of this revival movement, such as Jonathan Edwards (1703–1758), promoted the establishment of schools to train people for ministry. Denominational colleges, such as Princeton, Brown, and Dartmouth, were founded to serve this need. A similar pattern occurred during the Second Great Awakening in the early 1800s.[22]

As people were impacted by this revival movement, many became concerned for the physical, social, and spiritual needs of others around them. Many laypeople began looking outside their churches for ways to bring the gospel to bear on the needs of society. This fueled the growth of parachurch ministries, including the Sunday school and the Young Men's Christian Association (YMCA).

Robert Raikes (1736–1811), a newspaper publisher and social activist, began the Sunday school in Gloucester, England, in 1780. The initial purpose of these schools was to provide literacy and spiritual training to children who were working in the factories. Their only day off from work was Sunday, and there was no other educational opportunity available for them. The first schools were for children ages six to fourteen. The school ran from 10:00 A.M. to 5:00 P.M. and included reading from the Bible, catechism, and worship attendance. Discipline was strict, and the teachers were paid. At first, many church and community leaders were not supportive of Raikes's efforts, fearing a growing dissatisfaction of the working class and violating the Sabbath. However, with the support of businessmen like William Fox, the Sunday school grew in popularity. In 1785 the Sunday School Society was formed, followed in 1803 by the Sunday School Union, which promoted the spread of the schools and the development of curricular and training materials.[23]

Christian Nurture versus Revivalism

By the mid-1800s, the Second Great Awakening had been going on for several decades. One of the outgrowths of this movement had been the tendency for some churches and parents to neglect the spiritual instruction and nurture of their children due to their understanding of human depravity. Instead, they relied on the work of the Holy Spirit in revivals to bring their children to faith in Christ through a radical conversion experience. Horace Bushnell (1802–1876), a pastor in Connecticut, challenged this practice. Based on his understanding of a Christian's covenant relationship with God and the organic unity of the family, he championed a view that "the child is to grow up a Christian and never know himself as being otherwise."[24] From Bushnell's perspective, children of Christians should be encouraged to exercise faith in Christ from the earliest age and learn from the example of their parents how to live the Christian life. If this was done well, by God's grace these children would not need a radical conversion experience later in life because their faith would have grown through a gradual process. While quite controversial at the time, Bushnell's views have had a tremendous impact on the present understanding and practice of children's ministry (see chapter 22 for further discussion of this topic).

THE AMAZING TWENTIETH CENTURY: DRAMATIC GROWTH IN CHRISTIAN EDUCATION MINISTRIES

As the nineteenth century drew to a close, there were different movements that added to a growing renewal and expansion of the church's educational ministry. The missions movement of the late 1800s encouraged the development of Bible institutes and colleges for training young adults to evangelize and disciple others in the faith. Within public education religious instruction became minimal, causing church leaders to consider how they might provide biblical and theological instruction to their children and youth. Some church leaders began to experiment with ways of using children's free time to provide moral and religious instruction, including the first organized Christian camping experiences.

Early Twentieth Century

As the new century began, these concerns and experiments focused the attention of educators and church leaders alike on the educational ministry needs of church and society. In 1903 a convention was held in Chicago at which the Religious Education Association was formed. Under the leadership of people like William Rainey Harper and George Albert Coe, this group promoted sound educational work in the church and religious education in the public schools. It served as a rallying center for people concerned with moral and religious educational efforts of all kinds.

Within a few years, colleges were offering programs in religious education, and churches were hiring staff members to oversee their educational ministry efforts. These directors of religious education provided professional educational leadership in much the same way that a principal led a school—guiding curriculum development, staffing and staff training, facilities development, and program leadership. This marked the dawning of a new era for the Christian education professional and the dramatic expansion of the church's educational ministries.

One educational ministry innovation of the early twentieth century was the Vacation Bible School (VBS). While some efforts along these lines had been tried out in various cities in the United States before, Robert G. Boville launched the modern VBS movement in 1901 in New York City. During the summer months, when many children had little to occupy their time, Boville set up Bible schools taught by college students where the children participated in worship, Bible instruction, crafts, and recreational activities.

While most VBS programs today run one week and are staffed by church volunteers, these schools lasted four to six weeks and were led by paid staff. By 1922 there were approximately five thousand VBS programs in operation, and by 1949 the number had grown to over sixty-two thousand.[25] Today, churches all over North America utilize some form of VBS in their ministry with children.

Late Twentieth Century

As the century drew to a close, there were many changes and initiatives in educational ministry. The success of many child and youth parachurch organizations stirred church leaders to revitalize their own ministry with youth. Youth pastors were hired to lead in developing ministries modeled after those of groups like Young Life and Youth for Christ. Colleges and seminaries began to offer youth ministry majors, and curriculum publishing companies pumped out a wealth of resources to support these efforts. As baby boomers began raising their own families, demands for top-quality children's ministries increased, leading many churches to hire children's ministry directors. Professional organizations, programs in Christian higher education, training conventions, curriculum resources, and professional magazines have mushroomed for children's and youth ministries. Never before has so much been available to support those who minister to children or youth.

Adult ministries have also seen a number of innovations and developments. Single adult and small group ministries have been popular for several decades, providing informal times for fellowship, Bible study, caring, and prayer. Men's ministries have seen a resurgence, with Promise Keepers a prime example of the attempt to encourage men to grow spiritually. The combination of large group rallies and small support groups in the church is one model being used to reach and teach men.

Other educational ministry emphases during this time include: (1) the growth of short-term missions experiences where youth and young adults work to serve others and encourage their own spiritual growth; (2) the growth of the homeschooling movement with many Christians opting to teach their own children, including biblical studies as part of their curriculum; (3) the "seeker-sensitive" church ministry phenomenon, bringing more adults to the church who have little or no biblical knowledge and are in need of learning the basics of the Christian faith; (4) the growth of church-based day care and preschools serving congregational and community needs; (5) a growing use of Sunday school and other church settings for parent training classes and marriage enrichment efforts; and (6) the cell-church movement, which utilizes small groups for instruction and spiritual growth and challenges the use of traditional educational models such as age-graded Sunday school classes and large adult classes. The face of Christian education in the evangelical church has become more diverse, with many methods being employed toward the same goals.

Entering the Twenty-First Century

As this overview of the history of Christian education comes to a close, it is important to look at some of the developing trends and opportunities the church faces at the beginning of the twenty-first century. First, the profession of Christian education itself is splitting into a variety of more focused educational ministry areas, including youth ministry, children's ministry, family ministry, and others. Colleges and seminaries are responding to this demand, offering more focused programs of study than in the past. Second, advances in computer technology and the Internet are just beginning to be explored for educational ministry purposes. Third, the rapid growth of Christian music and other media is impacting the Christian culture, providing different kinds of resources for aiding instruction and encouraging spiritual growth. Fourth, the secularization of North American society has accelerated, causing many parents to desire church ministries that strengthen the family and provide distinctly Christian instruction for their children. Christian private schools and homeschooling continue to grow, creating unique challenges for churches attempting to serve both the needs of children from public school and Christian/homeschool backgrounds.

Some of the challenges we face are new, but many of the basic needs in Christian education have not changed. People still need to hear and respond to the good news of salvation in Jesus Christ and to learn how they can know God and follow him in their daily lives. We, like church leaders throughout the past two thousand years, need to be clear on our purpose and creative in our design of educational strategies and use of methods that promote the knowledge of God and a growing relationship with him. Those who have come before us have accomplished much that we can learn from.

NOTES

1. Lewis Joseph Sherrill, *The Rise of Christian Education* (New York: Macmillan, 1944), p. 33.
2. Ibid., pp. 44–47.
3. Ibid., pp. 144–51.
4. James E. Reed and Ronnie Prevost, *A History of Christian Education* (Nashville: Broadman and Holman, 1993), pp. 77–78.
5. Cited in D. Bruce Lockerbie, ed., *A Passion for Learning: The History of Christian Thought on Education* (Chicago: Moody, 1994), p. 49.
6. Reed and Prevost, *History of Christian Education*, pp. 95–97.
7. Harold W. Burgess, *Models of Religious Education* (Wheaton: Victor, 1996), pp. 35–36.
8. Augustine, "The First Catechetical Instruction," in *St. Augustine on Education,* ed. George Howie (South Bend, Ind.: Gateway Editions, 1969), pp. 279–97.
9. Kenneth O. Gangel and Warren S. Benson, *Christian Education: Its History and Philosophy* (Chicago: Moody, 1983), pp. 100–104.
10. Sherrill, *Rise of Christian Education,* pp. 211–15.
11. Ibid., p. 239.
12. Barbara W. Tuchman, *A Distant Mirror: The Calamitous Fourteenth Century* (New York: Ballantine, 1978), p. 60.
13. Sherrill, *Rise of Christian Education,* p. 263
14. Reed and Prevost, *History of Christian Education,* pp. 137–39.
15. Clarence H. Benson, *A Popular History of Christian Education* (Chicago: Moody, 1943), p. 83.
16. Reed and Prevost, *History of Christian Education,* pp. 199–200.
17. Ibid., pp. 205–7.
18. Ibid., p. 250.
19. Gangel and Benson, *Christian Education,* pp. 174–80.
20. Ibid., pp. 260–61.
21. H. S. Ninde, J. T. Bowne, and Erskine Uhl, eds., *Young Men's Christian Association Handbook* (New York: YMCA, 1892), pp. 30–34.
22. Reed and Prevost, *History of Christian Education,* pp. 303–5.
23. C. B. Eavey, *History of Christian Education* (Chicago: Moody, 1964), pp. 222–29.
24. Horace Bushnell, *Christian Nurture* (New York: Charles Scribner and Co., 1861), p. 10.
25. Eavey, *History of Christian Education,* pp. 348–51.

PHILOSOPHICAL FOUNDATIONS OF CHRISTIAN EDUCATION   2

Warren S. Benson

THE PHILOSOPHICAL LADDER

The philosophical foundations of Christian education are derived from systematic theology, which in turn emerges from biblical theology. For many years of teaching, I have utilized the philosophical ladder constructed by Norman DeJong (see figure 2.1). The first and most fundamental rung, the Basis of Authority, is Holy Scripture. The Word of God is the "basis upon which all thinking rests."[1] A high view of Scripture is the Christian educator's ultimate frame of reference. A high view is one that accords with Christ's view of the Bible. Jesus said, "I tell you the truth, until heaven and earth disappear, not the smallest letter, not the least stroke of a pen, will by any means disappear from the Law until everything is accomplished" (Matt. 5:18). In John 10:35 the Savior states unequivocally, "The Scripture cannot be broken" and in John 17:17, "Sanctify them by the truth; your word is truth."

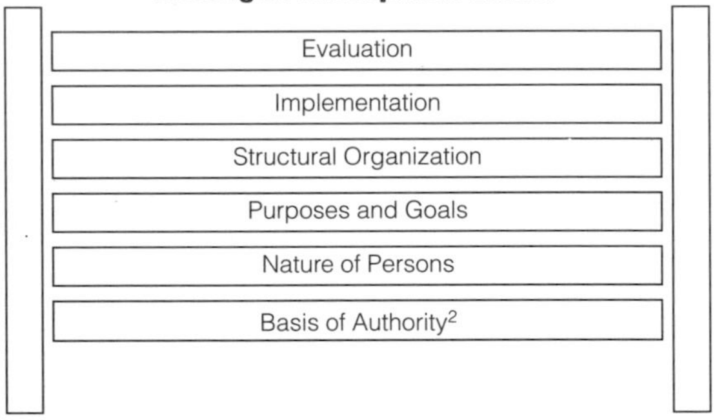

The second rung is the Nature of Persons—what and who people are, which is explicated in Scripture. The third rung, Purposes and Goals, is based on theology, for theological constructs give direction to goals, purposes, and objectives. Rungs four through six are: Structural Organization, Implementation, and Evaluation.

James Wilhoit closes this discussion with clarity when he states that the study of theology is crucial to a broad and comprehensive understanding of Christian education. He states,

Figure 2.1
DeJong's Philosophical Ladder

| Evaluation |
| Implementation |
| Structural Organization |
| Purposes and Goals |
| Nature of Persons |
| Basis of Authority[2] |

Often Christian education has been accused of drifting far from orthodox theological teaching, particularly in regard to the Christian view of human nature and spiritual growth. This drifting is unfortunate, for Christian education is lost unless grounded in biblically based teaching. No matter how much zeal a Christian educator may have, it is of little use without an awareness of the essential theological underpinning of the faith.[3]

A DEFINITION OF CHRISTIAN EDUCATION

Several evangelicals have attempted to formulate a biblical definition of Christian education. Certainly one of the most satisfying is formulated by Robert Pazmiño. He leans heavily on the work of his former professor at Columbia University, Lawrence Cremin. Cremin defined "education broadly as the deliberate, systematic, and sustained effort to transmit, evoke, or acquire knowledge, attitudes, values, skills, or sensibilities, as well as any learning that results from that effort, direct or indirect, intended or unintended."[4]

Pazmiño thus defines Christian education as the

> deliberate, systematic, and sustained divine and human effort to share or appropriate the knowledge, values, attitudes, skills, sensitivities, and behaviors that comprise or are consistent with the Christian faith. It fosters the change, renewal, and reformation of persons, groups, and structures by the power of the Holy Spirit to conform to the revealed will of God as expressed in the Old and New Testaments and preeminently in the person of Jesus Christ, as well as any outcomes of that effort.[5]

In effect, then, Christian education is the work of the church, the Christian home, the Christian school, and Christians in whatever societal setting they find themselves.

The home should be viewed as the primary agency of Christian education. As the companion agency, the church's programs, structures, and ministries should flow from biblical principles. The evangelical does not view the Bible as an educational handbook per se, but its principles will always be contemporary and relevant because they are transcultural when adapted properly. Such a construct should not be seen as disregarding the insights that may be gained from secular education or other disciplines bearing on the process. All truth is God's truth wherever it may be found. This is particularly appropriate of the social sciences, which enrich our understanding of Christian education. In essence, we examine the findings presented to us from the social sciences through the primary lens of Scripture (see figure 2.2).

Metaphysics is the most speculative and abstract area of philosophy. It inquires about the nature of ultimate reality. Ontology is the branch of metaphysics that investigates reality, and cosmology is the branch that studies the origin and

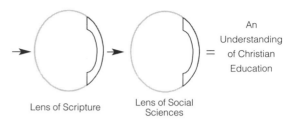

Figure 2.2
Areas of Systematic Philosophy

Lens of Scripture → Lens of Social Sciences = An Understanding of Christian Education

structure of the universe. Therefore, theology serves as the basis for these inquiries and further illuminates these concerns, including education, from God's perspective.

Epistemology presents the theory of knowing and knowledge and therefore is closely related to teaching and learning. It probes questions such as "What is knowledge?" and "How do we learn?" While metaphysics attempts to establish the content of our knowledge, epistemology discloses the process of knowing. Revelation is one of the oldest and major theories of knowing. It is the Bible that reveals God's constructs of metaphysics, epistemology, and axiology.

Empiricism is subsumed under the epistemological umbrella, for it develops the quest for knowledge on the foundation of experience and observation. Empiricists agree that knowledge "originates in sensory experience of the environment and that ideas are formed on the basis of observed phenomena."[6]

Axiology is concerned with values and aesthetics that prescribe what is good and right. The categories of ethics and aesthetics are subsumed under axiology. Ethics is the philosophical study of moral values in the dimensions of beauty and art. Scripture stands as the impregnable source of knowledge. While it certainly does not address all issues, where it does enter the arena of judgment it speaks with finality. Hence, Christian education is understandably absorbed with how values are formed with all age groups and how these values may be encouraged with biblically consistent behavior as the result.

As the following chart illustrates, our metaphysical and epistemological beliefs and commitments are crucial to the formation of our axiological judgments. The formulation of all three adjudications—metaphysical, epistemological, and axiological—rests firmly on the Bible. When these beliefs emerge and are consistent with our scriptural convictions, we are on the way to building a Christian philosophy of education.[7]

George Knight has cited seven hallmarks of a Christian epistemology. In a slightly adapted form, they are:

1. The biblical perspective is that all truth is God's truth. Therefore, the distinction between sacred and secular truth is a false dichotomy.
2. The truth of Christian revelation is true to what actually exists in the universe. Therefore, the Christian can pursue truth without the fear of ultimate contradiction.
3. Forces of evil seek to undermine the Bible, distort human reasoning, and lead individuals to rely on their own inadequate and fallen selves in the pursuit of truth.
4. We have only a relative grasp of the absolute truths in the universe. In other words, while God can know absolutely, Christians can know absolutes in a relative sense. Thus, there is room for Christian humility in the epistemological enterprise.
5. The Bible is not concerned with abstract truth. It always sees truth as related to life. Therefore, *knowing* in the biblical sense is applying perceived knowledge to one's daily life and experience.
6. The various sources of knowledge available to the Christian—the special revelation of Scripture and the person of Jesus Christ, the general revelation of the natural world, and reason—are complementary and should be used in light of the biblical pattern.
7. Given the unity of truth, the acceptance of a Christian epistemology cannot be separated from the acceptance of a Christian metaphysics and vice versa. The acceptance of any metaphysical-epistemological configuration is a faith choice, and it necessitates a total commitment to a way of life.[8]

JOHN DEWEY'S REVOLUTION IN EDUCATIONAL THOUGHT

At least two revolutionary events took place in 1859. First, Charles Darwin's *The Origin of Species* was published. Its impact is felt in almost every educational discipline. Second, and possibly as important as Darwin's volume, was the birth of John Dewey, who without question was the most influential educator in North America during the twentieth century.

For fifty years, process theologian Randolph Crump Miller has been urging that someone has to make a Christian out of John Dewey, by which

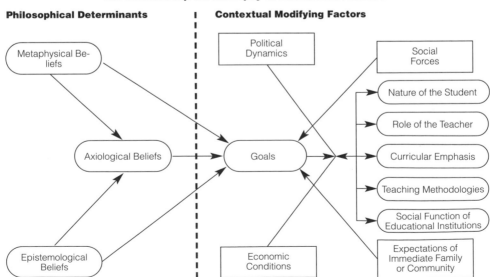

Figure 2.3
The Relationship of Philosophy to Educational Practice

he means that some of Dewey's best educational ideas should be harnessed to good theology. Miller wrote two books to attempt that feat himself—first as a neoorthodox theologian in *The Clue to Christian Education* (1950) and then as a process theologian in *A Theory of Christian Education Practice* (1980). To the evangelical, they have not made the grade.

The following discussion is not another attempt to solve that dilemma. But with this volume coming shortly after the close of an amazing century, Dewey deserves to be adequately recognized and, hopefully, fairly evaluated with grace and a firm biblical hand.

John Dewey's mother was a committed Christian who probably pushed her son too intensely about becoming a follower of Jesus Christ. She expected him to memorize Scripture and follow biblical teaching. Dewey recalls that the religion of his childhood "centered about sin and being good" and on the love of Jesus Christ "as savior from sin."9

As John grew older, his mother would frequently ask him, "Are you right with Jesus? Have you prayed to God for forgiveness?" John Dewey did teach Sunday school and later became president of Christian Endeavor, his church's young people's group. (Possibly the most extensive discussion of his religious convictions, or lack of same, are found in Steven C. Rockefeller's biography, *John Dewey: Religious Faith and Democratic Humanism.*10)

It is safe to say that Dewey never personally espoused an evangelical faith. His biographer also asserts that after he used the term *God* in "My Pedagogic Creed," this would be the "last time that Dewey would employ that word in a positive fashion in his own philosophical vocabulary for almost forty years, i.e., until the publication of *A Common Faith* in 1934."11

Democracy, experimentalism, and instrumentalism are then seen as some of the major concepts and designations by which Dewey's educational philosophy is known. They are the "ideal values that lie at the heart of Dewey's mature philosophy and personal unifying moral faith."12 Dewey viewed the school as a miniature community or embryonic society, in effect, a democracy. School is the indispensable laboratory, the testing ground, for both society and the building of a philosophy of education. In the school both individual and social problems are solved. It is the process of reconstructing the educational experience. To understand Dewey is to comprehend the way of naturalism, in which there is no place for God or supernaturalism.

Metaphysics

Traditional philosophies of education have always built their whole philosophical structure on a metaphysical base. Dewey took violent exception with this practice. Being primarily a naturalist, he cared little for "religious prejudice," which Dewey believed was the "molding factor of most metaphysics." Dewey asserted that natural science is forced by its own development to abandon the assumption of permanence and to recognize that process is the great universal.

Experimentalists view our Christian metaphysical base as nonverifiable because it cannot be exclusively tested in human experience. In a strict rejection of any kind of supernaturalism, Dewey rests humanity's purpose and possibility of survival upon people's relationship to nature.13

Epistemology

Dewey's pragmatic position leaves no room for absolute truth because his concept of truth was extremely relativistic. All knowledge to an experimentalist must be "considered temporary and conditional. Indeed, the word truth is an equivocal term that is hazardous to use in experimental theory.... To overcome this hazard, the qualifying adjective *tentative* is customarily placed before the word *truth*.... The point is labored at some length here because it is a crucial figure of experimentalist epistemology."14

To Dewey and his colleagues, an idea or construct is not true due to failure to prove or correspond to reality. Rather, reality serves in a utilitarian way and thereby assists the organism in adjusting to its natural environment. Pragmatists use the scientific method to solve problems. Dewey equated learning with problem solving. His stance on truth is a deliberate and substantial departure from that of Scripture.

In Scripture, truth is characterized by both qualitative and quantitative aspects. In the Old Testament, truth is equated with personal veracity and historical factuality. Truth is a fundamental characteristic of statements from the Lord

(John 1:17). In Romans 1:18, Paul indicates that truth is the message that humanity represses and has exchanged (1:25) for a lie due to their willingness and failure to worship the Creator God. As Christian educators, we belong to Jesus, who is truth (John 1:14, 17; 1 John 3:19). We who are of God know the Spirit of truth and are equipped to discern it from the spirit of error (1 John 4:6).

Axiology

After seminary, the first church in which I served as minister of education was in Winnetka, Illinois. At about the same time, a disciple of Dewey was offered the superintendency of the elementary and middle schools of Winnetka. This man, Carleton Washburne, developed what became known internationally as the Winnetka Plan. Washburne demanded absolute adherence to Dewey's experimentalist philosophy of education by administrators and teachers.

Van Cleve Morris, Young Pai, and Edward H. Reisner state categorically that

> Experimentalism . . . has spent by far the most time and energy on the problem of value. The philosophies previously considered have concerned themselves principally with ontology and metaphysics, spinning out from those bases their associated doctrines in epistemology and ethics. . . . The experimentalist has been indifferent to the problems of being or metaphysics and has confined his interest . . . to the analysis and description of experience, particularly to the problems of knowing and conduct—to the conceptions of truth and goodness.[15]

Again, we should be reminded of the pragmatists' penchant for relativism. Interestingly, in Winnetka, Illinois, seventy years later you may still observe the vestiges of the Washburne era. We are reminded of Morris and Pai's questions: "How, one might ask, can so scientifically oriented philosophy address itself systematically to value, the age-old renegade from science? Science can tell us what is true, but can it tell us anything about what is good? Science can give us knowledge, but can it tell us what we ought to do or what we ought to be like?"[16]

Progressivism

The English sociologist Herbert Spencer won a prize with his 1856 essay titled, "What Knowledge Is of Most Worth?" He contended that science was of the greatest value. As a result, the disciplines of music, art, history, and literature were demoted on the scale of value in the curriculum of many schools. At Yale, William Graham Sumner utilized Spencer's optimistic evolutionary worldview into the 1890s, when the United States was grasping for identity and direction. Frontier and rural America were in the throes of a national change to urbanization and industrialization. Rockefeller states that it was the emergence of the "Progressive movement as a political force at the turn of the century that lifted the nation out of its confusion and gave it a new sense of confidence and direction."[17]

The progressives were exemplified by Jane Addams (of Hull House fame in Chicago) and John Dewey. They embraced Darwin but rejected the social Darwinism of Spencer and Sumner. A new faith in the social sciences and social planning gained a foothold in the early years of the new century. Rockefeller says that "by 1894, his [Dewey's] psychological, ethical, social, and religious thought had come to a focus around the problems of individual self-realization and freedom, democratic social reconstruction, and the scientific search for practical truth including moral value. These three issues were closely connected in his mind."[18]

In 1903 the Religious Education Association (REA) held its inaugural meeting in Chicago. University of Chicago President William Rainey Harper convened the congress, which three thousand attended. John Dewey gave a lecture at the REA congress. It centered on the ideas of the Progressive Education Association and the progressive movement. In the overall context of the time, the national mood and attitudes as well as the evangelical wing of Christian education began to change, becoming more defensive in its stance.

In the public school domain, the Progressive Education Association established its own principles:

1. Children should be free to develop naturally.
2. Interest, arising from direct experience, is the best stimulus for learning.
3. The teacher should be a researcher into educational processes and a guide to learning.

4. There should be close cooperation between the school and the home.
5. The Progressive school should be a laboratory for educational reform and experimentation.[19]

As one can readily observe, the powerful handprint of John Dewey was evident in these principles. From a traditional role of lecture plus object lessons and other visuals, evangelicals slowly began to change their instructional methodologies and style.

Horace Mann

No two men have influenced American public education as have John Dewey and Horace Mann. Mann is sometimes regarded as the founder of the public school system. While a collegian he had turned to the writings of John Locke, who argued that almost all knowledge comes through experiential perceptions. Horace Mann came to consider Calvinism as sectarian, and he embraced Unitarianism. Believing that religion was moralism and not piety, he was committed to humankind's perfectibility through the process of education.

Mann promoted a policy of introducing "non-sectarian" religion into the public schools. In the 1830s America's cities and towns were still religious, homogeneous communities. Mann became the educational secretary of the state of Massachusetts and the editor of the *Common School Journal* in 1837. The *Journal* had an exceptional influence over public school mentality. Henry Barnard's *Connecticut Common School Journal* was its only competitor. With his preference for natural religion over revealed theology, Mann slowly removed Christianity from the public schools.

In the early twentieth century, the immigration factor and a burgeoning industrialization and urbanization produced staggering public education demands. John Dewey was certainly one of the chief theorists and formulators of the new patterns. Dewey advanced the concept that the school is the central agency for making sense out of life for the young. As we have already seen, he was not a Christian and was inexorably moving in another direction. However, he was of the opinion that his vision was religious even though, in essence, it opposed the Christian religion.

CONTEMPORARY PHILOSOPHICAL THEORIES OF EDUCATION

Essentialism

Rejecting much of progressivism, the essentialists insisted that education should transmit a core of knowledge and skills from past generations to our contemporary children. In addition, this knowledge and information should be arranged cumulatively and sequentially in a well-constructed and organized curriculum.

A discipline for mastering lessons should be favored over an undisciplined and ambiguous freedom to learn, and yet students should be engaged in individual experiences. The legacy of what past generations had learned should be prized. Essentialists charged progressives and experimentalists with worshiping the existential present. Therefore, the essentialists gave precedence to reading, writing, and arithmetic in curricular endeavors. The essentialists were quick to point out that children in countries whose educational philosophy was similar to theirs scored higher in national examinations in comparison with American children in the basic content areas. The debate still rages today.

Perennialism

Following the Aristotelian concept that people are rational beings, perennialists maintain that the main function of a school is to produce students who are growing intellectually. Like the essentialists, a prescribed body of knowledge is judged to be of the greatest value and should be imparted because its principles are lasting and continuing. Their classical progenitors are Aristotle and Thomas Aquinas. The twentieth century's exemplars were Robert M. Hutchins, Mortimer Adler, Jacques Maritain, and Allan Bloom.

The former president of the University of Chicago, Robert Hutchins, contended that the real purpose of education was to be the same in any time or place but also averred that: (1) education implies teaching; (2) teaching implies knowledge; (3) knowledge is truth; and (4) since the truth is everywhere the same, education should also be everywhere the same.[20] Hence, Hutchins and Adler desired to utilize established and universally recognized literature in recasting the curriculum at the University of Chicago in the 1930s and 1940s.

Reconstructionism

The early stage of the progressive education movement closely related educational reform to social reform. By the 1920s, however, the emphasis on social reform in progressive education was beginning to subside and was being eclipsed by the child-centered orientation that was actually part of the original progressive scheme. Social reconstructionists were attempting to build an ideal and more just social order. Therefore, these educators utilized the findings and methods of social sciences such as economics, sociology, psychology, and anthropology in determining content and methods for the public schools.[21]

Reconstructionists are committed to establishing a new society that demands the deliberate changing of the so-called obsolete ideas and values of traditional education. The late Paulo Freire is an admirable exemplar of this ambitious act of critically examining the culture, particularly the educational institutions. Freire, a well-trained educator at the University of Recife in Brazil, was motivated to assist the poor in becoming vocationally competitive with the middle and upper classes.

In John Dewey's magnum opus, *Democracy and Education* (1916), he delighted in castigating those who disagreed with his progressive and experimentalist educational views. Two of those he criticized were Johann Friedrich Herbart (1776–1841) and Maria Montessori (1870–1952). Herbart and his followers devised an eminently straightforward five-step program to assist teachers in knowing how to conduct education in the classroom. Dewey's ally, William Heard Kilpatrick, wrote a major attack on Montessori in 1914 in his *The Montessori System Examined.*[22]

Existentialism

Like another more recent development in educational philosophy—analytic philosophy or philosophical analysis—existentialism gained its greatest reception after World War II. Both of them fail to fit the contours of the metaphysical, epistemological, and axiological divisions of the usual philosophical systems. However, all Christian educators can benefit from the contributions of existentialist thinking.

In actuality, existentialist concepts reach back to Descartes and Pascal as well as Kierkegaard, Nietzsche, Husserl, and Heidegger. Existentialist theologians who periodically move into our discussions are Barth, Bultmann, Brunner, and Tillich. Gerald L. Gutek states, "Existentialist educators encourage students to philosophize about the human experiences of life, love, and death. The Existentialist teacher poses questions to stimulate self-consciousness. Such questioning, it is hoped, will grow into a dialogue among the students."[23]

Evangelical Christians share some of the same themes with existentialists. However, many evangelicals are disquieted by existential attacks on the certainties of faith, such as the authority of Scripture and a personal relationship with God through Jesus Christ. But their emphasis on "stimulating critical thought" can result in "significant insights regarding both educational theory and practice." Further, evangelicals agree with existentialists that people come to know truth through faith and action as well as by cognitive and objective processes. Finally, existentialists and Christians alike endeavor to facilitate inward growth, reflection, self-knowledge, ethical development, decision making, and courageous action. "Storytelling, role-playing, simulations, and discovery experiences are just a few of the educational strategies, . . . but they must be balanced by other methods and subordinated to the broader educational objectives of the Church and Holy Scripture."[24]

Analytic Philosophy

"Some would deny that analytical philosophy is a philosophy at all, but only a method of philosophical investigation. . . . The heart of the teachings of this philosophical method is a desire to clarify the language and methods used to communicate ideas."[25] The writings of Bertrand Russell, Alfred North Whitehead, and Ludwig Wittgenstein have provided some of the initial genesis for this movement, which remains disinterested in making metaphysical, epistemological, or axiological statements. It fails to answer the traditional questions of philosophy. It insists that one of philosophy's major tasks is clarifying the ways we use language, including language about educational matters. Analytic philosophers do not attempt to prescribe educational goals and therefore have little or nothing to say about curriculum, its structure, and pedagogical concerns.

Conversely, educator William Frankena claimed that analytic philosophy should not only "explicate the meanings of educational terms but map out the logic of educational philosophy as a whole region of discourse . . . which would assist us to build our own philosophy of education."[26]

Keeping in mind the weaknesses of the system, analytic philosophy may assist the Christian educator. While analytic philosophy claims no values inherent in its own system, the biblical educator can dig deeply in Scripture for values to be transmitted to the next generation. Further, analytic philosophy can assist us in writing much clearer outcome statements. "Precision can be very helpful in order to highlight what is intended as well as providing an adequate means to evaluate achievement."[27]

Postmodernism

While postmodern philosophers represent a wide spectrum of thought, they share a common dissatisfaction with modern thinking. Modern philosophers, such as René Descartes (1596–1650) and Immanuel Kant (1724–1804), disagreed with each other in significant ways, but there are certain distinctly "modern" aspects of their thought. First, both begin with the individual. Whereas Descartes bases his argument for the existence of God and the world on his own existence, Kant goes so far as to say that "enlightenment" (that is, "modernity") means that one "thinks for oneself." To be "mature" for Kant means that one relies on no authority or the wisdom of one's tradition or culture. One might say that the attitude of modernity is characterized by a confidence that "we moderns know better." Second, modern philosophers have a highly exalted sense of human reason. Although they may recognize its fallibility, they tend to assume that properly functioning reason is capable of understanding everything and solving all theoretical and practical problems. Third, a basic assumption of modernity is that reason ought to be "objective" in the sense of a detached observer. From the perspective of modernity, one thinks rightly when one's religious and moral commitments are kept at bay.

Postmodernity's diversity arises because there are different ways of responding to these modern ideas. On the one hand, neopragmatist Richard Rorty (b. 1931) represents the relativistic side of postmodern thought. Rather than believing that one can think for oneself and that reason should be objective, Rorty believes that one's identity and beliefs are contextual since they are based upon social and cultural norms. There is, in this view, no such thing as objective truth, even though some beliefs are more useful than others. But useful for what?

From a Christian perspective, one can affirm the modern conception of an objective truth that is God's truth. What is less clear is how far the Christian should go in affirming the idea of knowing that truth in an objective way. Scripture is clear that the unregenerate mind cannot know certain truths. So *who* one is matters in terms of *what* one can know. Further, Christians take Scripture to be authoritative. Thus the modern ideal of leaning on one's own understanding is at odds with Christian belief. A truly Christian education, then, should help us to understand and appreciate the authority of God's Word. It should also help us to see things not in a morally and religiously neutral way but from God's way of thinking.[28]

After summarizing these schools of educational thought, the Christian searches for a sure and definitive base for a philosophy of education. The elements to be considered in developing a Christian philosophy of education range from theological and doctrinal to social and educational. Initially, a biblical base of necessity must be developed. The importance of establishing a biblical base cannot be overemphasized.

WHERE THEOLOGY FITS IN

"Christian education must avoid teaching Bible and theology as ends in themselves, reducing them to purely cognitive constructs. Rather, studies must be designed so that students learn to think in biblical ways, using theology as a guide to categories of thinking."[29] Theology, rather than educational philosophy, must control Christian education. This leads us to a transformational aim in Christian education that is actualized most naturally within the context of community. Both the Old and New Testaments put particular stress on the interactive, interpersonal aspects that provide teaching and learning situations that transform our beliefs, attitudes, values, and behavior patterns (Deut. 6:1–9; 11:18–21; Acts 2:42–47; Eph. 4:15–16; Heb. 10:24–25).

Evangelicals will give no support to an educational philosophy that gives theology the second rung on its philosophical ladder. Theology is of primary importance. Instruction in theological matters is of great consequence for all Christians. However, it is quintessential that theological truth be taught in a manner that weds theory with life. This, then, gives direction to the way the Christian educator should instruct. Theology answers some of the most elementary and yet profound questions regarding educational theories and ministries, but it does have some limitations in constructing an educational philosophy. For example, how we understand theology proper (the person and nature of God) and human nature are theological constructs that give shape, definition, and texture to all of Christian education.

A high premium is placed on the teaching and preaching of the Bible. Fortunately, we are increasingly open to new methodologies. Informal approaches are being utilized to augment and supplement traditional or formal schooling.

Conclusion

There are many advantages in having a biblical philosophy of education. A biblical philosophy strives for coherence, the formulation of a worldview. Second, it brings the various spheres of life together in a coordinated whole. Third, in doing so, it relates knowledge systematically. Fourth, it examines the presuppositions, methods, and basic concepts of the various disciplines under consideration. And last, its method is to consult data from our total experiences.

A biblically informed philosophy of education will provide stability amid the incessant changes in our society. A commitment to a biblical view of reality provides direction for the future. The only constants in our world are God and Scripture. The Lord of the church is the Lord of theology and philosophy. And it is God who stands in the center of the intellectual universe, not us.

Notes

1. Norman DeJong, *Education in the Truth* (Nutley, N.J.: Presbyterian and Reformed, 1974), pp. 61–63. See Nigel M. de S. Cameron, "Authority of the Bible," in *Evangelical Dictionary of the Bible*, ed. Walter A. Elwell (Grand Rapids: Baker, 1996), pp. 55–58.

2. DeJong, *Education in the Truth,* pp. 61–63.

3. James Wilhoit, *Christian Education and the Search for Meaning* (Grand Rapids: Baker, 1986), pp. 59–60.

4. Lawrence A. Cremin, *American Education: The Metropolitan Experience* (New York: Harper and Row, 1988), p. x.

5. Robert W. Pazmiño, *Foundational Issues in Christian Education,* 2d ed. (Grand Rapids: Baker, 1987), p. 87.

6. Gerald L. Gutek, *Education and Schooling in America* (Englewood Cliffs, N.J.: Prentice-Hall, 1983), pp. 37–38.

7. George R. Knight, *Philosophy and Education,* 3d ed. (Berrien Springs, Mich.: Andrews University Press, 1998), p. 32.

8. Ibid., pp. 171–72.

9. Steven C. Rockefeller, *John Dewey: Religious Faith and Democratic Humanism* (New York: Columbia University Press, 1991), p. 37.

10. Ibid., pp. 35–40.

11. John Dewey, *A Common Faith* (New Haven: Yale University Press, 1934), cited in Rockefeller, pp. 234–35.

12. Rockefeller, *John Dewey,* p. 236.

13. Kenneth O. Gangel and Warren S. Benson, *Christian Education: Its History and Philosophy* (Chicago: Moody, 1983), p. 294. See pp. 292–304 for a more extensive treatment of Dewey's experimentalism and pragmatism.

14. Van Cleve Morris and Young Pai, *Philosophy and the American School: An Introduction to the Philosophy of Education,* 2d ed. (Boston: Houghton Mifflin, 1976), p. 147.

15. Ibid., pp. 248–49.

16. Ibid., p. 249.

17. Rockefeller, *John Dewey,* p. 222.

18. Ibid., p. 223.

19. Gutek, *Education and Schooling,* p. 61.

20. Ibid., p. 49.

21. Ibid., p. 64.

22. William Heard Kilpatrick, *The Montessori System Examined* (1914; Reprint, Arno Press and the New York Times, 1971).

23. Gutek, *Education and Schooling,* pp. 66–67.

24. Norman G. Wilson, "Existentialism and Education," in *Evangelical Dictionary of Christian Education,* ed. Michael J. Anthony (Grand Rapids: Baker, 2001), p. 274

25. Robert J. Radcliffe, "Analytic Philosophy of Education," in *Evangelical Dictionary of Christian Education,* p. 43

26. Michael L. Peterson, *Philosophy of Education* (Downers Grove, Ill.: InterVarsity, 1986), p. 74.

27. Radcliffe, "Analytic Philosophy," p. 44

28. I am indebted to my son, Bruce E. Benson, for his article on postmodernism in *Evangelical Dictionary of Christian Education,* p. 544–48, which has helped to inform my understanding of postmodern thought.

29. Perry G. Downs, *Teaching for Spiritual Growth* (Grand Rapids: Zondervan, 1994), pp. 64–65.

THEOLOGICAL FOUNDATIONS OF CHRISTIAN EDUCATION   3

Klaus Issler

Theology is the study of God—who God is and what he has provided for his creation, both now and forever. Studying theology is especially important for Christian educators, as illustrated in this definition of Christian education: "Christian education is a reverent attempt to discover the *divinely* ordained process by which individuals grow in *Christlikeness,* and to work with that *process.*"[1] First, to understand anything about life, we must begin with God and his revealed instructions. Second, human nature is designed by God to become Christlike—the goal toward which we educate (cf. Rom. 8:28–29). Finally, becoming like Jesus involves a "divinely ordained process" with which Christian educators must work. Each of these factors requires theological understanding and must inform how we educate Christians. This chapter presents a brief survey of commonly held beliefs among evangelical Protestants[2] to help inform the development of Christian education theory and practice.

BIBLIOLOGY: THE NATURE OF BIBLICAL REVELATION

The Bible is God's special revelation in written form and is open to public inspection. It is uniquely inspired ("God-breathed," 2 Tim. 3:16), rendering it authoritative for all times, the ulti-

mate standard of truth about God and his plan (John 17:17), providing the essential source for salvation (Acts 4:10–12) and God's explicit will for our lives (Matt. 4:4). God superintended the writing of the Scriptures by human authors (2 Pet. 1:20–21) so that, incorporating their individual personalities, literary styles, and interests (e.g., Rom. 9:1–3, free expression; Luke 1:1–4, research), these authors composed and recorded God's authoritative message in the words of the original manuscripts. Although the Bible consists of sixty-six books (thirty-nine in the Old Testament and twenty-seven in the New Testament) written over a period of approximately one thousand five hundred years by about forty human authors who wrote primarily in Hebrew and Greek, it speaks as one complete unit, having one ultimate divine author. No additional, equally authoritative revelation exists (such as the *Book of Mormon*) to which Christians must turn. Although the Bible does not provide exhaustive information on every topic, it is completely sufficient in what it teaches about God, our relationship with him, and his explicit will for Christian living.

The Bible is completely truthful, never affirming any falsehoods, even regarding incidental references.[3] The Chicago Statement on Biblical Inerrancy affirms that "the authority of Scripture is inescapably impaired if this total divine inerrancy is in any way limited or disregarded, or made relative to a view of truth contrary to the Bible's own; and such lapses bring serious loss to both the individual and the Church."[4] God's Word has been recorded for us in human language for our regular use and study. The words of the Bible are comprehensible to any reader, whether Christian or not. But the significance and application of the Word comes only to believers who interpret the Word accurately and welcome its truth by illumination of the Holy Spirit.

To interpret the Bible properly, believers must discover the author's main theme or big idea from the context and details of the paragraph or episode. Once the public meaning of the passage takes shape, we work on our personal response to the passage in light of the author's message to his readers. How were the original readers to respond? How do I respond in my situation today? God uses his "living and active" Word to "[judge] the thoughts and attitudes of the heart" (Heb. 4:12). Bible study is a dynamic process if we are willing to listen humbly and respond to the Spirit's ministry in our lives (Matt. 7:24–27; Luke 6:46–49; James 1:22–25).

Bible study is at the heart of Christian education. Our job is to take the living Word of God and write it on the hearts of believers. The result should be a slow process of life transformation that draws them closer in their relationship with God. Bible teaching requires a firm conviction of the origins and purposes of Scripture. As Christian educators, our lives must evidence this transformation before we can ever expect others to follow. Scripture teaches that it is impossible to know and understand the things of God (i.e., theology) without the Holy Spirit residing within us (Rom. 8:6–11). Once this relationship with God is established and one becomes a "new creation" (2 Cor. 5:17), an understanding of theology becomes profitable.

THEOLOGY PROPER: THE DOCTRINE OF GOD

How can we describe God, since God is unique (Isa. 40:25)? As the child's prayer frames it, "God is great and God is good." Millard Erickson employs these two focal points to outline the wonder and beauty of God's essential nature (greatness) and his natural and moral attributes (goodness).

The Greatness of God

God is personal—God thinks, feels, wills, and relates with others. God is life and the source of all living creatures. God is essentially an immaterial, nonspatial, invisible Spirit, existing without any physical body (John 4:24; Luke 24:39; 1 Tim. 6:15–16). Furthermore, God is immanent and present everywhere (omnipresent, Ps. 139:7–12). Philosopher Dallas Willard explains, "[God] occupies [space] and overflows it but cannot be localized in it. Every point in it is accessible to his consciousness and will, and his manifest presence can be focused in any location as he sees fit."[5] Wayne Grudem clarifies, "God is present in different ways in different places, or . . . God acts differently in different places in his creation."[6] Having no beginning and no ending, God is everlasting (Ps. 90:2; Isa. 43:13).

God is constant (immutable, James 1:17). Grudem notes, "God is unchanging in his being, perfections, purposes, and promises, yet God does act and feel emotions, and he acts and feels differently in response to different situations."[7] God is also all-powerful (omnipotent, Ps. 145:3; Isa. 40:21–26) and all-knowing (omniscient, Isa. 40:13–14, 28). Thus, whatever God plans to do, he will accomplish (Isa. 43:13; 55:11; Matt. 19:26).

The Goodness of God

Erickson identifies the goodness of God as consisting of ten attributes, clustered within three groups: (1) moral integrity—holiness, righteousness, justice; (2) integrity (truthfulness)—genuineness (real), veracity (speaks truth), faithfulness (keeps promises); and (3) love—benevolence, grace, mercy, and persistence. The basis of any Christian ethic is God's moral nature. Furthermore, Jesus Christ shows us who God is, for Jesus himself "is the radiance of God's glory and the exact representation of his being" (Heb. 1:3; see also John 14:7–9).[8] What all ethical theories critically lack, Christianity uniquely offers: the perfect, ethical example. Christians are not restricted solely to abstract principles for ethical conduct, because in Jesus we have a model for good living.

THE TRINITY—THREE PERSONS IN ONE GOD

God is one divine Being, but not one person, for he is an eternally existing "divine society" of three persons—Father, Son, and Holy Spirit—who love each other dearly and who comprise the one Christian God. The Bible makes reference to the three members of the Trinity in both the Old and New Testaments (e.g., Isa. 48:16; 61:1; Matt. 28:19; 2 Cor. 13:14).[9]

The Person and Work of God the Father

Lewis and Demarest state that God the Father "creatively designs and initiates relationships and activities. The point illustrated is not a time of origin, but a distinctness of activity with sameness of nature. The first person initiates and purposes."[10] Thus, the decrees and plan of God are from the Father (Ps. 2:7–9; Eph. 1:3–14). In addition, the Father uniquely answers prayer (Matt. 6:9; Eph. 3:14) offered by mankind, by the Spirit (Rom. 8:26–27), and by the Son (Rom. 8:34; Heb. 7:25).

Christology: The Person and Work of God the Son

At the center of Christianity is Christ. In Philippians 2:5–11, Paul narrates a basic outline: Who is he? What kind of person is he? What did he accomplish? Regarding his person, Jesus Christ is the preexistent, divine Son of God (John 1:1; 8:58), born of a virgin (Isa. 7:14; Matt. 1:16), who willingly took on human nature forever. Jesus became and remains the unique God-man, who displayed for the world to see both what God is really like and what the good potential of humanity is really like.[11] At the Council of Chalcedon (A.D. 45), the church officially acknowledged that "our Lord Jesus Christ [is] the same perfect in Godhead and also perfect in manhood; truly God and truly man, of a reasonable soul and body; consubstantial with the Father according to the Godhead, and consubstantial with us according to the Manhood."[12] Scripture cites references about Jesus' human body (e.g., thirsty, Matt. 25:35; hungry, Matt. 4:2; weary, John 4:6; died, John 19:30–34) and his experience of a full range of emotions (e.g., weeping, Luke 19:41; compassion, Mark 6:34; righteous anger,

Mark 3:5; frustration, Matt. 17:17; troubled, Matt. 26:37).

Heresies about Jesus are bounded by two extremes. Either his full deity is acknowledged, denying that Jesus was also essentially human (e.g., *docetism:* Jesus only appeared to be human), or his full humanity is acknowledged, denying his essential preexistent divine nature (e.g., *adoptionism:* Jesus was a good man but nothing more).

Regarding the work of Jesus, he performed the roles of prophet, priest, and king. As prophet (Deut. 18:15–19 [Acts 3:22–23]; Matt. 13:57; John 6:14; 7:40), Jesus was God's faithful messenger and teacher, communicating old and new truth about God and his plan (Matt. 4:17). As the unique priest outside of the Levitical lineage (Ps. 110:4; Heb. 7:11, 17), Jesus was both the once-for-all sacrifice *and* the one who offered the sacrifice (Heb. 10:11–14). During his first coming, Jesus took on the role of the suffering servant prophesied by Isaiah (Isa. 52:13–53:12), offering himself as a perfect atonement for our sins (1 John 2:2). "Christ died for our sins according to the Scriptures, . . . he was buried, [and] he was raised on the third day according to the Scriptures" (1 Cor. 15:3–4). Jesus is also the king, who veiled his glory during this first advent (Matt. 17:2; John 17:5), announcing the coming of the kingdom of God (Mark 1:15; John 18:36; Acts 1:3). After his resurrection, the Father laid all authority on Jesus (Matt. 28:18). We now await the moment when Jesus will return again, implementing an age when the will of God will be done on earth (Matt. 6:10) and Jesus reigns as the King of kings (Matt. 25:31–46; Rev. 3:21; 19:16; 20:4).

Pneumatology: The Person and Work of God the Holy Spirit

The most important aspect in studying the doctrine of the Holy Spirit is coming to terms with the personal nature of the Holy Spirit. Grudem notes, "After Jesus ascended into heaven, and continuing through the entire church age, the Holy Spirit is now the *primary* manifestation of the presence of the Trinity among us. He is the one who is most prominently *present* with us now."[13]

All the members of the Triune God are coequal persons. Thus, the Spirit is not a silent partner in the Trinity, for he speaks (Acts 8:29; 10:19) and may be "griev[ed]" by us (Eph. 4:30). Just as believers interact with the Father and the Son, in the same manner they can interact with the Spirit—in conversation and prayer, in worship and thanksgiving. J. I. Packer affirms that "prayer to the Spirit is equally proper when what we seek from him is closer communion with Jesus and fuller Jesus-likeness in our lives."[14] Jesus equated the Spirit with "rivers of living water" (John 7:38 RSV) within the believer. The Spirit is the Divine Counselor or Mentor sent by Jesus to indwell each believer, with whom every believer can develop a personal relationship (John 14:16–18; Rom. 8:6).

Regarding the work of the Spirit, he was involved in creation (Gen. 1:2), in the inspiration of Scripture (2 Sam. 23:2–3; Acts 1:16; Heb. 3:7; 2 Pet. 1:21), in selective indwelling in Old Testament persons (Gen. 41:38; Dan. 4:8), in the life of Jesus Christ (Luke 1:35; 4:18; Acts 10:38), in the ministry of conviction of sin throughout the world (John 16:8–11), and in the regeneration and renewal of sinners into saints (Titus 3:5). For New Testament believers since Pentecost, at the moment of regeneration the Holy Spirit indwells each believer forever (John 14:16; 1 Cor. 6:19), baptizes us (1 Cor. 12:13), seals us (Eph. 4:30), and inaugurates regular prayer for each believer (Rom. 8:26). As we walk with the Spirit (Gal. 5:16, 25), the Spirit fills (Eph. 5:18), teaches (John 16:12–15), guides (Rom. 8:14), and assures us (Rom. 8:16).

Furthermore, the Spirit dynamically empowers the believer (1) in deepening our relationship with God ("fellowship with the Spirit," Phil. 2:1; 2 Cor. 13:14); (2) for Christlike living ("fruit of the Spirit," Gal. 5:22); (3) for growing together into a healthy and mature Christian community ("unity of the Spirit," Eph. 4:3); and (4) for ministry to others ("spiritual gifts," 1 Cor. 12:1) and evangelism ("filled with the Holy Spirit and spoke the word of God boldly," Acts 1:8; 4:31).

The Holy Spirit plays a significant role in empowering the believer to perform works of service. The various gifts of the Spirit (Rom. 12:6–8; 1 Cor. 12:7–11, 28; Eph. 4:11) have been given for the express purpose of mobilizing the church to transform the world for Christ. Christian educators begin their role by first identifying their area(s) of giftedness and then using the gift(s) through the power which the Holy Spirit provides to do his work.

ANTHROPOLOGY: THE NATURE AND STUDY OF (REDEEMED) HUMAN PERSONS

Among all of God's creation, humanity is uniquely created in the image of God (Gen. 1:26; 9:6; James 3:9).[15] Furthermore, believers are now being renewed and conformed to the image of Christ (Rom. 8:28) in that Jesus has become the Second Adam, the pioneer of a new redeemed human race (1 Cor. 15:20–23, 45–49). Although the meaning of the phrase "image of God" is not easily discerned, three facts are clear. The focal point is on God as the prototype. As Charles Sherlock notes, "From the beginning of our discussion it is vital to be clear about how we image God, before we begin to explore what being made in the image of God as human beings may mean."[16] Secondly, human nature was designed so that God the Son could take on humanity. Erickson explains, "We know from the Bible, that God chose to become incarnate in a creature very much like himself. It is quite possible that God's purpose in making man in his own image was to facilitate the incarnation which would someday take place."[17] Furthermore, since Jesus was the only person ever to live fully within his humanity and also follow God's will, we must study more about Jesus to learn about our own humanity.

Anthony Hoekema draws together differing proposals regarding "being created in God's image" to suggest both *structural* and *functional* aspects for human nature. "By the image of God in the broader or structural sense we mean the entire endowments of gifts and capacities that enable man to function as he should in his various relationships and calling."[18] These gifts and capacities include self-consciousness, reasoning, self-determination, moral sensitivity, and aesthetic awareness. Regarding the functional aspect of the image of God, Robert Saucy identifies two particular dimensions, that of being God's unique representative on earth (Gen. 1:26–8; Ps. 8:5–8; cf. Rev. 22:5) and that of being uniquely able to have a relationship and be in communion with God (Deut. 6:5; Ps. 8:3–4; Matt. 22:36–37; Rev. 3:20).

"Being human involves community."[19] God is making a people for himself (1 Pet. 2:9–10; Rev.

21:3). From the beginning, God created human-kind as male and female (Gen. 1:26). The divine commentary "It is not good for the man to be alone" (Gen. 2:18) goes deeper than marital union to indicate an essential social aspect of our nature. "If we love one another, God abides in us and His love is perfected in us" (1 John 4:12 NKJV). In Western society and within Christian circles, an element of radical individualism hinders believers from growing more fully into a wholesome inter-dependency as a community of persons, rather than purely as an aggregate of human units. "We are to grow up in all aspects into Him, who is the head, even Christ, from whom *the whole body,* being fitted and held together by that which *every joint supplies,* according to the proper working of each individual part, causes the growth of the body for the building up of itself in love" (Eph. 4:15–16 NASB, emphasis added).

A proper view of Christian maturity must fit God's design of human nature. For example, Christian education programs based on truncated conceptions of "spiritual" maturity designed for isolated individuals will do more harm than good. We need Christian education programs that include whole-person, interactive-community, and Holy Spirit-mentored components in order to help believers grow to spiritual maturity.

SANCTIFICATION: GROWING TOWARD MATURITY IN CHRISTLIKENESS

At the moment of salvation, God begins a new work involving two distinct phases—*justification,* the declaration of the believer's positional righteousness in Christ based on Christ's substitutionary death and atonement; and *sanctification,* the process by which God the Holy Spirit and the believer participate together in the project of the believer becoming Christlike experientially. Grudem supplies the following table to heighten contrasts between these two aspects:[20]

Justification	Sanctification
Legal standing	Internal condition
Once for all time	Continuous throughout life
Entirely God's work	We cooperate
Perfect in this life	Not perfect in this life
The same in all Christians	Greater in some than in others

In an important sense, Christians have become "new creatures" in that certain "old things passed away; behold, new things have come" (2 Cor. 5:17 NASB). First, believers are no longer enslaved to sin, being freed from the power and obligation to sin (Rom. 6:6–23). Christians do not need to sin. Second, with God's grace believers have the potential and ability to grow in righteousness and actually sin less and less in this life (Rom. 6:12; 1 John 2:1). Although trials and temptations test us, Christians can overcome any trial (1 Cor. 10:13; James 1:2–4; Rev. 2:7, 11, 17, 26; 3:5, 12, 21) and can resist Satan at any moment (James 4:7; 1 Pet. 5:8–9; 1 John 2:14) by God's grace. Finally, God the Holy Spirit, who now lives within each believer forever (John 15:16), is ready to mentor each believer toward Christlike living (Rom. 8:6, 11, 16, 23, 26–27). As Henry Holloman notes, "Christlikeness is God's goal for Christians and . . . sanctification is His way for believers to become more like Christ."[21]

What expectations does God have for our part in the sanctification process? Although God has promised the completion of our growth (Rom. 8:29–30; Phil. 1:6) this side of death and heaven, the Bible clearly indicates a synergistic arrangement, a human participation with God's grace where both agents are operative (note the various Scriptural imperatives that urge believers to do something). Without our effort in response to God's initiatives and divine resources, no sanctifying will occur. For example, in the Old Testament, priests carrying the ark of God were explicitly instructed by God to walk forward, placing their feet in the Jordan River. Then God would dry up the waters for the Israelites to pass through on dry ground (Josh. 3:13–17). But until their feet actually touched the water, God would not stop the Jordan River from flowing. Similarly, though it is God who does the work, he still expects us to participate in the training process. The classic text is 1 Timothy 4:7–8, in which Paul charges Timothy: "*Train* yourself to be godly. For physical *training* is of some value, but godliness has value [in every way], holding promise for both the present life and the life to come" (emphasis added). Furthermore, the writer to the Hebrews lifts up Jesus' example to encourage our resolve: "You have not yet resisted to the point of shedding blood in your *striving against sin*" (Heb. 12:4 NASB, emphasis added).

ECCLESIOLOGY: THE NATURE AND WORK OF THE CHURCH

For some, "church" is a place or service one goes to on a certain day of the week. Biblically, however, the church is a community or family of people, with Jesus Christ as its Head (Eph. 1:20–23), its Savior (Eph. 5:25–27), its Teacher (Matt. 23:8; John 13:13), its Chief Shepherd (1 Peter 5:4), and its Lord (John 13:13). The church has a threefold focus—*upward* to God, to glorify, worship, love, and be in communion with God (Matt. 22:37–38; John 4:23–24; 1 Cor. 10:31; Eph. 1:12); *inward,* to grow and nurture itself in love and community and to care for the needs of the saints (Rom. 12:13; Eph. 4:1–3, 11–16; 1 Tim. 5:3–16); and *outward,* to bring the good news to a world without God (Matt. 28:19–20) and to do good in the world (Gal. 6:10).

The New Testament makes distinctions between the local (or visible) church, a gathering of believers in one location, and the universal (or invisible) church, the totality of all believers throughout the world, irrespective of the local church they attend.[22] Further matters related to the church can be clustered under three general headings: *Communion with God* (e.g., worship [Matt. 4:10]; prayer [1 Tim. 2:1–8]; participatory celebration [Eph. 5:19–21]; biblical instruction [1 Tim. 4:13; 2 Tim. 2:2]; ordinances of baptism [Matt 28:19]; and the Lord's Supper [1 Cor. 11:17–34]); *Organizational Aspects* (e.g., qualifications and roles of leadership [1 Tim. 3:1–7; Heb. 13:17; 1 Pet. 5:1–6]; giftedness for ministry of each believer [1 Cor. 12:7, 11; Eph. 4:16; 1 Pet. 4:10–11]); and *Relational Aspects.*

Relational Community

Jesus' own strategy of disciple making involved building communities (selecting the Twelve to be with him, Mark 3:14), through team ministry relationships (sending them out two by two, Mark 6:7), and through close personal friendships (Peter, James, and John, Matt. 26:36–38). Genuine community and various sets of close friendships always go together. Two kinds of lists indicate what healthy relationships look like: the famous "love" chapter in 1 Corinthians 13 and all of the "one another" verses scattered throughout the New Testament. Some of these exhortations can be experienced at almost any level of relationship, such as

"forgiving one another" (Eph. 4:32 KJV) or "be hospitable to one another" (1 Pet. 4:9 NASB). But some require a greater depth of trust and intimacy within close friendships to engage more freely in personal aspects of loving: "admonish one another" (Col. 3:16) or "confess your sins to one another" (James 5:16 NASB).

Reconciliation Ministry

To round out the church's community-building strategy, there is a great need for regular mediation and reconciliation among its members. The apostle Paul castigated the Corinthian church for not providing a means for resolving conflicts among members (1 Cor. 6:1–8), whether personal, financial, or business matters. Jesus encouraged the use of third-party mediation (the primary resolution mode in non-Western cultures) when a conflict cannot be resolved between the two parties by themselves (the primary resolution mode of Western cultures) (Matt. 18:15–17).[23] If we fail to plan here, we plan to fail by permitting non-Christian forms of relating and sinning among the church family. The healthy church family is not one that has no members who sin; that is reserved for heaven. Rather, it is the church that intentionally and regularly facilitates resolution for the customary differences and conflicts that arise among its members—members who are saints but not yet perfected (Phil. 4:2–3).

ESCHATOLOGY: THE CHRISTIAN'S HOPE AND DESTINY

When recommending a movie or novel to a friend, explaining how the story ends spoils the surprise. But with God, knowing how history ends makes all the difference in the world for living now (cf. Rev. 21, 22). In the future, God will permanently take up residence in the midst of his people (Rev. 21:3; cf. Jer. 31:33). He will be our God, and we will be his people—something God has been planning for a long time. Believers will experience the fullness of the glorious presence of God: "They will see his face" (Rev. 22:4; Num. 6:25; Isa. 25:9). In the future, God's kingdom will finally and fully be on earth as it is in heaven (Matt. 6:10). It will be a new day, a "new heaven and a new earth" (Rev. 21:1), with no night, no need of any lights (Rev.

Figure 3.1
From Here to Eternity

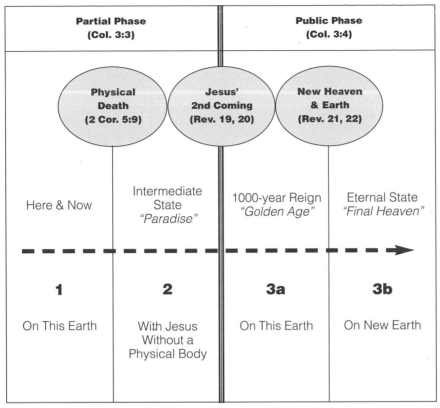

Note: Amillennialists and Postmillennialists believe Christians move from step 2 to step 3b, with no thousand-year reign after Christ's return. Premillennialists believe Christ will return to set up a thousand-year reign on the earth.

22:4–5), and no more pain or mourning or death (Rev. 21:4). Finally, believers shall serve God and reign with him forever and ever (see figure 3.1) (cf. Dan. 7:18, 27; Rev. 3:21).

What happens to believers who die now, before Christ comes? In God's eschatological program, there is both a partial phase and then a public phase initiated at Christ's second coming (see figure 3.1). Now believers only experience part of the full benefits of the new covenant (Jer. 31:31–34; Ezek. 36:22–32). All spiritual blessings are accessible (Eph. 1:3), but our physical bodies will not be redeemed until later (Rom. 8:23). Believers can look forward to physical death, since we are then ushered into a new phase of living to be with Jesus (2 Cor. 5:6–8). We enter what Jesus called "paradise" (Luke 23:43), or "Abraham's bosom" (Luke 16:22), also called the intermediate state, in which we exist without physical bodies (2 Cor. 5:6–8)

until the future resurrection. Then, at Christ's coming, the public phase begins, and all believers receive their renewed resurrection bodies (1 Cor. 15:51–58; Phil. 3:20–21). At some point, believers will individually stand before the judgment seat of Christ to give an account of their lives on earth (2 Cor. 5:10; cf. 1 Cor. 3:12–15; Matt. 25:14–30). Two additional eschatological events precede the second coming of Christ: the "rapture"[24] of the saints to be with Jesus (1 Thess. 4:15–17; John 14:2–3) and the great tribulation, a period of judgment on the earth (Matt. 24:21–22; Rev. 6:15–17).[25]

A difference is evident among theological traditions regarding the thousand-year reign of Christ (Rev. 20:1–6). Amillennialists and postmillennialists believe that when Christ comes again, the eternal state will begin. For premillennialists, prior to the eternal state Christ will inaugurate the thousand-year reign, a golden age on this earth as promised in the Old Testament (e.g., Isa. 25:6–9; Ezek. 37:21–28; Zech. 14:16–21) during which Satan will be bound (Rev. 20:1–3). Near the end of this reign Satan will be loosed, and Christ will defeat Satan and permanently assign him to hell (Rev. 20:7–10).

INTEGRATING THEOLOGY AND THE SOCIAL SCIENCES

When relating theology to the social sciences, the challenge for Christian educators is to maintain an evangelical affirmation of the final authority of the Bible while allowing other legitimate sources of knowledge to inform the practice and content of Christian education (e.g., how best to learn or teach, particulars about good parenting practices).

The biblical record is the central hub around which any theological interpretation is made. Yet each interpretative statement must also be checked by past theological tradition, by reason, and by experience.[26] When assessing the truth or falsehood of the advice of a friend or the claim of a neighbor, we regularly consult such tests of truth by checking our understanding of Scripture along with the teachings of respected pastors and Bible scholars, by discerning whether the claim makes sense or is logically consistent (Luke 24:11), and by deciding whether it fits with daily living (John 20:24–25).[27]

Theology and social science may be integrated in a number of ways.[28] In some cases, theology or the social sciences may provide the rationale or presuppositions for the other (e.g., being created in the image of God [Gen. 1:26], all persons must be accorded equal dignity, justifying the ethical treatment of persons in research). In some instances, either theology or the social sciences fills in details for general principles offered by the other (e.g., empirical research may suggest more detailed guidance for understanding how best to raise children without provoking anger [Eph. 6:4]). But in some critical arenas, theology and the social sciences offer competing explanations of reality, and only one explanation can be true (e.g., Christianity affirms that human nature is created in God's image and consists of both immaterial [spirit/soul] and material [physical body] aspects,

while the majority of social science publications understand human nature solely within macroevolutionary, antisupernaturalist, and physicalist terms). Christian educators must let both theology and the social sciences enlighten them, while still permitting the Bible to have final authority in all matters. Ultimately, all truth is God's truth, no matter what source uncovers it.

THEOLOGICAL DISTINCTIVES

One's theological tradition may also inform the interpretation of Scripture. It is unfortunate that these differences have been used among believers as a source of division rather than as a way to frame an intellectual debate among trusting friends. It is often best to differentiate between theological distinctives when applied to a particular doctrinal area. We'll demonstrate by using the topic of eschatology. For our example, differing scenarios are offered to explain what takes place prior to Jesus Christ's second coming. Two prominent eschatological views, amillennialism and premillennialism, actually fit into larger theological systems that attempt to explain the unity of God's overall plan.

Covenant Theology and Amillennialism

God's kingdom project encompasses two major covenants: the covenant of works (Gen. 1–2) and the covenant of grace (Gen. 3–Rev. 22). In the Garden of Eden, God offered Adam and Eve the opportunity to obey him and thus enjoy the blessings of his provision. Due to Adam's disobedience, however, God instituted the covenant of grace for all subsequent believers. The relationship between the Old Testament and New Testament is one of continuity, although certain symbols have been altered. God's church was established in the Old Testament, especially through the nation of Israel with symbols (circumcision) and ordinances (Passover). Yet, Israel's continual disobedience severed it from God's grace. God then instituted the international New Testament church, the "new Israel" (1 Cor. 12:13; Gal. 6:16). The ordinances of baptism and the Lord's Supper replace circumcision and the Passover. Since the church continues the traditions from the Old Testament, all Old Testament promises to national Israel now apply directly and solely to the church, not Israel. In the future, Christ will come to set up his eternal kingdom, not just a thousand-year reign.[29]

Dispensational Theology and Premillennialism

Dispensationalism offers another way to tie together the unity of God's plan by highlighting certain unconditional covenants God established in the Old Testament. The Abrahamic covenant (Gen. 12:1–3) provides the overriding framework to explain God's plan. God unconditionally promises to bless the nation of Israel, but through Abraham and his descendants, God will bless all nations. In time, God entered a conditional covenant with the nation of Israel at Mount Sinai (Exod. 19)—the Mosaic covenant. Israel eventually rebelled against God and was exiled from the land.

During these later disobedient years, God promised to make an unconditional new covenant with the house of Israel. In the future, after Israel has been judged by God and scattered around the globe, God will then gather them together again (Ezek. 36:22–32) and "put My law within them, and on their heart I will write it" (Jer. 31:31–34 NASB). Centuries later, Jesus came to institute this new covenant with his death and resurrection (Luke 22:20; 1 Cor. 11:25; 2 Cor. 3:6; Heb. 8–9). The new covenant was implemented in two phases relating to the two comings of Jesus. First, all New Testament believers after Pentecost are beneficiaries of the spiritual blessings of regeneration during this church age. Then, Jesus' coming will be premillennial to inaugurate a golden messianic reign of one thousand years (Rev. 20:1–6). Here, all the promises of the Old Testament will be fulfilled, with Jesus reigning in Jerusalem and national Israel having special prominence. All church-age believers will be resurrected at this time to share in God's bounty and provision in this golden messianic era.

CONCLUSION

To maintain evangelical distinctives in formulating both theory and practice in Christian education, we must become more aware of how our presuppositions and approaches influence the development of curriculum, instructional design, programmatic development, and so forth. As Christian educators, we can help our people enter into Christlike living and a deeper relationship with God by letting sound theology have its proper role in Christian education theory and practice.

One's theology must be predicated upon a solid conviction that God's Word is trustworthy. Many evangelicals hold to an inerrant view of Scripture. This is the belief that the Bible alone is authoritative and speaks for God. Without such a view, one's theological moorings are as firm as the latest fashion trend. Christian education begins with sound theology rooted deeply in the pages of Scripture. Its programs are designed with an understanding of the sinful nature of humans and the holy nature of God.

The astute Christian educator sees his or her work as an extension of Christ's mission to draw humankind into a saving and intimate relationship with a loving God. This is done in partnership with the Holy Spirit and in cooperation with other believers. How long does this take place? Perhaps that depends on your particular theological distinctives as they influence your understanding of the end times. Regardless of what those may be, we would do well to heed the admonition of our Lord that commands us to "make disciples of all the nations, baptizing them in the name of the Father and the Son and the Holy Spirit, teaching them to observe all that" we have been commanded (Matt. 28:19–20 NASB).

NOTES

1. Nevin Harner, *The Educational Work of the Church* (New York: Abingdon-Cokesbury, 1939), p. 20 (emphasis added).

2. Within Christianity there are three general families: Roman Catholicism, Eastern Orthodoxy, and Protestantism. The Orthodox Church of the East and the Roman Catholic Church of the West separated in A.D. 1054. Among the issues dividing the Western and Eastern Church was the so-called *filioque* clause. The West affirmed the procession of the Holy Spirit from the Father "and the Son" (Latin, *filioque*), whereas the Eastern Orthodox denied this. The Nicene Creed was later edited to include the filioque clause. The Protestant Reformation began when Martin Luther proposed his Ninety-five Theses for debate in A.D. 1517. Within the Protestant family, evangelicals tend to emphasize the following theological distinctives: "(1) the Reformation doctrine of the final authority of the Bible, (2) the real historical character of God's saving work recorded in Scripture, (3) salvation to eternal life based on the redemptive work of Christ, (4) the importance of evangelism and missions, and (5) the importance of a spiritually

transformed life" (George Marsden, *Understanding Fundamentalism and Evangelicalism* [Grand Rapids: Eerdmans, 1991], pp. 4–5).

3. "Scripture in the original manuscripts does not affirm anything that is contrary to fact," (Wayne Grudem, *Systematic Theology* [Grand Rapids: Zondervan, 1994], p. 90).

4. The Chicago Statement on Biblical Inerrancy (1978), printed in Grudem, *Systematic Theology,* appendix 1, p. 1204. Affirming complete inerrancy recognizes the figurative use of language, that some scribal errors may have been incorporated in the text we have today during the copying of manuscripts [although no critical doctrines are affected by these scribal errors], and the supposed "problem passages" for which reasonable explanations have been proposed (cf. J. P. Moreland, "The Rationality of Belief in Inerrancy," *Trinity Journal* 7 [spring 1986]: 75–86).

5. Dallas Willard, *The Divine Conspiracy* (San Francisco: Harper, 1998), p. 76.

6. Grudem, *Systematic Theology,* p. 175.

7. Ibid., p. 163.

8. Millard Erickson, *Christian Theology* (Grand Rapids: Baker, 1985), p. 737.

9. Ibid., p. 339.

10. Gordón Lewis and Bruce Demarest, *Integrative Theology,* vol. 1 (Grand Rapids, Zondervan, 1994), pp. 275–76.

11. Erickson, *Christian Theology,* pp. 737, 736, respectively.

12. Cited in Grudem, *Systematic Theology,* p. 1169.

13. Ibid., p. 634 (Grudem's emphasis).

14. J. I. Packer, *Keep in Step with the Spirit* (Old Tappan, N.J.: Revell, 1984), p. 261.

15. Since this chapter is written for Christian educators primarily working with Christians, we explore human nature as redeemed and regenerated. What is human nature like for Christians, following their conversion?

16. Charles Sherlock, *The Doctrine of Humanity* (Downers Grove, Ill.: InterVarsity, 1996), p. 19.

17. Erickson, *Christian Theology,* p. 737.

18. Anthony Hoekema, *Created in God's Image* (Grand Rapids: Eerdmans, 1986), pp. 70–71.

19. Sherlock, *Humanity,* p. 90.

20. Grudem, *Systematic Theology,* p. 746.

21. Henry Holloman, *The Forgotten Blessing: Rediscovering the Transforming Power of Sanctification* (Nashville: Word, 1999), p. 94.

22. Robert Saucy, *The Church in God's Program* (Chicago: Moody, 1972), p. 18.

23. Duane Elmer, *Cross-Cultural Conflict: Building Relationships for Effective Ministry* (Downers Grove, Ill.: InterVarsity, 1993).

24. Regarding the timing of the rapture, three options have been proposed: (1) *posttribulational* (e.g., Matt. 24:22, 29–31), in which the end of the tribulation, the second coming of Christ, and the rapture take place around the same time; (2) *midtribulational,* a rapture sometime during the tribulation in which the church is removed prior to the most difficult part of the tribulation, (e.g., Rev 12:6, and as represented by the rapture of the two witnesses, Rev. 11); or (3) *pretribulational,* at a point before the tribulation, removing the church from experiencing any of God's wrath upon the earth (e.g., Rev. 3:10). For further study, see Gleason Archer et al., *The Rapture: Pre-, Mid-, or Post-tribulational?* (Grand Rapids: Zondervan, 1984).

25. Prior to inaugurating the eternal state, all nonbelievers will appear before God at the great white throne of judgment, where they will be judged for their deeds and assigned to hell, a place away from God—what is called the "second death" (Rev. 20:11–15).

26. This four-factor interpretive framework was articulated by John Wesley (d. 1791), thus the label "Wesleyan quadrilateral." This framework consists of four sources of knowing God: Scripture, reason, tradition, and experience. See Kevin Lawson, "Theological Reflection, Theological Method, and the Practice of Education Ministry: Exploring the Wesleyan Quadrilateral and Stackhouse's Tetralectic," *Christian Education Journal* n.s. 1, no. 1 (spring 1997): pp. 49–64.

27. John Feinberg, *The Many Faces of Evil* (Grand Rapids: Zondervan, 1994), p. 72.

28. J. P. Moreland, "Introduction," in *Christian Perspectives on Being Human: A Multidisciplinary Approach to Integration,* ed. J. P. Moreland and David Ciocchi (Grand Rapids: Baker, 1993), pp. 7–14.

29. The *Westminster Confession of Faith* (1646) remains the standard systematic statement of covenant theology.

CROSS-CULTURAL PERSPECTIVES ON CHRISTIAN EDUCATION   4

Lillian Breckenridge

The distribution of racial and ethnic groups within the United States is expected to shift dramatically over the next several decades. Since 1970, ethnic minority groups have dramatically increased in proportion to the total population. The 2000 census form had fifteen potential boxes to check for ethnic identification. The American Council on Education projects that ethnic minority students represent approximately one-third of the current school-age population.[1] The Bureau of the Census predicts that approximately half of the population will be Hispanic, black, American Indian, or Asian by 2050. Asians are currently the fastest growing group, but Hispanics are expected to become the second largest cultural group in the country as early as 2010. It is predicted that the majority population in America at the end of the next century will be a "majority of minorities."[2]

The tapestry of American culture has changed dramatically in recent years due to this increasing ethnic diversity of America's citizens. With this varying demographic picture, the culture has gained an added richness that diversity provides. At the same time, churches face the challenge of providing adequate ministry opportunities for all. Many ministers and staff personnel trying to meet this challenge have experienced frustration over the past decade. These cross-cultural concerns include both individual and group contact and arise because interaction occurs between people who are dissimilar. The dissimilarity most often applies to skin color, communication via a different language, and/or different ethnic backgrounds.[3]

This diverse cultural scenario raises serious questions regarding the church's responsibility. What possible barriers or obstacles may be present that discourage members of an ethnic minority group from attending church? Is it acceptable for church congregations to represent only one culture when society represents diversity? Do members of culturally different groups become disillusioned with elements of the educational programs or worship service? If so, what strategies or action plans are needed to correct this?

Although diversity awareness is a responsibility of all agencies of the church, educational ministries will be one of the most efficient avenues for informing and changing attitudes. For this reason, educators and educational programs within the church may need to assume more responsibility for this task than other administrative positions or program units.

THE CHURCH AND CULTURAL DIVERSITY

Churches in the twenty-first century should assume that cultural differences of individual members will be a normal part of congregational life. Along with other institutions, the church will include a variety of races, genders, ages, ethnicities, classes, physical abilities, and religious backgrounds. The impact of ethnic differences on organizations and the people in them should not be underestimated. People representing different cultural backgrounds bring different assumptions, values, and behaviors with them into the congregation. Furthermore, those assumptions, values, and behaviors shape how others perceive and respond to them, how they respond to specific situations in the life of the church, and how they interact with other people. During general church meetings or committee meetings, members of different groups or cultures may talk past each other, never truly hearing the other's voice or acknowledging the truthfulness of the other's position. In such cases there may appear to be a surface consensus on an issue, when in actuality some members of the group leave believing that they were not heard or with feelings of defeat and frustration. Ineffective communication occurs, and division and controversy may arise in the church.

Christians lack agreement on how the church should express its openness to diversity and how that openness will look in contemporary society. Aubrey Malphurs insists that realistically our church culture will exclude some people, even though it is the desire of most congregations to reach everyone. According to Malphurs, "Attempts to reach everyone in general will reach no one in particular. Once your church's culture is set, you'll exclude some people. This can't be helped." However, he reminds us that an important concept to remember is that no culture is superior to another.[4]

The Challenge of Diversity

Churches consciously or unconsciously use various approaches to relate to members of subordinate groups. Placed on a continuum, these approaches range from a complete lack of acceptance to complete acceptance. Richard Schaefer uses seven approaches to describe varying degrees of acceptance for subordinate groups. Although not all of the approaches would have a direct application to the church, six of them do seem to appropriately identify possible reactions by church communities or organizations.[5]

The first approach, and the most extreme consequence for a subordinate group, is expulsion. Expulsion, an unacceptable consequence of minority-group status, occurs when dominant groups directly or indirectly force a specific subordinate group to leave.

A second approach is secession, in which a subordinate group formally withdraws from a church or denomination. The subordinate group may form a new group in which it ceases to be a subordinate group, or it may move to an already established church or denomination.

Segregation is a third possible approach for subordinates. It refers to the physical separation of two groups in physical location and social functions. This often occurs at the initiation of the dominant group. Segregation in America is still pervasive. The majority of blacks and Hispanics attend predominantly black or Hispanic schools and live in sections of metropolitan areas that are highly segregated.

The fourth approach is illustrated by the melting pot concept that was first used in 1782 by the French observer Crévecoeur to describe America.[6] The analogy was based on the attempt during the Middle Ages to melt less costly metals together in order to create gold and silver. The goal was to homogenize ethnic differences into one mainstream American identity that represented a new culture. In 1963, Daniel Moynihan and Nathan Glazer attacked the homogenization ideal. They maintained that it was a misconception that unity depends on uniformity rather than the strengths that come from diversity.[7]

Although this approach is moving in the direction of being more tolerant and accepting, it has its weaknesses. A church may choose to ignore individual differences in order to stress the similarity of oneness in Christ. It has the same weaknesses that are true of a marriage relationship that represents fusion. On the surface, this may appear to be a desirable union, but it often represents the losing of individual identities in order to take on the couple identity. Another illustration is the declaration that one is color-blind relative to skin color. It may sound advantageous to transcend skin color but not if it involves the denial of differences that are important distinctives in personal identity.

The fifth approach a church might take in relating to individuals of a subordinate group is assimilation, the attempt to absorb ethnic minority group members into the dominant group. This approach requires members of the subordinate group to take on the characteristics of the dominant group in order to eventually be accepted as part of that group. With this approach, minority groups usually lose some or most of their distinctives and values. Individuals who refuse to take on the characteristics of the dominant group may be considered disloyal.

The sixth and final approach which could be used by a church is multiculturalism or mutual acceptance. Its goal is to maintain and appreciate the cultural differences of all groups. It involves mutual respect for one another's culture. Rather than the melting pot approach of one identity, ethnic differences are woven into a tapestry or mosaic of American identities. Some would view this as more ideal than reality, and it has been the source of many controversial issues. An example is whether or not all languages should be valued equally in the United States or whether English should be the official language.

A FOCUS ON ETHNIC GROUPS

The church congregation that reflects contemporary society will have opportunity to interact with various subcultures, each of which represents different life experiences and socialization processes. A general understanding of the basic cultural groups is necessary in order to recognize and appreciate the distinct styles of communication and types of behavior unique to groups. Some of the more prominent ethnic subcultures by population are the Hispanic-American subculture, the African-American subculture, and the Asian-American subculture. The cultural assumptions of these selected groups will be considered below. General descriptors are used to provide the conceptual base needed to understand particular groups. They are not intended as a list of identifiable characteristics assigned to group members, for culture is not monolithic but is representative of broad differences across the ethnic group.

A description of the characteristics of cultural groups provides what sociologists refer to as the ideal type. The concept, introduced by Max Weber as a hypothetical model, consists of the most significant characteristics, almost in extreme form, of a social phenomenon. It does not mean the best possible version but rather a pure, distilled form, so pure that it probably does not exist in reality. If descriptions of cultural groups are viewed as hypothetical models, it lessens the possibility of stereotyping.

Hispanic-American Culture

The Hispanic culture includes groups that represent a diverse range of religions, ethnicities, languages, and skin colors. To identify all groups as Hispanic or Latino may be convenient in research but is often unfair in that it tends to overlook the uniqueness of the many groups identified within the more inclusive label. It is said to be "an adequate term but there is no one term satisfactory to everyone."[8] Mexicans are the largest Hispanic group in America, Central and South Americans are the next largest group, and Puerto Ricans are the third largest Hispanic group. Cubans represent only about 5 percent but are an especially strong economical and political factor in southern Florida. Although inadequate knowledge of the English language may cause difficulties in employment opportunities, the Spanish language is a marker of Hispanic pride for most. The majority of Hispanic Americans are bilingual in Spanish and English. Skin tones in the Hispanic cultures vary from white through shades of brown to black.

The Hispanic culture is collectivist, with the individual's dignity depending more upon internal spiritual qualities than external material accomplishments. Truth is grounded in interpersonal reality rather than in objective reality. Interpersonal relationships and spiritual values are very important. In one study, Hispanic managers valued the group over the individual, showed more need for consensus than their Anglo counterparts, and placed more value on interpersonal behavior than task achievement.[9]

Puerto Ricans are unique in comparison with other ethnic groups in that they can travel freely between their homeland and mainland America since they are considered citizens of the United States. Racial identity in the Puerto Rican culture is not determined primarily by physical characteristics (as is so often the case in the United States) but by nonracial factors such as socioeconomic status. They often express surprise at the prejudice based on skin color that they experience when first coming to the mainland.

African-American Culture

African-Americans have been a part of the American culture since the first Europeans reached this country. As a result, the African-American culture has had a strong role in shaping the language, art, music, and literature of America.

In the African-American culture, there is a strong sense of community and identification of the self within the group. Three social groups are especially important: the family, the community, and the church. Community is central to the identity of the individual, and high priority is placed on collective responsibility. In the African-American culture, individuals are encouraged to find self-identify within the group.

The emphasis on community entails a strong encouragement to resolve conflicts as they arise rather than allowing them to continue. This is in contrast to the mainstream American culture that tends to suppress or smooth over conflict. One study of managers found that white managers tend to value the "appearance of tranquility," while African-Americans wanted to achieve tranquility, even if it caused the appearance of disharmony temporarily because the conflict was dealt with openly.[10]

The church is the central social group for African-Americans. Organizations or individuals that want to reach the African-American culture today often begin by contacting black churches. Church leaders are commonly the spokespersons for black issues and concerns. The majority of black Americans are Protestant, with nearly half identified as Baptist.

Asian-American Culture

Asian immigrants to the United States represent a large number of nationalities and cultures. Five of the larger groups are Chinese-Americans, Filipino-Americans, Japanese-Americans, Asian-Indians, and Korean-Americans. Besides these groups, the Census Bureau identifies the Vietnamese, Laotian, Cambodian, Bangladeshi, Bhutanese, Bornean, Burmese, Celebesian, Cernan, Indochinese, Iwo-Jiman, Malayan, Maldivean, Nepali, Okinawan, Sikkimese, Singaporean, and Sri Lankan. Two Asian groups with the longest historical tradition in the United States are the Chinese and the Japanese. Collectively, Asian-Americans form the third-largest ethnic minority, after African- and Hispanic-Americans. To use the same set of descriptors with these diverse groups does them a great injustice, for they have distinct linguistic, social, and geographic backgrounds.

Many Asian-Americans have concentrated on achieving financial independence and academic success for themselves and their children, earning them the "model-minority" image. As members of a collectivist culture, long-term personal relationships are important to Asians.[11] Ken Fong, a pastor of a Baptist church made up mostly of Asian-Americans, writes that "reaching this group with the gospel requires a less confrontational, more relational style of evangelism."[12]

The status of Asian-Americans in general is as varied as the many groups represented. In a 1994 report, Asian-Americans as a group had the lowest divorce rate (3 percent), lowest unemployment rate (3.5 percent), lowest rate of teen pregnancy (6 percent), and highest median family income of any racial group in America. At the same time, 25 percent of the families in New York City's Chinatown live below the poverty level, and as many as 77 percent of Cambodian and Laotian households in California are receiving welfare.[13]

Within each of the ethnic groups considered, a great deal of diversity exists. A wide range of languages, religions, value patterns, and skin color is found in each cultural group. African students at our seminary often mention that it is difficult for them to identify with members of the African-American culture, even though others tend to place them in that category. This example demonstrates the importance of a shared symbolic community to establish cultural identity; it is not automatic due to ethnicity or skin color.

CHRISTIAN EDUCATION IN A CROSS-CULTURAL SOCIETY

The interactive study of culture and education is a phenomenon of the twentieth century. The topics of cultural diversity, multiculturalism, and diversity training in their specific relationship to education have received increased attention in research literature during the past two decades.

Principles and Goals for Multicultural Christian Education

Only more recently has Christian education been examined in terms of cross-cultural issues. Church school teachers face the same challenges as public school teachers do when their classes include students whose cultural backgrounds differ from their own. Such students have had different experiences, may not share the same values and attitudes, and may give different interpretations to the teacher's explanations than do other students in the class. Cross-cultural perspectives of Christian education include a consideration of the principles and practices that provide effective teaching for all members of a group when diverse cultures are included.

Multiculturalism is the term often used when cross-cultural perspectives are applied to education. However, there has been little agreement during the past century about how the concept should be defined. The following operational definition of multicultural Christian education that examines the subject in terms of its purpose should suffice as a beginning point for discussion:

> Multicultural Christian education has as its goal the embodiment of a system of beliefs, attitudes, and behaviors that recognizes and respects the presence of individuals from diverse groups, acknowledges and values their differences, and provides an inclusive context that empowers all members of the church family so that they are encouraged and enabled to make a personal contribution to Christ's ministry.

When a program of Christian education in the local church is truly cross-cultural in its approach, it will be viewed as a process that affects the structural organization of the church, directs instructional strategies, and changes personal values of members of the congregation.[14] The purpose of such a program goes beyond the boundaries of the local church. Martin Marty writes that the purpose of multicultural Christian education is "to provide the widest scope and fairest representation of the surrounding world."[15]

Cross-cultural sensitivity is sufficiently important to warrant its own mission, vision, and goal statements. These will need to be consistent with the general statements for the overall church ministry as well as with the specific statements for Christian education. The objectives listed below are suggested to assist the local church in developing a more inclusive approach for its educational ministries:[16]

1. To develop an increased awareness of cultural diversity
2. To assess practices and attitudes in the church that are ethnocentric in nature
3. To encourage positive interethnic relationships within the church and community
4. To develop cross-cultural skills for the teaching-learning setting and for intercultural communication
5. To assist parents in encouraging children to appreciate and value diversity in others
6. To develop a sense of social responsibility to reduce inequalities and promote justice for members of minority groups

Cognitive Styles and Ethnic Groups

Cognitive styles have been extensively researched to determine cultural differences in education. A learning style is defined as the pattern of behavior and performance by which an individual most consistently experiences and demonstrates learning. (See chapter 14 for more detailed information on learning styles.) Research has shown some correlation between cognitive style and cultural differences.

The cognitive learning style is concerned with the learner and his or her relationship to the learning environment. All learners tend to differ in the degree to which they are field-independent as opposed to field-sensitive. Field-independent learners tend to be more analytical and are less bound to their immediate environment. Field-sensitive learners find it more difficult to separate themselves from the surrounding field and consequently show a strong interest in other people and in interpersonal relationships. Studies have found a tendency for Mexican-American children and African-American children to be more field-sensitive and for European-American children to be more field-independent.[17] It should be noted that public schools in America generally plan curriculum goals around learning styles that are more analytical or field-independent, creating a potential obstacle for students whose style tends to be more relational or field-dependent.[18]

The analytical or relational mode of conceptual organization is another facet of the cognitive learning style that is also associated with cultural groups. Research has found that African-Americans, Asian-Americans, Native-Americans, and Hispanic-Americans are more likely to reflect relational thinking than European-Americans.[19] Analytical learners are believed to be task-oriented and favor individuality and independent thinking. Individuals with a relational mode are more aware of the whole picture and appreciate learning situations that are more personal and are experientially relevant. They will appreciate learning that provides a social encounter rather than one that is purely cognitive.

Another behavior related to ethnic influence is the difference in value placed on affiliation. Research has shown the tendency for Asian-Americans, Native-Americans, and Hispanic-Americans to place greater value on group identity, conformity, and collective behavior than is demonstrated by European-Americans.[20] This is consistent with another study in which European-American children showed a tendency to score higher in their need to achieve than Mexican-American children, who placed greater value on affiliation.[21]

Diversity and the Instructional Process

Unfortunately, researchers have spent more time attempting to ascribe characteristics as learners to members of cultural groups than determining the effectiveness of instructional procedures for specific groups. In a search for "teacher education" and "black education," the ERIC database produced only 27 references for the years 1980 to 1990.[22] That same search for the years 1990 to 2000 only provided 116 sources.

Over the past ten years, however, greater attention has been given to how the academic performance of diverse students can be improved. General implications can be drawn from such research to provide helpful guidelines for the impact of diversity upon educational instruction in the church.

1. Classroom preparation should include consideration for those who represent cultures different from that of the teacher. This means preparing and planning both curriculum and classroom presentation that will be most conducive for all students present.

2. The teacher of diverse students needs to utilize a variety of pedagogical procedures that acknowledge diverse learning styles. This may include procedures that are not considered the most effective for students of the dominant culture. For example, the Anglo styles of teaching place value on active participation in class discussions. However, a more passive role may be both preferred and valued by Hispanic-Americans and Asian-Americans.

3. Both visual and verbal cues are especially important for students who speak English as a second language. Charts, graphs, line art drawings, and transparencies provide additional information and can be used as direction indicators for lectures. Printed outlines giving the general direction of the lecture are also helpful. The teacher can call attention to concepts that are significant by using the terms *first, second,* and so on.

4. Church teachers must be especially careful when dealing with abstract concepts. Those who use a style of thinking that differs from the teacher and others in the classroom may have difficulty understanding theoretical ideas. This is a special concern in religious education since most of the primary theological concepts are abstract in nature. Providing examples and being sure to make clear and thorough explanations for the concept are important. Sufficient time for questions that truly deal with understanding the concept will help those who are struggling to move with the flow of the class. A Korean student in my "Women in Ministry" course shared that other students were involved in such a rapid exchange of complex ideas throughout each class that she invariably suffered from a physical headache at the end of the hour due to the constant strain to stay with the class discussion.

5. Pedagogical methodology should be evaluated in terms of the ethnic heritage that students represent. In her book *Soul Stories:*

African American Christian Education, Anne Wimberly advocates the story-linking process to apply Christian education to the life experiences, history, and liberation of African-American Christians.[23] Jung Young Lee writes that his theology of marginality is a result of his living as an Asian in North America; he describes his faith from the perspective of a marginalized existence. He goes on to state that "marginality is not only the context of marginal theology but also the *method* of marginal theology."[24]

WHAT IT MEANS TO HAVE A CHURCH THAT EMBRACES DIVERSITY

North America has changed from being described as an industrial society concerned with nationalism and uniformity to being currently described as an information society concerned with diversity. The global society is predicted for the twenty-first century. The truth is that our world is changing rapidly. This cultural revolution may tempt churches to follow the example already set by a number of major denominations and, in the words of Cheryl J. Sanders, to develop "increasingly exclusive memberships, defined along economic, class and ethnic lines."[25]

Some churches will not achieve diversity transformation because leaders fail to conceptualize and articulate the need to their constituency. Others may underestimate the complexity of the task. Still others will not move beyond conceptualization. Unless action follows conceptualizing and strategizing, churches will fail to reflect Christ's model of diversity in which all are accepted regardless of race, gender, or class. The magnitude of this task dictates that a local church must prioritize the development of a Christian education program that is multicultural in perspective. The process begins with assessment and proceeds to articulation and action plans. The desired outcome will be interrelationships of equality and respect among the collections of "people groups" that reflect an awareness, acceptance, and appreciation of differences.

Ronald C. Potter, in his essay on race and theological discourse, provides the Christian response to cross-cultural issues. He declares that resolu-

tion occurs when individuals genuinely place themselves at the foot of the cross where they "begin to see themselves as they really are: one new humanity, the people of God. In this regard there are no we-versus-them categories. We see ourselves literally as family members."[26]

The truly multicultural Christian education program is not found in methods, materials, or programs. It is found in changed attitudes of individuals as they interact with one another. It is found in relationships of acceptance and appreciation for individual differences and in the desire to represent the unified family of God. As Christian educators articulate the relationship between cross-cultural perspectives and the significance of the cross of Calvary, the stage is set for others to connect that meaning with their personal lives and to commit themselves to become one in Christ.

NOTES

1. George M. Gazda et al., *Human Relations Development: A Manual for Educators,* 6th ed. (Boston: Allyn and Bacon, 1999), p. 35.

2. Mearle Griffith, *A Church for the Twenty-First Century: A Planning Resource for the Future* (Dayton, Ohio: Office of Research, the General Council on Ministries, 1989), p. 3.

3. Sandra J. Mumford, "The Cross-Cultural Experience: The Program Manager's Perspective," in *Handbook of Intercultural Training,* vol. 2, ed. Dan Landis and Richard W. Brislin (New York: Pergamon Press, 1985), p. 83.

4. Aubrey Malphurs, *The Dynamics of Church Leadership* (Grand Rapids: Baker, 1999) pp. 138–39.

5. Richard T. Schaefer, *Racial and Ethnic Groups,* 7th ed. (New York: Addison Wesley Longman, 1998), p. 20.

6. Philip Gleason, "American Identity and Americanization," in *Harvard Encyclopedia of American Ethnic Groups,* ed. Stephen Therstromm (Cambridge: Belknap Press of Harvard University Press, 1980), p. 31.

7. Nathan Glazer and Daniel Patrick Moynihan, *Beyond the Melting Pot: The Negroes, Puerto Ricans, Jews, Italians, and Irish of New York City* (Cambridge, Mass.: MIT Press, 1963).

8. Veronica Méndez, "Formation in Religious Communities," in *Perspectivas, Hispanic Ministry,* ed. Allan Figueroa Deck, Yoland Tarango, and Timothy M. Matovina (Kansas City: Sheed and Ward, 1995), p. 67.

9. B. M. Ferdman and A. C. Cortes, "Culture and Identity among Hispanic Managers in an Anglo Business," in *Hispanics in the Workplace,* ed. S. B. Knouse, P. Rosenfeld, and A. L. Culbertson (Newbury Park, Calif.: Sage, 1992), pp. 246–77.

10. A. K. Foeman and G. Pressley, "Ethnic Culture and Corporate Culture: Using Black Styles in Organizations," *Communication Quarterly* 35 (1987): 297.

11. David L. James, *The Executive Guide to Asia-Pacific Communications* (New York: Kodansha International, 1995), p. 14.

12. Ken Fong, "Current Innovations," *Leadership* (fall 1999): 51.

13. Schaefer, *Racial and Ethnic Groups,* p. 314.

14. James Breckenridge and Lillian Breckenridge, *What Color Is Your God? Multicultural Education in the Church* (Grand Rapids: Baker, 1995), pp. 76–83.

15. Martin E. Marty, "Christian Education in a Pluralistic Culture," in *Rethinking Christian Education: Explorations in Theory and Practice,* ed. David S. Schuller (St. Louis: Chalice, 1993), p. 22.

16. Breckenridge and Breckenridge, *What Color Is Your God?* pp. 75–83.

17. Manuel Ramírez III and Douglas R. Price-Williams, "Cognitive Styles of Children of Three Ethnic Groups in the United States," *Journal of Cross-Cultural Psychology* 5, no. 2 (1974): 216–17.

18. James E. Plueddemann, "World Christian Education," in *Christian Education: Foundations for the Future,* ed. Robert E. Clark, Lin Johnson, and Allyn K. Sloat (Chicago: Moody, 1991), p. 358.

19. Janice E. Hale-Benson, *Black Children, Their Roots, Culture, and Learning Styles* (Baltimore: Johns Hopkins University Press, 1982), pp. 30–31.

20. Breckenridge and Breckenridge, *What Color Is Your God?* pp. 116, 149, 191.

21. Deborah L. Bainer and Jeffrey W. Peck, "Effective Teaching and Multicultural Religious Education," in *Multicultural Religious Education,* ed. Barbara Wilkerson (Birmingham, Ala.: Religious Education Press, 1997), p. 299.

22. Gloria Ladson-Billings, *The Dreamkeepers: Successful Teachers of African American Children* (San Francisco: Jossey-Bass, 1994), p. 8.

23. Anne Streaty Wimberly, *Soul Stories: African American Christian Education* (Nashville: Abingdon, 1994).

24. Jung Young Lee, *Marginality: The Key to Multicultural Theology* (Minneapolis: Fortress, 1995), pp. 2–3 (Lee's emphasis).

25. Cheryl J. Sanders, "How We Do Church," in *The Gospel in Black and White: Theological Resources for Racial Reconciliation,* ed. Dennis L. Okholm (Downers Grove, Ill.: InterVarsity, 1997), p. 148.

26. Ronald C. Potter, "Race, Theological Discourse, and the Continuing American Dilemma," in *The Gospel in Black and White,* ed. Dennis L. Okholm (Downers Grove, Ill.: InterVarsity, 1997), p. 36.

EVANGELISM AND DISCIPLESHIP   5

Jerry Root

Though the focus of this chapter is evangelism and discipleship, the attention here is not directed toward techniques or "how to" information. There are already many evangelism and discipleship guides and manuals, and some are very helpful. An underlying assumption of this chapter is that the gospel is the most relevant message that a person can receive in this life. By the term *gospel,* we mean the good news of Christ reconciling the world to himself. This message may be simplified to the extent that a child can understand it, or it can be developed to such complexity that the greatest of scholars will remain perpetually fascinated by its riches and depth.

THE MISSION: GO AND MAKE DISCIPLES

Jesus said, "Go therefore and make disciples of all the nations, baptizing them in the name of the Father and the Son and the Holy Spirit, teaching them to observe all that I commanded you; and lo, I am with you always, even to the end of the age" (Matt. 28:19–20 NASB). The word *disciple* literally means "to become a learner or pupil."[1] It may safely be assumed that Christ wanted his followers to produce disciples, not of themselves, but of Christ.[2] The unity of the body of Christ is found when each member of the church seeks to tune his or her life to Jesus Christ.[3] The whole process of disciple making may be understood as beginning and ending in evangelism. It should be natural for a follower of Christ to develop a style of life that places a high priority on leading others to Christ and nurturing them to maturity.

Dawson Trotman, founder of the Navigators (an organization committed to making disciples), developed the follow-up program for the Billy Graham Evangelistic Association. He once observed that a person was physiologically mature when he or she could physiologically reproduce. So, too, Trotman noted that a person was considered spiritually mature when he or she could spiritually reproduce.[4] If this is so, then spiritual maturity may be seen as the acquisition of that set of capabilities that makes it possible for an individual to lead another person to Christ and to nurture that other person so that he or she is capable of reproducing as well.

Philemon 6 reads, "I pray that you may be active in sharing your faith, so that you will have a full understanding of every good thing we have in Christ." Often when we set out to share our faith in Christ, we will be asked questions. And, as often is the case, we may not know the answers to these questions. In looking for answers, we will be stretched to discover and grow in our own understanding of the Christian life. This happens because we choose to make evangelism a part of our lives.

Sharing faith in Christ makes the evangelist vulnerable to scrutiny. Jesus said, "By this all men will know that you are my disciples, if you love one another" (John 13:35).[5] The world has a right to judge the quality of our discipleship to Christ based on the love we have toward one another. The evangelist lives a life that is at risk of being scrutinized by the world. This is not a bad thing. Though it may at times be painful, it calls us to greater authenticity as disciples of Christ commissioned to make disciples of others.

MOTIVATION

Jesus said, "You did not choose Me, but I chose you, and appointed you, that you should go and bear fruit, and that your fruit should remain" (John 15:16 NASB). Christ expects his followers to be fruitful, but often we are not. It might be helpful, though humbling, to briefly investigate the reasons for our lack of fruitfulness. This is done not to increase guilt or shame but to grow and improve. Certainly, the causes of fruitlessness in the church are complex. Even so, it is good to begin to comprehend some of the reasons behind our lack of spiritual fruit.

One reason may be that the vitality of our witness for Christ is lacking because we are not abiding in Christ. Jesus said, "I am the vine, you are the branches; he who abides in Me, and I in him, he bears much fruit; for apart from Me you can do nothing" (John 15:5 NASB). If we are not getting to know the heart of God through prayer and his Word, it is unlikely that we will have a heart of compassion to reach the lost. If we learn to love him, we will begin to love what he loves. Those who followed Christ and observed him firsthand recorded that when he looked on the multitude, "He felt compassion for them" (Matt. 9:36 NASB). To abide in Christ means to learn and experience firsthand the compassion of Christ toward those in need. It also means we will be transformed by that compassion.

Another reason could be that we have not known the joy of fruitfulness in our lives simply because we have never been coached how to be effective in evangelism and mentoring. Robert Coleman, in his book *The Master Plan of Evangelism,* observes that Christ was intentional in the way he trained and equipped his disciples for fruitful service.[6] Of course, it is best to be taught and coached how to effectively share one's faith, but if we have no one to mentor us, it is better to learn through trial and error than to let the mission of the church go unfulfilled. Written resources are available to help us grow in this area. They also leave us without excuse if we do not cultivate fruitfulness in our lives.

Sometimes fruitlessness is the result of fear. Perhaps we fear to share our faith because we know so little and we are intimidated by questions people ask. This fear can be overcome through study. Each question we find difficult and perplexing provides a new area where we can grow in our understanding of what it means to be a follower of Christ. These questions should not be intimidating to us but should challenge us in a healthy way. No matter how much we know about God, there will always be more to know. Perhaps we're afraid to share our faith because we feel our behavior falls far short of the life we should be living for Christ. This fear can be overcome by learning to confess our sins before God and perhaps before some close friends who will love us and hold us accountable in these areas of struggle. Perhaps we fear to share our faith because we worry what others might think of us. This fear can be overcome when we grow in our sense of security in Christ. While having a good reputation is a thing to be valued, a good reputation before the world can be such a fleeting thing and can lead to inappropriate compromises when pursuing it becomes an end in itself. We can be tempted to make inordinate sacrifices and embrace certain kinds of pretense in order to gain it and maintain it. Scripture reminds us that "perfect love casts out fear, because fear involves punishment and the one who fears is not perfected in love" (1 John 4:18 NASB). We must learn the grace of being transparent before God and others.

Sometimes we are unfruitful because we do not really believe that people are interested in the gospel. We may pride ourselves on our interest in spiritual things. We may become cloistered with others like ourselves and form church communities that look more like social clubs, generating programs for members only, removed and distant from those around us who do not yet know Christ. This is unfortunate, for it is appropriate for us to assume that there are people around us who do want to hear an honest and thoughtful explanation of the gospel. Jesus called his own disciples to be mindful of this when he observed that "the fields . . . are white for harvest" (John 4:35 NASB). Even those who appear to be hostile to spiritual matters may be in the midst of a pilgrimage that will eventually lead them to Christ. Augustine wisely advised, "Let this city [the City of God, the community of believers] bear in mind that among her enemies lie hid those who are destined to be fellow citizens, that she may not think it fruitless labor to bear what they inflict as enemies until they become confessors of the faith."[7] It was Rebecca Manley Pippert who reminded the church that we are to get "out of the salt shaker and into the world."[8]

A final reason that we are not fruitful may be because we lack motivation. This is a tricky topic. Ask yourself, "Have I ever had a perfectly pure motivation for anything I've ever done"? I doubt that any of us could say we have acted from absolutely pure motives. After confessing the truth of this, we should then ask ourselves, "If I waited until my motives were pure, would I ever get around to doing anything at all"? I think the answer to this question is clearly no. And yet God calls us to serve him, even with our deficiencies in motive and action. Perhaps our best efforts are to be compared with Andrew's offering of a boy's five loaves and two fish for the feeding of the five thousand. Though seemingly menial in light of feeding five thousand, Christ was able to use it in a miraculous way. Imagine what Christ will do with our efforts for his kingdom, even though our motives may not be perfectly pure. This is no excuse for mediocrity or laziness with respect to our motives; we want to approximate the best motives we can while seeking to grow wherever we might.

HUMILITY AND EVANGELISM

A humble spirit is an essential character quality and prerequisite for soul evangelism. Honesty does a great deal to prepare one for reaching a lost and needy world. There are a number of reasons for this, several of which will be reviewed in this section.

Honesty as a Synonym for Humility

The posture of the evangelist should be one of humility if he or she is to enjoy maximal credibility in the proclamation of the gospel. Humility is necessary in the life of the evangelist lest he or she becomes arrogant in his or her work. It is an important component to any sincere evangelistic enterprise because it leads to honesty. Perhaps honesty and humility are synonyms. Honesty prevents an "us-versus-them" approach to evangelism that is always condescending and far from expressing the heart of Christ. An honest evangelist is mindful of the struggles of life and the relevance of the gospel in those struggles.

When a church marginalizes the experiences of those who are struggling in life, whether they be inside or outside of that fellowship, severe consequences follow. The implication of such a practice is the belief that everyone in that community must be perfect. Of course, no one is perfect, so a kind of pretense is bred among the membership. People will find that community too unsafe to share the honest struggles of their hearts. Pretense can give birth to legalism.

Humility and the Way of Grace

Humility goes so much further. It leads us to be honest and open to the constant need for grace. If someone seeking to justify his or her disinterest in the gospel makes the charge that there are hypocrites in the church, that criticism may have some validity. An honest person can openly admit that hypocrites may exist. In fact, we can go further. We can admit that we know firsthand there are hypocrites in the church because when we honestly evaluate our own lives we are aware of inconsistencies and compromises of which we are ashamed. Such honesty usually invites honesty in return. The person who was ready to reject Christianity will often respond that he or she also recognizes hypocrisy in his or her own life. When both the Christian and the non-Christian acknowledge they struggle, they have something in common. Honesty and humility will begin to characterize the conversation. There is no need for either to be condescending toward the other because they are two pilgrims on the same road, trying to make sense of life's complexities. The Christian can share openly and humbly how he or she has found the Bible to be relevant in life's complexities and struggles. The non-Christian's objection has provided the very opening for an honest explanation of the gospel.

Humility and Sin

Scripture says that we tend to suppress the truth in our unrighteousness (Rom. 1:18).[9] It is possible for us to reconstruct the way we perceive the world around us. This is sometimes due to sin. We make bad choices. At that moment, we can become sad in the face of our deficiencies, repent, and, by God's grace, seek to do better next time.

C. S. Lewis recognized a tendency in his own culture to live in denial of personal fault and culpability. He was concerned with how a sense of sin might be awakened in the lives of those he sought to evangelize. It is no small consideration, since an essential element of the gospel is the forgiveness of sin, and the whole message of the cross is irrelevant to the one who thinks he or she has no sin. Lewis observed,

> I cannot offer you a water-tight technique for awakening the sense of sin. I can only say that, in my own experience, if one begins from the sin that has been one's own chief problem during the last week, one is very often surprised at the way this shaft goes home. . . . Whatever method we use, our continual effort must be to get their mind away from public affairs and "crime" and bring them down to brass tacks—to the whole network of spite, greed, envy, unfairness and conceit in the lives of "ordinary decent people" like themselves (and ourselves).[10]

Humility and "Scratched Records"

There may be other factors that can affect the way the evangelist looks at life. Developmental theorists remind us that we pass through various phases of development. Scripture is written with an awareness of these processes. For example, in Samuel we read, "Now the boy Samuel was growing in stature and in favor both with the Lord and with men" (1 Sam. 2:26 NASB).[11]

It might be helpful to think of the process of development using the analogy of an old phonograph record. When we are born, it is as if someone put the needle of the phonograph into the groove of our record, and we begin to play the theme of our life. Unfortunately, in a fallen world our record will get scratched. As with the old records, when a scratch is particularly deep, we

tend to recycle in that rut over and over again. This phenomena can be called repetition in search of mastery. We look for surrogates with whom we might replay, often in projective ways, the events surrounding our having been scratched. We can spend significant periods of our lives trying to resolve the spiritual, psychological, and emotional conflicts related to these disorders.

Healing and Forgiveness

I am familiar with a true story of a young man whose "record" was horribly scratched in several places. When he was only four, the boy's mother died while she was giving birth to a younger brother. He may likely have struggled with abandonment issues. He was raised in a very large family that was also abusive. I do not believe the family was sexually abusive towards this particular boy, but they were certainly physically abusive, and he suffered much. At around age seventeen, he was kicked out of the home and had to make it on his own. It was a very traumatic experience for someone so young. This young man found work and was industrious at his job. Over a period of years he proved to be successful and moved up the ladder at his place of employment. But his problems were not over.

When he was of prosecutable age, someone filed a sexual harassment suit against this man. I believe he was innocent. Still, falsely accused, he was declared guilty and sent to prison for a crime he did not commit. One wonders if a person with these circumstances could ever recover.

The young man's name was Joseph. His story is told in the Bible in the Book of Genesis. It was his mother Rachel who died while giving birth to his younger brother Benjamin. It was his brothers who abused him. They were jealous of Joseph because their father Jacob had favored Joseph and given him a colorful coat. Jacob should have known better, for he had been the unloved son of his father Isaac, who preferred his brother Esau over him. The sins of the parents are often visited on the children to the third and fourth generations. Joseph does get better and Scripture tells how.

When he was at last elevated to the second-highest position in ancient Egypt, the names which Joseph chose for his own two sons provide the clues to his healing process. He named his first son Manasseh, which means "forget." Joseph said, "God has made me forget all my trouble and all my father's household" (Gen. 41:51 NASB). I do not think that Joseph meant that he forgot about his family altogether. Later, during a famine, when members of his family came to Egypt in hope of buying food, Joseph disguised himself and provided a banquet for his brothers. He had not forgotten them, seating each one of them in the chronological order of his birth. Certainly, he remembered them well. So what did he mean by naming his son Manasseh? Perhaps he is indicating by this that God gave him the power to forgive his brothers to the degree that he no longer made decisions based upon his painful past. In essence, he was able to make decisions based on what was in everyone's best interests rather than based on resentment or past pain. He forgave them and moved on.

These two things—the freedom to grieve rather than suppress the pain of past wounds and the power to forgive—are particularly relevant to the presentation of the gospel. If we lack these in our lives, we are most likely to gain them by discovering God's grace in forgiveness toward us. The gift of his forgiveness makes our unwillingness to forgive others appear rather petty by comparison. In fact, this is exactly what Christ taught his disciples in the parable of the unforgiving slave (Matt. 18:21–35).

Joseph's second son was named Ephraim (Gen. 41:52). The name Ephraim means "to be fruitful." God wants us to get on with the purposes for which he created us. To work through the issues and begin the lifelong process of healing is vital. It will add tenderness and patience to the demeanor of the Christian worker. The best evangelists and disciple makers are the those who are in touch with many of the operations of grace in their own lives. They are aware of their own deficiencies and revel in the kindness of God that he still chooses to use them for his purposes and pleasure.

CONNECTING: MAKING THE MOST OF OPPORTUNITIES TO SHARE THE GOSPEL

As men and women who are committed to fulfilling the Great Commission, we must find ways to connect with the lost of this world in order to begin the process of evangelism and discipleship. Without a relationship with the lost, it is difficult to win them for Christ and therefore impossible to disciple them into fruitful and mature believers.

Looking for Places to Connect

Humility brings a kind of sight to evangelists whereby they can discover openings to present the gospel. Evangelists are not out to win arguments but to communicate, as clearly and as effectively as possible, the love, forgiveness, and grace of God to all they meet. The greater general knowledge evangelists have, the more widely they will be able to connect the gospel to the life of any particular person in everyday conversation. In light of this, evangelists should be people whose natural curiosity about the universe that God has made should be always expanding. They should be lifelong learners.

Discovering Christian Answers to Complex Problems

In his book *Christianity and Classical Culture,*[12] Charles Cochrane sought to understand why Christianity spread so rapidly in its first few centuries under the Roman Empire when it seems that circumstances were politically and culturally antithetical to its growth. Some, taking their lead from Galatians 4:4 ("But when the fulness of time came, God sent forth His Son" [NASB]), might suggest that the fullness of time meant efficient Roman roads under the protection of Roman soldiers. This would have made transportation both easy and safe. Some have suggested that this refers to a common trade language, Koine Greek, which extended across the Roman Empire. This common language made it possible to communicate any message more quickly than had ever been possible before.

However, Cochrane builds a case throughout his book that the reason Christianity spread was because classical culture was asking questions for which it had no answers. The following questions plagued classical thinkers: Can civilization be safe? How can human nature and temperament be tamed or subdued in order to make life in the commonwealth secure? Can you have ethics without God? If it is not possible to have ethics without God, then whose god should it be? And if it is a matter of arbitrary choosing, then why can't Caesar be god? If a certain god is necessary for ethics, then how do we know which god is to be preferred? Are questions of religion clarified by nature, or are questions of nature clarified by religion? Can reason stand on its own, or must it be held in check by that which is real? Are questions of right and wrong, truth and error, a mere fantasy, or are they matters worthy of consideration and resolution? According to Cochrane, the answers Christians put forth to these and many other questions led to the rapid growth of Christianity.

This fact ought to intrigue the evangelist and prod him or her to discover the probing questions of this present age and culture, wrestling to understand what the Bible has to say about certain issues. Certainly some questions will emerge that are peculiar to particular times and places. On the other hand, some questions will reflect perennial concerns. These provide an opportunity for the evangelist to connect with individuals at a deeper level.

MORE PLACES TO CONNECT

In her book *Mysticism,* Evelyn Underhill identifies three categories that underscore the deepest human longings. While Underhill's categories are not exhaustive, they are helpful in enabling us to see places where we might connect those we meet with the gospel message. She says that there are

> three deep cravings of the self, three great expressions of man's restlessness which only mystic truth can fully satisfy. The first is the craving which makes him a pilgrim and a wanderer. It is the longing to go out of his normal world in search of a lost home, a "better country"; . . . the next is that craving of heart for heart, of the soul for its perfect mate, which makes him a lover. The third is the craving for inward purity which makes him an ascetic, and in the last resort a saint.[13]

Underhill is suggesting that these longings are universal. If it is possible to connect with another person at the point of one or more of these "cravings," it may lead to an opening for the presenta-

tion of the gospel. Most people can identify within themselves a kind of homesickness. It is a desire for home that haunts us even in our own homes. That thirst to satisfy nostalgic cravings and reconnect with people and places once familiar cannot seem to be quenched in the here and now. Perhaps the longing is ultimately for heaven. When these notions are brought to light in the midst of a conversation, it is surprising how the doors for entry to the gospel fly open.

Most people have a longing to connect relationally on a deep level, to love and be loved. The quest for a soul mate—as a spouse to share the adventures of life with or as a friend who, knowing all our faults, still remains faithful—is near to each of us. Unfortunately, geographic relocations, the passing of time with all of its capricious mutability, and even death itself lead us to wonder if the deepest relationship we long for might be with God. This disquietness within, when it bubbles to the surface in a conversation, leads obtrusively toward the rich themes of the gospel.

Each of us longs to have what is broken in us repaired. No honest person denies the dark side of all humanity. Our histories witness to it. Our cultures are continually shocked by it. Our sociopolitical institutions are clouded by it. When the longing to be mended remains a mere abstraction, generalized to the condition of the masses, it does not stir us as dramatically as it might. But in honest, vulnerable moments, when the participants in the conversation unmask themselves, owning their own sense of inner darkness, the points of contact become obvious and strengthen our presentation of the gospel message. In those moments, relationships cultivated by humility and honesty will look thoughtfully at the themes of grace. To share Christ in those circumstances should be easy and natural. Evangelism and spiritual nurturing need not be an awkward endeavor but a delight. Michael Green has observed, "When men have the will to speak of their Lord, they find no shortages of ways in which to do it."[14]

CONCLUSION

As we go about our journey in life, regardless of where it may take us, we must look for opportunities to share Christ along the way. Some opportunities will come about as a result of our own intervention and appointment while others will come as a result of God's sovereign timing. Regarding our preparation, the apostle Paul admonishes us to be ready in season and out of season for opportunities which come our way (2 Tim. 4:2).

The fulfillment of the Great Commission is dependent on human intervention. God largely has chosen to place his work in the hands of humanity. We have become his body, with our lips as his means of communication. In spite of our flaws and imperfections, he has chosen us through his own sovereign planning. Such a partnership is accomplishing his task of world evangelism and also contributes to our own personal and spiritual maturity. Our task is to obey his command and be actively involved in the disciple-making process.

NOTES

1. Henry George Liddell and Robert Scott, *A Greek-English Lexicon, Based on the German Work of Francis Passow* (New York: Harper and Brothers, 1871), p. 876.

2. This is a matter of deep concern for the apostle Paul in 1 Corinthians 1:1–17. The Corinthian church was divided. Factions or parties had formed in the church around certain personalities. Paul wants an end to these artificial identities; he wants a church united around the Lord Jesus Christ.

3. This is an image used effectively by A. W. Tozer in his book *The Pursuit of God.* How do you tune one hundred pianos? If you tuned the second to the first, the third to the second, the fourth to the third, and so on until you had tuned all hundred, it would result in discord. To tune one hundred pianos

so that they will each be in harmony with one another, you must tune them to a common tuning fork. In the same way, unity in the body of Christ is approximated when we make disciples of Christ and not of ourselves. (See A. W. Tozer, *The Pursuit of God* [Camp Hill, Pa.: Christian Publications, 1982], p. 96.)

4. Dawson Trotman, *Born to Reproduce* (Colorado Springs: NavPress, 1993).

5. This is a point developed by Francis Schaeffer in *The Mark of the Christian* (Downers Grove, Ill.: InterVarsity, 1974).

6. Robert Coleman, *The Master Plan of Evangelism,* 2d ed. (Grand Rapids: Spire, 1995).

7. Augustine, *The City of God* 1. 35. See also 2 Timothy 2:10.

8. Rebecca Manley Pippert, *Out of the Salt Shaker and Into the World: Evangelism as a Way of Life* (Downers Grove, Ill.: InterVarsity, 1979).

9. This is not an observation peculiar to Scripture. Aristotle noted that "vice is unconscious of itself" (*Nicomachean Ethics* 1095B). C. S. Lewis noted that "continued disobedience to conscience makes conscience blind" (*A Preface to Paradise Lost* [London: Oxford, 1954], p. 10).

10. C. S. Lewis, "Christian Apologetics," in *God in the Dock: Essays on Theology and Ethics,* ed. Walter Hooper (Grand Rapids: Eerdmans, 1970), p. 96.

11. In Luke 2:52, the Scriptures say that Jesus "kept increasing in wisdom and stature, and in favor with God and men" (NASB). We can observe in this: (1) experiential and intellectual development ("increasing in wisdom"); (2) physiological development ("stature"); (3) spiritual development ("in favor with God"); (4) social development ("and men"). Certainly it would be fair to add that there is also psychological and emotional development as well.

12. Charles Cochrane, *Christianity and Classical Culture: A Study of Thought and Action from Augustus to Augustine* (Oxford: Oxford University Press, 1940).

13. Evelyn Underhill, *Mysticism: The Preeminent Study in the Nature and Development of Spiritual Consciousness* (1911; reprint, New York: Image Books, 1990), pp. 126–27.

14. Michael Green, *Evangelism in the Early Church* (London: Hodder and Stoughton, 1970; reprint, London: Highland Books, 1990), p. 338.

PART TWO

Developmental Perspectives on Christian Education

LIFE SPAN DEVELOPMENT 6

Ellery Pullman

Those interested in studying developmental psychology today recognize the importance of viewing development from what is commonly known as the life span perspective. Development here is best understood as the study of change in behavior over the whole life span from birth until death. A life span view of development takes into consideration the multitude of changes that occur over time as a result of many factors interacting together. It also understands that developmental change occurs throughout the different phases of the life span, and that change tends to be cumulative, that is, earlier events affect later development. Development also occurs within various contexts and cultures.

The major contributions to human development come from the social science disciplines of cultural anthropology (i.e., the study of human developmental process in a variety of different cultures); sociology (i.e., the study of the role of the family, the church, education, and so forth, and their effect on the development of individuals); psychology (in particular, developmental psychology); and the natural science of biology (i.e., genetic and cellular development, the study of the effects of aging on development, and so on).

A developmental theory not only attempts to describe and explain changes in behavior as people develop over the life span but also attempts to show individual differences in these changes—for example, differences related to gender, race, and place in society. In other words, an effective theory should be able to describe and explain the course of development generally as well as specifically over the course of the life span. A good theory will help to explain why your best friend is changing but in a different way than you are, and why your children, though from the same family, may have different characteristics. A good theory may also help you understand the differences between yourself and those around you.

Theories of human development add new levels of understanding by suggesting causal relationships, unifying diverse observations, and identifying the importance of events that may have initially gone unnoticed. Theories of development can offer explanations regarding the origins and functions of human behavior and the changes that can be anticipated as the individual moves from one period of life to another.

Generally, developmental theory can be divided into several different categories, each with its own unique perspective. The theoretical perspectives that will be reviewed here will be the psychodynamic, cognitive, intellectual-ethical, and social learning theories.

PSYCHODYNAMIC THEORY

Psychodynamic is a classification used to differentiate several schools of thought, among them psychoanalytic theory and psychosocial theory. Psychodynamic theories of development are concerned primarily with personality and emotional development. The focus of such theories is on the way in which peoples' emotional and biological needs adapt to the expectations of the society in which they live.

Traditionally, psychodynamic theories have emphasized the role of early experience in the development of personality. As a result, this perspective has stimulated a great deal of inquiry into early childhood socialization processes and impending adolescent and adult adaptations. Much of the early research was based upon the works of Sigmund Freud and Erik Erikson. More recent additions to psychodynamic theories might include the works of Mary Ainsworth and her theories of child-parent attachment, James Marica concerning the development of adolescent identity, and Daniel Levinson and his perceptions of adult life structure.

Psychosocial Development

Perhaps the most important and influential theory for understanding life span development has been developed by Erik Erikson. He drew heavily upon the work of Freud in his early theoretical development but began to part ways with him over time. For example, Freud placed a great deal of emphasis on the role of sexuality (libido) and on the importance of the role of conflict involving the id, ego, and superego in determining personality and ensuing mental health. Freud referred to his theory as a psychosexual theory of development and tended to take a somewhat more pessimistic view of the developing individual, whereas Erikson's psychosocial theory is much more positive in its orientation, being concerned with the healthy development of the self.

Psychosocial theory represents human development as a product of the interaction of individual needs and abilities with societal expectations and demands. Psychosocial theory is also based on several organizing concepts. This theory depicts one's development as a building process that incorporates several key concepts.

The first concept is the progression of stages that occurs throughout the life span. A developmental stage is a period of life that is characterized by a specific underlying pattern. At each stage of development, the accomplishments from previous stages provide necessary resources for encountering and mastering the challenges of the next stage. Each stage is unique and leads to the acquisition of new skills and capabilities.

Erikson originally described human development as unfolding over eight stages, the first five spanning infancy, childhood, and adolescence; the last three describing adulthood. More recently, eleven stages of development have been identified.[1] The revised theoretical construct takes into consideration the emergent changes in society and how they impact human development.

As noted earlier, theories of development emerge and change within a cultural and historical context. For example, it is not unusual to view adolescence as a stage of development encompassing the ages of twelve to twenty-four. The changes in the timing of the onset of puberty, the changes in educational structures, as well as issues related to choices affecting one's education, vocation, and possibly marriage, all contribute to an expanded view of adolescence. As a result, adulthood is also affected, where old perspectives are replaced with new views of what it means to be adult at various ages. Figure 6.1 summarizes an expanded version of Erikson's earlier work. Specific changes involve the inclusion of a stage addressing the needs and concerns of a prenatal stage, a second stage of adolescent development, and a very old stage in adulthood.

Figure 6.1
Psychosocial Crises

Life Stage	Age	Psychosocial Crisis
Prenatal period		No apparent crisis—normal prenatal development
Infancy	Birth–2 yrs.	Trust versus mistrust
Toddlerhood	2–4 yrs.	Autonomy versus shame and doubt
Early school age	4–6 yrs.	Initiative versus guilt
Middle childhood	6–12 yrs.	Industry versus inferiority
Early adolescence	12–18 yrs.	Group identity versus alienation
Later adolescence	18–24 yrs.	Individual identity versus identify confusion
Early adulthood	24–35 yrs.	Intimacy versus isolation
Middle adulthood	35–60 yrs.	Generativity versus stagnation
Later adulthood	60–75 yrs.	Integrity versus despair
Very old age	75 until death	Immortality versus extinction

Erikson identified a series of issues or psychosocial crises that must be encountered and resolved if the person is to develop in a healthy manner. A developmental crisis arises when one must make adjustments to the demands and expectations of one's environment at each stage of development. Adjustment might call for the acquisition of new information, the development of a new skill, or the refinement of personal goals. The word *crisis* in this context refers to a normal process of understanding and adjusting to a new set of expectations rather than an extraordinary event in one's life.[2] Each developmental encounter may result in a positive or negative outcome.

Prenatal Stage. Although the prenatal period does not involve a stated psychosocial crisis, this stage of development can have long-term consequences following the birth of the child. Pregnancy may affect a woman's social roles and social status and may influence how people treat her. A woman's physical well-being and emotional state, as well as her attitude toward her pregnancy and her developing attachment to her unborn child, may very well set the stage for the quality of her parenting after the child is born.

Infancy Stage. In infancy the psychosocial crisis that exists is that *of trust versus mistrust* (birth–two years). The focus is on the development of a sense of connection to the larger social world. For infants trust is an emotion, that sense of confidence that they are valued, that all is well in the world, and that needs will be met. The nature of parental interaction with the child is crucial here. This sense of trust, initially established between mother and child, eventually expands to include other significant caregivers in the child's life.

Toddlerhood. The third stage, approximately two to three years of age, involves the accomplishment of autonomy versus shame and doubt. Children at this stage begin to realize that they can be the authors of their own actions. With the increasing development of physical and mental capacities, the child now begins to seek a greater degree of independence. If this growing urge to explore and investigate is encouraged, children grow more confident in themselves and become more autonomous in general. However, if their developing independence is met with parental disapproval or discouragement, children may question their own abilities and begin to harbor doubts about their adequacy.

Early School Age. During the ages of four to six, children experience the psychosocial crisis of initiative versus guilt. An increased capacity for taking responsibility for oneself prompts children to self-initiate greater investigation of their environment. Judicious parental support and encouragement increases the likelihood of a sense of initiative. Undue parental restriction or lack of parental support and approval is likely to promote a sense of guilt in children and leads to a lack of confidence in their ability to explore the world on their own.

Middle Childhood. Industry versus inferiority (approximately ages six to twelve) is characterized by the child's desire to manipulate objects and learn how things work. The task is to develop a capacity for industry while avoiding an excessive sense of inferiority. This is the early school age where children enter into the larger world of knowledge and work. Industry is an eagerness to acquire skills and perform meaningful work. The skills that are learned are new. They bring the child closer to the capacities of adults. Each new skill allows the child some degree of independence and may even bring new responsibilities that heighten his or her sense of worth. Inferiority may result, however, if adults perceive and communicate that such behavior is childish or troublesome.

Early Adolescence. During the initial years of adolescence (twelve to eighteen years), one confronts a new psychosocial conflict in which pressures to ally oneself with specific groups and to learn to be comfortable functioning as a member of a group are major preoccupations. This conflict is referred to as group identity versus alienation. Adolescents experience a search for involvement and question the type of groups they should belong to. They may seek commitments to church groups, reevaluate their family ties, and begin to understand the unique characteristics of their role in the community and the world at large.

Alienation, as defined by Mau, is a sense of social estrangement, an absence of social support or meaningful social connection.[3] The adolescent who experiences alienation does not have a sense of belonging to a group; rather, he or she is continually uncomfortable in the presence of peers and others.

Later Adolescence. The concept of <u>individual</u> identity versus identity confusion is probably one of Erikson's most famous concepts, and it is within that construct that this stage will be discussed. The years from eighteen to twenty-four are often characterized by a growing sensitivity to the process of identity development. Personal identity is developed as an individual struggles with questions such as: What is the meaning of my life? Who am I? Where am I going in life? Identity development during this period is a cornerstone of the unique individuality of adulthood. With the ever-increasing choices and life roles that are facing the later adolescent today and taking into consideration that more adolescents are living at home longer than ever before as well as delaying many of the decisions related to education, vocation, and marriage, the issue of identity is probably more important today than it was in the past.

Early Adulthood. Between the ages of twenty-four and thirty-five, the task of intimacy versus isolation is to develop close and meaningful relationships with others. Having attained a greater sense of personal identity in the previous stage, individuals are now able to share themselves with others on a greater moral, emotional, and sexual level. Intimacy is the ability to experience an open, supportive, and caring relationship with another person without fear of losing one's own identity in the process. The negative outcome of the crisis in early adulthood is isolation. Those unable or unwilling to share themselves with others suffer a sense of loneliness and distance, as well as a fragile identity.

Middle Adulthood. Generativity versus stagnation or self-absorption is the psychosocial crisis between the ages of thirty-five and sixty years. These years bring with them a new capacity for directing the course of action in one's own life and in the lives of others. Generativity implies the desire to attain a sense of sharing, giving, or productivity. Caring about the well-being of future generations and the world in which they live is embodied in the concept of generativity. The force counteracting generativity is stagnation. Stagnation suggests a lack of psychological growth, which may take the form of egocentrism or self-indulgence. Stagnation and self-absorption imply caring exclusively about oneself. A sense of emptiness often characterizes this person's life, and abilities are not used to their fullest extent.

Later Adulthood. Erikson suggests that the key to harmonious personality development in the later adult years (sixty to seventy-five years) is the ability to resolve the psychosocial crisis known as integrity versus despair. Integrity versus despair is resolved through the process of life review and self-evaluation. Factors such as health, family and peer relationships, and role loss are integrated with an assessment of one's past and present hopes and dreams. The achievement of integrity is the culmination of a life of psychosocial growth.

Whereas feelings of integrity and satisfaction result from a positive evaluation of one's life and acceptance of it, despair is characterized by regret over the past, fear of dying, and the frustration that accompanies the realization that it is now too late to do anything further. People resolving the crisis of later adulthood in the direction of despair cannot resist speculating about how things might have been or about what actions might have been taken if conditions had only been different.

Very Old Age. The last stage to be considered here is a more recent addition to Erikson's scheme. The fact that an increasing number of people are attaining advanced years means that some consideration must be given to a new stage of psychosocial development. For lack of a better term, this stage is referred to as *very old age,* taking into consideration the years from age seventy-five until death. Even though this stage was not specifically identified in Erikson's original theory, he later wrote a book about the dynamics of psychosocial development for the very old.[4] If older adults have achieved integrity, they believe that their lives have made sense. They are now more able to accept the end of life and view it as a natural part of the life span. The psychosocial crisis here is one of resolving the issue of immortality versus extinction.[5] The adult in this stage is faced with a new challenge—the potential conflict between the acceptance of death and the hope and desire that one's life has been spent in such a way as to leave a sense of legacy.

The potential negative outcome here is one of extinction.[6] The implication is that in place of a belief in continuous existence and transformation, one views the end of life as an end to attachment, change, and meaning. Instead of faith in the ideas of connection, continuity, and community, one experiences a great fear that death brings nothingness.

The challenge for the aging adult is to come to grips with a sense of the meaning and significance of life that involves not only one's past but also one's present role in society. Part of the challenge of the mature years is the necessity to transcend the several sources of personal identity and significance that characterize the adult years.

Psychosocial theory provides a unique and comprehensive way to understand and develop strategies for working with any age group. Very few theories give as complete a picture of development as does the psychosocial theory. It not only seeks to understand the uniqueness of the individual but also places a great deal of emphasis on the role of the context(s) that the individual is involved in.

We need to provide safe and caring environments for children that will encourage them to make and act on choices. Judicial guidance needs to be extended in light of the options and alternatives allowed for healthy choice making and relative to the abilities and understanding of the children involved. Involve children in activities that allow them to utilize all their senses and motor abilities. We need to make sure that children have the opportunity to experience various measures of success, whether through a new skill being learned or a game being played. We also need to be tolerant of accidents and mistakes, particularly when children attempt to do something on their own. Encourage completion of that which is begun; recognize efforts and accomplishments. Extend praise at every opportunity.

The central issue for early through later adolescents is the development of a healthy identity. For those who are believers, this must be developed from the perspective of who they are in Christ. The adolescent years mark a time when a greater conscious effort is made to answer the more pressing questions, "Who am I?" and "Where am I going?" Adolescents need positive role models who can provide mentoring support. Parents, teachers, coaches, and pastors can be of great help in assisting adolescents in this regard. Be willing to give realistic feedback to them as well, remaining aware that adolescents are often exhibiting characteristics from a variety of different identity status types. Since adolescents are trying on many different roles, use these as teachable moments to affirm and gently correct.

The psychosocial issues of intimacy, generativity, integrity, and immortality become driving forces throughout the adult years. The adult years are characterized by a need for growth in personal identity, achievement in one's vocation, growth in intimacy with others and with God, understanding the necessity for play and creativity, searching for meaning and significance, and finding ways to make lasting contributions. The church can help by pointing individuals toward Christ and assisting them in their search for meaning from God's point of view. Inner peace, happiness, and meaning are found in seeking the things of God rather than through the avenues of the world.

ADULT DEVELOPMENT

Daniel Levinson has sought to trace the course of adult development. Although he initially limited his study to forty males,[7] he has since added to our understanding of adult development by doing research with women as well.[8] Levinson suggests that our lives are divided into eras of approximately twenty-five years each, and each era consists of developmental periods marked by a distinct biopsychosocial character. A major transition occurs between each era, and there are also several transitions within each era.

The central concept in Levinson's theory of adult development is that of the life structure, the "underlying pattern or design of a person's life at any given time."[9] The key components of the life structure are relationships with one's spouse or significant other, children, work colleagues, or significant social groups, such as church or community clubs.

Levinson refers to the first stage of development, ages seventeen to forty, as early adult transition. This stage deals with the issues of independence, establishing an identity and a life separate from one's family. The young adult must now understand what it means to be an adult, find work, and create relationships. The midlife transition in the early forties deals with another set of issues—an awareness of mortality and the realization that certain dreams may not come to fruition. A further major transition, at around age sixty to sixty-five, focuses on the loss of physical powers, possible illness, and accepting that one may have achieved as much as one can. Late adulthood in Levinson's scheme is characterized by the cognitive and physical adjustments that one must make at this time. The ultimate task is finally coming to terms with the self, particularly knowing it and accepting it reasonably well, and being prepared for the end of life. A brief overview of Levinson's stages can be found in figure 6.2.

Figure 6.2
Levinson's Stages of Adult Development

Stage	Age	Description
Early Adult Transition	17–22	Leave the family and adolescent groups and make preliminary choices for adult life.
Entering the Adult World	22–28	Initial choices in love, occupation, friendship, values, and lifestyle; conflict between desire to explore and desire to commit.
Age 30 Transition	28–33	Period of reworking, modifying life structure; smooth transition for some, disruptive crisis for others; growing sense of need for change before becoming locked in because of commitment.
Settling Down	33–40	Establish a niche in society; progress on a timetable in both family and career.
Midlife Transition	40–45	Life structure comes into question, usually at a time of crisis in the meaning, direction, and value of each person's life. Neglected parts of the self such as talents, desires, and aspirations seek expression.
Entering Middle Adulthood	45–50	End of appraisal; time of choices, forming of new life structure in relation to occupation, marriage, locale; wide variation in satisfactions and extent of fulfillment.
Age 50 Transition	50–55	Work further on the tasks of midlife transition and modification of structure formed in the mid-40s; crisis if there was not enough change during the midlife transition.
Culmination of Adulthood	55–60	Build a new life structure; time of great fulfillment for middle adults; those who can rejuvenate themselves and enrich their lives.
Late Adult Transition	60–65	Reappraisal of life; moments of pride in achievement are interspersed with periods of despair.
Late Adulthood	65–80	Confrontation with self and life; need to make peace with the world; fewer illusions, broader perspective on life.
Late-Late Adulthood	80+	Final transition; period of further psychosocial development; preparation for death.

COGNITIVE THEORY

Cognitive development refers to the orderly changes that occur in the way people understand and cope with their world. Cognitive theorists are concerned with how we know, that is, with how we obtain, process, and use information. The design of cognitive (mental) growth was proposed by Swiss psychologist Jean Piaget.

Piaget maintained that there are four major periods of cognitive development. Each period is age-related and has certain characteristics that permit various types of knowing and understanding. Figure 6.3 gives a brief overview of Piaget's theory.

The following descriptions of development should be prefaced by a word about Piagetian terminology. Although Piaget refers to stages of development, each of the four major stages is designated as a period, for example, the sensorimotor period. When Piaget identifies substages within these four major periods, they are designated stages.

Figure 6.3
Piaget's Stages of Cognitive Development

Stage	Age	Characteristics
Sensorimotor	0–2	Develops schemes primarily through sense and motor activities.
Preoperational	2–7	Gradually acquires ability to conserve and decenter but not capable of operations and unable to mentally reverse actions.
Concrete Operations	7–11	Capable of operations but solves problems by generalizing from concrete experiences. Not able to manipulate conditions mentally unless they have been experienced.
Formal Operations	11–15	Able to deal with abstractions, form hypotheses, solve problems systematically, engage in mental manipulations.

Piaget's stages of cognitive development are summarized briefly as follows:

Sensorimotor Stage. According to Piaget, in the first period of cognitive development, thinking is limited to immediate sensory (perceptual) experience and motor (physical movement) behaviors; therefore, the first two years are given the label sensorimotor period. Children learn about their bodies and the immediate environment through direct manipulation and experimentation. For the infant, the world exists here and now. It is real only when it is being acted upon and sensed. At the beginning of this period, out of sight is out of mind. For example, a toy that is not being played with at present does not exist. Of particular importance at this stage are the basics of language acquisition toward the end of this period. Language acquisition helps the child in making the transition from this period of sensorimotor intelligence to a more cognitive intelligence.

Preoperational Stage. This is a period marked by a time when children become increasingly capable of thinking, using symbols such as words to represent the objects and events they experience. The use of the imagination comes to the forefront of their thinking. During this period, thinking and feeling are tied together. The preoperational child can mentally represent information through the senses but does not yet integrate this information with other knowledge in a logical manner. The following are some of the key characteristics of this period:

1. *Symbolic representation* is the ability to create and use symbols or images to represent objects, people, or events.
2. *Symbolic play* occurs when children pretend and engage in make-believe play.
3. *Animistic thinking* happens when children attribute feelings and intentions to objects that are not alive.
4. *Realism* is the tendency to attribute real physical properties to mental events.
5. *Egocentrism* is the inability to distinguish easily between one's own perspective and the perspective of others.
6. *Centration* is a process whereby children have a tendency to focus their attention on only one detail or aspect of an event.
7. *Irreversibility* is the inability of children to mentally reverse their thinking and return to the point of origin.

Concrete Operations. The major acquisition of the next period of development (approximately seven to eleven years of age) is the ability to think operationally; therefore, this period is referred to as concrete operations. An operation is a thought or mental action. Children are able to think more logically about their environment and execute mental operations that they previously had to carry out physically. More importantly, concrete operations represent a time where children are now able to reason more consistently. An especially important element is the ability to begin planning ahead before taking a course of action. Two key characteristics of this period are *decentration,* where the child can deal with several aspects of an issue simultaneously, and *reversibility,* which enables a child to work backward from a conclusion to the beginning point of a problem.

Formal Operations. The fourth period of cognitive development is formal operations which begins around age twelve and ends at approximately age fifteen and is characterized by the ability to manipulate abstract ideas. Formal operational thought arises from a combination of maturation and experience. A distinguishable feature of formal operational thought is the ability to think outside the box—to think of possibilities, not just present reality.

Formal operational thinking becomes an integral component of the adolescent's movement toward adulthood. The adolescent begins to implement various responsible behaviors in his or her preparation for future adult roles and is also increasingly viewed as one who reflects on his or her own thinking processes. In essence, the adolescent thinks more about thinking. Such reflection and reasoning becomes vitally important for the adolescent as he or she begins to construct a personally meaningful value system or worldview that incorporates beliefs, opinions, and attitudes.

It should be noted that a number of studies have pointed out that not all older adolescents and adults attain or exhibit formal operational thinking. It has been argued by some that only 40 to 60 percent of first-year college students can do so. Also, some people may attain formal operations only in certain areas of personal interest and expertise. Even Piaget notes that different individuals may attain formal operations at different ages and that the manner and age at which this ability is displayed may depend on aptitude and experience.

There are several guidelines for applying Piaget's concepts. First, the teaching of biblical concepts needs to focus on what learners at each stage can do and avoid what they cannot meaningfully understand. This implication needs to be understood very carefully, as recent research has shown that children in the preoperational and concrete operational stages can do more than initially believed by Piaget. Second, children in these stages should be given ample opportunity to describe and explain things through the use of artwork, body movement, role play, musical performance, and speech. Third, be sure to arrange situations to permit social interactions so children can learn from one another. Fourth, encourage problem-solving processes where the student is asked to draw on that which is already known and to make application to new experiences. This becomes vitally important in the development of higher levels of thinking, particularly as they relate to issues of faith development. Fifth, encourage students to develop their metacognitive knowledge and skills by thinking about the various conditions that affect how they learn and remember. Here we are helping the learner to reflect on not only the importance of the principles being learned but also how they might be applied to present-day circumstances. This becomes increasingly important when working with adult learners who may tend to organize and transfer learning based on prior experience.

INTELLECTUAL-ETHICAL THEORY

William Perry, building on the work of Piaget's concept of formal operational thinking, studied the intellectual-ethical development of college students. Perry's scheme of cognitive and ethical development posits that later adolescents and early adults move through four categories of development:

1. Dualism: They view the world in polar terms.
2. Multiplicity: They begin to see the possibility of several right positions.
3. Relativism: They identify themselves with sources of authority and values.
4. Commitment: They make value choices from among various alternatives and commit themselves to those choices.

According to Perry, the majority of college freshman fit in the dualism category. This position carries with it certain attitudes that have considerable impact on students' learning styles. At this stage, students will seize upon structure and organization as supports to help them make sense of their learning. They may be somewhat overwhelmed by assignments that ask for their opinion, in-class activities that carry the expectation that they learn from their peers, any signs of confusion or lack of organization in their teachers, and assignments that call for undirected, independent learning.

Obviously, it is in these students' best interest to move beyond the dualism stage. Those working with students in this stage of development can help them by designing strategies that consciously take students to another level. For example, a teacher could provide structure in a sequence of assignments that leads from supervised to more autonomous learning or teach multiple perspectives on a single issue, thus helping them to see more than one point of view on a matter—to move beyond the black-and-white issues. These are techniques that accommodate the students' developmental stage and entry to the next stage of intellectual development.

Not every college-age young adult moves beyond the dualism stage, however. There are several alternatives for those who choose not to develop. Some may retreat and draw back. This occurs when they avoid making tough decisions about integrating their faith with their living. A second alternative to healthy progression is to escape at level two (multiplicity) by avoiding adult responsibilities and commitments. At this point, students may verbalize a cynicism about spiritual matters. They may take the position of devil's advocate when discussing spiritual matters with others. A final alternative to healthy development is temporizing. This manifests itself as a delay at the same sublevel within one of the three main categories of intellectual-ethical development. Temporizing may be a result of young adults' unwillingness to explore relevant issues of the faith in relationship to their own worldviews.[10]

Helping college-age young adults come to a mature faith in Christ can be a significant challenge. Many of these young people have moved away from home for the first time and are actively exploring new frontiers of living. They are on a search for answers to some of life's most perplexing questions. Issues such as the ethical use of force to solve global conflicts, the depletion of the rain forest, world poverty, the AIDS epidemic, and global warming are just a few of their concerns. Many of these problems do not have simple answers. College students need to be provided with God's principles of decision making and then guided toward the proper application of Scripture to life's dilemmas. They need to be challenged to think critically about the answers posed by postmodern philosophies steeped in naturalism and relativism. God's Word provides moral absolutes that, if violated, produce long-term consequences. This newfound freedom of choice requires a large measure of responsible decision making.

SOCIAL LEARNING THEORY

A theoretical perspective that is considered behavioristic in nature is social learning theory. The position taken by social learning theorists is that behavior involves the interaction of people, with many different environmental conditions affecting a person's role and learning within a given context.

Albert Bandura, who has done the greatest amount of work with this theory, does not dispute the role that reinforcement plays in guiding behavioral outcomes. However, he believes that such concepts as imitation, modeling, and observational learning account for many of a person's behavioral patterns. For example, some behaviors can be imitated and learned without any form of reinforcement. Much of what children learn occurs through their natural tendency to imitate or model the behavior of others. This would also include the use of various cognitive skills and strategies that have tended to be minimized in the behavioristic approach. As a result, Bandura has established a number of themes unique to the social learning approach.

Some of the key elements are as follows: (1) An individual is continuously engaged in two-way interaction with the self and the environment. In other words, we influence our environment as well as being influenced by it. (2) We can learn through observation without any immediate external reinforcement. (3) Our cognitive expectations and perceptions affect what we do, and our awareness of the consequences of such behavior influences our choices of behavior. (4) We are active processors of information and not the mere robot-like people that earlier behaviorists would have us believe we are. We do have the ability to use various cognitive strategies to engage in processing information to evaluate potential outcomes of various chosen behaviors.[11]

Much of the research in social learning theory has sought to specify the conditions that enhance learning through imitation and modeling. For example, researchers have shown that people are more likely to imitate a model they admire and perceive as being similar to themselves than someone who is not highly regarded. Parents and other significant caregivers are children's most effective models during the early periods of development. As development continues and the person's world expands, peers, coworkers, and other significant people have the potential to be effective models as well. This process eventually leads a person to the realization that he or she is able to be a model and example for others.

The concepts of modeling and imitation are continuously referred to in Scripture. Two examples that are well-documented in the Bible are the role of our Lord with the disciples (John 13:15) and the writings of the apostle Paul (Acts 20:35; 1 Cor. 4:16; 11:1; 1 Thess. 1:6–7; 2:14), both of which encourage us to look at their examples and to be imitators of those examples in all we do and say. The implications for anyone involved in working with individuals or groups are tremendous. Relationships are crucial for furthering the gospel no matter what the context might be. We dare not underestimate the importance of being examples worthy of imitation.

CONCLUSION

This chapter has sought to provide a brief overview of several life span developmental theories in use today. No one theory is adequate in and of itself to give us a complete understanding of life span development. However, when viewed from different points of reference, each contributes something to our understanding of the needs and issues of those to whom we are called to serve. An understanding of these developmental perspectives allows us to be deliberate in our planning and implementation of various strategies for ministry. Ministry, whether it involves forms of communication, curriculum planning, discipling and mentoring, counseling, or parenting, can be done with confidence. We have the Holy Spirit's guidance as we seek to be intentional and effective in understanding and meeting learners' needs.

NOTES

1. B. M. Newman and P. R. Newman, *Development through Life: A Psychosocial Approach* (New York: Brooks Cole Wadsworth, 1999), p. 37.

2. E. H. Erikson, *The Life Cycle Completed: A Review* (New York: Norton, 1982), p. 31.

3. R. Y. Mau, "The validity and development of a concept: Student alienation," *Adolescence* 27 (1992): 731–41.

4. E. H. Erikson et al., *Vital Involvement in Old Age* (New York: Norton, 1986).

5. Newman and Newman, *Development through Life,* p. 529.

6. Ibid.

7. D. J. Levinson, *The Seasons of a Man's Life* (New York: Knopf, 1978).

8. D. J. Levinson, *The Seasons of a Woman's Life* (New York: Ballantine, 1996).

9. Levinson, *Seasons of a Man's Life,* p. 6.

10. D. Dirks, "Foundations of Human Development," in *Foundations of Ministry: An Introduction to Christian Education for a New Generation,* ed. Michael J. Anthony (Grand Rapids: Baker, 1992), p. 79.

11. A. Bandura, "Social Cognitive Theory of Moral Thought and Action," in *Handbook of Moral Behavior and Development: Vol. 1. Theory,* ed. W. M. Kurtiness and J. L. Gewirtz (Hillsdale, N.J.: Erlbaum, 1991), pp. 45–103.

MORAL DEVELOPMENT THROUGH CHRISTIAN EDUCATION   7

James Riley Estep Jr. and Alvin W. Kuest

What is moral development? This question is often asked throughout society. Interest in the development of morals in children and adults has even reached into the arena of public education. Such bestsellers as Robert Coles's *The Moral Intelligence of Children,* William Kilpatrick's *Why Johnny Can't Tell Right from Wrong and What We Can Do about It,* and most recently William Bennett's *The Educated Child* all highlight current interest in moral development among parents, counselors, and educators.

What makes a moral decision right or wrong? What is the reasoning that goes on within each decision? Are morals individually developed or adopted from society? Do children make the same moral decisions as teens or adults? Are there gender differences in moral decision making? Is morality concerned with actions, virtues, behaviors, reasons, motives, or a combination of these? What factors drive the developmental process? Do Christians approach moral development differently than non-Christians? Why or why not? How does spiritual formation relate to moral development—or does it? How influential are religious beliefs in moral development? These are but a few of the questions being asked throughout society today. The answers have implications for the way we teach, live in society, and raise our children.

DO MORALS REALLY DEVELOP?

Various approaches to moral development have been presented in the twentieth century. Each of these approaches to moral development represents the assumptions and theoretical issues of the theorists. Four general approaches to moral development, as noted by Bonnidell Clouse, are the psychoanalytical, learning/conditioning, cognitive/moral reasoning, and moral potential (see figure 7.1).[1] Each of these approaches represents a fundamentally different understanding of morality and its development.

A foundational issue is whether morals develop, which implies a unilateral, progressive, standard process, or whether they are formed, which implies the opposite. This is not an issue of mere semantics. Words convey concepts with implicit assumptions and limitations.

Similarly, the means of moral development reflect the theoretical approach to it. Moral development has been described in a variety of ways, each with its own distinct understanding of the nature of morality. For example, advocates of character education regard morals as teachable constructs of content, whereas values clarification assumes that morals are implicit within the human being and simply need identification and explanation. Similarly, those supporting moral behavior principally regard morality as action, whereas moral conflict provides a more Freudian/Jungian psychological motif for moral development.

Figure 7.1
Contemporary Approaches to Moral Development

Approach	Proponents	Description	Morality results from . . .
Psychoanalytical	Sigmund Freud	Development occurs due to psychological conflict between the ego, superego, and id.	Conflict
Conditioning	B. F. Skinner, Behaviorists	Development occurs due to the individual being exposed to external stimuli and is conditioned with a behavioral response to a given situation.	Action
Cognitive/ Moral Reasoning	Jean Piaget, Lawrence Kohlberg, Carol Gilligan	Development is a process that accompanies cognitive/intellectual development, with each level representing a "higher" level of authority by which moral decisions are made.	Knowledge
Moral Potential	Carl Rogers, Abraham Maslow, Humanists	Development of morals is innate to humanity and is progressed through the process of self-actualization as needs, basic and advanced, are fulfilled.	Potential

PREDOMINANT COGNITIVE MODELS OF MORAL DEVELOPMENT

The theories of moral development with the most impact on education have been those relying on cognitive development, beginning with Jean Piaget. His basic concept of moral development was one of internalization of external rules. According to Piaget, morals begin as external, heteronomous elements and move toward autonomous internal elements as they are appropriated by individuals.[2] From Piaget's basic concept, Lawrence Kohlberg and Carol Gilligan later advanced and promoted their theories of moral development. Figure 7.2 provides an overview of their levels/stages of moral development.

Jean Piaget (1896–1980)

Piaget believed that "all morality consists in a system of rules, and the essence of all morality is to be sought for in the respect which individuals acquire for those rules."[3] Though perhaps better known for his work in cognitive development (see chapters 6 and 10), he also assembled some notable findings in the realm of moral development. His work in moral development and cognitive development was centered in studies of children. Piaget's interest was in how children learn to think and reason, and his work has made a lasting impact on how to understand and teach children. His research has provided the basis for many ongoing studies. The impact of Piaget's work not only affected children. His work also led to a better understanding of adult learning and thinking processes.

Piaget's work on the moral development of children was first published in 1932. In his work he analyzed children's spoken responses to questions about the rules of games, clumsiness, lying, stealing, and justice. Two broad modes (stages) of moral thought were identified in children ages six to twelve: heteronomy (or moral realism) and moral autonomy. The youngest children were in the stage of heteronomy. Here the rules of the game and of life were laid down by adults and were held as sacred "laws of the gods" that one must not transgress. This stage of moral development gradually gives way to autonomy.[4] Here the rules are seen as the outcome of a free decision and worthy of respect to the degree that they have enlisted mutual consent. No longer seen as the requirements set down by a superior, they are seen as requirements for group relations.[5]

Piaget conducted extensive observations and interviews with children in an attempt to understand the manner in which they set up and interpreted the rules of the games they played. He observed them playing common games, which the children developed with little formal training and minor adult influence. Marbles was the primary game used. From his studies he concluded that children up to two years of age used marbles as a physical activity. The concept of rules for the game did not exist. The game was a copycat of what they had seen but was used exclusively as a motor activity.

Piaget watched as older children developed rules, and he asked them questions about the rules and structure of the game. He then tried to introduce a new set of rules and observed the children's reactions. The moral realist, or heteronomist, believes

Figure 7.2
Comparative Cognitive Models of Moral Development

Piaget's Modes

Moral Realism (Ages 4–7)
Moral Autonomy (Ages 10+)

Kohlberg's Levels/Stages

Level 1: Preconventional (Ages 4–10)
    Stage 1: Punishment Orientation
    Stage 2:: Naive Reward Orientation

Level 2: Conventional (Ages 10–13)
    Stage 3: Good-boy/Good-girl Orientation
    Stage 4: Authority Orientation

Level 3: Postconventional (Ages 13+)
    Stage 5: Social Contract Orientation
    Stage 6: Morality of individual principles and conscience

Gilligan's Levels

Level 1: Preconventional Morality (Ages 4–10)—Concern for self and survival

Level 2: Conventional Morality (Ages 10–13)—Concern for being responsible, caring for others

Level 3: Postconventional Morality (Ages 13+)—Concern for self and others as interdependent

that all rules are unchangeable and are handed down by all-powerful authorities. When Piaget suggested new rules be introduced into the game of marbles, the young children became troubled; they insisted that the rules had always existed as they were and could not be changed. The moral autonomist, by contrast, accepts change and recognizes that rules are merely convenient, socially agreed-upon conventions, subject to change by consensus.[6]

Piaget believes that adolescents usually become formal-operational thinkers. As such they are able to compare the real to the ideal and create contrary-to-fact propositions; are cognitively capable of relating the distant past to the present; understand their roles in society, in history, and in the universe; and can conceptualize their own thoughts and think about their mental constructs as objects. It is at ages eleven and twelve that youth begin to spontaneously introduce concepts of belief, intelligence, and faith into their religious identities.[7]

Thus, the cognitive development of adolescents has a significant bearing on their moral development and needs to be considered. Nevertheless, Piaget did not formally report on the moral development of the adolescent. However, two other significant researchers in moral development, Lawrence Kohlberg and Carol Gilligan, included all age groups in their work.

Lawrence Kohlberg (1927–1987)

Kohlberg's work on moral development complemented and expanded Piaget's research, so much so that when the subject of moral development is brought up, Kohlberg's name comes to the forefront, not Piaget's. Kohlberg began his research with a group of fifty American males, ages ten through twenty-eight, whom he interviewed every three years for eighteen years. As a result of this research, he established three levels of morality with six stages of moral development. The rate of development varied for each of the participants and none reached the upper developmental levels.

Kohlberg loved moral dilemmas. He built his research around a series of scenarios in which participants had to make decisions based on their own frame of reference. Perhaps his most famous scenario is the one involving Heinz:

In Europe a woman was near death from a special kind of cancer. There was one drug that the doctors thought might save her. It was a form of radium that a druggist in the same town had recently discovered. The drug was expensive to make, but the druggist was charging ten times what the drug cost him to make. He paid $200 for the radium and charged $2,000 for a small dose of the drug. The sick woman's husband, Heinz, went to everyone he knew to borrow the money, but he could only get together $1,000, which is half of what it cost. He told the druggist that his wife was dying and asked him to sell it cheaper or let him pay later. But the druggist said, "No, I discovered the drug, and I am going to make money from it." So Heinz got desperate and broke into the man's store to steal the drug for his wife.[8]

The interviewees were then asked a series of questions about each of the dilemmas. Should Heinz have done that? Was it actually wrong or right? Why? Is it a husband's duty to steal the drug for his wife if he can get it no other way? Would a good husband do it? Did the druggist have the right to charge that much when there was no law actually setting a limit on the price? Why? Kohlberg does not concern himself with the statements about whether an action is right or wrong. What shows the differences in moral maturity is the reasoning given for the action, why it is right or wrong.

To bring the dilemma into a Christian context, Charles Sell, in his book *Transitions through Adult Life,* suggests a different scenario with a similar set of questions. In his scenario he asks the reader to "imagine being in Corrie ten Boom's house. The Nazis, who are occupying her country, stand at the doorway. They ask, 'Are there any Jews in this house?' Knowing that several are cowering under the dining room table, what would you say?"[9]

Kohlberg's Moral Development Stages. Level one is preconventional morality, wherein children are responsive to cultural rules and labels of good and bad but interpret these based upon the punishment or reward they will receive for their decisions.[10] The two stages of level one are punishment orientation and naive reward. Stage one would be indicated by the fear of punishment: "It is wrong to lie because I will be punished." Stage two is shown by the attitude that the action is okay if it satisfies my needs: "It is okay for the druggist to charge so much money. He made the drug, so he deserves to get rich."

Level two is conventional morality, where maintaining the child's family, group, or nation is seen as valuable in its own right, regardless of immediate or obvious consequences. Loyalty is of utmost importance.[11] The two stages of level two are good boy/good girl orientation and authority and social order orientation. A stage three person would justify his or her action out of a desire to gain approval from others: "I would tell the Nazis the truth because good citizens do not lie," or "Heinz should steal the drug because he is a good husband, and it would be the natural thing to do considering his love for his wife." Stage four is indicated by a desire to maintain the rules of society: "Heinz should not steal because stealing is wrong." Most of Kohlberg's participants remained in stages three and four. He surmised that women, because of their desire to care for others, seldom, if ever, rose above stage three.[12]

In later studies, Kohlberg discovered that students moving from level two to level three passed through an additional stage. In this stage, simply called stage four, students moved from heteronomous decision making to autonomous decisions. This stage is exemplified by college students who have seen conventional morality as relative and arbitrary but have not yet discovered universal ethical principles. They then may drop into a hedonistic ethic of doing their own thing, as noted in the hippie culture of the 1960s. In essence, stage four maintains, "Whatever decision Heinz makes is okay as long as it is his decision."

Level three is postconventional morality, where the person is able to make autonomous decisions. Up to this point all moral decisions have been influenced by those around the person. Now moral decisions are made solely by the individual based on his or her own beliefs and ideals. Level three includes stages five (the social-contract orientation) and six (morality of individual principles and conscience). In stage five, right action is based on avoiding the violation of others' rights. For example, "Taking the drugs in this situation was not wrong. The laws were not set up for this situation." Stage six is considered by many to be a purely theoretical stage. Kohlberg mentioned only three individuals who may have reached this level: Martin Luther King Jr., Mahatma Ghandi, and Jesus Christ. At this stage the decision is made based on the principle of justice to which the individual has dedicated himself or herself. The good of the cause transcends law and considers the good of the people served. In deciding whether to steal the drug or let his wife die, it is morally right to steal.

Kohlberg's research into moral development is based on justice, which ultimately is based on abstract, rational principles by which all individuals can be treated fairly.[13] Justice also carries with it the element of personal integrity, exemplified by statements such as "I have standards that must be maintained." Caring only appears briefly in stage three and would prevent the participant from advancing any further. Because his work deals mainly with American men and took place only in laboratory situations, Kohlberg's research has come under a great deal of criticism in recent years.

Carol Gilligan (b. 1936)

Gilligan is quoted as saying that "men feel secure alone at the top of a hierarchy, securely separate from the challenge of others. Women feel secure in the middle of a web of relationships; to be at the top of a hierarchy is seen as disconnected."[14]

Kohlberg's study involved mostly American males, and the characteristics of the stages are those of men and not women. One of his students, Carol Gilligan, became concerned about this biased treatment of the moral development of women by Kohlberg, Freud, Piaget, and Erikson. The disturbing factor was that their research always concluded that women were deviant or deficient. Basing her work on Nancy Chodorow's research on personality differences between males and females, Gilligan found that males and females make moral decisions on different bases. Chodorow's research found that children are generally raised by the mother, and the father is basically absent. Therefore, girls identify with the nurturing of the mother, whereas boys must separate themselves in order to find their own identities. Not having a father to identify with, they learn to keep an emotional distance from others.[15]

As Gilligan began her research, she was surprised to discover that studies on moral development only included young boys and men, resulting in an obvious (albeit unintentional) bias toward men. That women do not rise above Kohlberg's level two is not surprising considering that the list of desirable feminine characteristics are tact, gentleness, awareness of the feelings of others, strong need for security, and an easy expression of tender feelings. In her definitive work *In a Different Voice: Psychological Theory and Women's Development,* Gilligan says that the voice of women has been left out of moral development theory. She concludes that there are two basic approaches to moral reasoning. In the justice perspective, people are differentiated and seen as standing alone—the focus is on the rights of the individual. In the care perspective, people are viewed in terms of their connectedness with other people, and the focus is on their communication with others. As they mature,

women become more nurturing, and the ethic of caring becomes the basis for their moral development. From Gilligan's point of view, Kohlberg has greatly underplayed the importance of the care perspective in the moral development of both females and males.[16]

Gilligan's research follows the same three levels that Kohlberg developed, but her reasoning differs, and she does not recognize intermediate stages. Level one, preconventional morality, is an orientation toward self. At this simplest level, women are pragmatically and egocentrically preoccupied with self-interest and survival: "I will not steal the drugs because if they catch me I will go to jail." Level two, conventional morality, identifies goodness with responsibility toward others: "I think there must be other ways besides stealing it, like if he could borrow the money or make a loan or something, but he really shouldn't steal the drug—but his wife shouldn't die either."[17] Level three focuses on the dynamics between self and others. Self-interest reemerges, combined with the need to please others: "Even if I must sacrifice myself, I am compelled to seek the medicine that my wife needs."

According to Gilligan, what is needed is a rethinking of our understanding of morality. Women view the moral domain differently than men do, and these differences need to be incorporated into our theories about morality. Current moral theory too easily dismisses the specific relationships that exist between individuals. We need a moral theory that will take this into account and will on occasion allow the rights of a person to be sacrificed for the sake of maintaining such a relationship.[18]

CHRISTIAN REFLECTION ON MORAL DEVELOPMENT THEORY

Christian educators have both praised and pilloried contemporary moral development theories, particularly those of Kohlberg and, by association, Piaget and Gilligan.[19] Several basic criticisms of their theories have arisen. First is the simple, narrow, and solitary definition of morality used by theorists. The assumption of Kohlberg and Gilligan is that morality can be simply and narrowly defined and that it rests on the reasonableness of a moral proposition, for example, the decision made during a moral crisis. This assumes that morality is merely a cognitive process. However, this is far too simple and narrow. Morals are more than just cognitive. What of behavior? Moral reason alone does not make an action correct, just, or merciful. Are morality and intellectual development inseparably linked? Does moral reason equal moral decision or action? Doesn't the situationality of moral dilemmas make it impossible for morality to form with any consistency?

Second, is morality situation or dilemma driven? Paul Vitz comments that Kohlberg's dilemma approach to moral development "makes all morality ... seem both abstract and difficult," assessing that his "approach doesn't bring about the internalization of Christian morality, because it is fundamentally in conflict with that morality."[20]

Third, the philosophical assumptions regarding morality and human nature are often questioned by Christian educators. Paul Vitz comments that "Kohlberg has put a great deal of political and social philosophy into his theory," describing him as having "unconsciously smuggled" an ideology into his developmental theory.[21] This does present Christian educators with some issues. For example, Iris Cully critiques the implications of Kohlberg, stating that "the Christian could not affirm, with level [stage] five thinking, that the social contract is an ultimate form of morality."[22] Similarly, the assumption that humanity is intrinsically good gives insufficient attention to the "dark side of the human self" and is often questioned by Christian educators.[23]

Fourth, many Christian educators find Kohlberg's view of religion, or lack thereof, a barrier to making use of his theory. While Kohlberg did remove religion from the concept of moral development, paradoxically, his final stage of moral development resorts to a tenet similar to religious mysticism such as that articulated by the Catholic theologian Teilhard de Chardin.[24]

Kohlberg's theory of moral development provides a form or structure for moral reasoning, but without substance it is an empty vessel. However, faith could provide the content for the structures, and hence the idea of "religious inquiry" is given credence for moral reasoning on a theological basis.[25] Ironically, while Kohlberg and Fowler utilize the same structure for moral and faith development, they are divided as to which is causative

of the other.[26] Kohlberg maintains that moral development precedes faith development, and therefore faith is not an element of moral development, while Fowler maintains that faith development precedes moral development.[27] Thus, the place of religious belief in moral development is not given credence by Kohlberg.

VOICES FOR MORAL DEVELOPMENT THEORY IN THE CHRISTIAN EDUCATION COMMUNITY

Christian educators have often turned to Scripture and theology to supply the foundation for understanding moral development. Dennis Dirks notes the developmental framework (not theory) presented in the metaphor of moral growth throughout the New Testament (1 Cor. 2:1ff.; 13:11; Heb. 5:12–14; Phil. 2:14; Eph. 4:15), as well as the concepts of internalization of values (Eph. 6:6; Matt. 5:1ff.) and moral transformation (Rom. 12:1–2).[28]

Several theological tenets have likewise been employed as foundational bases for moral development within the Christian community. For example, Bonnidell Clouse has suggested the *imago dei* as a theological foundation for moral development theory. Similarly, Joel Brondos suggests that the theological premise of sanctification has been used to provide a suitable portrait of moral growth in the New Testament.[29]

However, moral development theory requires more than foundational premises. Can the Christian education community articulate a theory of moral development that is consistent with evangelical theology and the findings of the social sciences? Stanley Hauerwas contends that the reason Christians adopt moral development theories is "because of their lack of conceptual paradigms" for morality.[30] Three major voices in the Christian education community have spoken out regarding moral development theory.

Donald Joy describes the path of moral development as a pilgrimage. He affirms the value of Kohlberg, particularly in regard to his levels of moral reasoning (not necessarily the stages) but sees the social sciences as "myopic, if not blind" to what "ought to be," having been fixated on what is observable.[31] Hence, moral development must have insights from theology, not just the social sciences, in order to provide a comprehensive view of the process.

For Joy, moral development must be perceived through the lens of the pilgrimage-life, which "consistently is dynamic, relational, aspirational, epochal, and cumulative."[32] He comments that "ethical development on the pilgrimage tends to be characterized by two features: (1) an eagerness to move ahead to better perspectives and solutions . . . and (2) a magnetic attraction for advanced ways of interpreting reality . . . in which the 'vision' is embraced well before matching 'performance' is attained."[33] He uses concentric spheres of moral levels to parallel Kohlberg's levels.[34] Figure 7.3 contains an adaptation of his moral development theory, and figure 7.4 explains the various shells within the moral sphere or levels. Theologically, Joy maintains that the incarnation was "an adventure of reverse transformation," wherein Jesus breached the developmental process of humanity, and "hence an entry station is opened at every stage and level by which any person might encounter and engage the redeeming Prince."[35]

Figure 7.3
Donald Joy's Levels of Moral Development

Level	Label	Example	Description/ Explanation
Level 1	Egocentric	Taboos	Response to physical consequences
Level 2	Hetero-centric	Laws	Response to respect persons and their rules and laws
Level 3	Logo-centric	Principles	Corporate contracts and vows voluntarily entered into and faithfully sustained

Bonnidell Clouse presents a biblical paradigm of moral formation that is responsive to and reflective of the four approaches to moral development discussed in her book *Teaching for Moral*

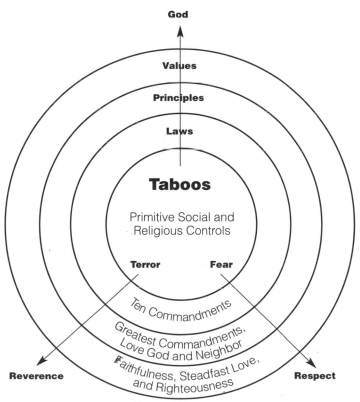

Figure 7.4
Donald Joy's Paradigm of Moral Development

Adapted from Joy, *Moral Development Foundations*, p. 24.

Growth (i.e., psychoanalytic, conditioning, moral reasoning, and moral potential). According to Clouse, the biblical approach to moral formation is comprehensive, whereas the four previous approaches are fragments of the whole (figure 7.5). "Each of the major psychologies . . . emphasizes one of the four expressions of morality: conflict, action, knowledge, and potential. By contrast, the Bible stresses all of them, *thus presenting a more complete picture of what it means to be a moral person.*"[36]

Clouse presents a biblical approach to moral development that has four components:

1. *Conflict,* which can be approach-approach (Josh. 24:14–18) or approach-avoidance (Rom. 5:17; 7:21–24)
2. *Action,* which is an integration of personal and social morality (Ps. 15:1–4; Amos 5:11–12, 21–22; Matt. 25:31–40; James 1, 2)
3. *Knowledge,* which is linked to conduct (Ps. 119:34; John 13:7; Eph. 2:12; Phil. 4:9; James 2:17)
4. *Potential,* because of the *imago dei* (Phil. 2:7; Col. 1:17) and redemption (Ps. 138:8; Rom. 8:17; 2 Cor. 3:18; 1 Peter 2:2; 2 Peter 1:1; 3:8)

Hence, moral development is the result of a combination of conflict, action, knowledge, and potential, as denoted by the social sciences and exemplified in Scripture.

While advocating the developmental approach to morality, Ted Ward provides a more comprehensive perspective on the field of moral development. He has an appreciation for Kohlberg's findings, particularly the three levels of moral development. According to Ward, one's view of authority is indicative of one's moral developmental level. For example, obedience to law is a factor that marks one's passage from level one to level two, while trust marks one's passage from level two to level three.[37] Although Ward makes use of the three levels devised by Kohlberg, he does not limit moral development to a cognitive process.

Ward suggests that the metaphor of a bridge leading from moral truth to moral action provides a more comprehensive concept of moral development (figure 7.6).[38]

The bridge itself has three parts: (1) moral reasoning or cognition (*à la* Kohlberg), which leads to (2) moral will or volition, which leads to (3) moral strength to act upon the truth (what Ward calls "character").[39] What motivates an individual to cross the bridge from moral truth to moral action? According to Ward, moral development is driven by four factors: (1) experience of justice, (2) experience of social interaction, (3) open discussions of moral concerns, and (4) opportunities for role play.[40] Hence, Ward provides a model of moral development that can make use of, but is not restricted to, developmental insights.

MORAL DEVELOPMENT AND CHRISTIAN EDUCATION

The concept of moral development presented by Christian educators is broader and more com-

Figure 7.5
Approaches to Moral Development

**Contemporary Approaches
to Moral Development**

**Clouse's Biblical Approach
to Moral Development**

Figure 7.6
Ward's Moral Development Bridge

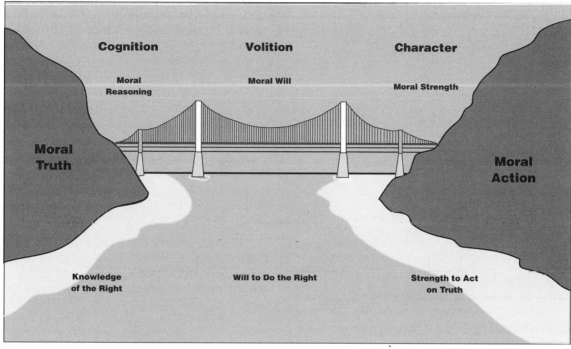

The Bridge from Moral Truth to Moral Action

prehensive than those concepts presented by developmentalists and other moral development theorists. One reason for this broader definition is the inclusion of theological insights with insights from the social sciences. For this reason, moral development is not perceived as merely a cognitive process or moral reasoning. It must include reasons, actions, and characters that require knowledge, behavior, virtues, and principles.

Conclusion

Moral development is a critical concern for Christian educators, both in theory and practice. By gleaning insights from Scripture and the social sciences, we are better able to fashion a more complete understanding of moral development as well as provide more effective ministries in our local church. We are called to be salt and light in a dark and needy world. Understanding the development processes associated with moral development will allow us to be better educators in the classroom, in our Christian schools, and in our homes. As we

live out our moral convictions in an increasingly postmodern world and help our children stand strong against moral relativism, we will make a difference in our communities.

Notes

1. Cf. Bonnidell Clouse, *Teaching for Moral Growth* (Downers Grove, Ill.: Victor/Bridgepoint, 1993).

2. Cf. Bonnidell Clouse, "The Teachings of Jesus and Piaget's Concept of Mature Moral Judgment," in *Psychology and Christianity: Integrative Readings,* ed. J. Roland Fleck and John D. Carter (New York: Abingdon, 1981), pp. 200–210.

3. Jean Piaget, *The Moral Judgment of the Child* (New York: Free Press, 1965), p. 13.

4. This is not the ultimate autonomy of the Kohlberg stages. Rather it is the basis for social interaction that is necessary for moral development. Cf. Ronald Duska and Mariellen Whelan, *Moral Development: A Guide to Piaget and Kohlberg* (New York: Paulist, 1975), p. 8.

5. Ibid., p. 11.

6. John W. Santrock and James C. Barlett, *Developmental Psychology* (Dubuque, Iowa: Brown, 1986), p. 476.

7. Ibid., p. 477.

8. Lawrence Kohlberg, "Stage and Sequences: The Cognitive-Developmental Approach to Socialization," in *Handbook*

of Socialization Theory and Research, ed. D. Goslind (Chicago: Rand McNally, 1969), p. 379.

9. Charles M. Sell, *Transitions through Adult Life* (Grand Rapids: Zondervan, 1991), p. 93.

10. Lawrence Kohlberg and P. Turiel, "Moral Development and Moral Education," in *Psychology and Educational Practice,* ed. G. Lesser (Glenview, Ill.: Scott Foresman, 1971), p. 415.

11. Ibid.

12. Santrock and Bartlett, *Developmental Psychology,* p. 484.

13. Henry Gleitman, *Basic Psychology,* 3d ed. (New York: Norton, 1992), p. 397.

14. Carol Gilligan, *In a Different Voice* (Cambridge: Harvard University Press, 1982), p. 42.

15. Jack O. Balswick and Judith K. Balswick, *The Family* (Grand Rapids: Baker, 1999), p. 289.

16. Santrock and Bartlett, *Developmental Psychology,* p. 484.

17. Gilligan, *In a Different Voice,* p. 28.

18. Balswick and Balswick, *The Family,* p. 289.

19. Most critics of moral development theory respond directly to Kohlberg as the representative of the field of study, since he formulated a more advanced theory of moral development than Piaget and Gilligan, who simply duplicated his research with females. Hence, Kohlberg is often sectioned out as the moral developmental theorist when in fact critical reflection on the subject also includes Piaget and Gilligan.

20. Paul Vitz, "The Kohlberg Phenomenon," *Pastoral Renewal* 7, no. 8 (1982): 65, 67.

21. Ibid., p. 64.

22. Iris V. Cully, *Christian Child Development* (San Francisco: Harper and Row, 1979), p. 86.

23. Nicholas Wolterstorff, *Education for Responsible Action* (Grand Rapids: Eerdmans, 1980), p. 89.

24. Gabriel Moran, *Religious Education Development* (Minneapolis: Winston, 1983), pp. 73, 78.

25. Lisa Kuhmerker, "The Kohlberg Perspective on the Influence of Religious Education on Moral Development," in *The Kohlberg Legacy for the Helping Professions* (Birmingham, Ala.: Religious Education Press, 1991), pp. 164–65.

26. Kohlberg's and Fowler's six stages are directly parallel to one another, with Fowler adding a seventh stage to faith development based not on social science findings but on the theology of Tillich.

27. Jack T. Hanford, "The Relationship between Faith Development of James Fowler and Moral Development of Lawrence Kohlberg: A Theoretical Review," *Journal of Psychology and Christianity* 10, no. 4 (winter 1991): 306–10.

28. Dennis H. Dirks, "Moral Development in Christian Higher Education," *Journal of Psychology and Theology* (winter 1988): 324–26.

29. Joel Brondos, "Sanctification and Moral Development," *Concordia Journal* (October, 1991): 419–39.

30. Stanley Hauerwas, *A Community of Character* (Notre Dame: University of Notre Dame, 1981), p. 130.

31. Donald Joy, *Moral Development Foundations* (New York: Abingdon, 1983), p. 23.

32. Ibid., p. 16.

33. Ibid., p. 20.

34. Ibid., p. 21.

35. Ibid., pp. 23, 33.

36. Clouse, *Teaching for Moral Growth,* p. 49 (emphasis added).

37. Joy, *Moral Development,* p. 25.

38. Ted Ward, *Values Begin at Home* (Wheaton, Ill.: Victor, 1989), p. 108.

39. Ibid., pp. 108–9.

40. Ibid., pp. 89–92.

FAITH DEVELOPMENT 8

Dennis Dirks

I s faith something that is fixed and unchanging? Or is it typically active and undergoing alteration? Is faith a body of knowledge that must be mastered? Is faith a lifestyle? Or is it both knowledge and lifestyle? What happens to the knowledge and lifestyle of faith as it matures? Does growth in faith mean becoming more intimate with God and deepening one's relationship with him? Are there other ways in which faith develops that are predictable? These questions are at the heart of a body of knowledge that has come to be known as *faith development*.

FOUNDATIONS OF FAITH DEVELOPMENT THEORY

The founder of faith development theory, and its most notable researcher, is James W. Fowler.[1] Fowler has devoted his academic career to studying the nature of faith and its development. For its developmental foundations, faith development theory draws heavily upon the cognitive development theory of Jean Piaget, the cognitive-structural theory of moral development identified by Lawrence Kohlberg, and the psychosocial development theory of Erik Erikson. Theologically, Fowler's theory is based on the work of H. Richard Niebuhr, Paul Tillich, and Wilfred Cantwell Smith.[2]

To understand Fowler's theory of faith development, it is necessary to realize that his primary conceptualization of faith is generic. That is, Fowler assumes that all human beings have some form of faith that proceeds through a rather predictable process of development. Even atheists have something that provides meaning to their experiences and draws them toward deeper understanding and commitment. The ways in which Muslims, Hindus, or atheists create meaning in life are similar. Although Fowler allows for Christian faith and finds deepest application of faith development understandings in that realm, his theory is intended to apply to the development of all forms of faith.

Beliefs and Faith

In faith development, a distinction is made between beliefs and faith. Beliefs are significant means by which faith is expressed. But faith is much deeper and includes both conscious and unconscious motivations. Fowler defines faith in terms of loyalty and trust, which are expressed in several areas. First, there is devotion to those ideas or persons that have much worth to us. These are described as "centers of value."[3] A center of value is "something that calls forth our love and devotion and therefore exerts ordering power on the rest of our lives and our attachments."[4] God, along with other value centers, is included in this category. Second, there is loyalty to power centers in life that give us a sense of security. Family or a savings account may represent nonreligious sources of security. Finally, Fowler believes that each person is devoted to a "master story" that gives direction and hope in life. This master story, which involves other people with whom values are shared, transcends human experience; that is, it goes beyond the limitations of life that can be experienced through the five senses.[5]

Qualities of Faith

Two qualities define the nature of faith itself. It is, first of all, considered to be relational, occurring in a triadic pattern. The first part of the triad is relationship to "centers of value." The second part of the triad is ourselves, while the third part is others. Faith is experienced with others in relationships that are characterized by mutual trust. This relational nature of faith makes community central to expressions of faith. Faith is not a privatized, individualistic matter. Relationship with others, while at the same time having mutual relationship with a center of value, forms the triadic pattern.[6]

Second, faith is seen as knowing that leads to being and doing. Knowledge is not something that is merely tucked away in the memory to be called up whenever needed. Rather, the knowing aspect of faith means that it is to be acted upon. It is to be experienced by shaping who we are and what we do. Faith is active, not static. Here, Fowler accepts Piaget's and Kohlberg's understandings of cognitive and moral development (see chapters 6 and 7) and relates them to faith development. He holds that knowledge is developed through interaction with people, ideas, and experiences.[7]

Structures of Faith

The means by which the content of faith may be understood is through structures of thinking, valuing, and knowing. These structures undergo change as faith development occurs. In this way, the structures that give meaning to a child's faith are typically different from those of an adult.[8] Each succeeding structure provides stability (equilibrium) that is needed to deal appropriately with the issues of life in a context of life change.[9] In part because faith involves structures, images associated with structures hold great importance. Fowler maintains that virtually all our knowing begins with images and that most of what we know is stored in images. Thus, childhood images of faith have a permanence and continue throughout one's life.[10]

While faith development theory focuses primarily on the human side of faith, the psychology of faith, Fowler acknowledges the importance of what he generically calls the Transcendent, or "the ultimate conditions of existence." These terms, which roughly correspond to concepts such as God or some other supreme being or idea, allow his theory to be applied to faith of any kind. Still, Fowler allows for the Christian understanding of God and considers it to be the ultimate source of faith.[11]

STAGES OF FAITH

Faith develops through identifiable stages that represent increased complexity and comprehensiveness. Greater capacities for understanding differences and making distinctions result. Likewise, stage growth results in greater flexibility in dealing with differences of faith. Fowler found that the stages are *invariant* (each person progresses through the same stages), *sequential* (stages occur in the same order in each person), and *hierarchical* (each stage builds on and adds to previous stages). However, Fowler does not claim that the faith of persons in each culture has these same characteristics. Thus, his theory is not universal.

Fowler found that there are six stages in the development of faith. Although each stage can be reached during the ages Fowler identified, it is by no means certain that development through each stage will in fact occur.[12] The beginning of faith development occurs in a period that is not actually considered to be a stage. Fowler called this period *Primal or Undifferentiated Faith* (birth–3 years). It is shaped by experiences of love and care by primary caregivers (parents and other adults). These experiences result in a disposition of trust toward life. This trust orientation begins prior to the onset of language. Here seeds of faith are sown.[13]

The first actual stage is *Intuitive-Projective Faith* (2–7 years). Imagination emerges through stories, gestures, and other symbols. Joined with perception and feelings, imagination creates powerful faith images that continue over a lifetime. During this stage, moral emotions emerge. The child's understanding of God takes shape and is influenced by experiences with parents and other adults with whom emotional bonds have been formed. Here, the content of faith is largely missing, resulting in vulnerability and little that gives faith stability.[14] Faith experiences have an episodic quality; they are a collection of independent, generally unconnected events. This is in contrast with linearly connected faith experiences of later stages.[15]

Fowler gives the title *Mythical-Literal Faith* (8–11 years) to the second faith stage. Here, the child begins to take on the stories, beliefs, and practices of his or her faith community. A breakdown of literalism leads the child to become critical of teachers and ideas of former stages because they do not correspond with the child's beginning capacity for symbols.[16] The child is able to distinguish between reality and fantasy. The perspectives and feelings of others can be perceived. At this stage the child views God anthropomorphically. Right and wrong behavior are viewed through the lens of consequences: Right is whatever is rewarded, while wrong is whatever is punished.[17]

The third stage of faith development is *Synthetic-Conventional Faith* (12–22 years). Because formal thought in the cognitive domain of development emerges, the adolescent is able to use abstract ideas to determine meaning in life. Experiences of the past can be considered for their meaning, now and for the future. Mutual perspective-taking, an ability to see things as others see them, becomes possible, also making it possible to see ourselves as others see us. Relationships play a large role in shaping faith. This strong pull toward relationships in shaping personal identity leads to conformity to the expectations and judgments of others. Faith is also shaped by identity concerns. There is in addition a hunger for a personal relationship with a God who knows, accepts, and confirms.[18]

Individuative-Reflective Faith (young adulthood) is the fourth faith stage. This stage involves, first of all, a thoughtful examination, even questioning, that leads to reshaping earlier understandings of faith. Second, it involves taking charge of one's own life. While in the previous stage relationships gave greatest shape to faith, now individual responsibility becomes most prominent. This does not mean an individualistic faith is formed. Instead, personal ownership of faith emerges. Still, there are struggles that become evident. It can be frightening, for example, to sense one's movement away from earlier understandings of faith that provided security and stability. There is tension between individual responsibility and the faith that was defined by others in the previous stage. A struggle between self-fulfillment and service to others surfaces. Finally, there is contention between relativism and absolutes. These tensions are eventually resolved as the ability to critically examine beliefs emerges.[19]

The fifth stage of faith development is *Conjunctive Faith* (middle adulthood and beyond). In prior stages, the individual has become aware of faith symbols that give meaning to life. At this stage, a hunger surfaces for deeper relationship with the reality that those symbols represent. Faith can be examined from many perspectives simultaneously. A more profound awareness of inner inconsistencies develops, while at the same time there grows a commitment to justice for others of various ages, races, and so forth. A strong desire to assist others in the development of their own faith emerges.[20]

The sixth and final faith stage is *Universalizing Faith*. A deep sense of being firmly rooted in the Transcendent, "the ultimate conditions of existence," or God, develops. The process of decentration from self that began in the second stage reaches completion. An ability exists to fully take the perspective of others in self-abandonment without devaluing self. There is a striving to live out ideals of love and justice with all people in a sustained manner. Fulfillment in spending and being spent for the good of others becomes evident. While respect for human rules, expectations, and conventions continues, there is a freedom from the same that develops. Correspondingly, there is increased openness to truth in all faiths.[21]

Fowler's research determined that children and adolescents are unable to attain stages four to six. Most adults in the United States are at stage three or four, some even at stage two. Few adults over age forty attain stage five, while stage six is extremely rare. The years of midlife are significant for adults because they determine whether or not further development will occur.[22]

STAGES OF FAITH AND CONTEMPORARY CULTURE

It is clear to most observers at the beginning of the twenty-first century that massive tidal waves of postmodern change are sweeping across the cultural landscape. Responses to these changes in the United States have been classified in various ways.

One view identifies two broad opposing categories of response. The first category is concerned with maintaining fidelity to teachings and traditions that have been passed down historically. Scripture would be included here. The locus of authority is considered to be external. The second category rejects external authority, particularly that of traditions and historic teachings. Instead, universal ethical principles are claimed as authoritative. The locus of authority for this group is more internal.[23]

Fowler analyzes the two viewpoints above as representing competing worldviews of faith. He sees each as identified with a different stage of faith development. The first worldview is placed at stage three, Synthetic-Conventional Faith. It is a stage most commonly found at adolescence or beyond. At this stage, individuals are unable to grasp their own views conceptually, relying instead on slogans and rather simplistic ideas. There is strong reliance on authority figures. Fowler places the second worldview, on the other hand, at stage four, Individuative-Reflective Faith. Here, suspicion of teachings and tradition is strong. Traditional teachings are analyzed from the perspective of contemporary assumptions and understandings, making current perspectives more acceptable than historic perspectives. One's locus of authority is more inward, allowing for greater personal judgment, choice, and freedom.

While the views of the second response to postmodernism are supportive of postmodern thought, there are also individuals who enthusiastically embrace it. Fowler equates this more thorough postmodern perspective with stage five, Conjunctive Faith. He concludes that such people recognize the complexities of our era and have the capacity to hold in dynamic tension viewpoints that are opposing and contradictory. This is done with minimal internal dissonance or tension. It represents an ability to recognize and embrace truth from a variety of sources and perspectives. Fowler is convinced that modeling Conjunctive Faith in contemporary culture is compelling to a postmodern world.[24]

RELATIONSHIP OF FAITH DEVELOPMENT TO CHRISTIAN FAITH

In relating faith development to Christianity, Fowler emphasizes the importance of the calling of God upon believers. Vocation is the response a person makes to this call.[25] Fowler refers to the apostle Paul's letter to the Ephesian Christians, where Paul says, "I, therefore, the prisoner of the Lord, entreat you to walk in a manner worthy of the calling with which you have been called" (Eph. 4:1 NASB). Vocation has the idea of fully and completely embracing or giving our lives to Christ. But it is always to be done in community with others, never in isolation. To walk worthy of our calling is to conduct ourselves in vital relationship with God at the core of our beings in all situations of life. At the heart of this process, according to Fowler, is a narrative that gives meaning to life experiences in light of our calling. There is of course the master narrative of Scripture. But Fowler understands the unfolding or developing stages of faith as likewise having the effect of narrative, both shaping and giving meaning as we live out our calling.[26]

Fowler's view of Scripture as primarily narrative, a master story that provides meaning and guidance to the pilgrim journey of life, is not to say that he views it as fictional. However, this view of God's Word clearly leads to a particular hermeneutical, or interpretational, approach. This approach points Fowler beyond the unique work of God among his people and the priorities to which they have been called to seek to understand God's work throughout the world with people of diverse worldviews and faiths. The work and priorities of God are discerned by examining the experiences and events of all people, all cultures, and all religions. In this, Fowler embraces pluralism, the idea that all perspectives are valid and contribute to a more complete understanding of God. Diversity is welcomed and encouraged.[27]

Fowler affirms his conviction of the reality of the sovereignty of God. His view is that God is at work throughout his creation. The image of God is placed within each individual, and the stages of faith represent one way in which the potential of that image unfolds. Fowler's understanding of two aspects of faith growth—conversion and transformation—roughly correlate with New Testament teachings.

Growth through the stages of faith, according to Fowler, involves changing the way one views his or her relationship to God and others. Each successive stage brings added potential for partnership with God. At the same time, successive stages can lead toward greater personal autonomy, resulting in alienation from God. The result is a more effective means of self-directing one's life for the purpose of self-preservation and self-enhancement. Growth can become arrested at any stage. When this occurs, an egocentric perspective is clung to, or the narrow perspective of a particular group with which the person identifies is adopted. Likewise, there may be "a clinging to the formulaic interpretations of Scripture or to the leadership of authoritarian leaders or institutions."[28]

Because Fowler considers the successive faith stages to involve development toward maturity, it is helpful to review a biblical/theological perspective of growth toward spiritual maturity. The doctrine of sanctification states that the growth of believers is "a progressive work of God and man that makes us more and more free from sin and like Christ in our actual lives."[29] A moral change occurs in believers at the time of regeneration or becoming "born again" in Christ (Titus 3:5). There is a break from the ruling power of sin (Rom. 6:11, 14). This process of moral change continues throughout life as believers yield themselves more and more to righteousness (Rom. 6:19). It is a process of turning away from a sinful past and becoming increasingly conformed to the image of Christ (Phil. 3:13–14; Rom. 8:29). The process is never completed in this life.

Sanctification involves the cooperative work of both God and man. God's role is active (1 Thess. 5:23) while ours is more passive, comparatively speaking, in that we trust God to sanctify us and we yield increasingly to him (Rom. 6:13). But our role is not entirely passive; we are to be engaged in the process by "putting to death the deeds of the body" (Rom. 8:13 NASB) and striving for holiness (Heb. 12:14). Sanctification affects the whole person: intellect (Col. 3:10), emotions (Gal. 5:22), will (Phil. 2:13), spirit (2 Cor. 7:1), and physical body (1 Thess. 5:23).

The differences between faith development theory and the doctrine of sanctification are quite obvious. There is a difference in focus. As faith development places emphasis on human experience, it neglects the work of God. There is also a difference in purpose. Stages of faith lead toward greater appreciation for and acceptance of differences among fellow human beings. The purpose of sanctification, on the other hand, is to bring about Christlikeness in every aspect of one's being, leading to an appropriate realization of the exclusive claims of Christ.

Still there are elements of similarity. Just as becoming like Christ involves loss of self-centered-ness, so faith development yields greater concern for others. As sanctification produces greater conformity to God's expectations and less to human conventions, so does faith development. Christ emphasized the importance of changing from an external perspective to one that is internal. This was at the heart of the Sermon on the Mount. Fowler's theory has a similar direction. However, a central concern of sanctification for a deepening relationship with God seems to be lost in faith development's concentration on the human experience (although Fowler claims a more firm grounding in God in the higher stages).

Fowler's emphasis on the relational dimension of faith captures an essential aspect of biblical faith. Scripture consistently calls the people of God to worship and other faith-related activities with others in the family of God. In the Old Testament, the children of Israel gathered together regularly and frequently for sacrifices and celebrations. In the New Testament, under his new covenant with man, we see that God desires the church to be relational at its core. Worship continues to be an experience of community. The Epistles are filled with "one anothers," instructions for believers to be involved with other believers in living faith. Biblical Christianity is to be pursued in community, in relationships with other Christians.

Just as faith development emphasizes the human experience, so spiritual formation is a process that focuses on the human side of sanctification. Formation has been defined as "a process of being conformed to the image of Christ for the sake of others."[30] It is the process of reforming or restoring the soul.[31] Formation that is holistic involves the entire person: spirit, mind, heart, emotions, will, and body. It occurs in large measure through the practice of spiritual disciplines that include prayer, Scripture reading, silence, solitude, service, and worship.[32] Faith development, by contrast, takes place through general interaction with the environment, whether faith-related or not.

FAITH DEVELOPMENT AND EDUCATIONAL MINISTRY

Fowler's ideal church context for encouraging ongoing faith development is a body that he labels "public church." As the label suggests, it is a church that is significantly visible and understandable to the surrounding culture. A public church relates in nondefensive ways to others whose perspectives are different than its own. It is able to do this because it assists its members in forming clear identities in and commitment to the Christian faith. Yet, it is involved in efforts to transform culture by removing society's injustices, building up its members, and helping them grow. Its membership is diverse, representing various walks of life—ethnically, economically, and theologically—within certain boundaries. The church intentionally prepares believers to proclaim their beliefs and live out their calling. It acknowledges the gifts and calling both of laypeople and professional leaders. Fowler's research indicates that public churches such as these have adult members whose faith development is at or beyond stage four, Individuative-Reflective Faith.[33]

Each of the above characteristics of a public church is found in the various parts of church life, including preaching and teaching (kerygma), worship (leitourgia), experiences of community or fellowship with other believers (koinonia), service and mission (diakonia), and encouraging reflection among church members on the calling, or vocation, of Christians (paideia).[34] Fowler believes that faith development of individuals best takes place in a context in which Christians are involved in these activities together. Although there may be reasons for age-graded activities, much of Christian education needs to be done in intergenerational settings.

It is Fowler's conviction that as leaders understand the stages of faith, they are able to respond in more appropriate ways to believers who are living out their faith according to their current faith stage. But he cautions against using stages as a means of classifying or comparing believers in ways that devalue persons or lead to judgmental attitudes. Nor should leaders have as a primary goal the movement of individuals from one stage to the next. While this may be a rather fine distinction, leaders instead are to encourage Christians to live out their faith in ways that will naturally make it more likely that stage growth will occur. In this way, faith development is more a byproduct of the ministry of the leader rather than an explicit objective.

In any group in which leaders minister—whether a small group Bible study, a large class, or a congregation—a range of stages will be present. As few as two or as many as three or four stages will be found. This means that there will be a range of perceptions or understandings of what is being taught or experienced.[35] At the same time, each group of believers is characterized by a modal level of faith development. That is, there is a faith stage at which most members of the group may be found. Group members whose stage is beyond or below the modal level will feel somewhat alienated or nonconforming. It is the responsibility of leadership to work toward affirming all individuals in the group regardless of whether or not they are at the group's modal level.

Educational attention should be given not only to communicating the content of faith but also to the ways in which people process their faith. That is, leaders should identify the ways of understanding and living out faith that are implied by each stage.[36] As noted earlier, transitions between stages may involve a range of feelings of dislocation or misfit. Patient encouragement and reassurance during stage change is essential. Neither pressure to reduce time spent in transition nor admonition to "just have more faith" or to "take on the mind of Christ" will be particularly helpful at these times.

IMPLICATIONS FOR EDUCATIONAL MINISTRY

A number of implications of Fowler's faith development theory for educational ministry may be identified. First, it calls attention to the fact that the faith of adults has potential to continue to develop throughout adulthood. Growth is not simply a matter of enriching faith already possessed. Instead, it is possible for adult structures of meaning to develop. This is a strong reason for including adult ministries as an essential part of the educational ministry of the church. However, it is not sufficient merely to offer a range of activities that will interest adults or address adult needs. Adult educational activities must be created that are challenging in ways that encourage faith stage change.

Second, intentional educational experiences are to be designed that not only encourage growth toward the next stage but also nurture enrichment and fullness of meaning within the present stage. Anxious or compulsive desires to keep Christians moving on to higher stages will be counterproductive. Adequate time must be given for reflection and solidifying the benefits of the present faith stage. Without it, faith development will tend to be truncated or cut off.

Third, the temptation to substitute generic language and practices common to the surrounding culture in place of the unique language of faith is to be resisted. This is a practice rather common in contemporary seeker-sensitive evangelical churches. While this may prove effective in providing common points of identity between non-churched and those in the family of faith, the loss of distinctive faith language removes some of its power to draw toward higher stages.

Fourth, the difficulties associated with transition from one stage of faith to another should lead us to a deeper, more biblical understanding of pain. As Scripture clearly teaches, suffering is essential for the growth that it brings. It is not to be avoided, nor is it simply to be endured. This suggests that ministry must be about helping Christians acknowledge pain and accept its purpose in bringing about growth.

Finally, faith development theory reminds us that faith is to be related to all aspects of life. It is not to be isolated from day-to-day experiences. When compartmentalized from life, an unhealthy dichotomy forms that actually inhibits development.[37]

In considering strategies to nurture faith development, it must be remembered that faith competencies at any stage cannot be directly taught. Rather, they are the result of the individual's interaction with ideas, others, and the circumstances of life.[38] Strategies that provide opportunities for symbol breaking at one stage and the shaping of new symbols for the new stage assist in encouraging faith development. For example, inviting individuals to talk about their personal faith journeys may be effective. Here, it is especially helpful to ask them to identify ways in which current faith symbols are more helpful than previous ones. Faith development is also nurtured by encouraging Christians to take the perspective of others. This involves seeking to understand the other person's thoughts, feelings, and behavior. The result is a broadening of one's own perspectives and a prompting of stage growth. Involving Christians in decision making in matters related to their life experiences has similar benefits. This may be done in the home, in Chris-

tian education activities, and in the general life of the church.[39]

The role of parents and other adults is exceedingly important in the faith development of the child. Adults offer opportunities to the young child for interaction with others, which is at the core of growth in faith stages.[40] But Fowler goes beyond this concept to think of families as "an ecology of Christian consciousness."[41] By this he means that the family offers cross-generational interaction around the meaning and values that each family member possesses. Families are influential in faith development as they intentionally provide for mutual experiences and discussion of life's concerns in light of shared values. Research indicates that most Christian families structure family experiences around stage three, Synthetic-Conventional Faith. Most families would benefit from patterns that are more like stage four, Individuative-Reflective Faith.[42]

CONCLUSION

The insights of faith development theory have much to contribute to the Christian leader and the process of Christian education. Its principles enlarge our understanding of the human psychological aspects of spiritual development. But the discerning leader must also be aware of its weaknesses and limitations. God's perspective as given in Scripture must be the ultimate and most important benchmark by which faith development is measured. As we move into an increasingly postmodern world, evangelicals must be unequivocal in their rejection of pluralism, relativism, and naturalism and live distinctively Christian lives based upon a genuine biblical faith relationship with our eternal Lord and Savior. The degree to which faith may be empirically analyzed as a stage theory may be debated in the academy for years to come. However, the authenticity and integrity of our faith relationship must always remain pure, undefiled, and based upon sound doctrine and biblical imperatives.

NOTES

1. James W. Fowler III is the Charles Howard Candler Professor of Theology and Human Development, Candler School of Theology of Emory University (United Methodist Church)

and director of the Emory Center for Ethics in Public Policy and the Professions.

2. James W. Fowler, *Stages of Faith: The Psychology of Human Development and the Quest for Meaning* (San Francisco: Harper and Row, 1981), pp. 4–15, 38–39.

3. James W. Fowler, "Stages in Faith Consciousness," in *Religious Development in Childhood and Adolescence,* ed. Fritz Koser and W. George Scarlett (San Francisco: Jossey-Bass, 1991), p. 32.

4. James W. Fowler, *Weaving the New Creation: Stages of Faith and the Public Church* (San Francisco: Harper, 1991), p. 101.

5. Ibid., p. 100.

6. Fowler, *Stages of Faith,* pp. 16–18.

7. James W. Fowler, "Faith and the Structuring of Meaning," in *Toward Moral and Religious Maturity,* ed. Christiane Brusselmans and James A. O'Donohoe (Morristown, N.J.: Silver Burdett, 1980), pp. 57–64.

8. Ibid., pp. 64–66.

9. James W. Fowler, "Stages of Faith: Reflections on a Decade of Dialogue," *Christian Education Journal* 13, no. 1 (1992): 31.

10. Fowler, *Stages of Faith,* p. 25.

11. James W. Fowler, "Faith, Liberation, and Human Development," in *Christian Perspectives on Faith Development: A Reader,* ed. Jeff Astley and Leslie Francis (Grand Rapids: Eerdmans, 1992), p. 5.

12. James W. Fowler, *Faithful Change: The Personal and Public Challenges of Postmodern Life* (Nashville: Abingdon, 1996), pp. 56–57.

13. Fowler, "Stages in Faith Consciousness," p. 34.

14. Ibid., pp. 34–35; *Stages of Faith,* pp. 122–30.

15. James W. Fowler, "Moral Stages and the Development of Faith," in *Spiritual Development in Later Life,* ed. Bill Puka et al. (New York: Garland, 1994), pp. 358–59.

16. Ibid., pp. 145–46.

17. Fowler, *Stages of Faith,* pp. 135–39.

18. Fowler, "Stages in Faith Consciousness," pp. 38–39.

19. Fowler, *Stages of Faith,* pp. 178–82; *Weaving the New Creation,* pp. 38–40.

20. Fowler, *Stages of Faith,* pp. 185–88; *Weaving the New Creation,* pp. 40–41.

21. Fowler, "Stages in Faith Consciousness," p. 41.

22. Fowler, "Faith, Liberation, and Human Development," p. 39.

23. Fowler, *Faithful Change,* pp. 161–68.

24. Ibid., pp. 171–76.

25. James W. Fowler, "Keeping Faith with God and Our Children: A Practical Theological Perspective," *Religious Education* 89, no. 4 (fall 1994): 546–47.

26. Fowler, *Weaving the New Creation,* pp. 119, 126–27.

27. Fowler, *Faithful Change,* pp. 174–201.

28. Fowler, "Stages of Faith," pp. 18–19.

29. Wayne Grudem, *Systematic Theology: An Introduction to Biblical Doctrine* (Grand Rapids: Zondervan, 1994), p. 746.

30. M. Robert Mulholland, *Invitation to a Journey: A Road Map for Spiritual Formation* (Downers Grove, Ill.: InterVarsity, 1993), p. 12.

31. Dallas Willard, "Spiritual Disciplines, Spiritual Formation, and the Restoration of the Soul," *Journal of Psychology and Theology* 26, no. 1 (1998): 107–8.

32. Dallas Willard, *The Spirit of the Disciplines: Understanding How God Changes Lives* (San Francisco: Harper, 1991).

33. Fowler, *Weaving the New Creation,* pp. 151, 155–62, 169.

34. Ibid., pp. 179–89.

35. James W. Fowler, *Faith Development and Pastoral Care* (Philadelphia: Fortress, 1987), p. 82.

36. Scott Lownsdale, "Faith Development across the Life Span: Fowler's Integrative Work," *Journal of Psychology and Theology* 25, no. 1 (1997): 60–63.

37. Fowler, "Faith and the Structuring of Meaning," pp. 79–84.

38. James W. Fowler, "Faith Development Theory and the Aims of Religious Socialization," in *Emerging Issues in Religious Education,* ed. Gloria Durka and Joanmarie Smith (New York: Paulist Press, 1976), pp. 200–201.

39. Gary L. Chamberlain, *Fostering Faith: A Minister's Guide to Faith Development* (New York: Paulist, 1990), pp. 23–25.

40. James W. Fowler, "Strength for the Journey: Early Childhood Development in Selfhood and Faith," in *Faith Development in Early Childhood,* ed. Doris A. Blazer (Kansas City, Mo.: Sheed and Ward, 1989), p. 36.

41. James W. Fowler, "Perspectives on the Family from the Standpoint of Faith Development Theory," in *Christian Perspectives on Faith Development: A Reader,* ed. Jeff Astley and Leslie Francis (Grand Rapids: Eerdmans, 1992), p. 337.

42. Ibid., pp. 337–40.

SPIRITUAL FORMATION: NURTURING SPIRITUAL VITALITY

Nick Taylor

Attempting a biblical definition of spiritual maturity is an elusive quest. Over the years many have tried to define and describe the essential components of spiritual formation. Some have espoused a process of growth that mirrors the lifestyle of a monastic monk living an isolated existence deep in a desert cave. Others have prescribed a more simplistic step-by-step formula. Neither seems to satisfy or last the test of time. A fresh perspective is needed.

Spiritual formation is more than the transfer of knowledge from a teacher to a learner. It is a process concerned with the holistic growth and development of the individual. Whereas the goal of education is learning, the goal of spiritual formation is maturity. The biblical word translated "mature, perfect, complete" is the word *teleios*. In Matthew 5:48 we are exhorted, "Be perfect, therefore, as your heavenly Father is perfect." William Barclay makes the comment that "the basic meaning of *teleios* in the New Testament is always that the thing or person so described fully carries out the purpose for which it was designed."[1]

"Formation" is the root word *morphe* (Rom. 12:2; 2 Cor. 3:18), from which we derive the word *metamorphosis*. It concerns not only outward change but also a crucial development from one form to another. As Scripture describes it, we are "being transformed into his likeness." The first concern is with being.

In the traditional schooling model, a pedagogical learning method is often used exclusively. This is a teacher-directed process, wherein the student is passively engaged and becomes dependent upon the instructor for learning external truths. In a formational approach, the andragogical method is also fully utilized. Learning is self-directed. The student is actively engaged in his or her own process and becomes equipped from within to grow and develop spiritually.

Spiritual formation is not "postconversion maintenance." It is an ongoing path of developmental learning and experience. It gives structure and form to the maturity process. While spiritual growth can in no way be standardized and forced, it can be given direction. As we grow physically from infancy to adulthood, there are predictable phases of learning we must go through. Spiritual formation is a dynamic process focused on developing through similar phases of growth, healing, and renewal. It guides and equips disciples toward being as well as doing. It ultimately produces an authentic maturity in Christ—the true goal of our faith.

BIBLICAL FOUNDATIONS OF SPIRITUAL FORMATION

Old Testament

Deuteronomy 6:6–9 states, "These commandments that I give you today are to be upon your hearts. Impress them on your children. Talk about them when you sit at home and when you walk along the road, when you lie down and when you get up. Tie them as symbols on your hands and bind them on your foreheads. Write them on the doorframes of your houses and on your gates." From the time God gave the law to Moses, he encouraged his people to know him not as an intellectual exercise but rather as a lifestyle. Their learning was not prescribed to take place in formal settings or only during certain hours of the day. Instead, God's people were to make their understanding of him a process that never ended in their homes, on the road, in the morning, and at night. This principle of formation remains. It is in the larger arena of life that we learn of him. What may or may not begin in a schooled environment is fleshed out in the everyday situations of home life. There is no ringing bell to signal when it is time to stop being spiritually transformed. All of life is learning.

In Isaiah 29:13 we read, "The Lord says: 'These people come near to me with their mouth and honor me with their lips, but their hearts are far from me. Their worship of me is made up only of rules taught by men.'" God made it clear in the Old Testament that he was not interested in religious acts of rule keeping when they were not springing from a changed heart. He explained that it was possible for us to be far from him even when our external actions did not indicate so. He spoke in a relational language, not an academic one.

Spiritual formation begins first in the changes of the heart, where being begins. These changes primarily bring about relational depth with God and others. The by-product, not the goal, is secondary change in behaviors and attitudes. Rules cannot create worship. Relationship can. While the law provides necessary form, it takes a heart connection to provide a meaningful encounter with God in worship.

New Testament

The last words Jesus spoke to his followers before ascending into heaven, as recorded in Matthew 28:18–20, have been referred to as the Great Commission. In that text he gives an imperative to "go and make disciples of all nations." The mandate for spiritual formation resounds in this statement. As has been said, disciples are not born, they are made. It is that "making" that entails the art and action of formation.

The New Testament writers urge the followers of Christ to take on a dynamic view of the Christian life. It is presented as anything but a static belief system. James, for instance, challenged his audience saying, "Do not merely listen to the word, and so deceive yourselves. Do what it says" (James 1:22).

Paul came upon the scene of spiritual formation after his own conversion and often described his ministry as a calling to bring men and women to completion and maturity in Christ. One of the strongest images he used was that of a pregnant woman in Galatians 4:19: "My dear children, for whom I am again in the pains of childbirth until Christ is formed in you." He wrote this to those who were already believers. Obviously, he saw their spiritual lives as an ongoing process.

In Colossians 1:28 Paul resonates with the goal of perfection, or completeness, in the lives of his converts: "We proclaim him, admonishing and teaching everyone with all wisdom, so that we may present everyone perfect in Christ." He illustrates the Christian life as an ongoing process of calling and design that grows in depth. He says in Ephesians 4:1, "As a prisoner for the Lord, then, I urge you to live a life worthy of the calling you have received." And again in 2 Thessalonians 1:3, "We ought always to thank God for you, brothers, and rightly so, because your faith is growing more and more, and the love every one of you has for each other is increasing."

Other passages echo the principle of continual growth that leads to faith and holiness, such as 2 Peter 3:18: "But grow in the grace and knowledge of our Lord and Savior Jesus Christ." The writer to the Hebrews speaks of the work involved in formation when he says, "Make every effort to live in peace with all men and to be holy; without holiness no one will see the Lord" (Heb. 12:14). Jude 20 agrees: "But you, dear friends, build yourselves up in your most holy faith."

Paul speaks of the dual direction of spiritual formation, being and doing, in Romans 12:2 when he admonishes, "Do not conform any longer to the pattern of this world, but be transformed by the renewing of your mind. Then you will be able to test and approve what God's will is—his good, pleasing and perfect will." The process involves both a disciplined action ("do not conform") and an inner point of change ("be transformed" in your mind). These lead to a relational insight with God—knowing his good, perfect, and pleasing will.

But perhaps nowhere else in the New Testament is the goal and direction of spiritual formation made more clear than in Ephesians 4:13–14. Paul talks about each of us using the grace we have been given as Christ apportioned it "until we all reach unity in the faith and in the knowledge of the Son of God and become mature, attaining to the whole measure of the fullness of Christ. Then we will no longer be infants, tossed back and forth by the waves, and blown here and there by every wind of teaching and by the cunning and craftiness of men in their deceitful scheming."

Here is the blessing of Christian maturity. It leads us to the fullness of Christ in our own lives. Additionally, it serves as a safeguard against the confusion and spiritual deceit we so often encounter in the religious world. By being formed to his image, we are made stable and sound in contrast to spiritual infants who cannot steady themselves when blown about by schemes and heresies.

SPIRITUAL FORMATION ACROSS THE LIFE SPAN

Spiritual Formation in Childhood

Second Timothy 3:14–15 says, "Continue in what you have learned and have become convinced of, because you know those from whom you learned it, and how from infancy you have known the holy Scriptures, which are able to make you wise for salvation through faith in Christ Jesus." The process of Christian discipleship has never been restricted to adults. The Old Testament admonished parents to teach their children about their God from an early age. When Jesus began his public ministry, he included children both as audience and example. The church has long embraced its challenge to educate children. However, it has been pointed out that there is often a large difference between traditional education and spiritual formation.

Robert Clark defines spiritual formation in children as "a step by step and stage by stage process through which a child is guided, encouraged, nurtured, admonished, and disciplined to embrace Christ as Savior and be discipled to de-

velop as a Christian through the work and power of the Holy Spirit."[2] In particular, note the words "step by step and stage by stage." This is a key to all formation, but nowhere is it more important than in the area of children.

Theories of child development abound. Each one is like a pair of glasses that helps us focus on the one part being observed. Jack and Judith Balswick illustrate a few of these major theories in the following scene:

> Let us suppose that representatives of the major child development theories are observing a child playing in the family living room. Each will perceive the child's activity in accordance with a set of predetermined assumptions about human behavior. For example, the cognitive development theorist will be especially aware of the particular stage to which the child has developed; the Freudian theorist will look for unconscious motivations in overt behavior; the symbolic interactionist will concentrate on the child's self-concept; and the proponent of the social learning theory will pay special attention to what the child has learned from observing others.[3]

In all of the child development theories, there is a bias that explains behavior on the basis of environmental conditioning. However, the Bible presents the view that we are choice-making creatures who are responsible for our own behavior. While all of the major theories have differed upon whether children are passive or active in their development, all do agree that human input is necessary if children are to take on human characteristics.

Spiritual Formation in Adolescence

"Being a teenager in our society is like being Alice in Wonderland—not knowing what the rules and expectations are."[4] In much the same way that Alice attempted to negotiate the twists and curves of Wonderland, today's adolescents are faced with the momentous task of growing up in a world that sometimes makes no sense to them. Having outgrown the last steps of childhood and not yet entered fully into the adult world, they are in the midst of an often confusing life development stage.

When considering the spiritual formation of teens and preteens, it is essential to help them through this passage with both grace and truth. Scripture offers much to consider in evaluating the identity of a follower of Christ. It helps us take the first step by establishing the truth of who we are. Galatians 2:20 says, "I have been crucified with Christ and I no longer live, but Christ lives in me. The life I live in the body, I live by faith in the Son of God, who loved me and gave himself for me." As James Bryan Smith explains, "Christian spiritual formation is arriving at this awareness of our true identity and letting Christ live his life in and through us."[5] This awareness is integral at every age; however, adolescence is the time when that cry is first heard. Teenage disciples are ready to seek out this understanding with a unique edge of fervor and desire that comes from a natural fire within.

The adolescent self emerges through two primary ways: imitation and integration. Smith defines the two:

Imitation is the process of adapting to one's surroundings by patching together the beliefs and behaviors of others. Adolescents try to develop a sense of who they are by attempting to look, act, think, and sound like someone else. On the other hand, integration is the process of testing, separating, and discriminating between several types of beliefs and behaviors until one discovers that which is genuine and real. It involves interaction with others, personal reflection, and the freedom to explore.[6]

Imitation begins with parental models because home life deeply shapes identity. Research shows that adolescent rebellion is highest in very restrictive and very permissive homes.[7] In an extremely restrictive home, parents do not allow for the gradual development of independence in the child. Without the opportunity to experience individual freedom, a child's frustration may lead to outward aggression toward parents or society. Others may exhibit more subtle controlling techniques, such as developing eating disorders.

Teenagers may reject "institutional religion" but be quite open to spirituality in a general sense. They often choose to break away from their parents' views and beliefs and strike out on their own paths of discovery. For many, this is the beginning of their spiritual formation process. Adolescents are at an age wherein they may come to see religion as a very personal friendship with God. He is the one who gives protection, guidance, and purpose in a time when those things are sorely needed.

James Fowler tells us that adolescents both want and need mirrors.[8] Forming spirituality in a teenager is partly a process of showing them mirrors they can trust. Scripture speaks to them of who they are but only if it is taught in a way that captures their hearts as well as their minds. They need models of adults who will give them both grace and truth, people who will love them unconditionally while showing them the reality about themselves. These kinds of human mirrors are crucial in helping adolescents see not only themselves but also God.

Spiritual formation with adolescents also has much to do with empowering them with the ability to integrate Christianity into their everyday lives. This empowering process may have already begun at home. Ideal parents will have moved beyond merely telling and teaching and toward the delegation of responsibility. This enables teenagers to learn how to take control over their own lives.

The second half of the empowering process is offering opportunities for teens to exercise responsibility. Cognitive learning is important, but until it is translated into active experience, it will not finish its work of formation. The Balswicks state, "This is no less necessary in the church than in any other social institution. The youth programs of many churches do a great job of entertaining the young people and keeping them busy, but do little in the way of bringing them into responsible positions within the church community."[9]

The formation process offers unconditional love and an atmosphere of grace. Where there is grace, there is safety to fail without the threat of guilt or condemnation. Spiritual formation depends upon a place of safety and acceptance. At the same time, as adolescents are looking for direction and identity, the church offers to be a place of truth. As teens are loved, they are brought to understand the reality about themselves, about others, and about God. With these principles in mind, the Wonderland of adolescence may be navigated more smoothly and purposefully through the light of formation.

Spiritual Formation in Adulthood

Julie Gorman asks the penetrating question, "Why have so many Sundays of Bible teaching produced so few spiritually mature adults?"[10] For all the work that the church has done toward educating adults, we seem to have much less to show for it than one would expect. In terms of measuring the success of our efforts, we may assess weekly attendance, membership roles, giving records, or adult class participation, but none of these is enough to provide a clear measurement of genuine maturity.

To be spiritually formed is to be brought to an ever-deepening maturity in Christ. This process is continuous for adults, children, and adolescents. For children of all ages, churches tend to offer an incredible array of learning tools and opportunities through which they can discover Christ. Retreats, trips, and events for spiritual growth abound. Meetings are often designed to be interactive and application-oriented. Current issues are addressed, and cultural relevance is a given in all aspects of youth ministry.

Unfortunately, much of our adult education ministry has not continued in the same vein of creative learning. By adulthood much, if not all, of the educational process has narrowed toward the schooling model alone. Discipleship instruction becomes an offering of classes and the Sunday sermon. There is no guidance developmentally, no growth in intentional relationships, and no spiritual goals to press toward. Spiritual maturity is measured by church attendance and moral behavior, while the condition of the heart and conscience remain unchecked. Sin is viewed as a list of bad things to avoid rather than an internal nature to be reckoned with.

Scripture, however, doesn't applaud the results of this paradigm. Jesus spoke to this issue in Matthew 23:23: "Woe to you, teachers of the law and Pharisees, you hypocrites! You give a tenth of your spices—mint, dill and cummin. But you have neglected the more important matters of the law—justice, mercy and faithfulness. You should have practiced the latter, without neglecting the former." The writer to the Hebrews voiced a similar concern: "In fact, though by this time you ought to be teachers, you need someone to teach you the elementary truths of God's word all over again. You need milk, not solid food! . . . Therefore let us leave the elementary teachings about Christ and go on to maturity" (Heb. 5:12; 6:1).

If external actions and elementary teachings aren't enough to bring disciples to maturity, then what else is missing? How do we as educators direct adults toward a more holistic Christian faith? Let us begin by revising the education model we often use by default. Rather than follow the typical schooling process, we must expand our view and practice of adult formation in several areas.

First, the one who leads the formation process needs to view his or her role as a facilitator who helps bring about learning. This type of leader encourages participation from the student and demonstrates caring and acceptance. A lecturer, on the other hand, sees his or her role as being the only one who determines what the students should learn, do, and be. All power and authority rest in his or her hands.

Next, the setting in which a person learns must be expanded from a formal classroom in an official building or institution to anywhere and everywhere life happens. As Jesus taught in both the synagogue and on the sea, adults must see that learning is related to all of life, no matter when or where it is found.

The formational approach also goes beyond content orientation toward a concern with the development process. It doesn't rely extensively on organized, highly planned curriculum to transfer information. Spiritual formation is most concerned with the needs of the learner, not the teacher. It views all activities of the leader as teaching, and learning does not end when the course is over. It is a lifelong process.

In most traditional schooling situations, the only teaching method used is lecture, or telling. The students are given what the teacher has learned and only experience the information indirectly. However, transformation occurs when more methods are added to the process. When students not only listen but also practice doing and reflecting, they are much more likely to integrate what they are learning into their own direct experience.

This leads, lastly, to the view of knowledge held by the formational approach. Under the schooling model, knowledge is a product that is transferred from teacher to learner. The student's goal is simply to acquire as much of it as possible. This is usually done by using memorization skills, and often the knowledge gained does not become a permanent part of the learner's life or philosophy. Within the formational model, however, knowledge is a mutually discovered process between the teacher and the learner. The goal is not only to acquire but also to practice what is learned. The integration of ideas into life is a crucial element of spiritual formation.

Once we have switched to a model that is developmental in its approach, it is also important to consider the unique characteristics of adult learners and how they are different from children. Chapter 24 has a more detailed discussion, but a brief overview here may be helpful. Malcolm Knowles has determined that there are four crucial assumptions we must keep in mind concerning the adult maturity process:

1. The adult's self-concept moves from dependence toward self-direction. Adults prefer to be involved in the direction of their growth and learning. Don't expect them to take a passive role; create ways for them to be active in their formation. Offer choices, assess individual discipleship needs, and delegate responsibilities to the learner whenever possible.
2. The adult accumulates a growing reservoir of experiences that become an increasing resource for learning. Utilize real-life experience in the formation process. Celebrate personal history, draw out life lessons from past trials and crises, acknowledge former lessons learned, and move on to new ground.
3. The adult's readiness to learn becomes oriented increasingly to the developmental tasks of his or her social role. Adults are most concerned with the everyday roles they find themselves in—employee, parent, boss, sibling, spouse. The areas of discipleship that will provoke the most passion for them will involve these roles.
4. The adult's time perspective changes from one of postponed application of knowledge to immediacy of application, and accordingly his or her orientation toward learning shifts from one of subject-centeredness to one of problem-centeredness.[11]

When we understand and respect the realistic needs and views of maturing adults, we can design a spiritual formation strategy that will both interest and retain them in the process. It is not enough to teach a class and hope that people's lives will change as a result. Our mission is to make authentic disciples.

Adult formation does not end. It is an ongoing process that fosters continual growth and change. As Paul wrote, "Forgetting what is behind and straining toward what is ahead, I press on toward the goal to win the prize for which Christ has called me heavenward in Christ Jesus" (Phil. 3:13–14).

SPIRITUAL FORMATION THROUGH THE SPIRITUAL DISCIPLINES

In our quest as the modern church to stay on the cutting edge of development and discovery, many of us have overlooked the ancient insights and practices that fueled the faith of a multitude of believers before us. While our answers have become increasingly complex, the questions have remained simple. How does one practice to become mature? What actions may lead me to the throne of God more easily than others? How do I guide others toward the process of sanctification and spiritual formation?

Fortunately, there are well-worn paths we may walk down to nurture our relationship with God. Ancient practices known as spiritual disciplines have served generations in their quest for depth and renewal. They are simple to learn yet not easy to exercise. They serve to take us away from what is comfortable and distracting and lead us to new realities found in the kingdom of God that are "not of this world."

In helping others become spiritually formed, the spiritual disciplines are crucial. We may wish to avoid the work that it takes to employ these practices, but as Søren Kierkegaard reminds us in *For Self-Examination,* "It costs a man just as much or even more to go to hell than to come to heaven."

Dallas Willard explains the coworking of God's grace and our action:

True character transformation begins in the pure grace of God and is continually assisted by it. Very well. But action is also indispensable in making the Christian truly a different kind of person—one having a new life in which, as 2 Corinthians 5:17 states, "Old things have passed away and, behold, all things become new." Failure to act in certain definite ways will guarantee that this transformation does not come to pass.[12]

So what are the spiritual disciplines we seek to apply in our process of spiritual formation? Richard Foster, in his book *Celebration of Discipline,* explores thirteen areas of discipline that have been utilized by Christians throughout the centuries.[13] They are divided into three categories:

1. *The Inward Disciplines:* meditation, prayer, fasting, study
2. *The Outward Disciplines:* simplicity, solitude, submission, service
3. *The Corporate Disciplines:* confession, worship, guidance, celebration

Leading others in the practice of these disciplines will sometimes be difficult. For many of us, spirituality has long been an exercise in belief, not in inner or outer discipline. For others, discipline has been attached to meritorious works rather than relational intimacy with God. Christian educators have the opportunity to turn the tide of understanding and practice.

Reviving the spiritual disciplines in the lives of disciples will be a life-changing process. The disciplines will assist us to grow relationally with God, overcome sin, gain spiritual insight and direction, and love our neighbors as ourselves. This is the fuel of spiritual formation.

SPIRITUAL FORMATION IN SMALL GROUPS

Over the past few decades, there has been a great deal of effort and attention given to the ministry of small groups in the church. Pastors and researchers have developed varying models for small group ministry that have impacted scores of churches around the world. The small group ministry has truly been key in both the recovery and nurturance of community in the church. However, as in most things, we always run the risk of honoring the messenger above the message. Small groups are vital in spiritual formation, but they are not an end in themselves. They are a means to bring something about. They are a tool that can be used to accomplish a purpose. The real question in a healthy small group ministry is not "How many groups do you have going?" but rather "What is going on in your groups?"

Many forms of education and learning can take place in the life of the believer, but for the purpose of doing intentional spiritual formation in an educational sense, it is vital to include four components in all that we do. They are:

Information. Formation begins with receiving information, be it from a teacher, a book, a verse, or a movie. We start with receiving something new.

Experience. At some point we begin our quest to understand and integrate what we have taken in. This is the stage of experience. We practice being or doing the new thing. We "try it on" in daily life.

Reflection. After the experience, we reflect and examine what took place. What internal insights were gained? What new behaviors were attempted? Where did we sense success or failure? What was learned about God? Reflection will sometimes begin alone but is most effective in the shared company of other disciples.

Community. When we are together with other learners who are being taught, practicing new attitudes and actions, and sharing each other's experiences, there is a mysterious bond that is naturally developed. It is called community and is made up of shared history, mutual discovery, and group gains and losses. Community does not have to be forced, because it cannot help but occur under these circumstances.

Can and should small groups play a crucial role in helping this process occur? Absolutely! However, they are not capable in and of themselves to produce spiritual growth. They are merely vessels that help contain the process as it takes place in the lives of its members. Without all four elements present in formation, the small group may simply be a study or a social gathering.

The difficulty comes when small groups attempt shortcuts to genuine community. This often happens by excluding experience and reflection from the formation process and expecting that information alone will lead the group to a shared sense of love and growth with one another. These groups may focus on gaining information through study, teaching, reading, and so forth, without planning or asking for experiential change to occur in the lives of its members. This can take place with support groups, Bible studies, social clubs, and virtually any other form of small group gathering. But practicing the art of spiritual formation can happen powerfully and effectively utilizing the small group structure. When its members agree to do all that is within their power to make it a safe place for learning, practicing, and reflecting, it often becomes a place of true Christian community.

Jesus modeled this in Mark 6 and Luke 9 when he sent the Twelve out in pairs with instructions to proclaim the kingdom of God and to perform healing, as they had seen and heard him do. They returned with the stories of their experience, reporting to Jesus and to each other all that they had done and taught. Scripture tells us that during this reunion, there were many people coming and going about them, so many that they could not even eat. What was Jesus' response? He said, "Come away by yourselves to a lonely place and rest a while" (Mark 6:31 NASB).

Jesus gave them information and instruction. They were sent out to experience and practice what they had learned. They reassembled with the need to share and reflect what had happened with their teacher and with each other. And their reward was a safe place in which they could commune with one another in their newly shared bond of discipleship.

Small groups are dynamic forms in which the spiritual formation process can take place. The key to their success, however, is not their structure but rather the elements they contain for genuine growth and transformation.

CONCLUSION

The art of spiritual formation is ancient and yet feels new to many churches and Christian leaders in our time. There is a renewed concern that we not only evangelize the lost but that we also do the work to make authentic disciples from those who have believed.

The message of God never changes. He has given us the mission to mature and to equip others to do the same in Christ. We as Christian educators are challenged to do more than inform the people of God. We are called to help them be spiritually transformed and renewed in the image of Christ. That is an awesome task and one that we should approach humbly with prayer, wisdom, and passion.

The ministry of spiritual formation draws upon our ability to know God and make him known in ways that will permanently change the lives of his followers. Our goal, as Paul expressed, is the vision of a great day when we "all reach unity in the faith and in the knowledge of the Son of God and become mature, attaining to the whole measure of the fullness of Christ" (Eph. 4:13).

NOTES

1. William Barclay, *Letter to the Hebrews* (Philadelphia: Westminster, 1976), p. 26.
2. Robert Clark, "Spiritual Formation in Children," in *The Christian Educator's Handbook on Spiritual Formation,* ed. Kenneth O. Gangel and James C. Wilhoit (Grand Rapids: Baker, 1994), p. 234.
3. Jack O. Balswick and Judith K. Balswick, *The Family: A Christian Perspective on the Contemporary Home* (Grand Rapids: Baker, 1989), p. 110.
4. Ibid., p. 136.
5. James Bryan Smith, "Spiritual Formation in Adolescents," in *The Christian Educator's Handbook on Spiritual Formation,* p. 249.
6. Ibid., p. 251.
7. Balswick and Balswick, *The Family,* p. 142.
8. James W. Fowler, *Stages of Faith: The Psychology of Human Development and the Quest for Meaning* (San Francisco: Harper and Row, 1981), p. 151.
9. Balswick and Balswick, *The Family,* p. 146.
10. Julie Gorman, "Aiming for Maturity: Implications for Ministry" *Theology News and Notes* 21, no. 2 (Fuller Seminary, June 1984), pp. 6–10.
11. Malcolm Knowles, *The Modern Practice of Adult Education* (New York: Association Press, 1970).
12. Dallas Willard, *The Spirit of the Disciplines* (San Francisco: Harper and Row, 1988), p. 20.
13. Richard Foster, *Celebration of Discipline* (San Francisco: Harper and Row, 1988).

PART THREE

Educational Implications of Christian Education

LEARNING THEORY FOR CHRISTIAN TEACHERS

10

William "Rick" Yount

Learning theory targets classroom behaviors, values, and principles that in turn lead to more effective learning. While specific theories of learning do not translate directly into principles of teaching, they provide maps and compasses to aid the inexperienced teacher-traveler in charting the course to learning success.

THREE ASPECTS OF THE LEARNING PROCESS

I contend that the effective teaching-learning process intersects and transforms the lives of learners. Teaching is more than conveying subject matter, more than displaying the knowledge of the teacher. It is facilitating the confluence of learner need and subject substance.[1] Both learner need and subject substance fall into three fundamental areas of life: what we think (meaningful understanding), what we value (personal convictions), and what we do (skillful behavior). That is, learners need to deepen understanding, develop appropriate values, and hone skills. Subjects possess concepts and principles to be grasped, values to be embraced, and skills to be mastered. As such, this thinking-feeling-doing triad incorporates the entire learning process.

The approach of educational psychology texts in the 1960s and '70s emphasized learning theory systems (cognitive, humanistic, behavioral) as sep-arate schools of thought. Today these theories are normally addressed in chronological order of development in the United States: behavioral, cognitive, and humanistic.

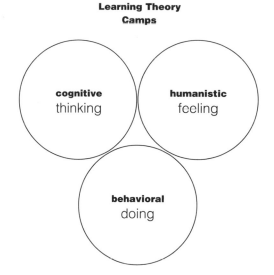

Figure 10.1
Learning Theory Camps

cognitive
thinking

humanistic
feeling

behavioral
doing

BEHAVIORAL THEORIES OF LEARNING

The most prominent theorists in behavioral learning theory include Ivan Pavlov (Classical Conditioning), E. L. Thorndike (Connectionism), and B. F. Skinner (Operant Conditioning).

Ivan Pavlov (1849–1936) was a Russian physiologist who discovered a simple connection between food (stimulus) and salivation (response) in dogs. His research on digestive reflexes in dogs earned him the Nobel Prize in 1904. In essence, his work revealed a connection between the sight and sounds associated with food and canine salivation rates. This connection is called a stimulus-response (S-R) bond. He further noticed the existence of both unconditioned and conditioned stimulus and response. That is, food caused salivation without training. But dogs also salivated when lab assistants entered the room, even when they had no food. The lab assistants had been associated with food and therefore became *conditioned stimuli*. Salivation in response to lab assistants was a *conditioned response*. Pavlov had discovered a technique for stimulating specific behavior. This link provided the foundation for behavior modification—behavior shaping as well as brainwashing. It is a little-known fact that Pavlov was a Christian. He believed he had simply discovered a principle of human behavior designed by God. So valuable was his discovery to the Soviet state that Lenin himself granted him immunity from prosecution as an "enemy of the state."[2]

Classical conditioning in classrooms focuses on involuntary behaviors that are outside conscious control. Students suffering from test anxiety do not consciously choose to feel this way. Their anxiety is linked to tests because of bad experiences in the past. The climate of a classroom provides a veritable ocean of possibilities for positive or negative associations. Whether the sea is stormy or calm depends on our teaching style. Is the classroom a warm, inviting place? Do students feel free to ask questions or share their thinking? Is the classroom emotionally safe? If it is, then positive associations will result. Or is the classroom tense? Are student questions handled as interruptions? Is the teacher gruff in demeanor? If he or she is, then negative associations will result and will generalize to the teacher, the subject, the school, and perhaps learning itself.

E. L. Thorndike (1874–1949) is known as the father of educational psychology. He did much to bridge the gap between psychological research and educational application. While Pavlov's work emphasized simple reflex actions, Thorndike demonstrated the mechanism by which new responses are formed. He showed that stimuli occurring after a behavior had an influence on future behaviors.

Thorndike postulated three laws of learning that have influenced American educational practice ever since.

1. *The Law of Readiness* states that learning proceeds best when learners are prepared to respond. If the learner is ready to respond, there is satisfaction (reward) in being allowed to respond and frustration (punishment) in being prevented from responding.
2. *The Law of Exercise* states that repetition ("drill and practice") strengthens S-R bonds. Thorndike later modified this law to require feedback on the quality of responses that were being made, since blind practice has no effect on learning.
3. *The Law of Effect* is the most important of the three. It states that any response (R) followed by pleasure or reward (S) is strengthened. Any response (R) followed by pain (S) is weakened. Learning is a function of the result of the response, not just the contiguity of the stimulus and response elements. Concrete rewards—such as gold stars on charts and verbal praise—have been widely used in classrooms because of this discovery.

Thorndike's view of learning was a mechanical process of stamping S-R bonds into the nervous system through repetition. His theory describes how bonds are strengthened or weakened. Thorndike saw little difference between animal learning and human learning and therefore had a decidedly dehumanizing effect on the American educational system. Still, Thorndike's contribution was profound. His Law of Effect underscored the importance of motivation in education and established the basis for operant conditioning and the dawn of modern behavioral learning.

B. F. Skinner (1904–1990) developed his Operant Conditioning theory in the 1930s as an expansion of Thorndike's Law of Effect. By the 1950s Skinner's views dominated psychology and learning.[3] Contiguity and classical conditioning account for only a small percentage of learned behaviors. They are inadequate to explain most human learning because people consciously generate behaviors rather than merely respond to stimuli. In classical conditioning, responses are *involuntary* and *elicited* by specific stimuli. Operant conditioning emphasizes the acquisition of new behaviors as organisms operate on their environment in order to reach goals. The responses are *voluntary* and *emitted* by people or animals.

Skinner placed pigeons in observation cages. When they behaved in a way Skinner deemed desirable, he reinforced their behavior with a food pellet. By providing reinforcing stimuli (S) for desirable behavior (R), Skinner was able to teach pigeons to differentiate among various colors, to play the piano, or even play a game of Ping-Pong.

The educational application of the theories of Thorndike and Skinner is best seen in programmed instruction. A learning program begins with a desired competency. The program breaks the competency into small steps of learning. As learners negotiate each step, they are provided information and prompted for a response. A correct response is rewarded and permits the learner to move to the next step. An incorrect response blocks advancement; learners are given another chance to process the required information. When learners have negotiated all the steps in the program, they possess the competency. Programmed instruction maximizes learner reinforcement (reward) and also the amount of interaction between learner and information. Programmed instruction systems are found in textbooks, computer programs, as well as some types of Christian school curricula, most notably Accelerated Christian Education (ACE).

Are we guilty of manipulation, brainwashing, or bribery when we use behavioral principles? Or, to put it more positively, can we use behavioral learning principles in an ethical way? The answer to the second question is yes, if we move away from Skinner's "empty box" view of learners and treat learners as individuals with dignity and personal worth. This can be done in a couple of ways.

First, avoid manipulation by using behavioral principles for justified purposes. Ethical use requires that the focus of behavioral techniques be helping students learn, not merely shaping them to teacher demands. Teaching embraces the beliefs and rational thought of learners, and is more than conditioning, which focuses on performance.[4] Second, changes in attitudes, beliefs, and values should occur for reasons that students accept. Behavior changes must have student cooperation.[5] If the end behaviors are honest and students are aware that reinforcers are being used, then reinforcement is not bribery.[6]

In light of these considerations, what suggestions might we make for using behavioral principles in the context of Christian education?

1. *Use cues and prompts to help establish new behaviors or warn of impending punishment.* A cue is a teacher behavior that elicits a proper student response. A prompt is an explanation of the cue-response link. For example, a Sunday school teacher might say, "It is fine to talk with your friends as you come into the classroom, but when I stand with my Bible open, I need to have your attention so we can begin." Standing with an open Bible is the cue. Explaining what the cue means is the prompt.

2. *Use an appropriate reinforcement schedule.* When introducing new material, give frequent reinforcements by asking questions. Specifically, praise good answers and provide corrective feedback on inadequate answers. After the new material has been learned, reduce the amount of reinforcement to encourage persistence of learning.

3. *Ensure that all learners receive some praise, but praise learner behaviors judiciously.* General praise of the class as a whole is ineffective. Those who are already motivated to learn and do well resent such praise. Those who are not motivated and do poorly ignore it, knowing they do not deserve praise. Praise individual learners for specific, well-defined successes.

4. *Provide clear, informative feedback on student work.*[7] Practice without corrective feedback does not, Thorndike discovered, improve performance. Remember that feedback is most effective when it involves both praise for correct answers and corrective information for wrong answers.[8]

5. *Use negative reinforcement rather than punishment to curb inappropriate behaviors.*[9] Negative reinforcement takes away something learners do not want and is sometimes called relief. For example, "Brendon, if you will work cooperatively with your project group for these last fifteen minutes, I won't tell your parents about your behavior today." Punishment can inhibit learning.

6. *Use removal punishment rather than presentation punishment.*[10] Removal punishment takes away something learners want (such as recess or extra credit) and is sometimes called "penalty." Presentation punishment gives something learners do not want (criticism, demerits, extra homework). For example: "Brendon, since you chose not to work cooperatively with your project group, please take your seat in the time-out corner."

7. *Avoid reinforcing the behavior you're trying to punish.*[11] A reprimand is a positive reinforcer to one who is ignored most of the time. Giving attention to misbehavior reinforces it. Use cues and prompts to minimize behavior problems. Ignore minor misbehaviors.[12]

8. *Focus on student actions, not personal qualities.*[13] A common problem with teacher praise is that it goes to the best students rather than the best answers.

COGNITIVE THEORIES OF LEARNING

Cognitive learning theories focus on the internal mental processes people use in their effort to make sense of the world.[14] Cognitive theorists believe these nonobservable cognitive processes can be studied in a scientific manner.[15] They view learning as a reorganization of perceptions. Perception is the meaning we attach to information we receive from the world around us. Perceptual reorganization allows learners to develop a clear understanding of the subject. Cognitive theories focus on the mind rather than the nervous system, insight rather than S-R bonds, and understanding rather than behavior. Fundamental perspectives in the cognitive learning theory system come from Gestalt psychology, Jean Piaget, and Jerome Bruner.

Gestalt Psychology

Gestalt psychology, which emphasized the whole of human experience, developed in Germany in the early 1900s and was brought to America in the 1920s.[16] This view held that learning takes place best when we can see the relationship or pattern of one element to another. Gestalt psychology stressed the significance of relationships

in the learning experience. Three early German gestalt psychologists were Ernst Mach, Max Wertheimer, and Wölfgang Köhler.

Ernst Mach (1838–1916) felt that human beings perceived the world around them in ways that animals did not. It was his belief that human learning was determined by interaction between the world and our perception of it, not by mechanical bonds. In this, he was in direct opposition to behaviorist John Watson, who dreamed of a psychological science as credible as physics. It was Watson's belief that just as physics observed the behaviors of planets and falling bodies, so psychology should focus only on outward behavior. Behaviorist Ivan Pavlov focused on the S-R bond as the building block for all human learning and personality. Mach felt that such a perspective was woefully inadequate to explain the complexities associated with both learning and human personality development.

Max Wertheimer (1880–1943) thought it meaningless to focus on the smallest parts of learning. Just as movement in a film cannot be studied one frame at a time, it was Wertheimer's conviction that the whole gave meaning to the individual parts.

Wölfgang Köhler (1887–1940) conducted experiments to refute the research findings and conclusions drawn by behaviorist E. L. Thorndike. Thorndike emphasized trial and error learning, in which correct responses were stamped into the nervous system by repetition. Köhler conducted experiments with chimpanzees that demonstrated learning, not by trial and error, but by insight. In one experiment, Sultan the chimpanzee was placed in a cage with a banana suspended from the top of the cage, just beyond reach. Two boxes of different sizes were also in the cage. Reaching the banana required moving the larger box into position, placing the smaller box on top, and then climbing to the banana. Sultan did not learn these steps by trial and error or by S-R bonding. He sized up the situation, understood the problem, and perceived the relationship (gestalt) between the boxes and their length of reach (i.e., the solution).[17] These differences underscore the vast divide between behavioral and cognitive learning theories. Such foundational research paved the way for two of the best known cognitive theorists who were to follow: Jean Piaget and Jerome Bruner.

Jean Piaget (1896–1980).

Piaget held that every individual functions within his or her environment in an interactive fashion. Intelligence is not simply poured into children; rather, they actively structure understanding—they help create it through their own activity. Piaget described the process with several central terms: organization, scheme, equilibration, adaptation, assimilation, and accommodation.

Organization is the natural tendency to make sense of experiences by integrating them into logically related cognitive structures. These structures are simple at first but are built up—by combining, arranging, recombining, and rearranging behaviors and thoughts—into ever more complex systems.

Schemes are the cognitive structures produced as a result of the development process. As organized patterns of behavior or thought produced through interaction with the environment, schemes represent the world as we know it.

Equilibration is the natural tendency to maintain a balance between what one already knows (the cognitive network) and what one experiences in the world. When this balance is disturbed—that is, when we experience something that does not fit what we know—we experience anxiety, discomfort, or confusion. This confusion is called *disequilibrium*. Equilibration compels us to reduce the disequilibrium by restoring the balance, or equilibrium, between our understanding of the world and our experiences with the world. An example of this in an educational setting is an exam. Students prefer living in a state of equilibrium. However, once the professor announces that an exam will occur in the class next week, the student suddenly develops anxiety and fear. This disequilibrium is only resolved by reading, studying, and memorizing the material that serves as the basis for the exam. In this example, the disequilibrium facilitates learning by serving as a motivating influence for study.

Adaptation is the natural process of adjusting our thinking or our environment so that balance exists between what we know and what we experience. It is creating a good fit between one's concept of reality (schemes) and real-life experiences. Adaptation consists of two parts. The first part, *assimilation,* interprets experiences so they fit what we already know. A child knows "cats" but not "skunks." When she sees a skunk, she identifies it, wrongly, as a cat. The second part, *accommodation*, adjusts schemes so they fit what we experience. After being sprayed by a skunk, she differentiates between cats and skunks. Adaptation combines these two processes so that our perceptions represent the world in which we live as closely as possible.

In summary, the drive to systematize our world (organization) causes us to create a mental niche for everything we experience. Creating new schemes or modifying existing schemes provides niches for experiences (accommodation). We do this so that we can put everything we experience in its place, even if we have to change the experience so that it will fit (assimilation).

Piaget's theory identifies four stages of cognitive development and the differential cognitive abilities of learners of various ages. (See chapter 6 for an expanded discussion.)

Jerome Bruner (b. 1915)

Bruner saw little value in studying rats, cats, or pigeons to understand how children learn in a classroom setting. He gathered his data from children in classroom settings.[18] He believes that the goal of teaching is to promote the general understanding of a subject and that the facts and relationships children discover through their own explorations are more usable and tend to be better retained than material they have merely committed to memory.[19] Bruner found that discovery learning develops better problem-solving skills and greater confidence in the ability to learn as they "learn how to learn."[20] A colleague of B. F. Skinner's at Harvard University, he became Skinner's most vocal opponent.

Bruner held that any subject can be organized so that it can be taught in a meaningful way to almost any student. Structuring a subject means to exegete its fundamental principles and determine how they relate to one another. These ideas can be reduced to a diagram or set of principles.[21] Structure is facilitated by three components: presentation, economy, and power.

Bruner wrote that people possess different modes of understanding at any age. He called these the enactive, the iconic, and the symbolic. Enactive understanding is based on actions, demonstrations, and hands-on experimentation. Iconic understanding is based on pictures, images, diagrams, models, and the like. Symbolic understanding is based on language and the use of words to express complex ideas.[22] Presenting material in the sequence of enactive, iconic, and symbolic helps students develop structural understanding of the subject.[23]

Bruner believed that external rewards were an artificial means to encourage students to learn. All children, wrote Bruner, have an innate will to learn.[24] Intrinsic motivation comes from the students' own curiosity, their drive to achieve competence, and reciprocity—the desire to work cooperatively with others. These are rewarding in themselves and thus self-sustaining.[25] The teacher's responsibility is to ensure that these natural motivators are not impaired by irrelevant and dry presentations, frustrating expectations, and unwholesome competition among students.

Discovery learning emphasizes student activity, student initiative, and student solutions. Bruner knew that students would learn fewer facts through this approach but would gain a deeper understanding of the subject that could well continue beyond the classroom. It is one thing to be able to answer a teacher's questions but a better thing for students to learn to ask questions of themselves and then find the answers.

Effective teachers are well-versed in the subject being taught so that they can move easily from concept to concept. They model thinking competence, weighing student questions before answering, reframing statements to make them more focused, pulling relevant examples into the class discussion, and asking probing questions to further student understanding. Teachers are group facilitators and presenters of problems more than tellers of facts. Teachers serve as guides for the student-centered learning process, and they take care not to short-circuit the discovery process by giving students the answers.

As years passed, Bruner's pure discovery approach, described above, was found to be too student-centered, too dependent on self-motivation of learners, and achievement declined. Bruner's approach was modified to include more teacher intervention and direction. This modified approach came to be known as *directed discovery*.

In light of these considerations, what suggestions might we make for using cognitive principles in a Christian context?

1. *Use explanations, demonstrations, and pictures to help students understand concepts.* Much teaching is verbal. We talk about concepts more than clarifying their meaning. Explain, illustrate, and visualize concepts. Use diagrams to give visual support to verbal explanations.

2. *Learning should be flexible and exploratory, allowing students to solve problems on their own.* The phrase "flexible and exploratory methods" stands against inflexible, sit-still-while-I-instill information transmission. Lecturing students on "five key truths" is less effective than asking questions and having the students construct those five truths from the information.

3. *Arouse curiosity and maximize relevance of the subject to students.* Arouse curiosity by asking questions or posing problems that are relevant to students' needs. If the questions or problems are correctly set, then the study will produce effective and relevant learning for the students.

4. *Periodically return to important concepts.* Keep a log of key concepts studied week by week. Use terms from past studies to reinforce their meaning and to emphasize their place in the subject structure of your students.

5. *Encourage informed guessing.* Cognitive educators encourage students to make educated guesses in answering questions. When answers are wrong or incomplete, teachers help students analyze them to determine how to make them better.

6. *Use a variety of materials.* Since motivation is based on the intrinsic value of curiosity, provide a variety of learning experiences. Mechanical teaching and rote memorization kill curiosity and the desire to understand.

7. *Let students satisfy their own curiosity, even if the ideas are not directly related to the lesson.* There are times when class discussion moves away from the lesson plan for the day into other areas of interest for learners in the class. "Chasing rabbits" can increase student motivation and also helps students know that their teachers care about them. Investigating related topics can also enhance the depth of learning by integrating the planned information with student interests.

HUMANISTIC THEORIES OF LEARNING

Humanistic learning theory developed in opposition to Skinner's mechanically rigid approach to learning. Educational humanism, or affective education, emphasizes the affective domain of learning: receiving (personal openness), responding (personal response), valuing (personal conviction), organizing (personal value system), and characterizing (personal lifestyle). True human learning involves learners' attitudes, emotions, and values and emphasizes the uniqueness of each learner.

The early roots of humanism can be traced back to Democritus and Aristotle of ancient Greece. When the Romans conquered Greece in 146 B.C., they quickly took over the educational system. Humanism in the Roman Empire drew heavily upon the stoicism of Cicero and the sophist approach of Quintilian. Shortly after the fall of Constantinople in 1453, Greek philosophy again became a significant factor in the educational thought of Western Europe. At this time there was a resurgence in Greek teachers, manuscripts, and spirit. Students returned to the classics. Those who did were referred to as humanists. During the period of the Renaissance, several scholars emphasized humanistic models of education. Among them was Erasmus. His educational aim was for each student to develop independent judgment. Reformation Christian educators such as Luther, Melanchthon, and Sturn each placed an emphasis upon students having a solid understanding of the Greek and Roman classics.[26]

Thus, in education, Protestantism demonstrated humanist influences by creating an atmosphere that was conducive to academic adventure, challenge, and scholarship. Its emphasis upon Greek and Hebrew, together with the Latin of its day, played a large part in opening up the works of Plato, Aristotle, and Cicero to eager minds. This emphasis continued on through the period known as the Enlightenment. When John Dewey (1859–1952), the father of progressive education, came on the scene in the late 1800s, the foundation had been laid for a new approach toward the teacher-learner process, one that placed the student at the center of attention. In contemporary educational thought, Abraham Maslow, Carl Rogers, and Arthur Combs are three leading psychologists who influenced humanistic methods of education more than any others.

Abraham Maslow (1908–1970) believed that too much psychological study had emphasized research on animals and the mentally impaired. Instead, he chose to focus his research efforts on those who were mentally healthy (self-actualized).[27] He believed that children make wise choices for their own learning when given the opportunity. Teachers arrange attractive and meaningful learning situations, and students select from those they find personally valuable. In this climate, teacher-directed classroom management becomes secondary to the motivating power of self-chosen activities.

Carl Rogers (1902–1987), a psychotherapist by profession, developed person-centered methods for his work as a counselor. Person-centered counseling revolves around the client and stands against directive therapy, which revolves around the counselor. Rogers's ideas were not based on objective data but rather personal answers to questions about individuals. How do they feel? How do they perceive their relationships with others? He transferred his ideas into his graduate seminars in psychology and counseling. He focused more on phenomenology (the world as it is perceived by individuals) than reality (the world as it may actually be).[28]

In Rogers's view, teachers should trust students to do their work to the best of their ability and provide opportunities for learning. Teachers should be sincere and transparent facilitators who view the learning experience from the students' perspectives. The result of these efforts, according to Rogers, is that students take responsibility for their own learning.

Arthur Combs (1912–1999) stressed that teachers should serve as facilitators of learning. His work parallels Bruner's pure discovery learning, but Combs placed more emphasis on sharing personal views and less on objective problem solving. Effective facilitators, according to Combs, are well-informed, sensitive, believe in their students' ability to learn, have a positive self-concept, and use many methods to engage students in the learning process.[29] For Combs, meaning is not inherent in the subject matter; it is the individual who instills subject matter with its meaning. His dilemma was not how to present subject matter but how to help students derive personal meaning.[30]

A central tendency for educational humanism is a desire to create a learning environment free from fear, punishment, harsh discipline, and manipulative methods. Teachers should be trusting, sincere, and empathetic with their students. They should prize their students and hold them in high regard.[31] Affective factors should be explored as much as the cognitive dimension of classroom instruction.[32] The relationship between the teacher and the student has an important impact on learning and should be characterized by an atmosphere of openness, caring, and mutual respect. Since the way students feel about themselves will greatly influence the manner in which they learn, teachers should use techniques to encourage students to explore their feelings and emotions and should encourage students to identify with others, empathize with them, and relate their feelings to the feelings of others.[33] They should help their students become more aware of their own attitudes and values.

Humanistic principles can have both positive and negative effects when implemented in the classroom. Consider the following suggestions:

1. *Use humanistic methods where appreciation of subjects—personal values, convictions, value systems—is the primary goal.* Humanistic methods focus on learner experiences, emotions, values, and choices. Such methods may improve attitudes toward school, may improve students' self concepts, and may even improve cooperation among students because subjects are made more relevant. But academic achievement suffers as objective meaning is deemphasized.[34]

2. *Use small group processes to maximize personal interaction.* The heart of humanistic methodology in the 1970s involved sensitivity training and encounter groups. Groups of learners spent large portions of class time expressing feelings, exploring interpersonal relationships, and sharing personal values. Simulation games and role-playing activities were used to help participants intensify their sharing.[35] With the fall of standardized test scores and the general decline of content mastery during the late 1970s and early 1980s, educators abandoned encounter-type group experiences for more productive cooperative learning strategies.

3. *Allow students to regulate their own learning.* Humanistic educators emphasized learning situations in which students control their own learning. Such control included selection of topics and resources, setting goals, and evaluating outcomes—all with little teacher guidance.[36] Formal educational institutions discovered that human tendencies toward convenience and personal comfort resulted in misused classroom freedom and failure to learn. Achievement declined. Still, this principle works well with learners who are self-motivated, self-controlled, and engaged in learning for their own personal development—such as adult education classes and voluntary learning groups.

4. *Promote a relaxed and safe class atmosphere where you demonstrate care for learners as individuals.* Classroom learning is enhanced when open communication, willingness to share, genuine empathy, and warmth are emphasized by teacher and students.

5. *Place teaching priority on affective outcomes.* Humanistic educators believed that providing an environment of freedom, responsibility, caring, and interpersonal sharing is more important than achieving a few additional points on standardized tests. Achieving personal growth, enhanced and clarified values, and better interpersonal skills took priority over standard curricula, testing, and academic achievement. In this, they were proven very wrong, and American education still suffers from the overindulgence of the affective side of learning. Affective outcomes are important but not at the expense of developing skills and deepening subject understanding.

6. *Promote individualized instruction.* Humanistic educators molded instruction to student abilities. It is useful to provide a wide variety of activities and choices for achieving academic goals. Encourage peer assistance—learners helping each other—and cooperative learning experiences.

7. *Use humanistic approaches in situations where relevance to learners is more important than cognitive understanding.* For example, most Bible students know that Jesus said, "Love your enemies." Most understand what Jesus meant when he said it. But do they love their

enemies? Use humanistic approaches to help learners embrace truths for themselves.

CONCLUSION

The hand of the LORD was upon me, and he brought me out by the Spirit of the LORD and set me in the middle of a valley; it was full of bones. He led me back and forth among them, and I saw a great many bones on the floor of the valley, bones that were very dry. He asked me, "Son of man, can these bones live?" I said, "O Sovereign LORD, you alone know." (Ezek. 37:1–3)

Have you ever stood before a Bible study or Christian college class on the first day of a new year or semester and wondered if the dry bones of inattention, of self-absorption, of convenience and comfort sitting before you could ever be brought back to life? It is enough to drain away all the enthusiasm we can muster.

Figure 10.2

How do we open the way for the Holy Spirit to teach from within, to transform heads, hearts, and hands in a tangible way? How do we engage the internal influence of the Lord? First, we regularly engage in prayer, asking the Lord to reveal himself to students, to help them understand his truths, to value his ways, and to act in accordance with his laws. We pray for students to have open hearts and minds. We pray for God's presence in the classroom and allow for spiritually related experiences to be shared. Second, we assume the position of ministering servant rather than controlling tyrant. Students do not attend class for our benefit, to pro-vide us a job. We attend class for their benefit, to help them learn. We are servants of our students, giving our lives for their growth. This position of servant frees the Holy Spirit to work in the lives of our learners. Finally, our priority in teaching is not our own classes but the kingdom of God. Cooperation with other teachers and departments, an other-centered approach, allows much more freedom for the Lord to work through our classes than does a self-centered approach. Learning theory is helpful. But the presence and power of the Lord, operating from within through channels of thinking, feeling, and doing, is essential for true life transformation (see figure 10.2).

Then he said to me, "Prophesy to these bones and say to them, 'Dry bones, hear the word of the LORD! This is what the Sovereign LORD says to these bones: I will make breath enter you, and you will come to life. I will attach tendons to you and make flesh come upon you and cover you with skin; I will put breath in you, and you will come to life. Then you will know that I am the LORD.' . . . So I prophesied as he commanded me, and breath entered them; they came to life and stood up on their feet—a vast army." (Ezek. 37:4–10)

NOTES

1. The left and right foundation stones of the Discipler's Model are Bible (content) and learner needs. Both are necessary elements of teaching that is both Christian and life changing. See my self-published *The Disciplers' Handbook* or chapter one in my book *Created to Learn* (Nashville: Broadman, 1996). Or go to my web site (http://members.aol.com/wyount) for an overview.

2. Pavlov was not allowed to attend church and so remained at home and studied his Bible. He was often scheduled by the University of Samara, Russia, to lecture on Sundays, but he refused. One day when confronted by his students—some three hundred in his lecture auditorium—about his status as a "hero of the Soviet Union" and his belief in "religious myths," he replied with Pascal's famous quote on Christians and naturalists: "If the naturalists are correct, then when we come to death, we all die and that is the end. Slava Bogu ['Praise God']. But if the Christians are correct, then we come to death very differently. Are you willing to place the future of your eternal soul in the hands of the naturalists?" The auditorium was silenced. And Pavlov continued his lecture on dog anatomy. From a conversation with Sergei Golovin, Christian apologist and pastor, Simferopol, Ukraine, May 1998.

3. Paul Eggen and Don Kauchak, *Educational Psychology: Classroom Connections,* 2d ed. (New York: Macmillan, 1994), p. 262.

4. Thomas Good and Jere Brophey, *Educational Psychology: A Realistic Approach,* 4th ed. (New York: Longman, 1990), p. 295.

5. Ibid., p. 296.

6. Ibid., p. 297.

7. Eggen and Kauchak, *Educational Psychology,* p. 281.

8. Norman Sprinthall, Richard Sprinthall, and Sharon Oja, *Educational Psychology: A Developmental Approach,* 6th ed. (New York: McGraw-Hill, 1994), p. 235.

9. Anita Woolfolk, *Educational Psychology,* 5th ed. (Boston: Allyn and Bacon, 1993), p. 217.

10. Eggen and Kauchak, *Educational Psychology,* p. 280.

11. Woolfolk, *Educational Psychology,* p. 217.

12. See Yount, in "Teacher as Classroom Manager," *Called to Teach,* for suggestions for disciplining classroom behavior problems.

13. Woolfolk, *Educational Psychology,* p. 217.

14. Eggen and Kauchak, *Educational Psychology,* p. 305.

15. Robert Biehler and Jack Snowman, *Psychology Applied to Teaching,* 7th ed. (Boston: Houghton Mifflin, 1993), p. 378.

16. *Gestalt* is roughly translated as "configuration" or "pattern."

17. Sprinthall et al., *Education Psychology,* p. 220.

18. Ibid., p. 243.

19. Ibid., p. 247.

20. Biehler and Snowman, *Psychology Applied to Teaching,* p. 427.

21. Woolfolk, *Educational Psychology,* p. 319.

22. Sprinthall et al., *Educational Psychology,* p. 247.

23. Ibid., p. 243.

24. Ibid.

25. Ibid., p. 244.

26. Michael J. Anthony, "Humanism in American Christian Education," *Christian Education Journal* 12, no. 1 (1991): 79–88.

27. Daniel Barlow, *Educational Psychology: The Teaching-Learning Process* (Chicago: Moody, 1985), p. 189.

28. Gary LeFrancois, *Psychology for Teaching,* 8th ed. (Belmont, Calif.: Wadsworth, 1994), p. 241.

29. Biehler and Snowman, *Psychology Applied to Teaching,* p. 476.

30. Myron H. Dembo, *Applying Educational Psychology,* 5th ed. (New York: Longman, 1994), p. 203.

31. Biehler and Snowman, *Psychology Applied to Teaching,* p. 399.

32. Thomas Gordon, *T.E.T.: Teacher Effectiveness Training* (New York: Wyden, 1974), p. 24.

33. Biehler and Snowman, *Psychology Applied to Teaching,* p. 400.

34. Good and Brophey, *Educational Psychology,* p. 471; Dembo, *Applying Educational Psychology,* p. 227.

35. LeFrancois, *Psychology for Teaching,* p. 250.

36. Robert Slavin, *Educational Psychology: Theory and Practice,* 4th ed. (Boston: Allyn and Bacon, 1994), p. 298.

JESUS: THE MASTER TEACHER   11

Robert W. Pazmiño

A fascination with Jesus as teacher has persisted down through the ages and rightfully so. The Jewish leader and teacher Nicodemus noted this fascination when he is reported in John 3 to have met Jesus at night. In this encounter, Nicodemus first said, "Rabbi, we know that you are a teacher who has come from God; for no one can do these signs that you do apart from the presence of God" (John 3:2 NRSV). A teacher coming from God calls for our attention, wonder, and awe if we are committed to the ministries of Christian education. For Christians, Jesus alone stands as the Master Teacher, as the exemplar or model for teaching whose life and ministry are worthy of both passionate consideration and emulation.

THE CONTEXT OF JESUS' TEACHING

The world in which Jesus taught has been the subject of scholarly inquiry in an effort to gain perspective on the setting of his ministry. First-century Palestine stood at the crossroads of numerous teaching traditions that were present in Hellenistic culture under Roman rule. Palestine was influenced by the traditions of Egypt, Babylon, Syria, Assyria, Greece, and Rome, and by the Jews themselves. As a Jew, Jesus grew up in this diverse and multicultural context. It is likely that Jesus himself was trilingual—speaking Aramaic in everyday conversation, Hebrew in the local synagogue, and Greek in his carpentry profession. His multiple lingual and cultural fluency served to enrich his teaching repertoire. Within these diverse traditions, Jesus primarily drew upon his Jewish tradition in teaching and was even recognized by Nicodemus, a Jewish authority, as a rabbi.

The very consideration of the tradition upon which one draws in teaching is important because of how education serves to pass these traditions on to others. People view and interpret traditions in the transmission process just as Jesus did in relation to his Jewish tradition.[1] While Jesus' teaching ministry was primarily to the house of Israel, he did interact with diverse cultural groups and at times even commended the faith of Gentiles (Matt. 2:1–11; 8:28–34; Mark 7:24–30; Luke 7:1–7; 10:25–37; 17:11–19; John 4:1–26; 12:20–26).

The value of a multicultural heritage and multiple lingual and cultural fluencies is affirmed by the apostle Paul as an asset for ministry in 1 Corinthians 9:20: "To the Jews I became like a Jew, to win the Jews. To those under the law I became like one under the law (though I myself am not under the law), so as to win those under the law." In addition, at the birth of the Christian church in Acts 2, the impact of the preaching and teaching was extended as persons heard the gospel in their own language. In relation to Jesus' teaching context, it is helpful to consider how he was rabbinic in following his Jewish tradition. However, it is also insightful to consider how Jesus was unrabbinic in moving beyond his Jewish tradition.

Jesus: Traditional Rabbi or New Teacher?

In comparing Jesus' teaching with his contemporaries, we discern how he related to the wider context of rabbinic teaching.[2] Robert Stein, in his work *The Method and Message of Jesus' Teaching,* provides a helpful discussion of the ways in which Jesus was both rabbinic and nonrabbinic. Jesus held to traditional rabbinic thought when he proclaimed the divine origin of the law (Mark 12:28–34); taught in the synagogues (Mark 1:21–28, 39; 3:1–6); gathered disciples in his teaching (Mark 1:16–20; 3:13–19); debated with the scribes (Mark 11:27–33; 12:13–27); was asked to settle legal disputes (Mark 12:13–17); sat as he taught (Mark 4:1; 9:35; Matt. 5:1); and supported his teachings with reference to the Scriptures (Mark 2:25–26). In all of these ways, Jesus followed the norms for rabbis as they shared their wisdom and spiritual insights.

However, Stein also notes ways in which Jesus taught using new and distinctive instructional content and methodology. Jesus taught out of doors (Mark 2:13; 6:32–44); he taught women, tax collectors, sinners, and children (Mark 2:14–17; 10:13–16; Matt. 11:16–19; Luke 7:39); his disciples were protégés of himself and of a new tradition (Luke 9:21–27); he was greater than Jonah and Solomon in relation to his wisdom and impact (Matt. 12:38–42); and he was viewed as both prophet and teacher (Mark 6:1–6). These distinctives set Jesus apart from his contemporaries and resulted in a lasting impact upon all of his disciples or learners.[3] We must not fail to recognize Jesus' unique redemptive mission as the Son of God, which served to distinguish his teaching from all others.

Jesus was far more than a traditional rabbi, for he brought a new paradigm to the rabbinic tradition by embodying an expression of teaching that was distinctive and faithful to the spirit of the Hebrew faith. He broke through the bonds that prevented disenfranchised people groups such as women, children, sinners, and Gentiles from appropriating the new life offered freely by his heavenly Father. Those who sat at his feet and listened to him on a mountain peak or along the side of the lake discovered that new life. Jesus brought this new life to the cultural backwaters of Galilee, where his ministry was primarily centered. The question posed to Jesus' followers was, "Can anything good come from Galilee?" What could someone from Nazareth offer to those in culturally sophisticated first-century Palestine?

Galilee: A Multicultural Setting

In recent scholarship, the cultural context of Galilee has received attention in relation to multicultural realities. Galilee was a region composed of Gentiles and foreigners. It was a region that was constantly experiencing infiltration and migration. At various times in its history, Babylon, Persia, Macedonia, Egypt, Syria, and Assyria controlled Galilee. In the first century, Galilee had a population of approximately 350,000 persons. This number included a large number of slaves and about 100,000 Jews, who were largely Hellenized. The primary language at this time was Koine (common) Greek, although most Jews spoke Aramaic. Galilean Jews were lax in their attendance at the Jerusalem temple. There were two reasons for this. First, the obvious distance made it inconvenient; and second, a secularized attitude was indicative of the "orthodoxy" that Jews in Galilee were practicing. It is significant that much of the teaching of Jesus, directed primarily to those living in the Galilean context, was not acceptable to the orthodox interpreters of Judea, for he gained a reputation for unusual interpretation. Jesus manifested a freshness and independence of mind as to the meaning and application of the law, which was consistent with the spirit of Galilee. This region was occupied by a mixed population and had a reputation for racial variety in and around its borders.[4] Its cultural diversity posed a direct challenge to the perceived cultural purity of Judea and Jerusalem. Why would the Son of God choose to be incarnated in and identified with such a setting? What does the commitment to and engagement with a multicultural reality suggest for teaching strategies enamored with homogeneous groupings and a press for cultural conformity? The motley and diverse collection of Jesus' inner circle of twelve apostles may also confound the usual recruitment strategies for Christian discipleship efforts.

Multicultural education is an area of need among Christians who are committed to the education of the whole people of God. Multicultural education suggests a type of education concerned with creating educational environments in which participants from all cultural groups will experience educational equity.[5] "Educational equity" can be defined in terms of access to educational resources, respect for differences, space to be heard, appropriate role models, and shared power to make educational decisions. Jesus did not experience this equity in being identified as a Galilean in John 7, despite his birth in Bethlehem of Judea. Nicodemus was an advocate for this equity before the chief priests and his fellow Pharisees, the cultural insiders, in John 7:45–52. This brief introduction into the historical and geographical context of Jesus' teaching ministry provides us with a lens through which we can explore the content of his teaching. The two must be considered together.

The Content of Jesus' Teaching

One classic in the study of Jesus as teacher is the work of Herman H. Horne (1874–1946), who taught for many years at New York University. Horne's work was originally titled *Jesus: The Master Teacher* and was republished after 1971 as *Teaching Techniques of Jesus*. In its current incarnation, its title is *Jesus the Teacher: Examining His Expertise in Education.*[6] The summary of this work is worth quoting at length in introducing the content and methods of Jesus' teaching:

> The teaching situation is complex, though it may easily be resolved into its essential elements: teacher, student, lesson, aim of the teacher, method of teaching, and environment.
>
> The conversation of Jesus with the woman of Samaria is an object lesson in teaching in all these respects.
>
> Jesus began by winning attention through openers that centered students' interests; then he established some point of contact with his hearers on the physical or spiritual plane.
>
> As a teacher, he was not only a tactician with methods but also a strategist with objectives. His greatest objective was to share with people that sense of union with the Father that he enjoyed.

> Jesus based his teaching on the vital problems in the lives of his students.
>
> Though he was not a Greek, he was ready to converse in a profitable way as was Socrates, and he led a more public life, though shorter, than did Socrates.
>
> He asked and answered questions to stimulate self-expression, desiring conviction rather than persuasion on the part of his followers. His questions are better than those of Socrates because they are mostly of a kind other than leading.
>
> He used discourse at many different times before many different groups on many different themes, but always in a more or less informal way.
>
> He told stories with a point, the parables, which his listeners did not always understand but which always made them think and led the spiritually minded to inquire into their meaning.
>
> He knew and used the Old Testament Scriptures, both for the needs of his own soul and as a common meeting ground with the religious minds of his day.
>
> He never let an occasion slip but utilized it as it arose to clarify thought and to guide life.
>
> The principle of true learning is recognized in his words: "He who has ears, let him hear," and all his parables present the less familiar in terms of the familiar. Even so, he was often misunderstood.
>
> He used the principle of contrast to make real the portrayal of truth, concrete examples to bring the abstract near, symbols to make, if possible, difficult meanings plain, and wonderful imagery to enhance the appeal to the imagination and so to lead people to conviction.
>
> He cared more for individuals than for crowds, though he would often minister to crowds, perhaps with a view to reaching individuals.
>
> He trained his disciples as witnesses of him, by personal association, individualizing instruction, and meeting the needs of each one.
>
> The work accomplished by Jesus and through others, under his tutelage, was based on high motivation because of the awaken-

ing spiritual and altruistic impulses rather than those of personal advancement.

In a most interesting way, Jesus probed the depths of human nature and touched on most of the innate reactions of man, though some, like rivalry, he did not conspicuously appeal to, and some, like sex, he sublimated.

All the methods of impression he used were but means to expression. Jesus was far more pragmatic than either idealistic or mystic.

Jesus appreciated childhood and made its characteristics identical with those of membership in the kingdom.

In a way not surprising but confirming our previous impressions, Jesus embodies those qualities of the teacher commonly set up as ideal.

As we followed these discussions, we doubtless discovered repeatedly that the problems of teaching that we ourselves face are similar to those that Jesus faced and that the solutions he found will greatly assist us in our work.

Jesus is the master teacher. Have we made him ours?[7]

Horne's insights point out the unique content and instructional methodology of Jesus' teaching. Once having been exposed to his insights, the crowds marveled at his teaching for he spoke and communicated in ways which were distinct and unique. He spoke with persuasive passion yet exuded a respectful authority. His words could stir the hearts of sinners, quiet the hearts of the tormented, and bring peace to the turbulent minds of his listeners. At the same time, these words spoken before humble sinners and the downtrodden brought scorn and rebuke to those who opposed his mission. The Pharisees became jealous, the scribes were perplexed, and the priests were enraged. Each audience had a different response to the same content. The difference was brought about by the condition of the learner's heart. Herein lies the meaning behind the parable of the four soils (Mark 4).

Principles of Jesus' Teaching

From a broad review of the content of Jesus' teaching and instructional methodology, together with Horne's excellent summary, it is possible for us to identify five principles of Jesus' teaching practice that can guide our own practice.

1. *Jesus' teaching was authoritative.*[8] Jesus taught as one who had authority (Mark 1:27), a fact demonstrated by his actions and words. His authority was authenticated by the content of his teaching and by who he was as a person. The content of his teaching was the revelation of God, for he spoke with the words of God the Father (John 14:23–24). In addition, Jesus' life and ministry authenticated the authority of his teaching.

2. *Jesus' teaching was not authoritarian.* While being authoritative, Jesus' teaching was not forced or imposed upon his hearers (John 6:60–69). Jesus specified the costs and demands of discipleship and encouraged his followers to make personal commitments of their choosing. Once having delivered the message, he allowed the individual to confront the truth and come to his or her own conclusions.

3. *Jesus' teaching encouraged people to think.* Jesus stimulated serious thought and reflection in his teaching content. He expected his hearers to carefully consider their response to the truths he shared. In response to many inquiries, he did not provide simple, ready-made answers to life's problems. Jesus expected his students to search their minds and hearts in relation to his teachings and to consider the realities of life. In encouraging others to think for themselves, Jesus posed questions and allowed for questioning.

4. *Jesus lived what he taught.* Jesus incarnated his message faithfully in his life and ministry. Before commanding his disciples to serve and love one another as he had loved them (John 13:12–17, 34–35), Jesus demonstrated the full extent of his love by washing his disciples' feet. He then further demonstrated his love by laying down his life for his friends (John 15:12–13). No one had ever personified or embodied instructional content as much as Jesus.

5. *Jesus had a love for those he taught.* Jesus loved his students, his disciples, in a way that indicated the deep longings of every heart for an intimate relationship with another person and with God. This relationship of love

with Jesus was also characterized by an equal concern for truth as the Master Teacher communicated it.[9]

These principles help us understand the character and nature of the Master Teacher and provide insights for us as we seek to further his cause of making new disciples of all mankind.

The Master Teacher as Viewed by His Disciples

Each Gospel writer provides a distinct and fascinating portrayal of Jesus as a gifted teacher. Much like a painter adding color from the palette to the canvas, each Gospel writer depicts Jesus in a slightly different color. Together they provide us with a beautiful portrait of a skilled oratorical craftsman at work. Each presentation has a distinct purpose and is seen as unique from the others. It is only when each is explored in detail that a comprehensive account of Jesus' teaching can be developed.

Matthew's Gospel is written to those who would value and appreciate Jesus' Jewish heritage. Countless references to the Old Testament provide the New Testament reader with a bridge from the old to the new writings of Scripture. Matthew's account of Jesus portrays him as one who organizes his thoughts around five oratorical presentations. The five discourses are organized as follows:

1. Vision for participation in God's kingdom (5:1–7:27)
2. Mission directives for the disciples (10:1–42)
3. Outline of redemptive history (13:1–52)
4. Discipline which leads to reconciliation (18:1–35)
5. Vision for God's future kingdom (23:1–25:46)[10]

Mark's Gospel portrays Jesus as the teacher of authority and action who makes a difference in the lives of both individuals and society as a whole. Writing to the action-oriented Romans, Mark portrays Jesus as an individual with mission, purpose, and passion. Like an army sweeping across a great plain, Jesus is seen as a conquering leader who delivers mankind from the onslaught of the forces of darkness.

Luke's well-organized Gospel portrays Jesus as the inclusive and welcoming teacher who honors people of diverse ethnic and religious backgrounds. Directed toward a Greek audience, Luke is deliberate in his desire to portray Jesus as one concerned about injustice regardless of a person's country of origin. One will find Jesus welcoming Jew, Gentile, women, children, sinner, and saint. Each is invited to his table to share fellowship and receive unconditional love and acceptance.

John's Gospel portrays Jesus as a deeply personal and intimate teacher. In John's account Jesus is sensitive to the hearts and minds of each of his followers and establishes a special relationship with every person who is open and vulnerable to him. His Gospel is the tender story of a shepherd who laments over the loss of his sheep, which reveals the emotional nature of Christ.

Each Gospel account gives us a glimpse into a different side of Jesus' teaching ministry. Together they form a composite picture of a master craftsman at work, skillfully applying his trade of transforming hearts and reconciling a needy world with a loving God.

CONCLUSION

A consideration of the context, content, and persons of Jesus' teaching can provide the Christian teacher with new perspective for his or her ministry today. Roy Zuck, in his exhaustive work *Teaching as Jesus Taught,* proposes that we can incorporate some of the effective teaching principles and practices Jesus masterfully modeled.[11] They serve as benchmarks by which we can measure the effectiveness of our teaching ministries as well.

We can celebrate how Jesus was the Master Teacher in relation to the context, content, and persons of his teaching ministry. As the Master Teacher, Jesus continues to transform people today just as he did in the first century. This presence and power is made available to all Christian teachers who desire to replicate the life of Christ through their own examples while in partnership with the Holy Spirit. Jesus is a model for all those who are called to teach.

Notes

1. Bernard Bailyn defines education as "the entire process by which a culture transmits itself across the generations." See Bernard Bailyn, *Education in the Forming of American Society: Needs and Opportunities for Study* (New York: Norton, 1960), pp. 14, 45. This definition of education emphasizes the processes of socialization and enculturation in passing on a culture across the generations. In his study of colonial United States, Bailyn identifies four great axles of society that serve to pass on a culture: family, church, community, and economy. Bailyn does not name schools, although schools are what most persons associate with education. A question to consider is, Why does Bailyn not name them?

2. For an introduction to the rabbinic tradition, see James L. Crenshaw, *Education in Ancient Israel: Across the Deadening Silence* (New York: Doubleday, 1998).

3. Robert Stein, *The Method and Message of Jesus' Teaching* (Philadelphia: Westminster, 1978).

4. See my discussion of Galilee in Robert W. Pazmiño, *Latin American Journey: Insights for Christian Education in North America* (Cleveland: United Church Press, 1994), pp. 108–10, where I draw upon Kenneth W. Clark, "Galilee," in *Interpreter's Dictionary of the Bible,* ed. George A. Buttrick (Nashville: Abingdon, 1962), pp. 344–47. Also see Virgil Elizondo, *Galilean Journey: The Mexican-American Promise* (Maryknoll, N.Y.: Orbis, 1983) for a theological discussion of the significance of Galilee for understanding cultural realities.

5. Ricardo L. García, *Teaching in a Pluralistic Society: Concepts, Models, Strategies* (New York: Harper and Row, 1982), p. 8.

6. Herman Horne, *Jesus the Teacher: Examining His Expertise in Education,* revised and updated by Angus M. Gunn (Grand Rapids: Kregel, 1998).

7. Ibid., pp. 135–36.

8. For a study of authority in relation to teaching, see Robert W. Pazmiño, *By What Authority Do We Teach? Sources for Empowering Christian Educators* (Grand Rapids: Baker, 1994). Jesus' authority is discussed on pp. 24–26.

9. James Stewart outlines these areas in *The Life and Teachings of Jesus Christ* (Nashville: Abingdon, n.d.), pp. 64–71, which I elaborate upon in Pazmiño, *Principles and Practices of Christian Education: An Evangelical Perspective* (Grand Rapids: Baker, 1992), pp. 125–29.

10. These areas are elaborated upon in Pazmiño, *Foundational Issues in Christian Education,* 2d ed. (Grand Rapids: Baker, 1997), pp. 33–36.

11. Roy B. Zuck, *Teaching as Jesus Taught* (Grand Rapids: Baker, 1995).

THE TEACHING-LEARNING PROCESS

12

Ted Ward

The principles of teaching and learning are essentially the same regardless of the educational setting. Some readers may be expecting this chapter to deal with only one specific teaching-learning situation, whether home-schooling, Sunday school, youth leadership, the Christian school, or even Christian higher education. But to better serve the variety of settings in which Christian educators work, this chapter deals with principles more than methods, and it is not limited to one particular setting or form of Christian education.

The principles of teaching and learning are not unique because the setting is Christian. Good education is good education regardless of its locale. Effective teaching is effective teaching no matter where it takes place. Learning is learning. It is important to respect the way the Creator established human beings and the principles of human society.

In this chapter I intend to provide information about the relationship between teaching and learning and also to offer examples and practical suggestions about how to do it. It is my hope that this content will provide the reader with an encouraging reflection on how teaching can be carried out in such a way as to lead to effective and valuable learning.

TOWARD A BETTER UNDERSTANDING OF TEACHING AND LEARNING

Teaching and learning go hand in hand. Without the one, the other doesn't happen. This claim is commonly heard, but it provides a good starting place to build an understanding of teaching and learning. But a well-prepared educator also needs something else: an understanding of how teaching and learning relate to each other. How does the process of teaching interact with the process of learning?

The Christian who has accepted responsibility for educating others should bring more to the task than amateurism. Knowing something about educational processes will assist in the effective achievement of competency in this ministry. For a Christian, there is no excuse for leaving to chance and guesswork matters that are basic to human development and spiritual maturation. These matters are well-described in journals and books. The vast army of researchers working on matters of teaching and learning should not be ignored.

In the effort to clarify, we must be careful not to jump too quickly from the concept of teaching to the role of teacher or from the concept of learning to the role of learner. *Teaching* is a process; *teacher* is a social role. *Learning* is a process; *learner* is a social role. In most of the educational applications of these four terms, it is assumed that they refer to human and usually individual processes and roles. This assumption, especially in a media-centered society, leads to inadequate generalizations that hinder the development of the professional educator.

The Process of Learning

Do we really know what learning is and what makes it happen? Research studies of the human brain have increased over the past fifty years. The functions of brain cells, neurons, and synapses and how they support learning are widely discussed. The human brain, perhaps the artifact in nature that argues most persuasively for an intelligent Creator, is yielding little by little to the inquiries of neurologists, psychologists, psychiatrists, therapists, surgeons, and educators. Monitoring these various disciplines and studying their journals reveal that each is looking at a part of a much larger and more mysterious whole. One is reminded of the Indian legend of the five blind men describing an elephant. One of the least understood aspects of the human brain is how we learn.

Perhaps the most apparent gap in the understanding of learning is the role of social experience. Learning is clearly more than a cause-and-effect process in the mechanisms of the brain. Learning is a natural phenomenon, capable of being increased or decreased, brought intentionally to the center of purposeful activity, or allowed to recede into a default mode. But learning cannot be turned off and on by choice any more than breathing or the beating of one's heart. The competent educator needs to understand learning but cannot expect to be a specialist in the physiological or psychological details.

Learning involves a series of interrelated complex processes. While these processes can be listed in sequence, any such attempt is certain to be incomplete and to some extent misleading. The simple list that follows illustrates the immensity of the task of learning and suggests some of the ways that the human mind is engaged in its functions. Note that far more than remembering information is at stake in these processes.

> *Perceiving.* Turning sound and sight into meanings and feelings. Connecting the meanings and feelings with previous experiences and feelings.
>
> *Remembering.* Attaching the newly perceived meanings and feelings with the collected "files" of previous learning. Attaching the recall index of symbols and cues that will allow the new experience to be accessed appropriately in the future.
>
> *Applying.* The ability to use new information, whether in concrete reality or by imagining or hypothesizing. Projecting ways to use meanings and feelings. Applying ideas and information in physical reality or in conjectural anticipations of uses and applications.
>
> *Valuing.* Assessing the worth of meanings and feelings; discerning their merit in terms of previous habits of thought and decisions about what is good. Altering (strengthening or otherwise changing) one's values and convictions as a consequence of the worth and merit of the meanings and feelings.

The Process of Teaching

Contrasted with the complexity of the mental processes associated with learning, the apparent simplicity of the social process of teaching seems welcome. However, teaching is not one process but many. It is more than a skill; it is an art. Many teach well even if they have no technical knowledge of the process. By contrast, many who have read widely in the scientific literature on the teaching process have difficulty putting their knowledge into the actions of effective teaching.

Teaching requires that a person not only knows but feels. Any teaching, even teaching through mediated means such as television or computer programs, involves a human relationship of some sort. The relationship between teacher and learner is both intellectual and emotional. Perhaps it would be better to say that teaching is more dependent on human relationships within the learning context than upon the intellectual or informational components of the knowledge being taught.

The art of teaching is reflected in a competent teacher's excellence in balancing the complementary, though often conflicting, attributes of the teaching task. The teacher as artist is constantly working out the right combination of exhorting and complimenting, warning, reassuring, and supporting. The teacher must avoid the desire to control or to remake another person in his or her own image. Integrity demands that an artist-teacher should take very seriously the responsibilities of the career. Any marks of insincerity are displaced by a more thoughtful style marked by realistic judgment calls and underlined by warmth and gentle humor. This sort of sincerity can become warmly appreciated, even eagerly anticipated. Ultimately, it will come to reside in the learner's own capabilities for self-direction.

The Social Role of the Learner

In many ways, the social role of the learner is a continuous role for almost everyone. The learner role is a part of the personal development process. One can resist the role, deny the worth of the role, and strive to get oneself out of the role whenever possible. However, one consequence of being alive is interaction with the ideas and results of experience. Experience leads to learning, and in the process it puts the person in a variety of positions as a learner. Thus, the role is persistent and inescapable.

Learning can be a solitary experience or an intensely community-oriented experience. Professional opinion and educational research in recent years increasingly recognize the value of interactive learning and thus are biased toward the valuing and encouraging of communities centered on shared learning experiences.

The Social Role of the Teacher

If the emphasis on the social nature of learning is growing, what then is the importance of the teacher? Clarifying some of the casual thinking about teaching and learning is necessary for effective educational understanding and planning. To approach this matter logically and critically, consider the following questions. They may serve to deepen the reader's understanding of teaching and learning and how the two processes relate.

Is the teacher's superior knowledge of what is being taught the key to competency? No one should minimize the importance of a teacher's cognitive knowledge and understanding. But equally important are the affective matters of warmth, empathy, encouragement, support, stimulus, and judgment.

Does the teacher create the learning? The teacher's "bag of tricks" is not magical. The teacher brings a capability of being pleasant and encouraging. The teacher organizes the learning materials so that the learner can more easily comprehend. Not every teacher has conscientiously developed these skills nor does every teacher recognize their value. The teacher can bring a partnership to the learner so that interaction and reflection can occur. This mutual trust relationship is the basis of the teacher's value to the learner. The teacher does not create learning; learning must occur within the learner. It must be built of

experience, and it must be within the learner's comprehension.

Does the learner's capacity to learn limit or determine the teacher's capacity to teach? Surely the capacity of the learner is important. A well-grounded, knowledgeable learner will make any teacher look better. But the learner's capacity to learn is always an unknown factor. Therefore, the teacher should approach each situation with an open mind. If the teacher assumes that the learner is not competent, perhaps the teacher has heard stories about this person from previous teachers. Thus, the learner will not be expected to do well, which often translates into not being encouraged to do well. Now and then a really effective and skilled teacher can get through to a person who is not in the habit of learning well, and the teacher gains the reputation of being a miracle worker.

CLARITY REGARDING THE TEACHING-LEARNING PROCESS

For far too long teaching has been viewed as a science that can be isolated from its context and dissected into working elements. What people fail to remember is that teaching is also an art. It is a dynamic process that involves living, breathing subjects. Perhaps the following reminders will help to clarify the complex nature of the teaching-learning process.

Teaching is important. Teaching is considered effective if it leads to effective learning. Because of the erratic nature of school learning, many students have developed a dependency on the teacher and will learn very little of the curriculum without a teacher.

Teaching leads to learning. If teaching is competently done, it will lead to learning more often than not. Note that teaching is far more than telling.

Teaching is necessary for learning. However, teaching does not always require a teacher. The tendency to personalize teaching into the person of the teacher creates misunderstanding. Much of what a person learns in life is learned from the experience itself, perhaps assisted by some reading or reflective thought. Teachers are important, but life itself does a rather good job of teaching.

Teachers keep the excitement alive. The human side of the teaching-learning process is well represented in the teacher who can breathe life into even the dullest learning task. This is the point of challenge to media: Can computers and entertainment-style visualizations effectively substitute for the spontaneity and human touch of a teacher?

Teachers support, encourage, shape, and guide. Many things in life are learned without a teacher. Teaching may occur because of a teacher, despite a teacher, or regardless of whether or not there is a teacher. Teaching does not always depend on what a teacher does or says. In any given situation, the teacher may or may not be the cause of the learning. Teachers encourage, guide, and correct. At their best, teachers provide role models and skill examples. Teachers teach information, skills, habits, and values. They usually teach far more than they realize. They generally are teaching an intended curriculum plus an unintended curriculum.

THE INTENDED CURRICULUM

What do you teach? The best answer is "I teach children (or adults, or teenagers)." But that probably will not satisfy the questioner, who is really asking, "What is the content or the name of the course or program that you teach?" It is generally understood that you cannot teach everything. Some things must get more attention than others. One of the major reasons that a curriculum must be planned is that the choices of instructional methodology and emphasis are important.

The other major value of a well-planned curriculum is the matter of sequence. Learning is made easier if the teaching strategy adds ideas upon ideas and principles upon principles in logical order. The organization of knowledge and skills into concepts that contribute most to long-term development depends largely on the way that learning experiences are put into step-by-step increments. This is referred to as the scope and sequence of the content, and its importance must never be underestimated in the teaching-learning process.

THE UNINTENDED CURRICULUM

What do you teach? Try this reply: "I teach all sorts of things. Some things I have been assigned to teach, but other things just come along in the

bargain." No teacher ever stays exclusively within the intended curriculum. Lots of other things are slipped in, and often the teacher is unaware of the entirety of these extras or of the judgments that these choices represent. The way a teacher dresses, the moments of humor, the thoroughness of attention to some topics and the skimpy treatment of other matters—all of these tell the learners something about what is important and what is not important.

One of the clearest illustrations of the unintended curriculum is the way certain characters are developed thoroughly and others are barely mentioned. Abraham, Jacob, Moses, David, and Solomon are important. We teach about them explicitly. Ask any first-grade child who has grown up going to church for several years, and he or she can recite the stories verbatim to you. But although there is a clear biblical basis for giving attention to Barak, Jephthah, Jabez, and Rahab, we simply choose not to do so. Thus, our unintended curriculum tells our learners that these people are less important.

THE LEARNING COMMUNITY

At their best, learning environments provide situations in which learning can occur in ideal conditions. Although the folklore and traditions about schools and schooling are strong, the emerging evidence of the past thirty to fifty years strongly supports the following qualities and conditions. Learning occurs most effectively when:

- Learners are encouraged rather than coerced.
- Natural motivations of curiosity and exploration are recognized.
- A community of peers provides opportunities for sharing insights and questions.
- A teacher carefully extends and expands the learners' interpretations.
- The spirit of cooperation toward discovery and exploration is stronger than the motivation to compete and surpass others.
- Teaching one another is motivated by a spiritual unity toward eternal values.

Even in Sunday school, with its ill-advised tendency to mimic "schooling," the typical learning situation is called a "class," and the "classroom" is presumed to be where the important learning occurs. If only Christian education were to build its teaching-learning models around biblical examples from the ministry of Jesus Christ and biblical teachings about the church as a community, effective learning would be much more likely to result.

WHERE DOES THE TEACHING-LEARNING EXPERIENCE OCCUR?

How teaching and learning are understood has changed substantially since medieval times. Then it was typical for the few who were educated to be taught in tutorial and one-on-one situations. We are now experiencing a greater respect for peer relationships than for hierarchies and for equality rather than social systems based upon privilege and status.

The past two hundred years have brought about another dramatic transformation, especially with regard to where teaching and learning occur. Before education became widely available, most of the world relied on basic institutions as the central sources for education. Thus, home and church were particularly important. Whatever was learned in a systematic and formal way was the responsibility of these two institutions.

From these traditionally structured educational efforts—limited to reading, writing, religious catechism, and perhaps music and art, especially among the wealthy—grew the institutional forms that by the end of the twentieth century had come to dominate educational thought and practice. As we move into the twenty-first century, schools and schooling dominate our understanding of education.

The transformation from unstructured forms of learning to highly formalized institutions arose from the reliance on "factories" of teaching and learning in the style of the Industrial Revolution. This mechanical perspective has realigned the language of teaching and learning. The word *education* as commonly used today reflects this mechanical perspective. *Education* is almost always interchangeable with *school* or some other institutional delivery of teaching. In order to use the term more precisely, it helps to differentiate three major modes of education, as understood at the beginning of the twenty-first century:

Formal Education. This term identifies the many different forms of organized, planned, budgeted, staffed, and deliberate teaching and learning.

Informal Education. Perhaps even more common than formal education is the wide range of situations and relationships that result in important socialization. Learning one's first language is not the result of deliberate teaching; more likely, it is a natural process of learning from surroundings, people, and experiences. Walking, running, singing, understanding and using humor, and the multitude of commonplace things that we are not born with but that are ready to be used before we officially "go to school" are what informal education is about.

Nonformal Education. Every society provides a wide range of deliberate educational services, often free or at minimal cost, in order that the functional knowledge needed for contemporary life is more readily accessible. Swimming, automobile driving, job skills, outdoor and nature education, recreational sports, and religious education identify just a few of the specific educational needs that are met through nonformal education. Generally, nonformal education resembles formal education because it is deliberate, structured, planned, and staffed. But it is rarely linked to the credentialing system of credits, diplomas, and degrees represented in formal education.

CHARACTERISTICS OF THE PROFESSIONAL EDUCATOR

As always, integrity, truthfulness, and reliability are basic to professionalism. It was said of Jesus that he taught "as one who had authority" (Mark 1:22). Authority of this sort is evident in the educator's clear command of the material. Nothing can substitute for thorough preparation, but the educator should not emphasize personal knowledge and brilliant insight. The example provided by Jesus was that of a mature person whose self-confidence was evident. His claims to greatness depended on the credit he gave to the One who had sent him and whom he represented. The lesson for professional educators is clear. We can teach with authority to the extent that we give proper credit to valid sources and to those who have prepared us and sent us into the fulfillment of our responsibilities. We gain nothing from emphasizing our personal importance.

A teacher should possess an expanding knowledge of the material being taught. In today's world, firsthand experience with the content you are teaching is vital. A truly competent teacher needs to seek out opportunities to apply knowledge and to develop the skills that go along with the information communicated. Note that knowledge is not limited to the facts and figures that form the information base. The sort of knowledge that distinguishes a competent educator always shows a moral, ethical, and practical side.

An effective teacher has a broad acquaintance with a variety of related knowledge and experience. Any competent teacher, whether volunteer or salaried, certified or experientially qualified, needs the habits of seeking out learning experiences, reading, discussing, watching, listening, and becoming more actively acquainted with the real-world contacts that can keep him or her stretching and growing. This necessity for new learning should not only extend and deepen the knowledge and skills that are central to teaching assignments, but it should increase the teacher's range and variety of general information and skills.

Alert and creative teachers read to gain understanding of the specific information underlying current topics and to broaden and deepen their own academic frontiers. There are only a limited number of hours in the day, so deliberate decision making and setting conservative boundaries are important. But personal broadening and deepening is an educational task second only to directly feeding the knowledge base for one's primary teaching assignment. Many of the most competent teachers pursue three tracks of reading and discussion: (1) their personal frontiers of spiritual and social development, (2) the latest in the knowledge base related to teaching the assigned fields, and (3) the deliberate exploration of disciplines chosen because they are not already part of one's knowledge base. Through this combination, the teacher's world continues to grow and, especially because of the third track, will tend to develop into larger networks of connected knowledge.

Good teachers provide prompt feedback to learners. When any project or assignment has been put on the schedule, pay close attention to the expectations that the learners will have. Has the teacher made the assignment clear? Have the learners been reminded and reassured? Has the teacher set aside the time needed to promptly assess the paper or project after it is due? This habit endears a teacher to the learners. Nothing frustrates and disappoints them more than putting the effort into producing something valuable only to discover that their teacher is not ready to pay attention to it.

PROFESSIONAL COMPETENCIES OF AN EFFECTIVE TEACHER

The teacher must make time for social and professional interaction with students. Teachers do not gain prestige or create a reputation for fairness by remaining aloof and cold. The teacher should be considered as a member of the learner group. Though the teacher has special responsibilities and must behave as a responsible leader and example, relating effectively with each student brings a sense of unity and warmth to the learners. The teacher can be intentional about learning from the students just as students are expected to be intentional about learning from the teacher.

The teacher must seek out, learn about, and try out alternative approaches to teaching for various purposes and different bodies of content. Creativity as a teacher depends largely upon a steady and sure search for better ways to encourage and nurture learning. Predictable repetition is a sure sign of a teacher's incompetency. In today's world, and especially in the consciousness of younger learners, things are changing too fast to allow teachers to stand still. Freshness and creativity go a long way toward keeping learners interested. For example, a competent teacher can use role-playing, trying to dramatize events or relationships that need to be illustrated. The competent teacher asks questions that stimulate fresh thinking rather than repetition of facts. "How would you feel if . . . ?" "What could have caused that to happen?" "How does this event (or idea or fact) relate to what happened before?"

The key to course improvement for many competent college teachers is to deliberately trim away at least a fifth of the least-effective procedures and material each year and replace them with new and different teaching materials. Considering the rapidly changing and expanding substance of human knowledge, the teacher who does the same thing with the same material year after year is likely to become outdated and undereducated before age forty. Learners get damaged in this scenario.

A competent teacher will need to devote plenty of time and attention to gathering and using data for evaluating learners' progress. Teachers should be encouraged to commit themselves to a schedule of time-consuming assessment procedures. Even if the institution requires short-answer tests, the assessment menu can be supplemented with at least a few open-ended test items that will stimulate reasoning and effective communication.

Good teachers avoid the tendency to emphasize their superiority to their learners. While the teacher may be larger, older, wiser, and better informed, it is a good idea to avoid making oneself appear to be something special. Gaining the learners' respect and confidence will occur more readily by demonstrating basic humanity, not power. Emphasizing status, accomplishment, and prestige may isolate the teacher, create suspicion, and result in more and more distance from the learners. Good teachers develop a positive relationship with students. They make an effort to learn about and identify with the learners' own goals, purposes, and approaches to learning. Whether the concern is for teaching children, young people, or adults of any age, this suggestion may be the key to competence in handling the teaching-learning process.

DEVELOPING STORYTELLING TECHNIQUES

Within the art of teaching, nothing is more engaging than effective storytelling. Though some people naturally do it better than others, anyone can learn to do it better. Several guidelines are worth considering.

Feel the events of the story. Much of what we read in a Bible story, for example, describes real events concerning real people. While Jesus told some fictitious stories (parables), even in such cases he showed a careful concern for reality. Understanding these principles will help you become a better storyteller:

1. Real people have real feelings (emotions), not just disembodied information systems called brains. Thus, thinking always occurs within some combination of emotional colorations.
2. Various people's reactions and feelings about a certain situation are reasonably similar. Few differences occur simply because of the passage of time. The disciples' reactions to Jesus' declaration that "one of you will betray me" must have produced the same sort of shock, dismay, and suspicion among the disciples then as it would in our times.
3. Learn to find the central purpose in any basic story. Telling Bible stories gives excellent practice and appropriate illustrations of this skill. The entertainment value is secondary to the purpose revealed in the content. Imagine the reality of the story by personalizing it. Adopt the voice and the "lines" of one or more characters in the story. How does it feel to be there?
4. Learn to tell the story simply and clearly. Make it your own experience as you tell it. For example, in the central story of John 4, one apparent conclusion is that the Samaritan woman of Sychar became the first large-scale community evangelist. Discover and draw out the emotions and feelings of the situations described.
5. Learn to interpret a story well. This ability depends on being able to relate faithfully to both information and feelings.

EDUCATIONAL INNOVATION IN THE TWENTY-FIRST CENTURY

At the risk of sounding regressive, we must be aware that the beginning of the twenty-first century is based upon the experiences and innovations of the dramatically innovative twentieth century. Consider the following realities of our time that were unthinkable a hundred years ago.

There has been a substantial expansion of educational opportunity to all. Almost everyone in this country—and in most of the world—has the opportunity for formal education. How long a person stays in school has more than doubled since World War II. Dealing with racial and gender bias as well as changed policies of access to higher education have substantially widened the doors.

Expanded opportunities for higher education resulted from the G.I. Bill after World War II. Thus began the most significant change in higher education in our time: expanded access. No longer is there prejudice against older students. Curricular diversity, open enrollment, and part-time enrollment status have increased access.

New forms of teaching situations and experiences resulted from a combination of factors leading up to and following midcentury. As a result of the increase in educational research, the importance of applied learning within the academic curriculum has been generally accepted. Professional fields, especially through their accrediting associations, have brought pressure to bear on institutions that overbalance their degree programs with theoretical emphasis. The expansion of knowledge has demanded a more judicious and thoughtful curricular planning process. Field experience, internships, and in-service continuing education have become more widely recognized as valid concerns of the institution.

The explosion of knowledge and its long-term implications for the sustaining value of higher education have stimulated the demand for postbaccalaureate degrees and continuing education. The twenty-first century promises to bring strong demand for formal education, although not just for the ordinary forms of school and college. By the end of the century, most of the institutions that are locked into nineteenth and twentieth century practices will be gone, replaced by new models of instructional delivery and new standards of effectiveness in learning.

The higher expectations of more experienced students have forced institutions to give more attention to the quality of instruction and to the relevance of curricular content. Already the corner is being turned. Educators are taking a fresh look at ways to intensify the relationship between things theoretical and things practical. Teaching and learning will continue to move closer together in the years ahead.

THE HOLY SPIRIT IN THE EDUCATIONAL PROCESS   13

Gary Newton

THE UNSEEN CATALYST

When most people sink their teeth into a soft slice of bread, they seldom take the time to reflect upon the process of how the bread was made. Even if they can identify the sweet aroma of the yeast, they probably will not stop to appreciate the central role of that yeast in the bread-making process.

So it is with the Holy Spirit. Although he is the major catalyst to the educational process of learning and growing towards Christlikeness, the Holy Spirit's role is often overlooked or at least taken for granted. "The often neglected person in the teaching-learning process is actually the most important."[1] If we don't understand and actively seek the Holy Spirit's cooperation in our teaching, our efforts will fall short of raising up godly men and women who display the fruits of Christlikeness. A. W. Tozer makes this point in this timeless statement: "For the gospel is often preached and accepted without power, and the radical shift which the truth demands is never made. . . . The 'creature' is changed but he is not new."[2] Without intentionally cooperating with the Holy Spirit in the teaching-learning process, Christian education will fail to accomplish spiritual results. In order to take advantage of all he has to contribute to the teaching-learning process, we need to understand who he is, his role in the educational process, and how he works through the various aspects of the learning experience.

WHO IS THE HOLY SPIRIT?

In order to understand the significance of the Holy Spirit in the educational process, we must first come to an understanding and appreciation of his distinctive nature as the Third Person of the Trinity. While he possesses all of the attributes of God, he has a distinctive role and purpose. (See additional materials on this important subject in chapter 3.)

Jesus introduces us to the Holy Spirit as a teacher in John 14:26: "But the Helper, the Holy Spirit, whom the Father will send in My name, He will *teach* you all things, and bring to your remembrance all that I said to you" (NASB, emphasis added). The Holy Spirit expanded the ministry that Jesus had while he was on earth. The Spirit has the ability to be at work in many places at the same time because he is not limited by time or space. As a spirit he is able to fill each believer and develop an intimate relationship with his followers in every age. Intimacy with the Holy Spirit draws a person into an intimate relationship with Jesus Christ. The Holy Spirit testifies on behalf of the Son and brings glory to Jesus Christ through his words and actions. The Holy Spirit is synonymous with the Spirit of Christ (John 15:26).

The Holy Spirit took over a major role that Jesus had as teacher while he walked on the earth. Jesus was referred to as "Teacher" over seventy times in the Gospels. "Teaching was a major component of his ministry on earth."[3] The Holy Spirit took over a similar role as teacher in the lives of the disciples after Jesus ascended to the Father. Following Pentecost, when the Holy Spirit was given to the church, his role as teacher was of primary importance to the growth and health of the body of Christ.

Another dimension of the Holy Spirit's role is to bear witness to the truth about Jesus and to lead the disciples into all truth (John 16:13). The truth that Jesus speaks of here is objective, based in himself and his Father. The Holy Spirit testifies to this objective truth. This stands in stark contrast to the prevailing educational philosophy of this age, which defines the Holy Spirit as our inner light that reveals subjective truth within each individual.[4]

Contrary to the popular belief that the Holy Spirit's voice is primarily a subjective expression of a person's inner spirit, the Bible teaches that the Holy Spirit represents an objective manifestation of the truth of God that never contradicts biblical truth. While the Spirit often expresses himself in subjective ways within an individual, his voice can be tested as to its authenticity by comparing it to truth from the Word of God. The Holy Spirit's teaching never contradicts God's objective revelation in Scripture.

In a sense the Holy Spirit serves later generations of disciples by reminding them of the teachings of Jesus as recorded in God's Word. The Holy Spirit plays a vital role in the lives of Christ's followers today by reminding them of the principles and teachings of Scripture as they go through the normal activities of life. In this role, the Counselor not only reminds the believer what to do but also tactfully encourages the believer to do the right thing.

THE ROLE OF THE HOLY SPIRIT IN THE TEACHING-LEARNING PROCESS

The Holy Spirit desires to play a major role in every aspect of the teaching-learning process within Christian education. Unfortunately, his influence may be limited by our unwillingness to draw on his wisdom, truth, and power throughout our teaching experience. Hopefully, by understanding the depth and breadth of his involvement as the Teacher, we will be more apt to actively seek his help in every part the process. The Holy Spirit ministers through at least five elements of the teaching-learning process: the teacher, the learner, the Word, the participants, and the environment.

The Teacher

The first avenue through which the Holy Spirit works is the teacher. God chose to fulfill the Great Commission—to make disciples of Jesus—at least in part through teachers (Matt. 28:19–20). Paul instructs Timothy to pass on his teachings to reliable men and women who in turn would teach others (2 Tim. 2:2). God has chosen to use gifted men and women to be used by the Spirit to teach his truth to others. While in one sense all Christians have a responsibility to teach others what they have learned, some Christians are gifted by the Holy Spirit with special teaching abilities.

The spiritual gift of teaching is included in each of the lists of spiritual gifts in the New Testament (Rom. 12:3–8; 1 Cor. 12:7–31; Eph. 4:7–12; 1 Pet. 4:10–11). In Ephesians 4:12 the gift of teaching is closely related to the role of a pastor/teacher— "for the equipping of the saints for the work of service, to the building up of the body of Christ" (NASB). The Holy Spirit uses gifted pastor/teachers to prepare, equip, or train believers to serve one another within the body of Christ. Spiritually gifted teachers seem to have a holistic ministry in Scripture, teaching God's Word in a way that changes both individual lives and communities. Teaching that is anointed by the Holy Spirit focuses on teaching disciples to obey everything that Jesus taught (Matt. 28:20). "The spiritually gifted teacher helps the Spirit-directed learner to understand and apply the Word of God in the context of the community of other spiritually gifted Christians."[5] Such a teacher must possess not only a thorough knowledge of God's Word but also an ability to communicate it to people in such a way as to equip them to apply the Word within their lives and their relationships. The Holy Spirit uses the spiritually sensitive teacher to orchestrate every aspect of the learning experience toward the

Spirit's goals. As James Plueddemann states, the gift of teaching is the "art of compelling interaction between the various elements within the teaching-learning environment."[6] The Holy Spirit works most effectively through teachers who are gifted by God to oversee all the aspects of the teaching-learning environment in order to stimulate learners to learn and obey truth.

In addition to being gifted to teach, Christian teachers must be walking in the Spirit to be used effectively to accomplish his purposes. Fruitfulness in ministry is directly connected to our intimacy with Christ through the Holy Spirit (John 15:1–17). The Scriptures indicate that Christian teachers will be held to a higher standard of godly living (James 3:1). In order for teachers to be fully utilized by the Holy Spirit, they must be committed to live holy lives. As Paul states in 2 Timothy 2:20–22,

> In a large house there are articles not only of gold and silver, but also of wood and clay; some are for noble purposes and some for ignoble. If a man cleanses himself from the latter, he will be an instrument for noble purposes, made holy, useful to the Master and prepared to do any good work. Flee the evil desires of youth, and pursue righteousness, faith, love and peace, along with those who call on the Lord out of a pure heart.

Although the Holy Spirit often uses many different people and means to teach, those most apt to have a fruitful teaching ministry are those who are supernaturally gifted as teachers and who have an intimate relationship with Jesus.

Spirit-led teachers will cooperate with the Spirit throughout each phase of the planning, preparation, presentation, and follow-up of the teaching experience. They will maintain soft hearts to the prompting of the Holy Spirit and a continual attitude and practice of prayer. If the Holy Spirit is indeed the catalyst to effective teaching, then prayer opens the door to the knowledge, wisdom, and power necessary for an effective teaching ministry.

Yet a teacher should never allow prayer to cover up poor teaching methods. Since all truth is God's truth, we must utilize the wealth of knowledge that is available to us from the field of educational psychology in an effort to teach with excellence.[7] As Paul challenges us from his own statement of purpose in Colossians 1:28, "We proclaim him, admonishing and teaching everyone *with all wisdom*, so that we may present everyone perfect in Christ" (emphasis added). To teach with wisdom not only implies using the best content but also using the wisest methods to ensure that our efforts will partner with the supernatural work of the Holy Spirit in transforming students' lives.

The Learner

The second area of the Holy Spirit's ministry related to the teaching-learning process is that of the learner. No matter how gifted or spiritual a teacher may be, learning and growth towards Christlikeness will not take place unless a learner allows the Holy Spirit to work within his or her heart. Even Jesus' teaching ministry was limited at times by the hardness of his students' hearts (Matt. 13:15, 53–58). At one point he rebuked his own disciples for not having soft hearts to what he was trying to teach them (Mark 8:17–21). A learner must have a heart open to the Holy Spirit in order to learn.

Roy Zuck, in his classic study on the work of the Holy Spirit in teaching, asserts that the Spirit of God actively involves himself in the learner's heart in three ways: conviction, indwelling, and illumination.[8] When a learner's heart is open to God, the Holy Spirit instigates the conviction of sin (John 16:8). Through the indwelling of the Holy Spirit, a believer may learn the things of God, even without a teacher present; as needs arise (1 John 2:27). Although this text may be misinterpreted to insinuate that believers have no need for human teachers because of the Holy Spirit's direct teaching ministry, this is not the intent of the text. As was stated earlier, this text merely affirms the fact that believers who are walking in the Spirit have to be careful not to be seduced into following false teachers that violate the Word of God. Since the purpose of the Holy Spirit is to glorify Jesus Christ, and Jesus Christ is the incarnate Word, the Spirit's voice cannot contradict the Word of God (John 1:1; 16:14–15).

Once indwelt by the Spirit, believers are taught through the illumination of the Holy Spirit. In Ephesians 1:18, Paul prays concerning the believers "that the eyes of your heart may be enlightened" so that they may know the blessings of Christ on an experiential level. This illumination or enlightenment is the supernatural work of the Spirit whereby he enables the learner to perceive what God has revealed through his Word.

In order for learners to know and understand spiritual insights and apply them within their lives, they must have soft hearts toward God. When their hearts are soft before God, they are sensitive to the conviction of the Holy Spirit, causing them to confess sin and turn from sinful practices. The indwelling presence of the Holy Spirit allows them to enjoy the abiding presence of the Counselor to instruct, encourage, comfort, and admonish. As believers diligently study the Word, the Spirit illuminates scriptural principles for them to use in their daily lives. By continually seeking the fullness of the Holy Spirit each day, Christians open themselves up to all the power of God available for them to live holy and godly lives (Eph. 5:18; 2 Pet. 1:3).

The Word of God

The revealed truth of God is the third element in the teaching-learning process. Because of its objective nature, the Word provides the foundation for the work of the Holy Spirit. Second Timothy 3:16–17 states that "all Scripture is inspired by God and profitable for teaching, for reproof, for correction, for training in righteousness; that the man of God may be adequate, equipped for every good work" (NASB). Inspiration relates to this initial act of God sharing his truth in the original writings of Scripture. This objective revelation of God was not "made by an act of human will, but men moved by the Holy Spirit spoke from God" (2 Pet. 1:21 NASB). Since Scripture is directly inspired by God, it must be used as the final test of truth by which believers distinguish truth from error. In using the term "sword of the Spirit" to refer to God's Word, Paul emphasizes the Holy Spirit's aggressive use of the Word in accomplishing God's purposes (Eph. 6:17). Growth takes place as both teacher and learner interact with and obey the Word of God.

Interpersonal Interaction

The fourth element of the teaching-learning process that the Holy Spirit works through is the interaction between the participants in the learning situation. While the Holy Spirit often works within a person's heart individually, he also works within the interpersonal context of small groups and relationships. When the Holy Spirit first came to the church at Pentecost, he baptized the whole group of believers (Acts 2:1–4). After the major influx of about three thousand new believers, the newly established church formed a close learning community centered on the teaching of the apostles (Acts 2:42–47). The close, loving relationships within the church provided a vehicle for the Holy Spirit to move in a way that could never have been accomplished through a series of individual encounters with God. An interesting example of this principle can be found in Paul's prayer in Ephesians 3:16–19:

> I pray that out of his glorious riches he may strengthen you with power through his Spirit in your inner being, so that Christ may dwell in your hearts through faith. And I pray that you, being rooted and established in love, may have power, together with all the saints, to grasp how wide and long and high and deep is the love of Christ, and to know this love that surpasses knowledge— that you may be filled to the measure of all the fullness of God.

Paul's prayer not only focuses on individuals understanding and experiencing the blessing of being Spirit-filled but also on the saints learning together. A certain element of the Spirit's power and love can only be understood within the context of other saints who are seeking the fullness of God together. The healthy interpersonal dynamics of a class or group of Christians is an important factor in the Spirit's teaching ministry.

The nature of the church as the body of Christ suggests that it grows through its ability to learn and work together (Eph. 4:11–16). A major part of the Holy Spirit's teaching ministry relates to the interpersonal relationships within the church and other learning environments.

The Environment

The fifth dimension of the Holy Spirit's work in the teaching-learning process is the environment. Environmental or contextual factors in Christian education may include such things as seating arrangement, lighting, temperature, visuals, room location or size, colors, distractions, or smells. While some of these elements may seem too common to relate to the supernatural work of the Holy Spirit, we must remember that God has used such physical elements to set the environment for spiritual learning throughout history. Learning experiences such as Moses by the burning bush, Jews in the tabernacle or temple, Jesus and his disciples at the Sea of Galilee, the early disciples in the upper room, Paul and Silas in the jail at Philippi, or Paul and the philosophers in the Areopagus all illustrate the importance of environment as it relates to learning truth. Both the teacher and the learner cooperate with the Holy Spirit by strategically designing the physical and aesthetic aspects of a learning environment to allow the Holy Spirit freedom to accomplish his purposes.

Conclusion

The Holy Spirit works as a catalyst for learning through each of the five elements of the teaching-learning process. Although we may never totally understand the complexity of his role in the teaching-learning process, we must continue to depend on his wisdom and power to teach and learn God's truth. For the teacher, this means in-tentionally relying on the wisdom and power of the Holy Spirit within every step of the process of preparation and teaching. It also means utilizing the most effective teaching methods that have been tested through careful research. Only then— by walking in the Spirit, praying in the Spirit, and seeking his full presence—will both teacher and student effectively partner with the Holy Spirit in bearing fruit for the kingdom of God.

Notes

1. C. Fred Dickason, "The Holy Spirit in Education," in *Christian Education: Foundations for the Future,* ed. Robert E. Clark, Lin Johnson, and Allyn K. Sloat (Chicago: Moody, 1991), p. 121.

2. A. W. Tozer, *The Divine Conquest* (Old Tappan, N.J.: Revell, 1960), p. 34.

3. Roy B. Zuck, *Teaching as Jesus Taught* (Grand Rapids: Baker, 1995), p. 24.

4. Marianne Williamson, *Illuminata: A Return to Prayer* (New York: Riverhead, 1994), pp. 74–75.

5. James Plueddemann, *Education That Is Christian* (Wheaton, Ill.: Victor, 1989), p. 308.

6. Ibid.

7. Arthur Holmes, *All Truth Is God's Truth* (Downers Grove, Ill.: InterVarsity, 1977), p. 130.

8. Roy B. Zuck, *Spiritual Power in Your Teaching* (Chicago: Moody, 1972), pp. 45–52.

LEARNING STYLES   14

Marlene LeFever

Learning style can be defined as the way a student sees or perceives things best and then *processes or uses what has been seen.* When a student's preferred learning style is honored in the Christian classroom, that person will often be willing to attempt more for Christ, to become a stronger disciple. Learning styles move the focus away from "How can we maintain discipline long enough to get through this Sunday school class? How can we help these at-risk children?" to "We are so glad to be participating in this life-changing experience, called by God to teach so many at-promise children!"

The traditional view of learning was that all students learn the same way. Educators assumed that all students' minds process information in the same linear pattern. This pattern became the model or teaching template for countless decades of instruction. It had the same basic steps: (1) teachers presented the information while the students listened carefully; (2) students took notes and memorized them; (3) teachers interacted with the students through teacher-directed questions and answers; (4) students then returned the information to the teacher to prove they had learned the content of instruction. But learning is not an easily diagrammed 1–2–3–4 process. God was much more creative when he crafted our minds. Each of us learns best in a pattern that is uniquely ours. When we take into consideration the unique differences in learning preferences, students are able to learn faster, enjoy what they are learning more, and are more likely to put what they have learned into practice.[1]

When we as teachers fail to take these differences into consideration, we waste valuable learning opportunities. As students we may convince ourselves that we are not smart, and once convinced we may live down to those convictions. This detrimental mind-set can be learned early in life. As one public elementary school teacher quipped, "It takes no time at all for a child to understand the difference between being assigned to the Robin Reading Group or the Buzzard Reading Group."

Everyone has a learning style—both very smart people and people who struggle with any kind of learning. When students are taught in styles that match their individual learning styles, they will be much more likely to reach their full potentials.

LEARNING STYLES: A GROWING BODY OF RESEARCH

Picture a dandelion in seed. Carefully pick it and blow hard so that seeds fly off in the wind every which way. On even a moderately windy day, it would be impossible to follow each of those seeds. The same is true of information about learning styles. Many researchers are following different aspects of how people learn. Each confirmed new body of information makes Christian educators' jobs more difficult and at the same time more effective. We have a mass of new information. Volunteers may feel like the little girl who came home from Sunday school and stamped her foot, announcing to her mother, "I'm never going back there again." Her mother was not the least bit amused. "Why not?" she wanted to know. "Well," said the child, "I already know better than I behave." Yes, as teachers, we already know better than we behave, yet the more we learn, the more responsibility we have to put what we have learned into practice.

Here we will explore two aspects of learning styles.[2] First, we will look at the Natural Cycle of Learning, which gives us a pattern to follow as we teach. Second, we will look at the modalities or senses that we use most in learning. Knowledge of modalities can help us pick methods that appeal to everyone in a class, using them appropriately and effectively throughout the Natural Cycle of Learning.[3]

A NATURAL LEARNING PROCESS

It makes sense to most teachers that people learn in very different ways. "But how," the volunteer teacher asks, "can I possibly teach all these different students in the same classroom?" The answer is not as difficult as one might think. Learning follows a natural progression or cycle. When the teacher follows that cycle, he or she will find that every learner will have an opportunity to shine. The learner's preferred learning style will allow that student to participate and even take a leadership role in that part of the lesson. When the student knows that the way he or she learns will be honored at some point in the lesson, he or she is freed to listen and learn in areas that are not a preference.

Learning-style expert Bernice McCarthy has given names to students who enjoy one of these steps more than others and learn best when that step is included in every lesson.[4] She asserts that every student's learning style is defined by his or her favorite place on the cycle. In that place the student can say, "Here I am smartest. Here I can contribute best."

The Four Steps in the Natural Learning Process

Step 1: *Collaborative Learners* are learners who begin with what they already know or feel or need, easily sharing from their past experiences. They make connections with their lives outside of the classroom and bring those connections into class for everyone to discuss and examine. Quite simply, the students who contribute most to this first step of the learning process are adept at providing the context in which new learning takes place. They help the whole class understand why what is about to be studied is important. They answer the question, "Why study this?"

Step 2: Step 1 has prepared the whole class for learning something new. Now a second group of students, *Analytic Learners,* takes leadership for the next step. This is the group that enjoys answering questions such as "What new things do we need to know?" or "What does the Bible say about this issue?" Analytic learners need to learn something new in every lesson or see a new perspective on what they already know. Every student participates in every part of the natural learning cycle, but there will be one or two parts that each will enjoy most. A word of caution: It is here at the end of step 2 that many volunteer teachers stop. They have captured the interest of the class, and they have led that class into Bible study. Surely that's the end of their responsibilities. Their students, they feel, have learned. Wrong! They are only halfway through the learning cycle. If they stop here, students will be unlikely to put what they have learned into practice. Also, almost half their students will not feel a part of the class because they have not had an opportunity to use their minds in the ways that work best for them. In Western culture, 30 percent of our students prefer step 2 of the learning cycle. The other 70 percent are pretty equally divided among the other three steps.

Step 3: Step 3 is the safe laboratory where *Common Sense Learners* build on what has gone before. They know why the subject they are studying is important. They know what the Bible has to say about it. Now they want to know if what they learned makes sense today. Is it applicable? In the safety of the classroom setting, they want to practice finding answers to the hands-on, practical question, "How does this work?"

Step 4: A fourth group of students, the *Dynamic Learners,* will lead the whole class in finding creative ways of using what they have learned in the classroom. This final step moves students out of the safety of the classroom and into their Monday-through-Saturday lives.

Figure 14.1
Natural Learning Cycle

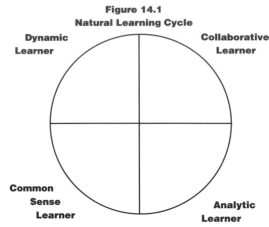

No student will fit perfectly into any one of the four quadrants (see figure 14.1). Our God was much too creative to limit his creation to just four kinds of learners. Each mind pattern will be slightly different, but for most of our students there will be one or two of the steps in the Natural Learning Cycle where they feel most at home and where they can contribute most to the class. Eliminate a step, devalue a student!

About this process McCarthy says, "It is natural to learn this way. In the process of my coming to understand the Natural Learning Cycle, I kept feeling I had always known it. I found myself recognizing how I had used it intuitively in much of my teaching. For the work of the researchers who helped me bring this cycle to my consciousness, I am grateful because now I can name it, now I can own it."[5]

A Predictive Evaluation

It would be very helpful for the student who is interested in further details on a learning style preference inventory to consider the Learning Type Measure (see figure 14.2).[6] Understanding your own style of learning will be a tremendous help to you in your ability to appreciate the variety of students you will have in your classroom.

Figure 14.2
What's My Learning Style?

The following learning style indicator will help you ascertain your own preferred style of learning.[7]

Directions: After reading each sentence, indicate if that statement is:

4 = Always like me   3 = Sometimes like me
2 = Rarely like me   1 = Not at all like me

After completing the statements, decide which predicts most closely the way you learn by adding the numbers in each of the four sections. The quadrant that has the largest numeric value is the one where you are most at home on the Natural Cycle of Learning. This prediction may confirm what you already know about how you learn best. Also pay attention to the parts of the cycle that are least like you. You'll want to pay extra attention to how you structure learning sessions to make certain that you are not overemphasizing the parts you prefer and underemphasizing those where you are not as comfortable.

Collaborative Learners

____ I do my best work when I'm with other people.

____ I like a colorful working environment.

____ I like to give essay-like answers to questions, rather than specific fill-in-the-blank answers.

____ I see myself as a friend to my students.

____ The worst thing that could happen in my class is that students wouldn't get along well together.

____ People describe me as a really nice person.

____ Part of my self-identity is wrapped up in the number of friends I have and the strength of those friendships.

____ Three words that describe me are *friendly, sharer, hugger*.

____ Total

Analytic Learners

____ I do my best work alone, gathering information I need from books or other teachers.

____ I like to work at a desk or table.

____ I like to solve problems by finding the right answers.

____ I see myself as an information giver to my students.

____ The worst thing that could happen in my class is that students wouldn't learn the basics of their faith.

____ People describe me as a really smart person.

____ Part of my self-identity is wrapped up in how smart others think I am.

____ Three words that describe me are *rational, analytic, smart.*

____ Total

Common Sense Learners

____ I do my best work alone, putting together information so it will work.

____ I like to work with my hands, as well as my mind.

____ I like to solve problems by checking out my own ideas.

____ I see myself as a trainer, helping my students do what needs to be done.

____ The worst thing that could happen in my class is that students wouldn't learn to live their faith in practical ways.

____ People describe me as a hard worker, a results-oriented person.

____ Part of my self-identity is wrapped up in how well what I do works.

____ Three words that describe me are *active, realistic, practical.*

____ Total

Dynamic Learners

____ I do my best work brainstorming new ideas and trying things not many people would dare to try.

____ I like playing with new ideas, making intuitive guesses on what works.

____ I like to solve problems by making guesses or following hunches.

____ I see myself as a facilitator for my students.

____ The worst thing that could happen in my class is that students wouldn't take what they have learned and make this world a better place.

____ People describe me as a highly creative person.

____ Part of my self-identity is wrapped up in how many new ideas I have.

____ Three words that describe me are *curious, leader, imaginative.*

____ Total

Based on these predictive lists, I suspect:

My strongest place on the Natural Learning Style Cycle is _____ . (This place may be your

"home base," the place where you are most comfortable teaching.)[8]

The students I am most likely to miss (those in the opposite quadrant) are those who are strongest in this section on the Natural Learning Cycle: _____ .

OVERVIEW OF THE NATURAL LEARNING CYCLE

Students who prefer different quadrants of the Natural Learning Cycle have very dissimilar learning characteristics. A study of each can help us meet the needs of all four distinct groups.

The Collaborative Learner: Why Do I Need to Know This?

The Collaborative Learner is at risk in many classrooms for two reasons. First, this learner is very good at looking at the broad picture but is not usually as good at details. For example, if the teacher asked for the names of the twelve disciples in the order in which Jesus chose them, this student would be totally lost. This is not the way his or her mind works. The student may not even value the answer. If, however, the teacher asks, "What is Christian discipleship, and how did you see Jesus' disciples growing in their understanding of discipleship?" this student is right in there talking about possible answers. For him or her, this is an important question.

Collaborative Learners base their in-class contributions on what they have seen outside of class. If they admire the pastor and see him or her as a person who is determined to follow Jesus even when it's difficult, they would be likely to answer the discipleship question by using the pastor as an example. They see things and generalize about them. They learn by listening and sharing ideas.

The second characteristic that puts Collaborative Learners at risk is that they have to talk in order to learn. The longer they discuss ideas, the smarter they often become. When a Sunday school teacher says, "Settle down and be quiet. We're going to study Christian discipleship now," these students may find staying focused on the lesson difficult. If instead the teacher said, "Get together with two other classmates and talk about people you know who are excellent disciples of Jesus today," these students are immediately engaged, often so much so that they bring the rest of the class along with them. These students function through social interaction. It is in the act of verbalizing that they discover what they think.

Collaborative Learners are people-oriented. They focus on facts primarily in terms of people. They are keen observers of human behavior and are able to show real interest and empathy for others. Along with their people skills, Collaborative Learners show great innovation and imagination, especially in areas that involve people contact.

Here is a partial list of characteristics that help define people who have a strong collaborative learning style.[9]

- Talk in broad overviews
- Learn by listening and sharing ideas
- Answer the questions "Why?" and "Why not?"
- Are sociable, friendly, sensitive
- Are empathetic
- Keenly observe human nature
- Enjoy listening and talking
- Work best in a noisy setting
- Dislike listening to long lectures, memorizing, working alone
- Are idea people
- Are in tune with their feelings
- See facts in relationship to people
- Learn by talking
- Like the feeling of "my gang"
- Get smarter the longer they talk
- Enjoy role play, simulation, mime
- Dislike win/lose situations (example: debate)
- Value people above product, friendship above grades
- Love a colorful classroom
- Define themselves in terms of friendship

The Analytic Learner: What Do I Need to Know?

Analytic Learners enjoy the part of the lesson where they learn something new or where they put something they know into a different context. They are the thinkers and watchers of our soci-

ety, the people who are most rational and sequential in their thinking. They like to sit back, listen, watch, and examine all sides of an issue before they venture an answer or conclusion. They start with an idea or an abstraction and allow their minds to play with it until they are certain they have the right answer.

In Western society, these are the students who are labeled "smart." Teachers love them. They love teachers. These are the children who, when the teacher tells them to sit down and open their books, actually sit down and open their books. Traditional classrooms suit them. They are quiet in class as long as they believe the teacher has something to teach them. They follow directions. They work for the A's in life, even in a Sunday school class where grades are not given. In other words, they want to be known as the ones who memorized every verse this quarter. They thrive on teacher affirmation: "I never have any trouble with Daniel. He always wins the Bible quizzes."

Yes, this group is smart, but those students who are stronger at other places in the Natural Learning Cycle are just as smart. Teachers need to make certain that while they are affirming this group, they are also affirming their other students as they move around the Natural Learning Cycle.

Here is a partial list of characteristics that help define people who have a strongly analytic learning style.[10]

- Like information presented logically and sequentially
- Value facts, figures, and the theoretical
- Debate to logically prove the correct stance or answer
- Value smart and often wise people
- Set long-range plans and see their consequences
- Are curious about ideas
- See themselves as intellectual
- Have a high tolerance for theory
- Think in terms of correct and incorrect answers
- Value being right
- Enjoy listening and taking notes
- Like teachers who are information givers
- Prefer a quiet learning situation

- Learn from traditional methodology
- Dislike situations and methods where no one wins
- Define themselves by how smart they are
- Enjoy reading the Bible for concepts and principles
- Are impersonal
- Need competition
- Prefer to work alone

The Common Sense Learner: How Does This Work?

Common Sense Learners are most at home in the third quadrant of the Natural Learning Cycle because in this section ideas are tested to see if and how they work. These students like to think about problems logically, breaking them down into parts and putting them together again to see how they work. They love to make the Analytic Learner's list of facts usable. They value strategic thinking. Action and doing are their strategies for learning. In this quadrant of the Natural Learning Cycle, students move away from knowledge for knowledge's sake to knowledge for Jesus' sake. Common Sense Learners would agree with Jewish educator Abraham J. Heschel, who said, "Thinking without roots will bear flowers but no fruits."[11]

Like their opposite—the Collaborative Learners—Common Sense Learners have two characteristics that put them at risk in the school system and also in our Sunday school and other church programs.

The first is their need to put what they have learned into some sort of usable form. If they can't use it today or tomorrow, they will ignore the information because it won't make sense to them to learn it. Their strength is their practical application of ideas. If what is being presented seems to have no immediate use, they may disregard it completely. Everything must be practical. Many of these students do not do well in school because they completely avoid classes that are preparation for the future. The attitude is, "I don't need it now, so I won't learn it now."

The second characteristic that puts the Common Sense Learner at risk is that he or she needs to move as part of the learning process. God seems to have put into these students' heads a direct connection so that when their bodies aren't moving, their minds are not working at full capacity either.

Many Common Sense Learners are more active than their counterparts with other learning styles. Their hands and bodies move constantly because they use all of themselves in the learning process. These learners strive to make things work, to make them right. They will be the first volunteers to clean up the church yard or get involved in a car wash to make money to buy a missionary a computer. While their bodies are moving and they are doing something that makes sense now, they are learning.

Here is a partial list of characteristics that help define people who have a strong Common Sense learning style. [12]

- Move during the learning process
- Value action, product development, "how-to"
- Are realistic and practical
- Deal with logical consequences
- Are goal-oriented
- See skills as knowledge
- Value teachers as instruction managers
- Prefer to work alone
- Are impersonal
- Do not enjoy lectures
- Value strategic thinking
- Restrict judgment to concrete things
- Grade success by how well projects work
- Resent being given answers
- Excel in problem solving
- Enjoy "how-to" reading
- See Christianity in terms of action
- Read the Bible to get hands-on information
- Dislike sitting quietly in a learning setting
- Teach and learn through demonstration
- Can be mechanically and computer literate

The Dynamic Learner: What Can This Become?

How sad it is when a teacher runs out of time before allowing this highly creative group of students to grapple with the question, What can this become? Dynamic Learners look at everything in terms of the future. "If we learned all this today and we know it works because we've practiced it in class, what good is it if we don't do something with it? Hey, I've got a great idea . . ." This group loves new ideas but has no difficulty moving from one idea to three new ones if the first doesn't work. The fun in learning for them is in flexibility, in trying new things that other people would never dare to try.

Unlike their opposites—the Analytic Learners—this group just plunges right into things without thinking them through. They have very experimental attitudes and accompanying experimental behavior. They would agree with humorist Jonathan Winters's quip, "I couldn't wait for success . . . so I went ahead without it." Dynamic Learners understand this mind-set. They have project after project started, but they often have difficulty finishing something. After all, there are so many other ideas to be tried.

In class, Dynamic Learners may run ahead of the teacher or want to do something totally different from what the teacher has planned. They don't want to do less; they want to do different. They would agree with Mike Yaconelli: "Christianity is not about learning how to live within the lines; Christianity is about the joy of coloring."[13]

Dynamic Learners have a curiosity about new ideas and a tolerance for ambiguity. In addition to their highly creative learning style, Dynamic Learners are often leaders. They have strong personalities and personal enthusiasm. Both characteristics make them easy people to follow. A caution to teachers: If you identify a strong Dynamic Learner, spend extra time being Paul to his or her Timothy. This person will be a leader. Teachers need to do everything possible to channel that leadership toward discipleship under Jesus Christ.

Here is a partial list of characteristics that help define people who have a strong Dynamic learning style.[14]

- Are leaders
- Have experimental attitudes and behaviors
- Cultivate a well-developed sense of humor
- Demand flexibility
- Take a long time to complete an assignment
- Need options
- Like student-directed classrooms
- Are curious and insightful
- Enjoy teachers who facilitate and stimulate creativity
- Are future-directed
- Want to do anything that is different or breaks the mold
- Make decisions based on hunches
- Enjoy people
- Communicate with great skill
- Enjoy dramatics or any art form that allows them to assert individuality
- Are unpredictable and willing to take chances
- Value creativity
- Have strong intuition
- Can see numerous ways of approaching a situation or problem
- Work to make these things different or better

MODALITIES: USING MODALITIES IN THE NATURAL LEARNING CYCLE

We can use the Natural Learning Cycle as our pattern for structuring a lesson that will allow each student an opportunity to do his or her best.[15] At this point we need to ask, "What methods should I use to help my students answer the four cycle questions: *Why study this? What do I need to know? How does it work? What can it become?*"

Our senses or modalities are our main avenues of sensation. Those who learn best by seeing are called visual learners. Visual learners may learn best through reading, but many of our students today are as picture literate as they are word literate. Those who learn best by hearing are called auditory learners. Those who need to move as part of the learning process are called tactile/kinesthetic (T/K) learners. Tactile refers to a sense of touch. Kinesthetic refers to large body movement that would be used in miming or playing kick ball. Seventy percent of all our students have a modality preference. The other 30 percent will stay focused no matter what modality is being used as long as they are interested in the topic. Students with modality preferences are smarter when they are taught with methods and materials that match how they prefer to learn, and they get even smarter when that teaching is backed up by their second preference.[16]

Auditory Learners

Twenty percent of students who have a modality preference are auditory. An auditory learner can remember 75 percent of what he or she hears in a 40- to 50-minute teaching session. Many more girls than boys are auditory learners. This single piece of information contains a clue as to why boys often don't enjoy Bible study groups or Sunday school classes as much as girls. If the teaching is primarily auditory, many boys don't learn from or enjoy what's happening in class, even when the auditory activity is intended to reach their preferred spot on the Natural Learning Cycle.

Researchers wired a playground for sound. They found that all the sounds coming from girls were recognizable words. Only 69 percent of the sounds made by boys were understandable words. The remaining were either one-syllable sounds like *uh* or *mmm* or sound effects like *Varoooom! Yaaaaah! Zoooooom!*[17]

Visual Learners

A visual learner can remember 75 percent of what he or she sees during a 40- to 50-minute class period. Forty percent of our students with a modality preference are visual learners. Some visual children, especially those who are picture literate, are thought less of because their visual aptitude is not valued as much as a verbal aptitude. Our society places a greater premium on verbal meaning, both spoken and written. We need to affirm the picture makers in our classes.

Many of our students are coming to class with unique picturing skills developed over years as they played video games and watched television. We need to use pictures in more creative ways to hold their attention and to capture and use the skills they have developed. Pictures and art are occasions for intelligence. For very young children, we use pictures, videos, and even flannelgraphs to help them see the story. But how do we continue to use pictures as children grow? For many teachers this will require an extra application of creativity.[18]

Tactile/Kinesthetic Learners

Many tactile/kinesthetic learners will have low visual and auditory skills. They have to move in order to learn. They will not be fully successful if taught in any other way. Forty percent of our students with a modality preference are T/K. Many more boys than girls have a strong T/K preference.[19]

Put yourself in the story found in Mark 9:35–37. "Sitting down, Jesus called the Twelve and said, 'If anyone wants to be first, he must be the very last, and the servant of all.' He took a little child and had him stand among them. Taking him in his arms, he said to them, 'Whoever welcomes one of these little children in my name welcomes me; and whoever welcomes me does not welcome me but the one who sent me.'" Jesus is dealing with men who learned as they walked around. Most were more comfortable working with their hands than with their minds. Jesus teaches them using T/K processes. First they all sit, probably on the ground. The ground is great for stretching out. Then Jesus picks up a child. Can't you imagine the disciples each holding the child and passing him around so that he can get his hair tousled? Jesus' lesson was heard.

Volunteers sometimes feel they have lost control when students are moving, but when movement is actually part of the process of learning, discipline will not be a problem. Students need to know the purpose of the activities and the rules (usually also including noise rules) involved.

Conclusion

Using the Natural Cycle of Learning and an educationally sound mix of methods throughout a lesson will not guarantee that every student will come to love Jesus and serve him. Only the individual students, led by the Holy Spirit, can make that decision.

"Teachers are called to view teaching as ministry to and with God as well as to and with others," says Christian educator Robert Pazmiño. "The gift of teaching requires speaking for God and serving the faith community with gifts and the strength that God provides. The ultimate end must always be in view, namely, the glory of God through Jesus Christ."[20] Dallas Willard writes, "We want to 'make the tree good.' We do not aim *just* to control behavior, but to change the inner castle of the soul, that God may be worshiped 'in spirit and in truth' and right behavior cease to be a *performance*."[21]

Learning styles should be viewed as one tool, one gift of understanding that teachers twenty years ago were not given. Learning styles can help volunteers teach students the way God made them, not the way we wish he had made them and not the way we used to think he made them.

A little girl was coloring a picture of Jesus healing a sick man. She colored Jesus' face all green, then his hands and his feet. The teacher said, "Tell me about your picture." The little girl had no trouble. "Well," she said, "green is healthy. Jesus is green because he's healthy, and pretty soon he's going to make that sick man green, too." Romans 15:13 echoes a teacher's prayer for a healthy, green ministry: "Oh! May the God of green hope fill you up with joy, fill you up with peace, so that your believing lives, filled with the life-giving energy of the Holy Spirit, will brim over with hope!" (THE MESSAGE).

NOTES

1. See Marilee Spenger's book *Learning and Memory: The Brain in Action* (Alexandria, Va.: Association for Supervision and Curriculum Development, 1999), an excellent resource for information on how the brain controls learning. "During the first year of life, the brain makes neuronal connections at an enormous rate. Some scientists say that after the first two years, the brain never again learns as much or as quickly.... It takes another 8 to 10 years to complete the wiring" (pp. 4–5).

2. For a concise overview of several bodies of learning style research, see my article on learning styles in the *Evangelical Dictionary of Christian Education*, ed. Michael Anthony (Grand Rapids: Baker, 2001).

3. Howard Gardner's book *Multiple Intelligences: Theory and Practice* (New York: Basic Books, 1993), while not covered in this chapter, is also worth the reader's consideration. His research, falling under the heading of "intelligence" rather than strictly learning styles, demands that teachers rethink classroom processes that facilitate learning, especially among those students who learn in wildly different ways. His theory of multiple intelligences (MI theory) suggests there are at least seven intelligences. They are linguistic, logical-mathematical, spatial, bodily-kinesthetic, musical, interpersonal, and intrapersonal intelligences. According to Gardner's research, "A person's learning styles are the pragmatic manifestations of intelligence operating in natural learning contexts. All students will exhibit all seven intelligences, and many of them may be developed to a level of competency. However, learners will be highly developed in some, modestly developed in others, and underdeveloped in the rest" (T. Armstrong, *Multiple Intelligences in the Classroom* [Alexandria, Va.: Association of Curriculum and Supervision Development, 1994]).

4. Bernice McCarthy, *The 4MAT System—Teaching to Learning Style with Right/Left Mode Techniques* (Barrington, Ill.: Excel, 1987). This essential resource introduces the reader to the 4MAT system. The book contains fifteen units showing 4MAT's applications in K–12 classrooms.

5. Bernice McCarthy, *About Learning* (Barrington, Ill.: Excel, 1996), p. 289.

6. For a more conclusive test, see the Learning Type Measure, developed by Excel, Inc. This excellent measure confirms what students already suspect—their preferred style. However, of even more importance is that the measure allows students to see how much ability they have in steps that are not their preference. For teachers this serves as a caution. Volunteers may weight their teaching toward the areas they personally enjoy, thus devaluing or ignoring opposite styles.

7. Adapted from Marlene LeFever, *Learning Styles—Reaching Everyone God Gave You to Teach* (Colorado Springs: David C. Cook, 1995) p. 29.

8. "Teaching styles should never be treated as a mere corollary to learning style. Teaching/learning styles are distinct, though complementary, and should be studied separately. They bear completely different objectives, goals and criteria. The nature of learning style describes the learner's learning. The nature of teaching style is not to describe the teacher's learning or even primarily the teacher's facilitation of the student's learning; rather, it is to describe the teacher and his or her behavior as a vehicle for teaching" (Grace M. H. Gayle, "A New Paradigm for Heuristic Research in Teaching Styles," *Religious Education* 89 [winter 1994]: 9).

9. LeFever, *Learning Styles,* p. 48.

10. Ibid., p. 56.

11. Quoted by Robert W. Pazmiño, *Foundational Issues in Christian Education* (Grand Rapids: Baker, 1997), p. 15.

12. LeFever, *Learning Styles,* p. 132.

13. Michael Yaconelli, *Dangerous Wonder* (Colorado Springs: NavPress, 1998), p. 124.

14. LeFever, *Learning Styles,* p. 74.

15. Rita Dunn and Kenneth Dunn, *Teaching Elementary Students through Their Individual Learning Styles* (Boston: Allyn and Bacon, 1992); idem., *Teaching Secondary Students through Their Individual Learning Styles* (Boston: Allyn and Bacon, 1993).

16. While we often think of methodology and modality preferences in terms of children, our modality preferences make a difference regardless of age. Michael W. Galbraith and Wayne B. James point out that "since learning styles impact the amount of information processed and retained, knowledge and utilization of an older learner's most effective learning style will enhance learning" ("Assessment of Dominant Perceptual Learning Styles of Older Adults," *Educational Gerontology* 10, no. 6 [1984]: 455).

17. Gary Smalley and John Trent, "Why Can't My Spouse Understand What I Say?" *Focus on the Family Magazine,* November 1988, p. 3.

18. Dynamic Learners/Teachers would enjoy taking on the challenge of brainstorming new ways to capture our students' picture literacy in class. Gather a group of people for this purpose and see what new ideas develop. Albert Einstein was diagnosed early and incorrectly as intellectually challenged. His exceptional gift for visual reasoning and visual perception was missed, even though he had a genius ability for visual-spatial perception, visual reasoning, and visual memory. Teachers today need to pray, "Lord, if you should ever allow me to touch the life of a child who has the potential of an Einstein, help

me to be ready. Help me recognize a visual gift and encourage it by the way I teach."

19. One out of every three women, black and white, attend church at least once a week. Only one of four white men and one of five black men do. Some men told researchers that they skip church because it is irrelevant and unmanly (National Opinion Research Center, Associated with the University of Chicago, reported in *The Christian Ministry* [Nov./Dec. 1990]).

One explanation is that the tactile/kinesthetic preferences of many men are often ignored in both adult church classes and in the actual worship service.

20. Robert Pazmiño, *By What Authority Do We Teach?* (Grand Rapids: Baker, 1994), p. 73.

21. Dallas Willard, *The Divine Conspiracy: Rediscovering Our Hidden Life in God* (San Francisco: Harper, 1998), p. 364.

Shelly Cunningham

WHY BOTHER WITH CREATIVITY?

Lynnette looked again at the passage she was preparing for the fifth- and sixth-grade girls. Across the table her husband, Jim, was preparing his lesson for the newly married group at church. They had begun their preparation time with prayer. Each had studied the biblical text for correct interpretation. They thought about personal application, and the truths of Scripture were taking shape. They became excited about their learning and now were at the point of "serving it up" to the learners. But how? How should they prepare to serve the living bread of God's Word? Should they regurgitate their own insights, add a sprig of parsley, and ask the students to swallow the pureed meal? Or should they arrange a buffet of carefully selected dishes, provide the utensils, and guide their guests to chew and crunch and savor the sights and aroma of hot, fresh spiritual food? The pureed meal takes little effort. The buffet takes time and energy—in a word, creativity.

For Christians, the starting place for thinking about all creative and imaginative endeavors is rooted in Genesis chapter one and a theology of God as Creator and humans as image-bearing cocreators.[1] God is creative. Are teachers made in the image of God? Are learners made in the image of God? Although it is not within the scope of this chapter to present a biblical defense for using creative teaching methods, the underlying assump-

tion is that creativity originates in the character of God and is expressed in his creative work. The teaching-learning process, then, is the engagement of God's truth with the learner's mind, will, and emotions. Creative teaching methods are a means to the end of leading learners, made in the image of a creative God, to know and follow their Creator fully.

WHAT IS THE PURPOSE OF CREATIVE TEACHING METHODS?

Included in the group of warriors who joined David and helped him in battle were "men of Issachar, who understood the times and knew what Israel should do" (1 Chron. 12:32). They were not described as carrying shield or bow but as people with a knowledge of the times and a grounding in truth so that they knew how to act. Creative teaching methods create cultural warriors and equip learners to handle a changing culture, to wrestle with understanding the times, and to discover how to respond as followers of God.

Given today's warp-speed culture, information overload, and strong audiovisual orientation, "the creative arts . . . poetry, music, art, literature, drama . . . are emerging to be significant elements of worship, ministry and communicating the Gospel in our 21st Century culture."[2] In a fast-moving and fast-changing culture, a creative approach to learning and living and tackling new problems may better prepare our children and youth for their future. Encouraging learners to develop their God-given talents and abilities in this context can be "instrumental in helping them learn to function as co-creators with God in bringing into existence cultural innovations which are socially as well as individually beneficial."[3] This requires a perspective that looks to the future with hope and anticipation. It may require using new methods or old methods in an innovative way. For some, anything new or different is not to be trusted. Although no method is to be employed without critical evaluation, neither should new or innovative ideas be suspect simply because they do not fit existing categories. "We may find that as Christians on this ship of life we are concerned about clean decks and flying the right flags when we should be preparing to dock in a whole new world that needs to be written, designed, painted, and danced."[4]

WHO CAN TEACH CREATIVELY?

Creative teachers participate with God as he moves and works in making all things new in the lives of the learners. What does it take to be a teacher who teaches with creativity? "From a Christian perspective, could it be that when a person has done all that he could do—i.e., worked through (the) creative process . . . the Holy Spirit graciously steps in to offer the answer?"[5]

Creativity is often described as a quality of person. It may be said, "Oh, he (or she) is such a creative person!" However, creativity is more a quality of ideas, behaviors, or products and can be developed. In fact, research shows that creativity can be fostered and developed in just about everyone.[6] The creative teacher is not the source of creative ideas. Instead, the creative teacher encourages learners to experiment and facilitates an environment where creative ideas, behaviors, and products may be discovered and experienced.[7]

Creativity also requires relationships. Creative teaching is highly interpersonal and involves being sensitive to the learner. Encouraging creativity in a learner requires that a teacher "nurture the uniqueness that lies within each student. He or she must be attuned to the potentialities as well as probabilities. This involves being ready to get

off the beaten track or break away from the predetermined lesson plan, and to relate . . . as persons."[8]

Teachers who are creative work closely with their learners. They talk with their students and are intentional about establishing positive relationships with them.[9] Creative teachers are open and honest. In the student-teacher relationship, flexibility encourages participation.[10] Listening and laughter is exchanged. A climate of mutual respect and acceptance among students and between students and teachers is facilitated so learners can share and develop in community as well as independently. Exploratory thinking is risked in an atmosphere of warmth and support.[11]

Finally, creativity takes commitment. Creative teaching methods are not by nature spontaneous and undisciplined, although the process may incorporate aspects of these elements. "A creative curriculum is a purposeful curriculum. . . . The power of the stated goal enables the teacher to evaluate the goal as well as to keep it in mind when planning and evaluating activities."[12] Creative teachers are intentional about guiding learners to develop and apply such creative qualities as curiosity, playfulness, and manipulativeness;[13] however, they are also able to separate their identities and personal value from the creative product of their learners.

Teachers often wish they were more creative; however, it is not an all-or-nothing attribute. More than a character quality, it is a commitment to personal growth and to development as a skilled teacher and communicator. "Most teachers who honestly *want* to teach creatively are on their way. . . . Creativity is developed through . . . discipline. . . . Do it! Pick new ideas and try them. Learn to brainstorm in groups (and perhaps just with yourself) to generate new ideas. And don't give up too quickly."[14]

The creative teacher appreciates the hard work and preparation necessary to facilitate a creative learning experience. Much of this preparation takes place outside of formal lesson planning time. According to Marlene LeFever,

It will happen as you expose yourself to all different aspects of life and become aware of how these things may be helpful in teaching. . . . If you really want to be a creative teacher, you can't limit your preparation to

Saturday night. It's life preparation. Every area of yourself will play a part in the building of a good teacher. . . . A good teacher is the person who cares enough to work hard to multiply the natural ability God has given.[15]

What does it take to multiply the natural ability God has given? Exposing teachers through training to creative activities and methods increases their creative teaching competencies and enhances their receptivity to students' creativity.[16] The next section describes in greater detail some of the competencies that may be used to apply creative teaching methods in a learning context.

How Do You Teach Creatively?

It might be expected that somewhere in a chapter on creative teaching methods a list of such methods would be provided.[17] Although there may be some teaching procedures that lend themselves more readily to creating a creative context, no method in and of itself is creative simply by definition. A method becomes creative as it is employed by the teacher in such a way as to elicit creative thinking and activity within the learner.

An atmosphere for creative learning must be established. A creative atmosphere is emotionally safe and nurturing. It is intellectually stimulating as questions are encouraged and new ideas are welcomed. Undeveloped ideas can be safely explored and tested. Alternative perspectives and approaches are presented, invited, and examined.[18] In this environment the teacher becomes a resource provider and a director of divergent learning activities.[19]

Creativity is inviting students to make sense of God's Word and God's world. If methodologies, curriculum, or structure of the learning environment are overly rigid so that data are merely "dumped," students have no opportunity to make sense of it. In a creative atmosphere, students are provided with enough content to face and challenge misconceptions. In the challenge, their biblical foundations are strengthened.[20]

Educational methods that facilitate creative learning and divergent thinking include such strategies as the following:

- Present ambiguities, uncertainties, and incompleteness.
- Heighten anticipation and expectation for what is to come.
- Look at the same thing from a variety of psychological, sociological, cultural, physical, or emotional points of view.
- Ask provocative questions.
- Encourage steps out of the comfort zone of the known and familiar.
- Explore missing elements and new possibilities.
- Use surprises.
- Work to make events and places concrete and visual.
- Experiment and test ideas.
- Encourage hypotheses.
- Transform and rearrange information.[21]

In many of these creative approaches, there is a move from one symbol system to another symbol system.[22] For example, to move from a verbal symbol system (language) to a visual, auditory, or tactile symbol system may involve having learners draw, sing, or dramatize content instead of talking about it. Instead of singing choruses during worship, perhaps participants use pantomime or photographs to express their love for God.

The basic considerations to be met in a creative learning experience are:

1. Provide the initial experience to interest students in inquiring about a problem, concept, situation, or idea. The use of media, role-playing, and demonstrations are generally successful investigative starters. Learning centers with a number of viable options are an excellent beginning.
2. Provide the students with manipulative situations and materials to begin avenues of exploration. Games, media, files, sourcebooks, and discussions are all good starters.
3. Supply information sources for students' questions. Outside sources, field trips, speakers, peers, and the teacher are good supplements to written sources. The community and the world at large are fair game in the information-seeking stage.

4. Provide materials and equipment that will spark and encourage student experimentation and production.
5. Provide time for students to manipulate, discuss, experiment, fail, and succeed.
6. Provide guidance, reassurance, and reinforcement for students' ideas and hypotheses.
7. Reward and encourage acceptable solutions and solution strategies. Use failing experiences as instructional motivators: Question why a solution will not work and ask open-ended questions. A supportive, positive climate will spawn the best results.[23]

These suggestions are for learners of all ages. Divergent thinking is not limited to adults nor is creative and hands-on learning limited to children. Young children have amazing capacities to explore their world creatively. They are capable of analysis at a level appropriate to their age and can be challenged to grasp the integration of related subject areas. They appreciate open-ended and long-term projects and desire to express their ideas through a variety of symbolic media and expressive avenues.[24]

In many people it seems that over the years these capacities become inactive, either through lack of development or through the pressure to conform to using nonexpressive avenues and media. However, older children, adolescents, and adults have the capacity to recultivate the capacity to approach learning and life creatively. When provided with the time, space, materials, and climate to be creative, and when encouraged by a teacher who provides the occasion for creative adventure, individuals who are made in the image of the Creator God can be invited to create with incredible results.[25]

TIPS FOR TEACHING CREATIVELY

As mentioned earlier, teaching creatively acknowledges that learning is interpersonal and intentional. Throughout this process, attention is given both to the accurate communication of biblical truths and to what is happening in the hearts of the learners. If learners are invited to participate in a creative learning activity that requires skills they do not have, they may lack the confidence necessary to explore something new.[26] When introduced to a new method, learners may at first be self-conscious and even uncooperative. It is important for teachers to acknowledge the learners' hesitancy while communicating an attitude of discovery and experimentation and excitement for trying something new. If possible, place the learners in a small group setting to work on a creative project. In this way everyone is learning and practicing creativity together.[27] Drawing on creative methods is often strategic whenever learners are feeling frustrated, bored, anxious, angry, or helpless. Identifying the root problem and beginning to tackle smaller subproblems with creative approaches may lead to the discovery of alternatives not seen earlier.[28]

Although a creative classroom encourages freedom of expression, it is not laissez-faire. Learners are aware of permissible behaviors and the basic parameters of the classroom.[29] In fact, learners are actively engaged in helping to shape the creative classroom.

In the creative classroom, students are allowed to make choices and to be part of age-appropriate decision-making processes. Learners take part in the control of their learning experiences.[30] Inviting learners to choose and design their own projects, individually or in a cooperative group, nurtures a sense of ownership and self-direction.[31] A self-motivating learning environment is established when the learner produces something (for example, an art, music, or writing project) and does something with the created product.[32] In this way, learners can see how creative teaching methods are a means to an end and how they can learn from an analysis and evaluation of the product.

Although the following caution may be obvious, it is critical enough to be stated. When working with creative forms of expression, be careful not to compare one learner's product to another's or one group's product to another group's. If it is a visual product, display everyone's in the room. Do not have rewards or contests for the best product.[33] This is not the intent of creative teaching methods within a learning environment.

A couple of procedural items, including space and time elements, may enhance the implementation of the creative approaches suggested in this section. Physical and structural issues supporting a creative approach to teaching include a well-lit and well-ventilated classroom with an attractive appearance and an ample supply of various craft and project materials available—some designated as ready for use at any time.[34] To create a classroom that encourages creative productivity may require changing the schedule to provide longer sessions. It may require rethinking the way classes are grouped and organized, and it may even require changing rooms so that materials can be left out prior to completion.[35]

Time must be provided for ideas to germinate, and then time must be provided for reflection on the new ideas.[36] Students need time to develop and express their ideas. While some creative ideas may surface spontaneously,[37] other creative projects of value may require longer to complete. Especially important in the creative process is the provision of quiet, reflective time for the learner's contemplation and work. Quiet time is not passive time. The learner is actively engaged in the material when the time is planned and intentional and the silence is guided towards creative thought. After biblical content has been presented and discussed in verbal, visual, and written forms, the teacher might conclude a class with five minutes of quiet time, then five minutes of writing or drawing.[38] For example, after studying the relationship between God and Adam and Eve in the Garden of Eden, students listen to nature sounds while recording a journal entry of Adam's or Eve's thoughts.

HINDRANCES TO USING CREATIVE TEACHING METHODS

Teachers committed to using creative methods in the classroom may face a variety of challenges in implementing these approaches. Challenges may be as general as the sacred/secular dichotomy in which creativity is considered appropriate for the school or the studio but not for the church or the ministry setting.[39] Or challenges may be as individual as doubt about one's creative abilities, resulting in the restriction of God-given gifts, talent, and potential.[40]

Each time a new creative activity is introduced, a measure of risk is assumed and a cost must be calculated. The tendency is to return to that which is known and familiar. "To infuse our teaching min-istries with excitement and perhaps to grow our own share of creativity, we need to be willing to look beyond the 'always done.'"[41] However, looking beyond often involves resistance, whether conscious or subconscious. "Creativity is in the surprise, the exception. Nearly everything in most classrooms mitigates against surprises; it is organized to insure consistency and often conformity."[42]

Some blocks to creative teaching include: conformity, overplanning, cookie-cutter approaches, dependence on the known and familiar and the way it has always been done, overuse of a lesson manual without the freedom to try original ideas, and a ministry setting or church context that discourages coloring outside the lines. Teaching behaviors that discourage creative and critical thinking include treating students as tape recorders and lecturing every class.[43]

Creative inertia may result if teachers become too:

1. Comfortable (Don't bother me.)
2. Complacent (I'll do it later.)
3. Contented (Why should I do it another way?)
4. Conceited (There are no other ways; my way is right.)
5. Customized (I have always done it this way.)
6. Resistant (Change is scary.)[44]

Creative methods themselves may become obstacles to learning if teachers become slaves to the method instead of owning it as the tool it was intended to be.[45] It has been said that your weakest teaching method is the one you use the most. There is a great deal of truth to this statement. You may be gifted and creative, but if your creativity becomes mundane and predictable, it becomes a weakness for future creative teaching.

CONCLUSION

There is no one way of teaching and learning creatively. If the more typical creative approaches of openness, fluidity, and high levels of interaction and engagement are used, these must not be regarded as the only way for children, youth, or adults to learn. Some students dislike open-ended curriculum assignments and may become frustrated and respond in unproductive ways. Other students dislike closed assignments that require little divergent thinking and no creative expression.[46] Then there are the students who do not necessarily dislike creative assignments so much as they dislike the discomfort of trying something different. Exploring creative teaching and teaching for creativity is a journey into the unknown and the untried for both teacher and learner.

These maiden voyages are rarely without adventure. The ship may rise and toss, struggling to navigate high seas, narrowly avoiding shallow bottoms and killer rocks. All on board may feel a bit sick, but if they can weather the first few days, they will find their sea legs. The green expressions will be exchanged for bright eyes, deep gulps of fresh, salt air, and muscles toughened by the demands of life at sea. Sure, there will be miscalculations. Weather is unpredictable. Shipmates will squabble. The ship may run aground. But the adventure is not over, just redirected. "We noticed that we learned as much from failure as from success. In fact, the way one learns from success is predictable and leads to repetition, but the way one learns from failure is always different and surprising, rich with nuances to be mined at a later date."[47] Digging out from the sand, the captain and crew press on, eagerly anticipating breathtaking scenery and unimagined discovery.

Creativity usually comes with a price. Adopting a commitment to engage the learner as holistically as possible with the truths of Scripture will require time, effort, and a willingness to risk and fail. Teachers must be willing to "dare students to dream!"[48] Navigating the creative seas requires that teachers:

- Try something new or different
- Take a stab at it
- Make believe you can do it
- Don't worry
- Hang loose
- Stay cool
- If you can't do something perfectly, it's okay to try anyway[49]

The price is worth it as teachers see learners enthusiastic about God's Word and committed to learning more about God's Son.

Taking a few liberties with a familiar passage in Hebrews, this discussion closes with the following challenge:

Therefore, since we are surrounded by such a great cloud of witnesses created in the image of the Creator God, let us throw off every teaching approach that serves up pureed, regurgitated food and the ruts that so easily strangle new and fresh insights, and let us run with perseverance and courage the creative race marked out for us as people made in the image of a creative God. Let us fix our eyes on Jesus, the author and perfecter of our faith and our creative attempts, and let us partner with the Holy Spirit as we follow Jesus Christ and lead others to follow the one, who for the joy set before him endured the cross, scorning its shame, and sat down at the right hand of the throne of the Creator God (Heb. 12:1–2, adapted).

NOTES

1. Leadership Network, "Interview with Musical Artist Charlie Peacock," *NEXT* 5 (July/August/September 1999): 5.

2. K. Allen, "Blessing the Arts: Engaging the Creative in the 21st Century," *NEXT* 5 (July/August/September 1999): 1.

3. L. D. Murphy, "Christianity, Creativity, and the Preschool Age Child," *Christian Education Journal* (1986): 15.

4. M. D. LeFever, *Creative Teaching Methods* (Elgin, Ill.: Cook, 1985), p. 22.

5. Murphy, "Christianity, Creativity, and the Preschool Age Child," p. 17.

6. M. Bozik, "Teachers as Creative Decision Makers: Implications for Curriculum," *Action in Teacher Education* (1990): 52.

7. J. L. S. Moore, "Strategies for Fostering Creative Thinking," *Music Educators Journal* 76 (May 1990): 39.

8. Murphy, "Christianity, Creativity, and the Preschool Age Child," p. 24.

9. J. S. Renzulli, "A General Theory for the Development of Creative Productivity through the Pursuit of Ideal Acts of Learning," *Gifted Child Quarterly* 36 (fall 1992): 170–82.

10. Murphy, "Christianity, Creativity, and the Preschool Age Child," p. 23.

11. J. F. Feldhusen and D. J. Treffinger, *Teaching Creative Thinking and Problem Solving* (Dubuque, Iowa: Kendall/Hunt, 1977), p. 14.

12. E. S. Marback, *Creative Curriculum* (Provo, Utah: Brigham Young University Press, 1986), p. 3.

13. Murphy, "Christianity, Creativity, and the Preschool Age Child," p. 20.

14. LeFever, *Creative Teaching Methods*, p. 18 (LeFever's emphasis).

15. Ibid., p. 26.

16. G. B. Esquivel, "Teacher Behaviors that Foster Creativity," *Educational Psychology Review* (June 1995): 190–91.

17. Two recommended resources for an introduction to creative methodology are *Creative Teaching Methods* by Marlene LeFever and *Creative Bible Teaching* by Lawrence Richards and Gary Bredfeldt (Chicago: Moody, 1998). Beyond these resources, almost all of the major Christian publishing companies that publish curriculum also offer a wide array of support materials that include a list of teaching methodologies and step-by-step procedures for implementing them in a variety of classroom contexts.

18. Bozik, "Teachers as Creative Decision Makers," p. 2.

19. Feldhusen and Treffinger, *Teaching Creative Thinking,* p. 14.

20. T. Cardellichio and W. Field, "Seven Strategies that Encourage Neural Branching," *Educational Leadership* 54 (March 1997): 34.

21. E. P. Torrance and R. E. Myers, *Creative Learning and Teaching* (New York: Dodd, Mead, 1970).

22. Cardellichio and Field, "Seven Strategies," p. 5.

23. Feldhusen and Treffinger, *Teaching Creative Thinking,* pp. 16–17.

24. C. P. Edwards and K. W. Springate, "The Lion Comes Out of the Stone: Helping Young Children Achieve Their Creative Potential," *Dimensions of Early Childhood* 23 (fall 1995): 26–27.

25. Ibid., pp. 27–28.

26. Torrance and Myers, *Creative Learning and Teaching,* p. 41.

27. B. Huitsing, E. McDaniel, B. A. Riley, and M. Tucker, *Adventures in Creative Teaching* (Wheaton, Ill.: Victor, 1986), p. 6.

28. G. M. Prince, *The Practice of Creativity* (New York: Harper and Row, 1970), p. 171.

29. J. A. Smith, *Setting Conditions for Creative Teaching in the Elementary School* (Boston: Allyn and Bacon, 1966), p. 132.

30. Feldhusen and Treffinger, *Teaching Creative Thinking,* p. 14.

31. S. Kay, "Curriculum and the Creative Process: Contributions in Memory of A. Harry Passow," *Roeper Review* 21 (September 1998): 5–13.

32. Torrance and Myers, *Creative Learning and Teaching,* p. 56.

33. J. Hale and J. Roy, "How Art Activities Can Be Used to Enhance the Education of Young Children," paper presented at the Southern Early Childhood Association Conference, Little Rock, Ark., March 16, 1996, ERIC, ED 394 937.

34. Smith, *Setting Conditions for Creative Teaching,* pp. 125–27.

35. Kay, "Curriculum and the Creative Process," pp. 5–13.

36. Ibid.

37. Feldhusen and Treffinger, *Teaching Creative Thinking,* p. 14.

38. D. J. Sill, "Integrative Thinking, Synthesis, and Creativity in Interdisciplinary Studies," *Journal of Education* 45 (1996): 148.

39. LeFever, *Creative Teaching Methods,* p. 22.

40. Ibid., p. 21.

41. Ibid., p. 14.

42. Kay, "Curriculum and the Creative Process," p. 8.

43. J. R. Downs, "A Mini-Workshop in Critical and Creative Thinking," paper presented at the International Conference on Critical Thinking, Sonoma, Calif., August 1, 1993, ERIC, ED 361 388.

44. A. Grupas, "Creative Problem-Solving," paper presented at the annual meeting of the Missouri Association of Community and Junior Colleges, November 15–17, 1990, ERIC, ED 343 813, p. 12.

45. Smith, *Setting Conditions for Creative Teaching,* p. 102.

46. Murphy, "Christianity, Creativity, and the Preschool Age Child," p. 26.

47. Kay, "Curriculum and the Creative Process," p. 7.

48. J. Flack, "Bringing Out the Best!" *Teaching PreK–8* 26 (May 1996): 58.

49. M. B. Chenfield, "Four Easy Nudges," *Phi Delta Kappa* 73 (Dec 1991): 333.

PART FOUR

Organization, Administration, and Leadership

Organizational Models of Christian Education

16

Mark W. Cannister

Organizing for Effective Ministry

In order for a church to effectively accomplish its mission, people, resources, and programs need to be organized and coordinated. While the magnitude of organization may vary from church to church, even the smallest church still needs some degree of organization in order to be a faithful steward of the resources that God has given it.

The concept of organization is sprinkled throughout Scripture. Moses organized people for the long journey to the Promised Land. Joseph demonstrated exceptional organizational skills in preparing for and then distributing food while governor in Egypt. In planning to rebuild the temple, Nehemiah organized families to distribute the construction workload in a fair and equitable manner. Jesus organized people and sent them out in pairs to proclaim the coming of the Lord. The twelve apostles organized the rest of the disciples to ensure that the widows would be fed without neglecting the ministry of the gospel. The early church organized people for ministry according to their giftedness and qualifications. Paul organized people to carry on the mission of the church by training leaders so that they would be able to continue the training process in others.

Good organization is essentially the coordination of human and material resources for the accomplishment of a given purpose. There are three basic elements common to any organization: human resources, material resources, and the tasks to be accomplished.

People are the church's highest priority. They are the reason why the church exists in the first place. God could have chosen to employ his angels to carry the message of salvation to a lost world, but instead he chose people for the task. People are eternal, whereas material resources are not. In the long run, only people count! Without people there would be no ministry. They bring life to the building and add meaning to the tasks at hand. Some church leaders forget about this priority in the rush to build a building that ends up as a monument to the pastor or some significant leader in the church. It is generally a case of misplaced priorities. Organization is needed to empower and focus the efforts of the people. A church can organize its people into a highly systematic group, but if these people do not accomplish their tasks, the purposes of the church will not be fulfilled. The people of the church must be equipped for and committed to the work of the kingdom.

Material resources are needed in order to facilitate the accomplishment of the tasks. Without a strategic plan, good people may perform a variety of worthwhile tasks that have nothing to do with the purposes of the church. Without some structure, people become Lone Rangers doing their own things without any corporate accountability. In such cases, material resources are wasted and become harder to replenish. Once people lose trust in how their resources are being used, it takes a great deal of time to regain that trust.

Good organization benefits the church in a variety of ways. Even in the smallest church the workload is far too great for one person. The work of the church is not the sole responsibility of the pastor. There must be a body of believers to share responsibilities, and those duties should be distributed wisely.

The church is a body with many talents. All the members of a congregation should use their gifts in proper relation to one another. Nominating committees cannot simply place warm and willing bodies on standing committees or in ministries without intentionally working to match a person's giftedness with an appropriate assignment. As each person develops his or her gifts and applies them to appropriate responsibilities, the whole body moves forward toward accomplishing its purpose (Rom. 12). The proper distribution of responsibilities according to giftedness also minimizes confusion, envy, and arrogance, as everyone knows the proper roles that they are to play in the church (Eph. 4:11–16).

Perhaps the greatest problem of stewardship in the church is the waste of time and resources caused by duplication of effort. This problem occurs more often in large churches when people do not communicate with one another. Simply coordinating all of the office supply orders in a large church, rather than each program ordering its own supplies, can result in significant financial savings. At times duplicity not only can be a waste of time, but it can also become counterproductive. This happens most often when the church overorganizes. Before implementing new organizational structures, church leaders should ask several questions. First, is there a task to be performed? If there isn't a job to be done, a responsibility to be taken on, or a need to be fulfilled, then increased organization may not be the answer to the problem.

If there truly is a need that requires attention, then a second question should be asked: Is it possible that this need could be met through the responsibilities of an existing staff member, committee, or program? All too often the church is quick to develop new positions, new committees, and new programs when existing structures are

more than adequate to meet the need that has arisen. There is no need to create a church sanitation committee when the custodian is capable of emptying the garbage. It is because of this trend toward increased administrative oversight that the position of executive pastor was created in the late 1980s.

If further structures do need to be developed to meet the need, the third question should be asked: How many people will it take to properly do the job? Often the church creates massive committees for a task that could be handled by one or two people. Sometimes the church saddles one person with a task that rightfully requires a full committee. One person may not be enough to plan the church's centennial celebration. On the other hand, it doesn't take a whole committee to ensure the candles on the communion table are replaced regularly.

Adding committees to the existing structure of the church should always be done with caution. Before appointing a permanent committee, the church should consider whether it is dealing with a short-term need or a permanent need. Often an ad hoc committee or a task force can deal with short-term issues. A pastor could become quite skeptical of his or her value to the congregation if the church maintained a permanent pastoral search committee.

The goal of any organization should be to effectively accomplish its purpose with the smallest amount of organizational structure possible. There is no virtue in having more organization than is absolutely necessary, and organization should never become an end in itself. The organization of any aspect of the church should always exist to further one or more of the purposes of the church.

TRADITIONAL MODELS OF ORGANIZATION

If we are to take seriously the interaction of Christian education with all of the purposes of the church, then we must consider some of the problems with the traditional models used for organizing Christian education.

There are basically two ways in which Christian education has been traditionally organized.[1] The *functional model* (figure 16.1) privileges the pro-

Figure 16.1
Functional Organization by Programs

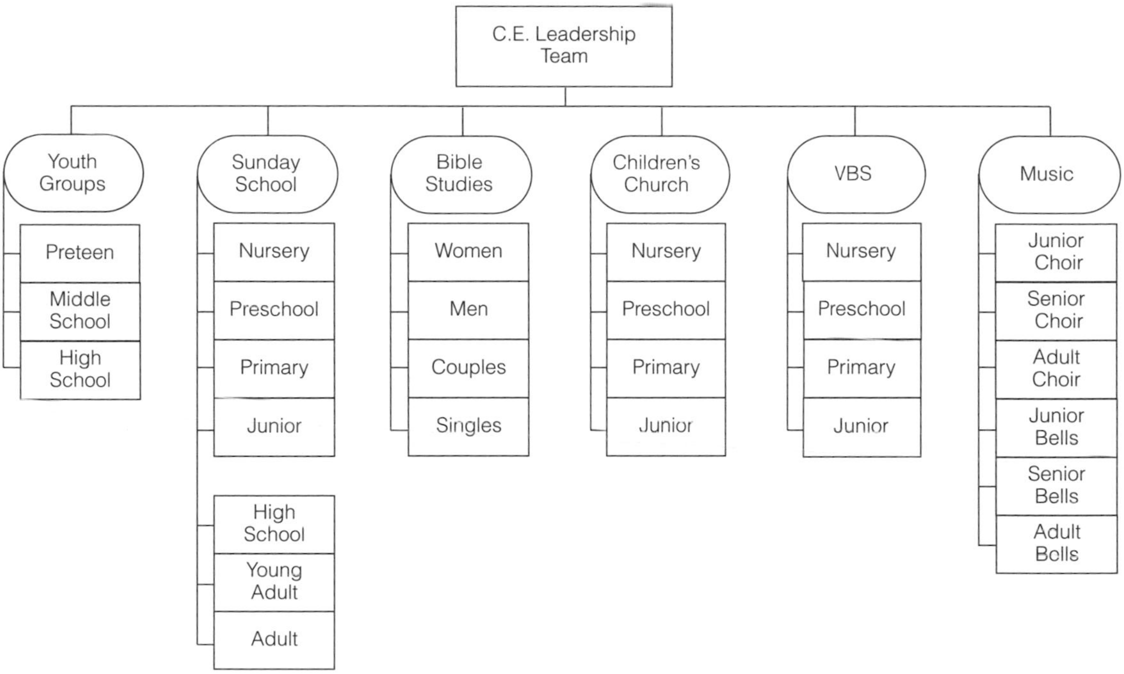

grams of Christian education. In this model the various programs are listed as headers, and each program is divided into age groups underneath. The leadership team of this model is often a committee made up of the various leaders (volunteer, part-time, and/or full-time) of each program. Typically this leadership team focuses on Christian formation, while other leadership teams or committees of the church are concerned with worship, evangelism, service, or fellowship. The work of this leadership team is typically overseen by the pastor, associate pastor, or director of Christian education and is ultimately responsible to a board of elders and/or the congregation, depending upon the particular model of church polity.

There are several issues to consider with this model. The greatest benefit of the functional model is the ability to maintain continuity of the curriculum across age groups. Theoretically, one person could be responsible for the education of a congregation from birth through death, if the leader stayed in the same church and lived long enough. This was the case of my father-in-law, who pastored the same church from the day he graduated from seminary until the day he retired forty-seven years later. The children in the church

at the time of his ordination literally grew up into middle-aged adults by the time he retired.

This type of staying power is rare in contemporary culture and may not be enough to counteract the problems associated with this model. The first problem is that there are built-in conflicts between programs that may have different leadership yet are targeting the same audience. It is not uncommon in this model for the music leader to schedule a youth choir program in conflict with a youth ministry program. The youth leader may plan a program at the same time the Sunday school coordinator or children's church coordinator was hoping to employ some teenagers to assist in the nursery.

Another problem with this type of organization is that of relationship building, especially among youth and children. It is difficult to build strong relationships when different leaders are responsible for each program. Children (and their parents) may be involved with a different leader for each children's program (e.g., Sunday school, children's church, VBS, and music programs). Likewise, teenagers may encounter different leaders in their programs as well (e.g., Sunday school, youth group, and music programs). While a variety of leadership across programs may seem appealing, consistency and continuity across programs is more important for students at these formative ages.

Finally, while continuity of curriculum may be achieved across age-groups, there is the problem of curriculum continuity across programs. It takes an extraordinary commitment on the part of each program leader to coordinate curriculum in such a way that the programs complement one another. While curriculums seldom conflict with each other, they often have no connection to each other or may even be redundant. From the participant's point of view, what is being learned in Sunday school may have nothing to do with what is being learned in youth group or Bible study, AWANA, or VBS. This lack of coordination makes for less than a congruent curriculum.

A more common model of organization is the *gradation or age-group model* (figure 16.2). This model privileges age-groups over programs.[2] Typically, groups are formed around children, youth, and adults, with each group having its own volunteer, part-time, or full-time leader. The leadership team in this model is similar to that of the previous model and would include the various leaders of each age-group ministry. The pastor, associate pastor, or director of Christian education would oversee the leadership team. Once again this leadership team would focus primarily on spiritual formation, while other leadership teams or committees would be concerned with worship, evangelism, service, and fellowship. In larger churches

that can provide more leadership, there might be as many as ten age-groups, each with its own leader (e.g., nursery, preschool, primary, junior high, middle school, high school, college, young adult, adult, seniors).

Organizing by age provides the benefit of what Gangel refers to as "unification."[3] From the participant's point of view, there is one leader overseeing each age-appropriate ministry. Within each age-group ministry, there would be a variety of programs. Similar to the way Paul suggested in 1 Corinthians 12 that the church is one body with many members created for a variety of purposes, so too each age-group is one ministry with many programs designed for a variety of purposes.

Programs can be scheduled to complement each other rather than conflict with each other. Music programs, Bible studies, Sunday school classes, and other activities can all be planned on a master schedule in consideration of the time commitments being placed on the particular age-group. No longer will the choir practice conflict with Bible studies.

Another advantage is in curriculum development. Leaders can work with their volunteers to develop a comprehensive curriculum for a specific age-group that cuts across a variety of programs. Junior church and VBS can complement each other. The teenage Sunday school classes and youth groups can be viewed as component parts of one ministry rather than isolated units. Adult Sunday school, Bible studies, and small groups can be coordinated to meet a variety of needs.

Perhaps the greatest advantage of this model is the relationship-building process that occurs with leaders, volunteers, and participants. Children see the same faces across all the programs in their ministry, and teenagers build meaningful relationships with adults who participate in the entire youth ministry rather than just one program. Relationship building, not only over a period of years (which is possible in the functional model) but also across a variety of programs, allows for significant mentoring relationships to be formed, especially for children and youth.

Using this model, some churches will utilize an individual or couple at a particular grade level and then promote that person or couple with the class as they move along. The result of such an approach is that the students can build consistent and mean-

Figure 16.2
Group Organization by Grade Levels

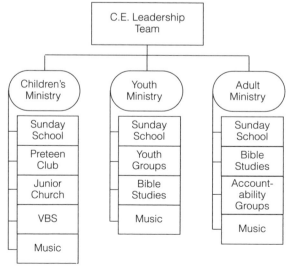

ingful relationships with the same people throughout their religious instruction at the church.

While this model provides a number of advantages over the functional model, there are still some difficulties. There may still be conflict between age-groups as younger groups attempt to recruit leadership from older groups (e.g., children's Sunday school recruiting senior high students as assistant teachers or youth ministry recruiting adult volunteers). However, these issues are typically easier to work out than scheduling and curriculum.

There is also the problem of continuity as children move into the youth ministry and teenagers move into the young adult ministry if the volunteer leaders remain with the previous age-group ministry. While the ministry coordinator, leader, or pastor should remain with the same age-group for the sake of program continuity, it is helpful to encourage volunteer leaders to "move up" to the next age-group so that they can continue in their volunteer roles with those children or youth with whom they have developed relationships. This of course creates a burden on the children's ministry, which will constantly need to replace those volunteers lost to the youth ministry, and not everyone will be able to make a decade-long commitment to the Christian education ministries. At the very least, it is always beneficial to have some volunteer leaders move across age-groups, even if they have only known the students for a short period of time and/or can only volunteer in the new ministry for a short period of time. These transitional volunteers can play an especially important role for students moving from children's ministry to youth ministry.

There also seems to be a theological problem with large churches that employ multiple staff according to function. A staff composed of one minister for Christian formation, one for evangelism, one for worship, and another for service creates the notion that these areas are distinct and separate. Biblically these areas are all interwoven and should be treated more holistically.

The greatest difficulty with this model of organization is that while it is unified within age-groups, programs drive this unification. Typically, a church moving from a functional model (or no model at all) to an age-group model simply attempts to unify the existing programs within an age-group and declare success. But how does the church know if it has unified the proper programs? This question brings us back to the earlier discussion about the purposes of church.

A NEW MODEL OF ORGANIZATION

While the age-group model provides unity, it does not guarantee the accomplishment of purpose. There may be a full complement of programs for each age-group, but the purpose of each program is not always apparent or clearly connected to the broader purposes of the church. Further, the traditional models have typically focused on spiritual formation and have left evangelism, service, worship, and fellowship to other committees within the greater church structure. It is time to rethink our approach.[4]

It may be helpful and especially appropriate in American culture to consider the three major age-groups of the church—children, youth, adults—as three distinct, yet related congregations. This is not a new idea—the Korean-American and Chinese-American churches have thought this way for years, and we have much to learn from them. In thinking this way, the church is forced to consider how each age-group should engage in the five purposes of the church. Figure 16.3 provides a Group-Purpose Organizational model that is helpful in developing programs that are both age-appropriate and meaningful in purpose.

This model is composed of four major elements: the Christian ministries leadership team, the three age-groups, the five purposes of the church, and fifteen empty program boxes.

The Christian ministries leadership team is perhaps the most radical departure from the traditional models. This leadership team replaces *all* the committees found in a traditional church leadership model, except for the board of elders/deacons. There is no need for separate committees on evangelism, outreach, missions, Christian education, and worship. The Christian ministries leadership team oversees all of these areas in a more unified and integrated manner. The leadership team is made up of at least four people and perhaps as many as a dozen. Essential to the team are the senior pastor and the ministers of each of the three age-group ministries. These age-group ministers may be volunteers, part-timers, or full-timers. They may come

Figure 16.3
Group-Purpose Organization

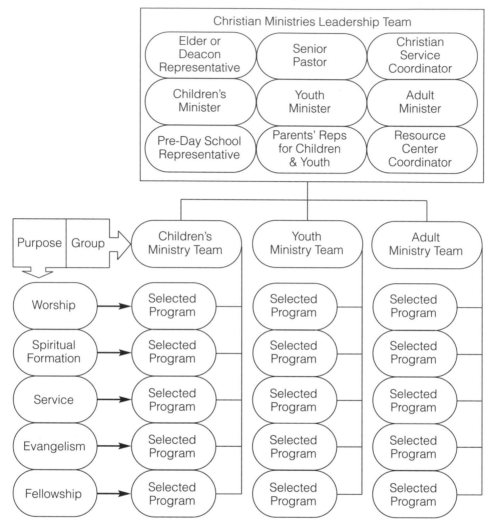

from the laity or be associate pastors. The key is that each age-group needs to have one leader who will coordinate the ministry.

While the senior pastor may or may not serve as a leader for one of the age-groups, the primary role of the senior pastor in smaller churches is to chair the leadership team and provide vision for the ministries of the church.[5] In a larger church, this task will probably be delegated to the executive pastor or the director of Christian education. The discussions of this leadership team would focus on the five purposes of the church. Since everyone on the leadership team has a stake in the area of worship for his or her age-group, a discussion on this topic will engage everyone. The same

is true for the other purposes of the church. This makes for a much more dynamic leadership team than the functional model where each team member is concerned with a single function, and the worship leader may not be concerned with evangelism nor the Bible study leader concerned with missions. A strong family ministry in the church will be a by-product of the leadership team working together to integrate the age-groups throughout a variety of ministries.

In addition, this leadership team would benefit from the input of an elder or deacon representative and parents who represent the concerns of families with children and youth. Large churches that operate day schools, preschools, and/or resource centers should include a representative from each area. Every church will benefit from a Christian service coordinator (sometimes called a networking coordinator) whose responsibility it is to identify the gifts and talents of the church members and match people with ministries that would benefit from their unique giftedness. Depending on the size of the church, this could be a volunteer, part-time, or full-time position. It is also possible that an associate pastor may serve in this capacity along with leading the adult age-group.

The first task of the Christian ministries leadership team in using this model is to fill in each of the fifteen program boxes with the existing programs of the church. Each program should fulfill at least one purpose for at least each age-group. There may be some programs that legitimately fit into more than one box, and there may be some existing programs that do not fit into any box and may need to be eliminated for lack of purpose.

Children's Ministry

Under the children's ministry column, worship may include a junior church program and all-church worship services. Spiritual formation may include Sunday school, after-school programs, or midweek evening programs. Service may include visiting a nursing home with the junior choir, sending note cards of encouragement to missionaries, and helping children discover their gifts and talents in Sunday school in preparation for ministry. Evangelism may include reaching out to the community through VBS, teaching children in Sunday school the importance of sharing their faith, or sponsoring a child or a missionary in a third world country. Fellowship may include all of the above programs, as well as Sunday school picnics and other intergenerational events.

Some churches may accomplish spiritual formation through after-school programs and use Sunday morning solely for worship while other churches may use after-school programs for service and evangelism. Churches that traditionally hold a Wednesday evening program may use this program for spiritual formation in place of or in addition to Sunday morning. This model forces the church to consider what age-appropriate programs are necessary for children in each of the five purpose areas. Emphasizing each of the five purposes equally is not the goal. The goal is that each of the five purposes be emphasized in an age-appropriate manner.

Youth Ministry

In youth ministry a church may decide that teenagers need to worship together with adults and develop a service that is meaningful to both age-groups. Another church that desires to maintain a more traditional adult service may decide to develop a youth service for their teenagers. Many churches have begun using the traditional Sunday school hour for such worship programs. Spiritual formation for teenagers may come in the form of weekly Bible studies and/or Sunday school. Local service opportunities may be designed as a monthly program for all teenagers or may be an outgrowth of small group Bible studies and student leadership meetings. Students at this age may be developing personal caring ministries of their own and certainly would be ready for significant personal ministry training. Some churches may design a midweek youth meeting with evangelism in mind, while others would consider their Sunday morning youth worship service as an evangelistic opportunity. Middle school students may serve on a domestic short-term mission trip, while high school students serve on an international short-term mission trip. Fellowship may be considered as part of all the above programs, or specific programs may be designed with this purpose in mind. Retreats and camps may serve to help fulfill any number of these purposes at the same time. In many instances, middle and high school students may have separate programs; however, there are places such as worship, fellowship, or service where they may come together.

Adult Ministry

In adult ministry the purpose of worship is typically fulfilled by a Sunday morning service, though some churches that use Sunday morning for evangelistic services have moved their worship to a midweek service. Spiritual formation may take place in a variety of small groups, Bible studies, and/or Sunday school classes. Service may include local caring projects, equipping people for personal ministry, and counseling and recovery programs, as well as meeting the physical needs of the poor. Evangelism could include special outreach programs,

Figure 16.4
Group-Purpose Organization (Traditional)

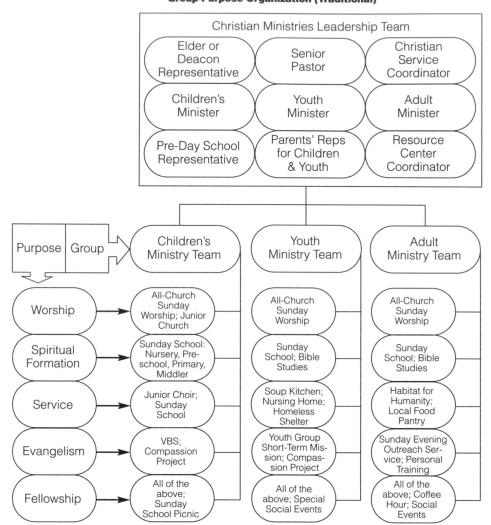

seeker services, personal evangelism training, evangelistic small groups, and short-term mission trips (either domestic or international), as well as the funding of career missionaries. Fellowship could be included in all of the above, along with social programs designed to foster relationships.

As each age-group develops programs to fulfill each of the purposes of the church, a variety of subcommittees or program teams may emerge. Many of the programs could be developed and maintained by an age-group leadership team under the direction of the age-group minister. To avoid becoming overorganized, it is important to understand that not every program of each age-group needs a program team. In larger churches the age-

groups may be divided further into as many as ten categories: nursery, preschool, primary, junior, middle school, high school, college/singles, young adult, adult, and senior adult.

Figure 16.4 details possibilities for churches with more traditional programs, while figure 16.5 details possibilities for churches with more progressive approaches to ministry.

These charts are simply examples and possibilities and should not be taken as prescriptive. Every church should prayerfully determine what programs would best meet the needs of their congregation and community.

There are two major risks in using this model of organization. The first is the possibility that

Figure 16.5
Group-Purpose Organization (Progressive)

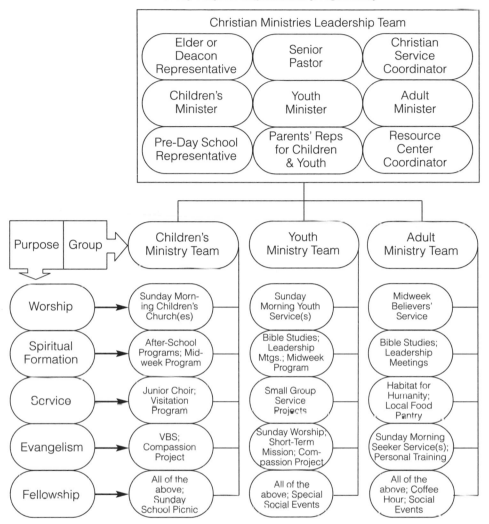

each age-group essentially becomes a church in and of itself, with no interaction between the age-groups. As mentioned earlier, it is the responsibility of the senior pastor and the Christian ministries leadership team to ensure that this does not take place. Communication among the age-group ministers is essential for healthy coordination. For example: Even if each age-group was to have its own worship service, there would be benefit in having all of the services at the same time in adjacent rooms of the same building.

The other risk is that of duplication of effort in similar purpose areas by each age-group. The administrative work for a comprehensive Sunday school program could be coordinated across age-

groups. It may also be advantageous to design local service opportunities in which all age-groups can participate. A church may commit to a particular region of the world or the country where all short-term mission trips would be taken, regardless of the age-group participating.

FAITHFULNESS AND EFFECTIVENESS

Too often effectiveness is measured through numbers. This is "the more, the merrier" approach. But Jesus never used numerical attendance to measure his effectiveness. In John 6, a massive crowd of Jesus' so-called disciples finally came to understand what was required of them if they were to follow the Master. To their amazement, they found Jesus' teachings too hard, and they turned and walked away. Jesus' reaction was not to chase after them, having lost his numbers. Instead, he turned to the Twelve and asked if they wanted to leave as well. Speaking for the Twelve, Peter declared that there was no other place that they wished to go, for they all knew that only Jesus possessed the gift of eternal life.

Jesus could have maintained the large crowd, but once they truly understood what it meant to follow him, he allowed those who were unwilling to make that commitment to walk away. Having communicated the gospel to the crowd, Jesus turned his attention to mentoring into full maturity those who had made a genuine commitment to follow him. Ultimately, the mark of a successful ministry is the percentage of the crowd that is genuinely maturing in their faith, not the number of the crowd itself. When seekers attend the entry-point programs of the church, they should realize instantly that they have encountered the home of the living God. The degree of this type of effectiveness is in no small part dependent upon the structures that a ministry chooses for carrying out its purpose.

An organizational structure that faithfully holds to the biblical purposes of the church and effectively coordinates the people, resources, and programs of the church, will ultimately be successful. Two outstanding publications that speak of the need for renewed organizational paradigms in the local church are Doug Field's book, *Purpose Driven Youth Ministry,*[6] and Mark DeVries's book, *Family-Based Youth Ministry.*[7]

CONCLUSION

There are clear biblical mandates for God's people to be faithful stewards of the resources that he has provided for them, both personally and corporately. Both the Old and New Testaments provide evidence of principles for biblical management. The managerial function of organization is an essential component of a local church's educational ministry. Learning how to better organize our ministries will help us to facilitate the accomplishment of the Great Commission.

NOTES

1. Cf. Kenneth Gangel, *Building Leaders for Church Education* (Chicago: Moody, 1982), pp. 177–88.
2. Cf. Michael Bechtle, "Organizational Structures for Christian Education" and "The Roles and Responsibilities of Christian Education Personnel," and Kenneth Garland, "Organizing Christian Education Ministry in the Small Church," in *Foundations of Ministry,* ed. Michael Anthony (Grand Rapids: Baker, 1992).
3. Gangel, *Building Leaders for Church Education,* pp. 177–88.
4. It is with deep gratitude I acknowledge the wisdom and insights of my colleague at Gordon-Conwell Theological Seminary, Gary Parrett, assistant professor of Christian education, who has sharpened my thinking in this area.
5. Cf. Richard Baxter, *The Reformed Pastor* (1656; reprint, Carlisle, Pa.: Banner of Truth Trust, 1981).
6. Doug Fields, *Purpose Driven Youth Ministry* (Grand Rapids: Zondervan, 1998).
7. Mark DeVries, *Family-Based Youth Ministry* (Downers Grove, Ill.: InterVarsity, 1994).

CHRISTIAN EDUCATION IN THE SMALL CHURCH

17

Mark Edward Simpson

O ne of the most common assumptions made by pastors and Christian educators, especially younger staff members and those less experienced with the working life of the church, is that the small church is essentially a scaled-down version of the larger church.[1] This assumption quickly leads to the conclusion that the role of pastoral leadership is to persuade the small church to adopt the successful purposes and practices of the larger church so it too can mature into a larger congregation. However, as staff members attempt to implement the vision and structures of the larger church in the smaller congregation, the differences between the two churches readily become apparent. Unfortunately, many church staff members will attempt to force the larger church philosophy on the small church rather than adapt that philosophy to the current needs of the smaller congregation. The end result is often a constant battle of wills between the staff and church membership rather than the advancement of ministry and the growth and development of the church.

A PROFILE OF THE SMALL CHURCH

Small is a relative term. If you compare a church with a membership of eight hundred to a congregation of ten thousand members, the former will appear small. But in many locales, especially rural communities, a congregation of eight hundred members is considered large. You must also take into consideration how you define membership. A church with eight hundred names on the membership role but only two hundred in average attendance is not the same size church as a congregation with eight hundred active people every Sunday. For purposes of this study, the small church will be defined as a congregation with fewer than five hundred active members in Sunday school or morning worship.

Small churches dominate the North American church scene. "In the year 2020, congregations averaging fewer than a hundred at worship will represent at least 40 percent of all the Protestant churches in the United States and Canada—and that proportion may be closer to 50 percent."[2] When churches with one hundred to five hundred in worship attendance are added to these percentages,[3] the number of small churches in North America is staggering.

Even so, at the dawn of the twenty-first century, some theological schools began to shift their focus from training men and women to serve in the "slow to grow" small churches to equipping men and women to serve in the increasing number of rapidly growing megachurches. Given the number of smaller congregations, their longevity, stability, and potential for growth, a fixation on rapid growth ministries may ultimately prove to be shortsighted.[4] Even the megachurch makes use of "small congregations" in its focus on the formation of cell groups for education and discipleship ministries.

THE DYNAMICS OF FAMILY AND TRADITION IN THE SMALL CHURCH

Small churches can grow into larger congregations. But for growth to occur, the minister of Christian education must both understand and learn to accommodate the dynamics that define the smaller congregation. Every church has its own unique character, but two dynamics appear to be common in small churches: Ministry is built around family, and ministry is built upon tradition.

Ministry Is Built around Family

It has been said that "small churches are often hard to get into and harder to get out of."[5] Why? Because one of the strengths of the small church is the family-like bond that holds the small congregation together. The Christian educator will find that almost every ministry of the small church is built around the biological family and a relatively closed system of "adopted" extended church family members. In the small congregation, especially in small communities, "everyone knows everyone or almost everyone else."[6] In some older congregations, many of the members will even be related to one another as distant relatives. Thus, participation and service in the local church is often viewed as much as a family obligation as it is seen to be a Christian duty.

Everyone in this extended family is considered important and needed.[7] This intimacy provides unique opportunities for education ministry that is difficult to duplicate in the larger church context.[8] "While the small church may not be proficient at turning out biblical scholars and theological sophisticates, it is well suited to 'enculturate' persons into the family and life of faith."[9] The challenge for the minister of Christian education is to tap into the family bond of the small church and build upon that relationship in the development of new ministries and the assimilation of new members.

The family intimacy of the small church also has its drawbacks. Remaining small is often the common expectation of the small congregation.[10] Because the focus of the church is on relationships within the existing family,[11] the inclusion of new members into the fellowship is often resisted. Christian education ministers who come into the small church from much larger congregations are usually surprised and confused by this resistance of friendly people to the welcoming of new members. Many educators will respond to this resistance by attempting to break the family bond of the small church in order to force the assimilation of new people into the congregation. Unfortunately, such efforts usually only reinforce the family mentality, leaving the new members feeling unwanted and treated as outsiders. A more productive assimilation strategy is to create a new family within the church from the new members and use that family to incorporate other new members into the congregation. Concurrent with this new family approach to assimilation, the minister of Christian education must be sure to pull members from both families into all areas of service and opportunities for leadership and fellowship to avoid the polarization of the church into two separate congregations. In this way the intimacy of the family bond is respected, new members are brought into the congregation, and the two families are gradually drawn together through the life of the church.

The family orientation of the small church also influences the way in which it responds to pastoral leadership and the leadership of associate staff. "A small church wants its minister to be a pastor, friend, and generalist, not a professional, specialist, administrator, or chief executive officer."[12] The longevity of the senior pastor is thus more often a function of his or her ability to be a member of the family than precision and excellence in ministry skills.

Ministry Is Built upon Tradition

In many small churches, ministry is built upon tradition. These traditions are often rooted in the family focus of the congregation and provide the small church with the stability that enables it to survive in the midst of hardship and turmoil.[13] Traditions range from annual events such as Christmas pageants, revival meetings, special programs, and appreciation banquets, to program details such as the order of worship, how communion is served, when VBS is held, and so on. The minister of education who suggests even the most minor change in a ministry built upon tradition invites immediate—sometimes vocal, other times covert—opposition to the change (and virtually anything else suggested in the same meeting).

Granted, some changes to tradition are necessary, especially when underlying theological presuppositions are in error or people are being genuinely hurt by the observance of the tradition itself. But many changes to tradition that are proposed by Christian educators are based on personal preferences instead of sound doctrine or educational theory. In these cases, what often happens is the exchange of the tradition of the small church for the emerging tradition of the educational pastor. This is painfully evident today in the sometimes blatant disregard by younger pastors for the traditions of senior adults.

The argument is made that senior adults are slow to change and thus are the cause for the failure of church growth strategies. Therefore, senior adults must change or discontinue their traditions so that new programs and ministries (that is, new traditions) can be created to meet the needs and concerns of younger families that will be the future of the church. After years of pouring their lives and financial resources into the church to create a stable foundation for ministry, it should not be so surprising that senior adults are unhappy with the changes being proposed as contemporary ministry.

Rather than ignoring the traditions of the small church, you can generate more change by working in and through existing traditions. The first step is to demonstrate to the congregation that you respect their preferences and traditions by participating in them.[14] The second step is to work within those traditions that need bona fide changes to introduce variations and new elements and to generate new ministries that can coexist alongside the traditional ones. The third step is to be patient and allow the changes and new ministries to take root. This will not happen overnight, and if people are rushed in adapting to these changes, they will likely reject them. If the new ministries are truly successful, interest in the traditional ministries will wane, allowing you to take the optional fourth and final step with great caution—discontinuing the old traditions. If the new

ministries are not successful, the traditional ministries are still in place, you have time to make necessary changes to the new ministries, and the family life of the church is maintained with minimal disruption.

LEADERSHIP CHALLENGES WITHIN THE SMALL CHURCH

The unique dynamics of the small church present the Christian educator with unique challenges in leadership within the small congregation that must be taken into account if efficient and effective educational ministry is to occur. Two challenges in leadership are common to Christian educators in small churches: defining a vision for ministry and working with volunteer leadership.

Defining a Vision for Ministry

The insights and wisdom of *The Purpose Driven Church* by Rick Warren and *Kingdom Principles for Church Growth* by Gene Mims have helped many churches find new life and a sense of direction for ministry. As a congregation moves through the stages of effectiveness over time—inception, growth, maturity, decline, and renewal (if the church can adapt to change before death sets in)[15]—understanding the purpose of the church and its local mission can help keep church growth alive or bring about renewal in the midst of decline.

"Small churches understand mission in personal and immediate terms."[16] The difficulty in implementing the *Purpose Driven* or *Kingdom Principles* models in the small church is that many of these congregations see their family focus and emphasis on tradition as their purpose for ministry. The education pastor who reads the Warren and Mims models and then immediately sets up ad hoc committees and research teams to move the church to define its purpose in preparation for defining new ministry most likely is engaging in futile behavior. Small churches would rather do ministry "their way,"[17] and all of the data in the world are not going to convince them to do otherwise. In church after church, pastors are spending hundreds of hours in helping the small church define its purpose, only to discover that the congregation has little enthusiasm for or energy left to implement the findings. How then do you create a vision for ministry and church growth in the small church? Capture the vision through action first, rather than through definition!

The first step in capturing the vision is to evaluate motives in framing a vision for ministry. Stagnation in church growth and dwindling effectiveness of discipleship ministries are good reasons for helping the church capture a clearer vision for ministry. But the pride of size also drives many pastors and educators to create this vision. "The small congregation does not need to feel obligated to become a megachurch, but it does have a responsibility to evangelize."[18] If the purpose of capturing a vision for ministry is to create the next megachurch, long-term conflict between the staff and the congregation is more likely to be the result than church growth.

The second step for capturing the vision for ministry in the small church is to build upon what it already does best—being small. By creating small group ministries without a great deal of fanfare or the elimination of existing ministries, change can be introduced and new members brought into the fellowship with minimal conflict. As the congregation sees the outcomes of these small groups as nonthreatening and indeed beneficial to them, they can begin to capture a vision for ministry. However, if small groups are introduced as the future of the church and/or the replacement for existing ministries, the Christian educator will trigger an entrenchment response in the congregation toward the status quo, as well as an adversarial response toward any new ministry created.

> The small church may be ambivalent about growth. Pastors usually focus on the positive consequences of numerical growth—a greater potential for ministry, an increased financial base, and a larger presence in the community. They sometimes forget that numerical growth is also painful for the congregation.
>
> As the church moves from one stage to another in its growth, it experiences a kind of death and rebirth. Its structure changes. The atmosphere changes. People experience more distance from both the pastor and the rest of its members. Even in the most successful transition, the church experiences real losses and must go through a period of disorientation and grief.[19]

If new ministries are introduced with patience, and the small church is given time to adjust to the resulting changes before other new ministries are introduced, a vision for ministry can be cast through action rather than the framing of definitions. As the church begins to grow, the vision for ministry can be expanded. Thus the time and energy usually invested in the framing of a vision for ministry that may or may not be followed is invested instead in immediate and nonthreatening action.

Working with Volunteer Leadership

The various editions of *Management of Organizational Behavior* by Hersey, Blanchard, and Johnson have helped business leaders and church leaders better understand how one's leadership style can and should be varied in working with others in the completion of a given organizational task. This situational approach to leadership assumes that an organization recognizes the role and authority of the leader to guide and direct the tasks of the organization. In theological education, the reclamation of the leadership role and pastoral authority is of primary concern. A new generation of pastors and educators is emerging from seminaries with the determination that role and authority cannot, should not, and will not be separated. These educators are now moving into the smaller church where role and authority have not necessarily been in the hands of the same person. A great deal of time will be wasted by dealing with change, power, and conflict issues on role and authority—delaying ministry advancement—if Christian educators fail to understand leadership from the perspective of the small church volunteer.

Christian educators in the smaller church are often given ministry roles without full corresponding authority due to the organizational structure of the traditional family-based congregation. "In broad general terms, larger congregations tend to function around an organizational structure that places heavy responsibilities on committees, while smaller churches tend to delegate responsibilities to individuals."[20] The resulting participatory democracy of volunteer leaders enables the small church to fill its ministry tasks. However, as the small church grows, that participatory democracy eventually becomes cumbersome. As new staff members are added to the ministry team, the representative system of church government common to larger congregations becomes more attractive to the staff but not necessarily to the volunteer leadership comfortable with a participatory democracy.[21] If a representative form of government is implemented by the staff and the roles of previous volunteer leaders begin to change or are eliminated, an "us versus them" mentality can set in if the transition period is not handled with great care and sensitivity. The problem is compounded if the volunteers sense that the representative form of government is but a smoke screen by the staff for rulership, not leadership.

Partnership also focuses more on relationships rather than organizational position. As noted earlier, the small church is often a family enterprise that thrives on relationships. In a partnership, the Christian educator manages by relationship, a method that the small church readily understands. If the authoritarian and relationally distant CEO business model is used in the small church, a new ministry may get accomplished, but it is often at the expense of building congregational ownership for that ministry. By building a partnership in the leadership of the smaller church, relationships can be built that generate an environment of trust and mutual respect. This environment then makes it possible to initiate change in less threatening and mutually agreeable ways.[22] Building this kind of partnership does take time and calls for patience on the part of the Christian educator.[23] However, for the continued development of the small church, that patience is ultimately time well spent in terms of long-term productivity and future cooperation in ministry development.

EDUCATION PROGRAMS IN THE SMALL CHURCH

Educational programming is the centerpiece of the small church ministry. The family orientation of the smaller congregation often results in a multiplicity of traditional programs and events throughout the week and the calendar year around which all other church ministries are held. These numerous and varied educational programs present the small church with unique challenges in educational management not faced by larger congregations. While it would be impossible to address every type of educational ministry found in smaller churches, there are programs and management issues common to these congregations: the role of discipleship and fellowship ministries; grouping and grading educational programs; and leading and managing educational ministries.

The Role of Fellowship in Discipleship Ministries

The megachurch movement has generated numerous educational programs and agencies that have brought vitality to Christian life and thought in those larger congregations. The success of these programs and agencies makes it tempting to bring them into the small church with the goal of bringing about that same vitality. But as has been observed, smaller churches have different dynamics that need to be taken into consideration when planning educational ministry. To ignore these dynamics is to invite unnecessary conflict that will most likely delay the growth and development of the congregation rather than advance it.

"Small churches are better at special events than they are at programs."[24] The family orientation of these congregations seems to draw church members toward special activities and fellowship events rather than long-term programs. In many small congregations, it is not uncommon to see numerous educational and fellowship ministries being offered each month of the year.

Much of the energy and focus of the educational leaders of the church will be on planning these special events. Programming such as Sunday school and Wednesday night Bible study will usually be consigned to self-maintenance modes requiring little attention, which is why these programs often become stagnant. Interest in developing new ongoing or long-term discipleship ministries may initially be met with resistance, because, in the perspective of the educational leaders, if it takes a lot of energy to do a one-time special event, how can they implement a ministry that meets every week?

The new education staff member will be tempted early in his or her tenure with the small church to discontinue or change many of the church's special educational and fellowship events in favor of developing a handful of more effective ongoing discipleship ministries. But in the smaller church where these events often define the church's identity, the education staff member should approach changes to these events with great caution.

A good rule for the small church today is to build the Christian education ministry initially by using the basic agencies which have proven successful over the years, replacing them only when it is clear that some alternative program will be more effective in meeting the needs of the congregation.[25]

A word of caution: Never assume that your alternative program will be more effective than the programs that have been in place for several years. In the smaller church where tradition and annual special events are ingrained in the life of the fellowship, your alternative program may be less beneficial in meeting their needs. This does not mean that you cannot change existing ministries. It does mean that any and all such changes should be approached with great care and sensitivity to the values and interests of those in your care. Too often Christian educators will create ministries that are educationally sound and interesting to them but not necessarily meaningful for those whom they serve.

In addition to Sunday school, church social events like potlucks, pitch-ins, holiday pageants, children and youth presentations, VBS, and so forth are often other major entry points in the small church for inviting nonmembers to join the fellowship. These events seem to be natural windows of opportunity to welcome visitors into the life of the smaller congregation.[26] They are time-consuming to implement, but the resulting relationships fostered in these activities are often stronger and longer-term than those generated through other forms of small group ministries.

Grouping and Grading Educational Programs

In the best of all possible worlds, a church would have sufficient numbers of each age-group to form classes appropriate to each age-level's needs. In the larger church, the congregation is usually sufficiently large to have a separate Bible class for each age-group, if not multiple classes for each. But in the smaller congregation, multiple age-levels can most often be put together to form viable small groups, particularly with children and youth programming.

When the education pastor in the small church is faced with grouping and grading classes for children and youth, the church's grading system should follow the grading system of the local school system as far as possible. Particular attention should be given to the grade break points in the school system where children and youth move from one school to another. For example, if middle school consists of the sixth through eighth grades and high school consists of the ninth through twelfth grades, the church should avoid a grouping and grading plan that puts eighth and ninth graders in the same class. Unfortunately, some churches are located within reach of multiple school districts with differing grading systems. If ninth graders are in the middle school in one system and in high school in another, the church's high school grouping and grading should include the ninth graders as far as possible. The basic grouping and grading principle should be to make a child or young person feel promoted, not demoted, in the grading system of the church classroom. This principle is especially important in communities where the extracurricular activities of the local school system predominate the academic and social life of the children, youth, and adults in the church.

One of the hardest challenges for the education pastor in the small church is grouping and grading youth classes when only one or two children are in each age-group. It is not uncommon in some small congregations to find a handful of elementary and middle-school students placed together in the same class to form a small group large enough to do the learning activities found in most Bible study materials. However, when too many young age ranges are placed together to form a large enough small group, the developmental differences between the ages often negates the value of many learning activities. In these cases, it would be better to form age-appropriate smaller groups, even with only two or three students, than to put too many ages together just to do a learning activity.[27] When the number of students is small, tap into the value of one-on-one approaches to discipleship and mentoring.

Grouping and grading of adults also has its challenges. Adults can be grouped by age, by friendship groups, by gender, or by interest and motivation.[28] A common misconception in grouping adults is that they learn best with others of the same age and that all other forms of grouping and grading are not as conducive to the assimilation of new members.[29] It is true that many larger churches have moved to grouping adults primarily by age and marital status to introduce and network newcomers with their peers. But grouping and grading options need not be limited to age and marital status.

In the smaller church, intergenerational Bible classes for adults are quite common, as are classes grouped according to topics of interest. In women's fellowship groups, and to some extent men's fellowship groups, classes will tend to form along the lines of similar age levels. The strength of the small church is that adult grouping and grading can be varied across programs, which encourages a more integrated and cohesive congregation. The family foundation of the small church also allows for using multiple types of adult age groupings.

Leading and Managing Educational Ministries

The family and tradition bases of the smaller church have generated leadership and management paradigms that both hinder and advance educational ministries. In the smaller congregation, organizational functioning is often simple rather than complex, communication is rapid, and short-term planning is the norm.[30] Thus, moving church leaders to engage in long-range planning for church growth is very difficult, since the small church will tend to focus on more immediate needs rather than those of the future.[31] In fact, it has been observed that the smaller the church, the shorter the outlook and time frame church leaders will follow when engaging in ministry planning.[32] Since most church growth strategies require careful long-range planning, the minister of education will be hard pressed to convince church leaders to begin planning for ministries that are beyond the current calendar year. Indeed, a common response used by church leaders when long-range planning is suggested is that it is contrary to the teaching of James 4:13–14 and puts the church in the position of getting ahead of God's will. That is a very real and possible danger if you fail to read further and take to heart verses 15–16, where James teaches the church how to engage in planning that always yields to the unfolding will of God.

Leadership and management habits, of course, are hard to break, and merely pointing out that long-range planning is appropriate for the church will not suddenly result in the adoption of a five-year ministry plan. The more productive response for the Christian educator is to create a long-range plan, subject to revision, that can be shared with the church leadership in increasingly larger and longer terms over time.

One management area often difficult for Christian educators in the small church is working with limited financial resources.

> When catalogs, curriculum, and seminary offerings are perused, one sometimes gets the impression that the typical church Christian education program is financed by an affluent, sophisticated church, housed in a many-roomed and well-equipped building, staffed by a large, trained team of enablers, and populated by many students who are led through a comprehensive learning program. Such an education program does not happen often.[33]

Governing boards in the small church often perceive themselves to be rationing or permission-giving/withholding bodies.[34] The Christian educator who is not sensitive to the flow of expenditures and the financial mind-set of the governing leadership will often run out of funds before the end of the fiscal year. Learning to plan and pace expenditures is thus essential in the smaller congregation.

There are a number of strategies that can be used to pace expenditures and spread the allocation of resources out over a longer period of time.[35] Learning to read the church budget and the monthly financial spreadsheet is the first step. Learning to honor budget parameters and respect the budget is the second step. Learning to report and interpret budget expenditures to other church leaders is the third step. Governing bodies tend to respect and support the education minister who is sensitive to the flow of monies, as opposed to the educator who spends every dime frivolously and yet asks for more. Deficit spending is usually anathema to small church leaders, since every dollar spent can impact the financial stability of the congregation.

CONCLUSION

Christian education in the small church is full of challenges and possibilities for the creative minister of Christian education. The unique needs of the smaller congregation require patience, persistence, perseverance, and faithfulness in prayer on the part of the Christian educator. Patience is required because changes may not be embraced quickly or completely when they impact the family orientation and traditions of the congregation. Persistence is required because new ideas, especially those regarding church growth, will take time to take root. Perseverance is required, for change invariably is threatening to some, and defensive responses to proposed changes often generate conflict. Faithfulness in prayer is required, for without it the Christian educator can end up building the wrong kingdom.

The small church is not the large church in miniature, but it can grow in size and influence in the ministry of the gospel. The key is to harness the unique qualities of the small congregation to help it grow and fulfill the Great Commission and not expect it to function as a large congregation prematurely.

Notes

1. Ron Klassen and John Koessler, *No Little Places: The Untapped Potential of the Small-Town Church* (Grand Rapids: Baker, 1996), p. 76.

2. Lyle E. Schaller, *The Small Membership Church: Scenarios for Tomorrow* (Nashville: Abingdon, 1994), p. 13.

3. David R. Ray, *The Big Small Church Book* (Cleveland: Pilgrim, 1992), p. 25.

4. Ibid., p. 27.

5. Ibid., p. 40.

6. Ibid., p. 36.

7. David R. Ray, *Small Churches Are the Right Size* (New York: Pilgrim, 1982), pp. 94–95.

8. Klassen and Koessler, *No Little Places,* p. 76.

9. Ray, *Small Churches Are the Right Size,* p. 92.

10. Ray, *Big Small Church Book,* p. 35.

11. Ibid., p. 38.

12. Ibid., pp. 38–39.

13. Douglas Alan Walrath, *Making It Work: Effective Administration in the Small Church* (Valley Forge, Pa.: Judson, 1994), p. 12.

14. Ibid., p. 2.

15. Norman Shawchuck and Roger Heuser, *Leading the Congregation* (Nashville: Abingdon, 1993), pp. 161–62.

16. Ray, *Big Small Church Book,* p. 38.

17. Ibid., p. 41.

18. Klassen and Koessler, *No Little Places,* p. 105.

19. Ibid., p. 104.

20. Lyle E. Schaller, *The Small Church Is Different!* (Nashville: Abingdon, 1982), p. 35.

21. Ibid., p. 36.

22. Klassen and Koessler, *No Little Places,* pp. 101–2.

23. Ibid., p. 103.

24. Ray, *Big Small Church Book,* p. 41.

25. Kenneth R. Garland, "Organizing Christian Education Ministry in the Small Church," in *Foundations of Ministry: An Introduction to Christian Education for a New Generation,* ed. Michael J. Anthony (Wheaton, Ill.: BridgePoint, 1992), pp. 248–49.

26. Schaller, *Small Membership Church,* p. 120.

27. Carolyn C. Brown, *Developing Christian Education in the Smaller Church* (Nashville: Abingdon, 1982), p. 33.

28. Ibid., pp. 33–35.

29. Ibid., p. 33.

30. Ray, *Big Small Church Book,* pp. 37–41.

31. Ibid., p. 41.

32. Schaller, *Small Church Is Different!* p. 24.

33. Ray, *Small Churches Are the Right Size,* p. 89.

34. Schaller, *Small Membership Church,* p. 15.

35. Donald L. Griggs and Judy McKay Walther, *Christian Education in the Small Church,* Small Church in Action Series, ed. Douglas Alan Walrath (Valley Forge, Pa.: Judson, 1988), p. 84.

Recruiting, Training, and Motivating Volunteers   18

Dennis Williams

One of the true tests of a successful church is the ability to involve others in the work of the ministry. This statement is much more than a simple call to action. It forms the foundation for a biblical philosophy of volunteerism. We need to look at Scripture for our marching orders as given by the Lord Jesus in the Great Commission (Matt. 28:19–20). Another helpful passage would be the instructions given by the apostle Paul in Ephesians 4:11–16.

In Matthew 28:19–20, the Lord gives the disciples the specifics of their ministry: to win people for Christ, baptize them, and then teach them his Word. Before the Great Commission passage, we find the Lord telling the disciples that the harvest is plentiful, but the laborers are few (Matt. 9:37–38). This is certainly the condition of many churches today. Their ministries have great potential, but finding needed workers is a difficult task. The Lord then commands the disciples to ask the Lord of the harvest to send out workers into his harvest field.

From a biblical perspective, the reason why we get more people involved in ministry is to obey God's command to equip and train the body for service. In this way, others are given the opportunity to serve as they mature in their walk with Christ. Spiritual maturity requires active involvement in some ministry capacity. When the workload is shared in a team fashion, God is honored and the work can be accomplished effectively.

Unfortunately, today some affluent church members would prefer to pay others to do the work that they themselves should be doing as volunteers. Two things are wrong with this approach. First, it is a violation of the biblical mandate for everyone to get involved in using their spiritual gift(s) to build up the local body of Christ. If one is not serving somewhere, he or she is out of God's will. It's as simple as that. Second, when paid professionals do all of the work themselves, they are preventing others from a path of spiritual growth. Leaders are to equip others to serve and give them the opportunity to do so.

Obstacles to Recruitment

Why is the recruitment of workers such a problem for churches? With such unparalleled opportunities in church ministries today and with God's blessing so evident, where are the needed volunteers to accomplish the ministry? Kenneth Gangel suggests that we face three basic problems in helping people serve Christ: misuse, disuse, and abuse. The first refers to enlisting unqualified teachers and workers; the second, to the many uninvolved Christians who occupy our church pews; and the last, to the problem of overburdened workers.[1]

My ministry experience has been in churches ranging from 50 to 6,000 members, and I've learned that recruitment is difficult for every size of church. We can be grateful for people who join as members already equipped. However, it is unlikely we can staff a church ministry on a consistent basis this way because the supply will eventually run out. Recruiting new workers is the key to keeping ministries functioning. This is a continual process, and churches that do not maintain a regular recruitment and equipping program for their volunteers will find their supply of recruits running dry. Remember, according to Ephesians 4:12 the role of vocational leadership is to prepare God's people for works of service. Keep in mind that the work of the ministry ultimately falls on the responsibility of the Lord Jesus Christ in partnership with the Holy Spirit. He does the calling. We simply present the opportunities for service and leave the internal desire up to God. This attitude will free us from any coercive or manipulative methods.[2]

It is important to state that in a philosophy of recruitment the entire church needs to work together to accomplish the task. In light of this, Margie Morris suggests that church leaders must use their influence to encourage and affirm the work of volunteers by supporting those who serve both publicly and privately.[3] Sometimes, even in spite of this public show of support, it can be a real challenge to recruit enough workers to accomplish the tasks at hand. Let's examine some of the more prominent obstacles to volunteer recruitment.

1. *Lack of prayer.* One possible answer to the crisis in recruitment we see in the church today is a lack of prayer. Remember, the Lord told the disciples to ask the Lord of the harvest to send out workers into his harvest field (Matt. 9:38). It is important to recognize that our prayers for finding people to serve in the church are not just to fill vacant positions. We want to be part of God's plan of finding the right place of service for individuals so that they can be equipped and fulfilled in their Christian walk. By providing places of ministry, the church gives individuals opportunity to exercise their spiritual gifts and minister to others.

2. *Insecurity of the senior pastor.* Ministry researcher George Barna sought to discover the reasons why so few people became involved in serving in their local church. He interviewed hundreds of people in his desire to find the reasons. Chief among their remarks was the attitude of the senior pastor. Much to Barna's surprise, he discov-

ered that many senior pastors and ministry leaders prefer to do the work of the ministry themselves and feel threatened by the presence and abilities of volunteer leaders. This in turn made it counterproductive or uncomfortable for many volunteer leaders to lead.[4] This runs counter to the spirit and intent of the Scriptures and certainly inhibits effective ministry.

3. *Competition among church staff.* The entire vocational ministry team needs to work together in the recruitment of volunteers without being in competition with one another. Unfortunately, that is not always the case. A minister of education came to me quite frustrated because he had to take the "leftover workers" who could not be used in the music ministry. Music in this particular church was the highest priority, and when new people came into the church, they were first approached to serve in the music program. Other ministries were secondary in importance and received little or no support from the church leadership. There was no sense of teamwork there. But this is clearly wrong. All ministries are important, and no one program should be allowed to dominate others.

4. *Expectations set too low.* "You get what you pay for" is an adage that permeates many business dealings. In some cases it is true. If something is free or too cheap, it probably isn't worth owning. The same can hold true to the work of the ministry. When we announce from the pulpit that we need workers and that any warm body will do, we sell ourselves short and diminish the importance of the positions we seek to fill. We want those who work in the church to serve with pride. When we tell people that teaching children in our Sunday school is an easy job and that they don't need any special training, we have undermined the value of working with kids. How important can the job be if anybody can do it and no training is required? Keep a high standard for the recruitment of volunteers, and do not lower expectations so much that you diminish the value of the position. If you do, don't be surprised if no one of quality volunteers to serve. Leaders, like all good businesspeople, have learned over time that anything that looks too good to be true usually is.

5. *We're hesitant to ask.* Church ministry leaders begin their careers fresh out of college or seminary with a belief that everyone enjoys working in ministry. They launch into their staff positions with

fresh zeal and enthusiasm. Then reality hits! Soon after starting their jobs, they begin recruiting people to serve in the various departments. Within a brief period of time, they discover that people avoid them in the hallway, screen their calls, and find reasons why they can't stop and talk after church. You'd think they had the plague. What leaders soon discover is that people don't like to be asked to help. Once you're on the receiving end of this treatment long enough, you become shell-shocked and avoid asking. But if you don't ask, you won't receive.

6. *Poor choices and misguided priorities.* It is true that some positions require more time than some people can give. There is no such thing as "one size fits all" when it comes to ministry. Some are able to spend several hours a week preparing to teach a Sunday school lesson and in contacting and ministering to people in their classes while others can give only a short amount of time to ministry opportunities. The key here is to try to place people in ministry positions that fit their abilities and time restraints. The principle is that everyone needs some kind of ministry, but not everyone can spend the same amount of time in ministry. A single parent who works one or two jobs cannot be expected to take on a ministry that will require twenty hours a week. That person, however, can contribute with a ministry that may take less time. Be creative and identify ways the entire congregation can serve. It is important to remember that everyone has the same 168 hours per week. It is how we choose to use that time and how productive we are in serving the Lord through the church that really counts. There are many good and wholesome things people can do with their time, and the church should not discourage positive activities for people. When the church is left out of the activities, however, there is a serious problem.

One reason for the shortage of workers today is the number of dual career households and the number of people working two or three jobs. Frankly, these people do not have the energy to add much of anything to their already busy schedules. Of course, this can be a symptom of deeper issues, and certainly we cannot solve the problem here. We must realize that many of our people are in situations like this, and it eliminates them from significant volunteer ministry in the church. This does not mean that these people cannot have any kind of ministry. Rather, they must volunteer in positions that do not require great amounts of time.

7. *Administrative roadblocks.* Another problem area in recruitment can be categorized as administrative issues. People are turned away from ministry opportunities because of poor planning, ineffective organization, weak leadership, and little or no evaluation. For example, planning includes setting objectives, designing strategies, scheduling, and budgeting. Organization includes structure, delegation, and relationships. Leadership involves casting a vision and motivating workers. Evaluation, one of the weakest elements in the church today, provides a measurement on how well we did in light of what we set out to do. When churches do not apply basic administrative skills to their ministries, the results are less than acceptable. People do not want to be a part of a weak organization. John Cionca states that the majority of people want to be part of something that is positive. They respond to something that is significant, something that will make an impact on their lives.[5]

8. *Church policies.* Many churches have policies that require volunteers to be members of the church before they can serve in the ministry. Though it is not a biblical requirement, it is a popular one. Another popular criterion is for all workers to be Christians before allowing them to serve. Not all churches have this requirement, and they use involvement in ministry as a stepping stone to lead these people to eventually join the church. Certainly, if membership is a requirement, it defines the pool of people from which you can select volunteers. Some policies are needed and are important. In this regard, an ounce of prevention can indeed be worth a pound of cure. However, choose your policies carefully, as they will also limit those who can serve.

9. *Limited vision of the future.* It is possible for us to eliminate potential workers by mentally placing people in certain positions with no thought of expanding them into other ministry areas. We need to learn to look at people from the perspective of potential and not just what they have done before. Sometimes it is important for us to think outside the lines when it comes to finding the right person for the right ministry. Maybe the person you need isn't ready yet and merely requires a little more training in another area before he or she can be moved into the position that is open. It would be helpful for us to adopt a long-term vi-

sion of volunteers, rather than one of short-sighted expediency.

10. *People's lack of confidence in themselves.* We live in an age where people come to the church with a host of broken relationships from their past. This baggage holds them back from being who God wants them to become. Due to past failures, some people do not accept ministry positions because they lack confidence in their ability to serve. Past failure prevents them from seeing beyond that to future success. How do you help foster confidence in the lives of your volunteers? Helping them prepare for the task at hand and giving them your full support and encouragement is the only way to develop confidence in your volunteers.[6]

Finding Potential Workers

Now that we have examined the top ten obstacles to recruitment, it would be helpful to look at the ways we can identify and locate new recruits. A little creativity can go a long way. Financial planners who work with people experiencing credit problems usually ask them to develop an asset/liability summary to describe where they are financially. This survey shows them their (1) sources and amounts of income, (2) how much is needed for living, and (3) how much is owed. Without these three pieces of information, a financial planner will not be able to develop a plan to lead the person back to financial stability.

Churches seeking to enlist volunteers for ministry should develop a similar approach. We are not looking at finances here but at the valuable resource of people. It would be helpful for church professionals to know (1) who is serving now, (2) where they are currently serving, and (3) who has never served before. Without this vital information, they have no way of discovering their untapped human resources.

The first step in developing this asset/liability form is to identify the personnel needs of the church. Every church agency or group should participate by identifying its ministry requirements, including those not presently filled. Often it is helpful to provide a chart or form for each ministry group. Figure 18.1 shows a sample chart for the Sunday school ministry.[7]

Figure 18.1
Ministry Inventory

Sunday School Staff	
Title	**Name of Person Serving**
General	
Superintendent/director	
Secretary	
Early Childhood Division	
Coordinator	
Cradle nursery director	
Secretary	
Teachers	
Teachers	
Helpers	
Nursery director	
Secretary	
Teachers	
Teachers	
Helpers	
Kindergarten director	
Secretary	
Teachers	
Teachers	
Helpers	

The same idea can be used for each age-group in the Sunday school ministry, and the form can also be used, with adaptation, for other ministry groups in the church.

As the list is developed for your particular church, fill in the names of those presently serving in the positions listed. From this you will begin to see how many people are currently serving in ministry positions and how many openings you presently have. This inventory will help you answer questions such as who is presently serving and at what effectiveness, what areas are in need of new workers, and what workers need additional training and encouragement. Plan ahead for possible future ministries, and include them on the inventory sheet. Planning is charting a course of action into the future, and without careful planning, the future ministries may not materialize.

Figure 18.2
Church Ministry Survey[8]

Dr   Mr   Mrs   Ms   Miss

Name _____

Sex: M   F

Address _____

City/State/Zip _____

Home phone _____ Business phone _____ Unlisted? _____

E-mail address _____

Occupation _____

Employer _____

Birthday___/___/___   Wedding anniversary___/___/___

Marital status: single   married   engaged   divorced   widowed   separated

Child(ren's) name(s) (living at home):

M _____ F _____ age _____

M _____ F _____ age _____

M _____ F _____ age _____

M _____ F _____ age _____

M _____ F _____ age _____

M _____ F _____ age _____

M _____ F _____ age _____

Relative/others living at the same address: _____

Sunday school department _____ class _____

Occupational status:

Employed   Self-employed   Unemployed   Student   Retired

Groups/Skills/Interests:

1=Active   2=Experienced   3=Trained   4=Interested

Groups
- ___ children's group
- ___ MOPS
- ___ recovery group
- ___ Bible study
- ___ men's group
- ___ women's group
- ___ youth group

Admin/Office
- ___ elder
- ___ trustee
- ___ deacon
- ___ finance committee
- ___ property committee
- ___ nominating committee
- ___ secretary

Worship
- ___ usher/greeter
- ___ sound technician
- ___ music committee
- ___ worship committee
- ___ decorations
- ___ sanctuary choir
- ___ children's choir

Education
- ___ Bible study leader
- ___ teach preschool
- ___ teach children
- ___ teach youth
- ___ teach adults
- ___ education committee
- ___ other

Outreach/Missions
- ___ missions committee
- ___ visitation
- ___ membership committee
- ___ evangelism committee
- ___ other

Fellowship
- ___ serving/helping
- ___ kitchen committee
- ___ social committee
- ___ other

Community Service
- ___ foster home
- ___ helping elderly
- ___ hospital volunteer
- ___ shut-ins ministry
- ___ hospice care
- ___ other

Spiritual Gifts
- ___ administration
- ___ exhortation
- ___ giving
- ___ mercy
- ___ prophecy
- ___ teaching
- ___ counseling

Promotion
- ___ advertising
- ___ poster art
- ___ public relations
- ___ public speaking
- ___ publicity/editing
- ___ sign painting
- ___ TV/radio
- ___ writing

Stewardship
- ___ estate planning
- ___ investments
- ___ foundations
- ___ other

Technical
- ___ media
- ___ computer
- ___ mechanic
- ___ printer
- ___ sound/lighting
- ___ video
- ___ chauffeur license

Repair/Construction
- ___ carpenter
- ___ carpet layer
- ___ electrician
- ___ gardener
- ___ handyman
- ___ glazier
- ___ janitor
- ___ landscaper

(continued)

Church Ministry Survey (continued)

Vocal Music	Instrumental Music	Child Care	Kitchen
___ soprano	___ piano	___ church nursery	___ cleanup
___ alto	___ organ	___ in homes	___ decorations
___ tenor	___ strings	___ in own home	___ receptions
___ bass	___ woodwind	___ days	___ other
___ soloist	___ brass	___ evenings	
___ small group	___ percussion	___ weekends	
___ other	___ guitar	___ other	

Drama
___ acting
___ choreography
___ directing
___ makeup
___ set construction
___ set design
___ stage crew
___ other

Once you have completed the ministry inventory, you are ready to design a ministry survey that is to be given to the entire congregation (see figure 18.2). Include all of the information listed on the ministry inventory, and include every possibility for ministry. Include specialized areas of skill such as carpentry, electrical work, plumbing, and painting. All churches need help in these areas from time to time.

Be certain to provide a way for workers to identify where they are presently serving, where they have served in the past, where they feel equipped to serve, and where they are interested in serving in the future. In the survey below, these are indicated by the words *active* (presently serving), *experienced* (have served in the past), *trained* (equipped to serve), and *interested* (possibly willing to serve in the future). Notice too that the survey asks for more information than is needed for recruitment purposes because this information is important for the church to have on hand.

After going to all of the work to develop the above survey, it is important that it be administered in the best way to assure the greatest results. The goal is to have as many church people as possible complete the survey so that you can have an accurate picture of the congregation. It seems that many churches that do get this far in the process fail to take advantage of the significant information available to them. Merely looking over the completed forms might help you discover some new workers, but the potential is much greater than that.

Establish a system to enter the data, creating files for every position and every person. Write a card

or letter of appreciation to each of them for completing the survey. State what they have volunteered to do, and tell them when you will be in contact with them about the position. Announce training opportunities. If there are no positions open in their desired area, assure them that they will be contacted as soon as a ministry position becomes available.

A volunteer ministry coordinator is a position that every church needs if there is no part- or full-time assimilation pastor at the church. This person, working with the staff and other church leaders, is the key to a successful recruitment ministry. The task carries major responsibilities and requires a great deal of time and spiritual maturity. This person will coordinate the above process on a continuing basis and will work to keep the information up-to-date. He or she will see that the survey is given to all new members, thus eliminating the need to complete a church-wide survey every year.

When a church adopts the philosophy that service is everybody's business, every ministry or group in the church will be on the lookout for potential workers. Adult class teachers and leaders have the responsibility of encouraging class members to find areas of service. The teacher should help in identifying these people to the church leadership. The same is true for church committees and ministry teams. New church members are an excellent source of volunteers, especially if in the new member orientation the importance of having a place of ministry is emphasized. Vacation Bible school is a good source of potential workers, and by serving a short time in this ministry, people can be observed and get their feet wet in ministry. Many times people who have volunteered for short-term ministries end up with long-term ministry positions.

Another effective way to introduce and find ministry volunteers is to have a ministry fair. Each ministry has a display explaining its ministry and how it contributes to the mission statement of the church. Handouts should be provided that include the church budget, the focus of the ministry, the current needs, and how interested people in the congregation can assist. Refreshments will facilitate an informal atmosphere for significant discussions. The ministry fair may not be the best time to recruit workers for ministries, but it does educate the congregation on the many possibilities available.[9]

Most church leaders agree that public announcements telling of the need for volunteers is probably the least effective way to recruit. It is necessary, however, to let people know of opportunities, and an announcement along with creative activities can be useful. Make the announcement general in nature, and tell people how they can find additional information on the positions. Announcing specific position needs may result in having unqualified persons volunteer.

TRAINING AND EQUIPPING WORKERS

We come now to the area of our study that will encourage and motivate workers not only to do a good job in ministry but to stay on the job. When you go to all the trouble of finding and recruiting individuals for ministry and after only a short time they leave their positions, you are faced with the enormous task of finding new people all over again.

Earlier it was stated that when volunteers are not doing a good job in ministry, it can often be traced to poor recruitment interviews where they were not given clear responsibilities for the task. To accept a position of ministry requires that the person be willing to be trained to do that ministry correctly. The tragedy is that many churches do very little if any training for their ministry positions. Recent surveys indicate that most churches are so involved in finding people for ministry positions that they have no energy left to provide the training and equipping necessary for effective min-

istry. Remember Ephesians 4, where the leaders were instructed to equip God's people for works of service. Without proper equipping, many volunteers will falter and fail in their ministries. Unfortunately, this is one reason for the poor quality of ministry in many of our churches. The situation does not have to be so bleak, however. There are ways to train and equip workers to do effective ministry, even with today's ultra-busy schedules.

In every ministry position, some kind of training should be provided for the volunteer prior to beginning the ministry. Depending on the position, training may take thirty minutes to an hour or a schedule of classes over several weeks or months. During the ministry year, the church should provide some kind of continuing education or ongoing training for the workers. Part of the position acceptance would be a willingness to participate in some kind of ongoing training each year. It is the responsibility of the church to offer several opportunities for training so the workers can choose a time that best fits with their busy schedules.

There are lots of methods that you could use to train your workers. There are many fine books and written training materials available through Christian publishers. Most Sunday school materials provide excellent training resources in the materials themselves or with separate books geared to specific age-group ministries. Training magazines are also available. For volunteers who are not able to spend several weeks attending training sessions, assign reading from these resources and have a leader meet with them to discuss the content.

Video and audio training resources on many areas of ministry can be used for equipping. Some publishers are providing resources and training materials on their Web sites. Churches can design their own materials to provide the necessary training. Like some of the resources listed above, these can easily be used in individual or group study.

A powerful opportunity for equipping prospective teachers is to take them to other churches that have outstanding ministries so that they can receive coaching and conversation from the leaders. Placing volunteers in positions alongside excellent workers for a period of time provides positive modeling in the proper way to carry on the ministry. In Sunday school ministry, it is always good to have prospective teachers working with experienced teachers so that they can be teachers in training. Years ago I did this with a young elementary class. After about four years, I discovered that every teacher in that department had been trained by this one outstanding teacher.

It is also valuable to bring in specialists to assist in the training from time to time. There are over two hundred Sunday school and Christian ministry conventions held in the United States each year. Add to this the number of denominational and publishing house conferences, and it is clear that many opportunities abound for leaders to find training for volunteer workers. These conferences provide workshops on nearly every topic of church ministry. Though it will take a special push to get people to attend these conferences, it will be worth the effort. Provide scholarships for some of the cost, assist with baby-sitting and transportation, and have a debriefing time following the conference to benefit even more.

Teachers' and leaders' meetings provide opportunity for communication, planning, ministry, and training. While these kinds of meetings were the mainstay of many successful Sunday school ministries in years past, the potential for today is just as significant. Whenever people meet together for ministry planning, no one should leave without learning at least one new and better way to do ministry.

MOTIVATING WORKERS FOR SERVICE

Have you ever gone into a place that just did not feel right? The atmosphere and attitudes did not make you feel welcome. The same problem can be found in some church ministry positions. The atmosphere for ministry must be positive, rewarding, and fulfilling. To make this happen, we must consider the needs of individuals, develop team efforts, affirm good work, and generate excitement about the mission of the church. Volunteer leaders should be given visibility and have the authority necessary to accomplish their ministries. Keeping volunteers working toward meaningful goals will help them maintain their enthusiasm. Certainly, receiving the personal attention of the leader as one does ministry will strengthen the climate for motivation.

Leaders are the prime creators, keepers, and cultivators of corporate culture.[10] This suggests that the climate for motivation is an important responsibility of the leader. Hal Pettegrew states that the motivation and satisfaction of volunteer workers is related to positive organizational climate factors. If the culture or climate of the church is a positive culture, then one might expect that the volunteers might be more positively motivated and satisfied.[11] If the climate is negative and critical, people will feel used and undervalued. Be on the lookout for burnout and overwork. When you see signs of depression, fatigue, lethargy, and tardiness, it is time for leaders to intervene and be of assistance. Otherwise these attitudes will be passed on to others and will be detrimental to the overall health of the church.

There are certain basics that people need and expect in their work. They want recognition as persons and fair treatment. If volunteers are treated merely as a means to get a job done without consideration of what it will do for them, it will affect their motivation. Leaders who play favorites by giving recognition to some and not to others will find disruption in their ranks.

People must also have suitable working conditions. Though this is part of the climate for motivation, it is also a basic desire for volunteers. In addition, people need a chance to be heard and to have pride in their ministry. Helping people develop pride in their ministries is a strong key to developing worker motivation. This can be accomplished by giving the workers the help of the leadership while they accept the challenge to prove themselves. Certainly, volunteers need a sense of belonging and acceptance by their fellow workers.

Though we have suggested some practical ways to facilitate worker motivation, we also need to indicate specific ways in which motivation is diminished. Most of these center on the way in which the leader functions in directing the ministry. If the leader's concern seems to stem from self-interest, if volunteers sense a lack of integrity on the part of the leader, if too much is put on too few, if leaders let workers flounder with no direction or encouragement, if goals are set too high or too low, if there is insufficient recognition, then workers will be demotivated.

Here are some specific suggestions to facilitate the motivation of workers for service in the church:

1. Church leaders must be person-centered and not task-oriented.
2. Ministry leaders must earn respect by demonstrating godly character.[12]
3. Every effort should be made to place persons where their wants and desires can be fulfilled.
4. Volunteers should be appointed for a definite period of time.
5. Sustained motivation requires that people know what is expected of them.
6. Praise, recognition, and appreciation should be given when merited.
7. Church leaders should emphasize teamwork rather than competition as a group incentive.
8. Sustained motivation occurs when workers have opportunity to participate in planning and decision making.
9. More attention should be given to effective supervision at all levels of church organization.

A believer's basic motivation for service is to serve God. It is a way in which we can be fulfilled as disciples.

CONCLUSION

In this chapter we have looked at recruiting, training, and motivating workers for ministry. From Ephesians 4 we discovered that this indeed is a major role in ministry. Church staff members and other church leaders must stress the importance of preparing God's people for works of service. As we do, ministries will be blessed with volunteers to perform the service, and the mission of the church will be accomplished.

NOTES

1. Kenneth O. Gangel, *Team Leadership in Christian Ministry* (Chicago: Moody, 1997), p. 321.

2. Dennis E. Williams and Kenneth O. Gangel, *Volunteers for Today's Church* (Grand Rapids: Baker, 1993), p. 21.

3. Margie Morris, *Volunteer Ministries* (Cincinnati: Standard, 1994), p. 154.

4. George Barna, *The Second Coming of the Church* (Nashville: Word, 1998), p. 49.

5. John Cionca, *Inviting Volunteers to Minister* (Cincinnati: Standard, 1999), p. 58.

6. Williams and Gangel, *Volunteers for Today's Church,* p. 40.

7. Ibid., pp. 48–50.

8. Adapted from Galilee Baptist Church in Denver, Colorado.

9. Williams and Gangel, *Volunteers for Today's Church,* pp. 59–60.

10. George Barna, *Leaders on Leadership* (Ventura, Calif.: Regal, 1997), p. 262.

11. Hal Kenton Pettegrew, "The Relationship of Organizational Factors and Motivation and Satisfaction among Volunteers in Evangelical Protestant Churches" (Ph.D. diss., Trinity Evangelical Divinity School, 1993), 150.

12. Barna, *Second Coming of the Church,* p. 166.

SMALL GROUPS IN THE LOCAL CHURCH

19

Julie Gorman

THE VALUE OF SMALL GROUPS

Newsweek introduced the decade of the '90s with a cover story devoted to the phenomenal popularity of support groups now undergirding our society. Near the middle of the decade, Robert Wuthnow published a book that argued "the small-group movement is beginning to alter American society, both by changing our understandings of community and by redefining spirituality. . . . Not only are small groups attracting participants on an unprecedented scale, these groups are also affecting the ways in which we relate to each other and how we conceive of the sacred."[1] Forty percent of adults in the United States claim membership in a small group for regular support and care. Roughly seventy-five million Americans regularly find strength in a small group source. This means there are approximately three million groups in existence, averaging one group for each eighty persons living in the United States today![2] There is no denying the fact that people value their small group experience.

In the race to survive, many churches have responded to this phenomenon by developing small group programs with a specific focus on accomplishing biblical mandates. The problem is that because these generic groups were often quickly added to the church's marketable menu without the benefit of deeply rooted theological convic-tion or direction toward the actual needs of local people, churches that saw this addition as the remedy for a declining membership discovered that these groups died as quickly as they had arisen.[3]

Still, the church cannot ignore small groups. As we move into the new millennium, the church finds itself struggling to live out its identity as a community reflecting its theological beginnings and seeking to portray what is uniquely Christian about relationships in a society that is content to blur its values. Though changing, small group programs will continue to play a major role in God's work throughout the next century. The challenge for the church is to find a way to integrate the benefits of small group ministry in such a way that it is done with theological integrity and programmatic quality. Such is the intent of this chapter.

WHY PEOPLE JOIN SMALL GROUPS

If you have never participated in a small group, you may be wondering what special attraction brings people together in such a manner. What contribution do small groups bring to our lives that make them so profitable to our individual and corporate well-being? There are as many different reasons for joining a small group as there are types of groups. Theologically and culturally, we recognize certain innate reasons for our desire to band together with others into small groups. There is something about a small group setting that stimulates us at the core of our being. After all, God created us to be relational, to crave interaction with our own kind. "Interpersonal relations are central to the quality of every person's life. . . . Evidence of the deleterious effects of isolation and the loss of important people in our lives reinforces the conclusion that relationships are critical to our well-being."[4] In essence, participating in small groups contributes to our personal wholeness and well-being while also making corporate contributions.

Interpersonal Contributions of Small Group Membership

Psychological well-being requires the presence of others. In detachment from others, we fail to develop in healthy ways and experience the detrimental influence of loneliness and isolation. To be excluded is excruciatingly painful. Indeed, it was the worst punishment a Hebrew could face. The threat of shunning and rejection caused people to behave according to their professed values. To feel loved makes life worth living. To know that I matter to someone gives life meaning and purpose.

Our sense of identity and self-worth is influenced by the feedback we receive from others. Most people find they need this interaction in order to feel secure in who they are and what they desire to become. Some studies have shown that people join groups to validate their attitudes, opinions, and beliefs about themselves. Relating to another tends to shape perspective, clarify thinking, and reassure a person that he or she has validity as a thinking, feeling, and acting individual. This is an important part of defining our identity and gaining a sense of worth, as a person gathers and processes information about self and one's experiences.[5]

Support and recovery groups are also proven methods for helping people develop new patterns of behavior. Freedom of disclosure leads to a desire to respond differently. The encouragement and supportive presence of others can encourage us to face up to difficult issues or areas where growth is needed and can cause us to move to new levels of obedience and growth. It is no accident that most programs that require discipline (e.g., weight loss, exercise) are accomplished by part-

nerships or group accountability. It is also true that most people would identify their spiritual growth periods in life with the accompanying presence of a supportive group community.

People also join groups for the assurance that others have felt pain similar to their own and have survived. The presence of others who have encountered similar pain and suffering brings peace and comfort to those still in need of consolation. Support and recovery groups bear out the truth of Ecclesiastes 4:9–12. Being able to disclose the truth one harbors about self or circumstances brings a freedom and sense of empowerment to move on in the midst of life's disappointments.

Corporate Benefits of Small Group Membership

Beyond these individual reasons, there are also a number of corporate reasons why people join small groups. Paul spoke of the need for all the members of the body (church) of Christ to relate together in a spirit of mutual dependence and respect (Rom. 12). The body of Christ is far more effective when it comes together in community and participates together in the functioning of ministry. It was the apostle Paul's conviction that when believers joined in community they could accomplish far more than when they lived in social, relational, and spiritual isolation from others.

It was fitting that after Peter and John were threatened by the religious authorities, they sought support from a group of believers who prayed that they all might speak the Word of God with boldness and power (Acts 4:23–31). Joining together in groups can help us accomplish what would be difficult or impossible alone. The combination of complementary giftedness, counsel of many, and united voice and effort, which join together to design and carry out ministry projects or to move to new depths of insight, is not available to the individual alone.

Another corporate benefit of forming and joining small groups is that these groups help equip us for the work of the ministry. "The personal attention and interaction possible within a small group setting make it an ideal equipping center. Sometimes the skill development is intentional, such as learning how to study the Bible, counsel other Christians, or evangelize. Many times a member is equipped with skills in subtle ways, simply by being an observer or participant in the group situation."[6]

People join small groups for both personal and corporate benefit. Our well-being as individuals and also as a local church body is enhanced as we meet together and discuss things that will improve the way we live and how we relate to those around us.

IMPORTANT CONSIDERATIONS IN THE DESIGN OF SMALL GROUPS

Snowflakes and small groups have something in common: No two are alike. The combination of variables in a small group is infinite. Many of the variables are identifiable, however, and tend to produce certain patterns of response in a group—whether that group be a Bible study, a recovery group, a committee, or a planning task force. Over the many years that small groups have been the target of research, we have learned what makes some groups highly effective and what can spell a quick death to the group. A summary of some relevant findings will guide us in the development of a small group ministry for the local church. Seven of the most essential elements of small group design will be discussed here. They are: purpose, commitment, size, configuration, timing, leadership style, and climate.

1. *Purpose.* Talking openly about a shared agreement of what a group will do and what it will not do is vital to the group's health. It is important to verbalize what the group hopes to achieve and to stress that it is only for those who want this as a purpose. "Too many times persons join a group thinking it will be one thing when there was no intention of going that direction. Or they get involved in a group that will ask from them something they are unwilling or unable to give."[7] Expectations and hidden agendas are some of the most deadly saboteurs of small groups, so it is important that the group's purpose be clearly communicated to all.

2. *Commitment.* In addition to clearly communicating the purpose of the group, it is also important that the expectations and responsibilities of group members be stated up front. Expectations need to be communicated to potential group members regarding such issues as frequency of meeting; attendance requirements; group status

(open or closed); confidentiality; accountability; each members' share in providing housing, food, or leadership in the group; and out-of-group requirements (e.g., homework, retreats, socials). The resulting group will be more effective once everyone knows the level of commitment that is required. When it comes to being responsible, what you don't know can hurt you.

3. *Size.* The size of the group will be influenced by factors such as purpose, available facilities, associated costs, frequency of meeting, and so forth. For example, the group will most likely be smaller if you (a) expect everyone to participate and assist in planning, (b) require accountability, and (c) hope for a deeper level of intimacy. The group may be larger if you simply desire broad exposure to a particular topic, desire greater diversity, have a larger pool for planning, and don't require everyone to participate (anonymity). "Most researchers agree that for optimum discussion and involvement five is an ideal number."[8] Keep in mind that an increase in size will also mean a multiplication of relationships that are possible.[9]

Group Size	Relationships
2	1
3	6
4	25
5	90
6	301
7	966

The size of the group influences the self-awareness, behavior, and level of communication among its members. When the number includes more than eight, there is a greater likelihood of experiencing silent members who don't contribute. This, in turn, affects the other dynamics of the group. Increase in size often means there is less follow-up to what a member says, some members appear to try to control others, and the leadership tends to take over. The larger the group, the less likely it is that vulnerable people will feel comfortable sharing their feelings and personal pain.

4. *Configuration.* The effects of space and seating have been well-documented and are easy to test. Being too close or too far away impacts comfort level, subject, and manner of sharing (e.g., facts over feelings). People sitting in a small room will usually sit farther apart than if in a large room where they will huddle together. Crowding is not just physical—it is also psychological. Rows, cir-

cles, facing one another, grouping around a table—each is a hidden persuader for how the person must act. Sitting at the corner of a table or behind someone will often signal nonparticipation. Sitting at the end or in the middle of a group and positioning in relationship to the leader influences the role a person will play in the group.

5. *Timing*. Frequency of meeting is a powerful predictor of response. The higher the frequency, the more likely the members will trust and open themselves to one another, which in turn affects other dynamics of the group. The duration of time spent together also impacts response. Groups that tend to meet for less than ninety minutes experience much less cohesion. Those that eat together, retreat together, and play together will bond more quickly. Likewise, the longevity of a group most definitely shapes its personality. Moving through stages is like growing up as a group and elicits its own unique phenomena. The beginning of a group creates expectations that are quite different from the period of confrontation, which is like night and day compared to the congenial cooperative and productive stage. When these groups, sometimes referred to as a cohort, have been together for years, they create their own culture. Having an awareness about the time factor can help identify and explain many attitudes and behaviors that can contribute to a small group's personality.

6. *Leadership style*. The leader's role, style, personality, and experience will influence the effectiveness of the group. An autocratic and controlling leader will likely produce a group that is dependent or in rebellion. The group may feel safe, but it will be immature in assuming responsibility. This group will have little vested interest because it is the "leader's group." Therefore, they will be hesitant to open up and share their innermost thoughts and feelings. A laissez-faire leader who fails to take charge may create frustration, insecurity, anarchy, and a feeling that "we aren't going anywhere." Groups led by this carefree approach may suffer from low morale and commitment. A leader who dominates the group as guru invites nonparticipation. A leader who needs to be seen as a messiah, fixer, rescuer, or resident counselor will condition the group to meet those roles. Effective group leaders will understand the need to be flexible in their leadership style as the

group grows and as individual group members gain confidence and skill.

7. *Climate*. Leaders and group members themselves determine what their group will become by establishing spoken or unspoken standards of behavior. Statements such as, "It's okay to disagree here," "The leader always occupies that chair," or "No one ever sits on the floor" all communicate standards of expectation. A major standard is whether the group is "open" or "closed." To be "open" means new persons can enter at any time, and it's acceptable to bring a one-time visitor. "Closed" means the group is limited for a designated period of time to those who committed themselves at the beginning. Both of these standards can affect the group positively and negatively.

Open groups work well for quickly assimilating people but often don't provide the stable relationships conducive to intimate sharing and caring. Closed groups are better for developing long-term, intimate relationships but can become exclusive. Content-oriented groups "lend themselves to a 'y'all come' approach. On the other hand, groups that stress relationships and are primarily process-oriented need to have fixed memberships."[10]

Closed groups often have smaller numbers and higher commitment to attend, while open groups may experience wide variation in attendance within a larger pool. Whether a group is open or closed is often determined by the purpose of the group. Many prefer to be open for the first few weeks and then closed once the group establishes some momentum.

Each of these important considerations has an impact on the effectiveness of the small group. A discerning student of small group dynamics will take these factors into consideration when designing the small group experience. Knowledge of these considerations will go a long way in helping to ensure a positive small group experience for all concerned.

ORGANIZING A SMALL GROUP MINISTRY PROGRAM IN THE LOCAL CHURCH

With any new program in a church, there will be a degree of suspicion regarding its usefulness and need. Other ministries are competing for limited resources, and some degree of education and communication is needed before the plan to develop a small group ministry in the local church is implemented. It is helpful to start with an understanding about just where this venture will fit into the existing Christian education program. Neal McBride suggests three types of churches that tend to shape and be influenced by a ministry of small groups. They are the Traditional Church, Transitional Church, and Transformational Church.

> In the Traditional Church groups are one programmatic option; groups must compete for resources and participants; groups are not viewed as essential to the nature or functioning of a local church; group membership is purely optional; none to moderate pastoral support for groups is present. In the Transitional Church groups are an integral part of the church; group membership is highly encouraged, if not expected; groups are viewed as being essential to the nature and functioning of the church; strong pastoral support for groups is evident. In the Transformational Church identity is focused in groups or house churches; group membership is equated with church membership; groups are the nature of how the church functions; pastoral leadership is focused on group facilitation.[11]

The origination and maintenance of groups falls on a continuum between *centralized control* (which offers total supervision with centralized decision making) and *decentralized control* (which encourages a grassroots ownership of the ministry). The former often hires professional staff to lead this emphasis and runs decisions through official church structures. The latter gives the power to initiate, determine, and maintain this ministry to the congregation, with paid staff serving only in a supportive position.[12] Leaders of a centrally controlled small group organization may assign group membership according to geography and determine that all members need to be in a group. Leaders of a decentralized small group organization limit their control and may not even know how many groups exist in the church.

The structure of the church's small group ministry can also fall on a continuum. On one end of the spectrum are groups that are spawned and exist as parts of existing structures (e.g., Women's Missionary Union, an adult Sunday school class), or they may be completely separate from any existing structures and draw membership across diverse lines (e.g., divorce recovery, grief recovery, parents of teens in crisis).

The themes of the church's small group ministry may be oriented around a particular emphasis such as spiritual maturity or church membership. They can be offered on a consecutive and repeating format, such as spiritual maturity: enfolding, discipling, equipping, and releasing, with each of the topics sponsoring a different group. Another approach to selecting themes for small groups is to have an emphasis on specialty groups. This allows for greater variety of topics that are chosen based on the needs of the group. Examples of this type of theme would include parents of mentally challenged children and veterans in career transition.

Likewise, in the structuring of the individual groups themselves, there are widely accepted ways of accomplishing what goes on. Some groups are highly structured to fit the exact same pattern, feeling this ensures quality control and keeps groups on target with the church's purpose for them. Others call for inclusion of certain generic elements such as loving, learning, doing, and deciding but allow each group to determine its own expression.[13] Still others allow the group itself to determine which elements and structure best fit the purpose and content.

When it comes to the types of groups that may operate in and through the local church, individual and corporate creativity are the only limits. There are many organizing formats. Some common types of small groups that are currently operating in many local churches across North America today include:

- Groups for belonging: evangelism, new member, house church, intergenerational
- Groups for knowing: new believers, Bible doctrines, discipleship
- Groups for healing: support, recovery awareness, self-help recovery
- Groups for serving: leadership development, missions, task/project, ushers

- Groups for enriching: covenant, affinity, worship, prayer[14]

Some of the different paradigms churches use to organize their small groups include:

- Relationship-oriented groups: assimilation, growth, recreation
- Content-oriented groups: Bible studies, discussion
- Task-oriented groups: leadership, service, advocacy
- Need-oriented groups: recovery, support, group counseling, self-help[15]

These organizational alternatives demonstrate the wide variety of methods that can be used to structure and staff the small group ministry of the local church. Since the leadership of the small group ministry is critical to its overall success, it might be advantageous to provide the reader with more detailed guidance regarding this important aspect.

LEADERSHIP DEVELOPMENT IN SMALL GROUP MINISTRIES

When it comes to small group ministries in the local church, there are two common approaches: professional leadership and volunteer leadership. Each has its advantages and disadvantages. Each requires a certain level of training and skill development. Any way you add it up, leadership is a major component, perhaps even the most important component, of a small group program.

There are many myths and misconceptions about the nature and use of leadership. Some of these misconceptions result from adapting a secularized business approach toward leadership to the ministry. Others prefer to adapt the autocratic military "chain of command" style to church governance. Regardless of how leadership is explained or defined in our present culture, it is regularly connected with such synonyms as *power, authority, control, influence, direction,* and *person at the top.*

However, the Bible doesn't seek the input from either the business or military models. It proposes its own style of leadership as a basis for ministerial oversight. This biblical model is called servant

leadership. The definition of leadership found in the New Testament incorporates three essentials: "Leadership is a servant ministry, based on spiritual gifts and always plural."[16] This radical style of ministry pictures a leader serving by being "so attentive to followers that he or she acts out leadership as a ministering to the needs observed in others. There is no ego building, no feeling of control or superiority—only a desire to fulfill the other in the relationship."[17] Groups need leaders who are attentive to God and willing to facilitate members becoming all God wants them to be.

Relational power not only influences but is open to the influence of another. There is an exercising of strengths and giftedness and a receiving from others what God has given them to contribute to community. This kind of leader does not have to have all the influencing potential. Rather, he or she serves and releases others to fulfill their roles as influencers and initiators in spiritual well-being, in equipping of one another, in processing issues, and in coming to decisions. "It is presumptuous to believe that God would expect one person to personify all that is needed by members of a community. . . . The gifts of group members join with the giftedness of the leader in bringing about the community God has designed."[18]

The kinds of leaders needed in a small group ministry are determined in large part by the size of the small group ministry and the diversification of responsibility. A large church model will be presented here so the reader will have a more comprehensive perspective. Obviously, in a medium-sized church one person may assume several of these roles. In a small church one volunteer leader may end up providing the leadership for all of these roles—though that would certainly not be the ideal situation.

1. *Small Group Pastor.* The pastor of small group ministries is the person who provides the primary oversight for the scope and breadth of the program. He or she is the strategist who designs and facilitates the overall small group design. This individual provides the mission, meaning, and purpose of the church's venture into small group ministries. He or she promotes understanding, awareness, and assessment of this ministry. He or she also plans intentional, ongoing development and stimulation of those who minister in small group settings, works with and equips the team of small group coordinators, and seeks to integrate

this ministry emphasis with other components of the Christian education program.[19]

2. *Small Group Coordinator(s).* Numerical growth leads to an expanded ministry necessitating some type of leader to care for and coordinate the leadership and work of these multiplying units. This person or team of persons is called the small group coordinator(s). This person is responsible for encouraging, problem solving, motivating, and facilitating the ministry of each small group under his or her care, as well as enabling communication and cooperation between groups. Coordinators work best when assigned no more than five to eight groups.

3. *Small Group Leader.* This lay minister plans and guides individual group meetings. This leader usually serves best when working within a predetermined structure, with format and materials provided. Leadership may be shared by a team made up of the content/process facilitator who plans and leads the group experience and a host/hostess who cares for logistical and relational details. Other roles may arise, such as event coordinator (retreats, socials, etc.), project coordinator, and childcare coordinator.[20] These leaders may be designated, leadership roles may be rotated among group members, or leaders may assume a combination of the roles above.[21]

The ways and means of helping people become more knowledgeable and proficient in their leadership ministry are numerous. Here is a sample of eight popular training methods that can be used:

1. The *training event* is a one-time workshop or seminar that focuses on teaching a particular skill such as "how to lead a discussion." It works to prepare leaders for a quick start-up of small groups.
2. The *group conference or retreat* may be a day or weekend and provides concentrated time for developing a skill or idea within the context of live relationship building. It is good for jump-starting and cultivating enthusiasm.
3. The *class* or *course* usually extends over a period of time and requires regular commitment. It is most effective when the methods used are reproducible by participants in their groups. A class needs adequate time prior to group start-up or can be integrated into ongoing small group ministry.

4. *In-service learning/apprenticing* is ongoing mentoring in an actual small group situation within a relational setting. This training method needs good, ongoing groups and leaders who know what they are doing and why.
5. *A model group* serves as a pilot experience of observing and copying the leader, along with explanation and feedback. This method is good for long-term small group effectiveness and overcoming old patterns.
6. *A self-study tutorial* using manuals, tapes, and books is ideal for self-starters who have an accountability source to keep them motivated.
7. *Existing groups and committees* can utilize regular gatherings to include group-building ideas and skills as part of their continued growth and effectiveness as a group.
8. *Using a professional consultant or attending a conference* are two means of being exposed to "experts" and "experienced practitioners." This teaching method builds enthusiasm as expanded awareness of group interest is encountered. The knowledge gained must be translated into the local situation. This method requires a budget.[22]

SMALL GROUP MINISTRY IN THE TWENTY-FIRST CENTURY

What is the future of small groups in the church as we enter a new century? While the role of the prophet is a precarious one, it might be worth the risk to point out what some feel will be the future of this ministry as we venture into the new millennium. I believe three trends will impact the future of the small group movement: (1) the desire for community, (2) demographic trends, and (3) how the church responds to a changing culture. These are by no means comprehensive.

Community is attractive to today's parishioner. Speaking of the appeal of community, futurist Lyle Schaller notes, "The word *community* has now surpassed the word *first* when choosing the name for a new congregation. . . . In one way or another, nearly every Christian congregation on the North American continent today boasts about the feeling of community the members enjoy."[23] The word exerts magic with the promise of supportive networks and a new definition of what constitutes family.

With spirituality a hot commodity and congruence a challenging dream in today's world, people have a hunger to process how their inner spirituality can be expressed in their outer lifestyles. Small groups will provide context and opportunity for this.

"Relating" is in. While rules have taken precedence in the past in our American culture, this emphasis has been replaced with the higher valuing of relationships. This is evidenced in the relational emphasis in teaching, preaching, evangelism, motivating, and supervising. The work of ministry now seems to center on people. The focus of newsletters is now on the stories of people and how their lives have changed or on citing people's accomplishments and thanking them for service.[24]

Generation X will significantly shape groups in the future. Among other things, Xers will challenge small groups with their quest for understanding truth in a world of ambiguity. Their questions are ultimately religious ones to which the Christian community must respond: "Will you be there for me?" "I believe; help my unbelief!"[25] Self-interpretation causes people to seek out others to hear and clarify their own stories.

The attractive multiplication of megachurches offering full-service ministries within a large congregational complex make it even more necessary for people to connect in small groups within their neighborhoods. Those communities will provide the closeness of belonging while enjoying the benefits of what these megaministries provide. The large number of people involved will foster increasing diversity in the different types of small group ministries available. The increase in house churches may be another response to this hunger to be a somebody in the midst of large numbers.

Seniors will the be fastest growing segment in the church, and their needs will significantly affect the kinds of groups that will be formed in the future. High on their priority list will be groups for the recently widowed, as well as for those coping with Alzheimer's, Parkinson's, aging parents, and retirement, and groups for empty nesters, mission project volunteers, and so on.

Diversity and choice will continue to be important. With both available in other spheres of living, people will expect the acceptance of diversity and the provision of many options, with frequent change acceptable as the norm in such groups.

Robert Wuthnow notes the following concerns relating to churches and small groups:

1. We face an overemphasis on "will it work" and tend to accept Scripture as truth only if it helps us get along better in everyday life. "Groups generate a do-it-yourself religion, a God who makes life easier."[26] "Sacred" is identified as little insights that the group intuitively embraces as right. Traditional insights compiled over the ages seem less important. There is the feeling that "if it works for me, it must be true."[27]

2. Likewise there is a tendency to "use" groups as portable support systems to "benefit me." They are disposable when I no longer need the kind of help they can give or they begin to make me uncomfortable in how I am living by challenging me to live by a higher rule.

3. People want community but not a community that is binding. They want the spiritual but not one that requires us to serve the sacred instead of the other way around.[28]

4. Will groups of the future continue to become the self-help tools that remain viable as long as they "support my goals?" Or will they hold forth a higher challenge to know and live in obedience to the higher One who created community to reflect himself?

It is far from clear what kind of society we will have in this new century. One thing is clear, however: The search for community and for the sacred will continue to characterize the American people.[29] This quest will bring many people to the church who might otherwise not be drawn toward a spiritual answer. Small groups have been referred to in theological circles as the "back door" to the church because those who enter the influence of the church through these avenues would not otherwise come through the main entrance. But regardless of which door they enter through, the church has a biblical mandate and moral obligation to provide for these individuals in grace, acceptance, and unconditional love. This is surely the model that was presented to us in the life of Christ. People long for a sense of connection to God and other people. Small groups provide an opportunity for people to make that connection. It is a vibrant and fast-growing ministry in many churches across North America today. Some churches use their small group ministry as the central organizing rubric for all other church programs. It may not be the elusive key to growth and happiness that many churches are looking for, but it certainly is one possibility among many that are being espoused by church growth experts today.

NOTES

1. Robert Wuthnow, *Sharing the Journey: Support Groups and America's Quest for Community* (New York: Free Press, 1994), p. 3.

2. Ibid., pp. 45–46.

3. Julie A. Gorman, *Community That Is Christian: A Handbook on Small Groups* (Wheaton, Ill.: Victor, 1993), pp. 284–85.

4. David W. Johnson and Frank P. Johnson, *Joining Together: Group Theory and Group Skills,* 4th ed. (Englewood Cliffs, N.J.: Prentice-Hall, 1991), p. 472.

5. Gorman, *Community That Is Christian,* p. 108.

6. Julie A. Gorman, "Dynamics of Small Group Ministries," in *Christian Education: Foundations for the Future,* ed. Robert E. Clark, Lin Johnson, and Allyn K. Sloat (Chicago: Moody, 1991), p. 513.

7. Gorman, *Community That Is Christian,* p. 135.

8. Ibid., p. 132.

9. William M. Kephart, "A Quantitative Analysis of Intragroup Relationships," *American Journal of Sociology* 60 (1950), cited in Rodney W. Napier and Matti K. Gershenfeld, *Groups: Theory and Experience,* 6th ed. (Boston: Houghton Mifflin, 1999), p. 40.

10. Neal F. McBride, *How to Build a Small Groups Ministry* (Colorado Springs: NavPress, 1995), p. 83.

11. Ibid., p. 46.

12. Gorman, *Community That Is Christian,* p. 300.

13. Carl George, *Prepare Your Church for the Future* (Old Tappan, N.J.: Revell, 1991), p. 89.

14. Gorman, *Community That Is Christian,* p. 308.

15. McBride, *How to Build a Small Groups Ministry,* pp. 75–76.

16. Gilbert Bilezikian, *Community 101: Reclaiming the Church as a Community of Oneness* (Grand Rapids: Zondervan, 1997), p. 262.

17. Gorman, *Community That Is Christian,* p. 265.

18. Ibid., pp. 265–71.

19. See ibid., pp. 265–72; cf. McBride, *How to Build a Small Groups Ministry,* pp. 109–16.

20. Gorman, *Community That Is Christian,* pp. 272–74.

21. McBride, *How to Build a Small Groups Ministry,* p. 89.

22. For further help in this area of training and factors to help determine which to implement, see Gorman, *Community That Is Christian,* pp. 276–80; McBride, *How to Build a Small Groups Ministry,* pp. 126–31. Both Pilgrim Ministries and Stephen Ministries also offer training information and assistance.

23. Lyle E. Schaller, *The Seven-Day-a-Week Church* (Nashville: Abingdon, 1992), p. 75.

24. Lyle E. Schaller, *21 Bridges to the 21st Century: The Future of Pastoral Ministry* (Nashville: Abingdon, 1994), pp. 29, 31.

25. Tom Beaudoin, *Virtual Faith: The Irreverent Spiritual Quest of Generation X* (San Francisco: Jossey-Bass, 1998), p. 141.

26. Wuthnow, *Sharing the Journey,* p. 357.

27. Ibid., pp. 358, 363.

28. Ibid., p. 365.

29. Ibid., p. 21.

LEGAL AND ETHICAL ISSUES IN MINISTRY

20

Ken Garland

Ministry has changed a great deal across North America over the past few decades. Pastors and church staff are having to face issues that they never dreamed possible while training in seminary. The litigious nature of society has crept into the church, forcing many congregations to defend themselves against challenging lawsuits. This chapter will discuss a host of contemporary issues that are being dealt with in many churches today. It is my hope that ministry leaders will learn from these principles in order to more effectively plan religious activities and foster a safer environment for ministry.

CASE STUDY #1

Don and Robert serve as pastors to young and single adults on the staff of a large church in their city. Recently, Doug, a young man in the singles group, came to each of them and asked if they would fill out a recommendation for him to enter a master's degree program at a local university. Doug had been part of their singles group for a few years, and since Don and Robert believed him to be a solid leader in the group with strong personal character traits, each of them agreed. They completed the reference forms and sent them to the university with accompanying letters extolling Doug's character and capabilities.

Doug was accepted into the program and began school.

Some months later, a young woman in the group came to Don and Robert and indicated that she had been having a sexual affair with Doug. The affair had lasted for several months, and she had not said anything about it because she believed Doug loved her and that she was the only love in his life. Recently, though, she had discovered that at least two other women in the group were also having sexual affairs with Doug, and she was devastated by the news.

Don and Robert discreetly investigated and discovered that as many as five different young women in the singles group had been having some kind of intimate relationship with Doug over a period of more than a year. When they confronted Doug, he admitted to the affairs after denying them at first.

In light of the new developments, Don and Robert contacted the university and notified the master's degree program director there that they would have to rescind their recommendations for Doug and explained why. Subsequently, Doug was dismissed from the master's degree program because of the actions of Don and Robert regarding the recommendations they had originally submitted. Doug retained an attorney and sued Don and Robert and their church for ruining his graduate degree program plans.

Case Study #2

Sandra serves on the pastoral staff of her church as director of women's ministries. She has been in that position for more than five years and has served with excellence and distinction.

Recently, she and her staff colleagues selected eight women to serve on a leadership council for the women's ministry program. Each of the women selected was interviewed regarding her personal life, spiritual depth, and leadership capabilities. The eight women were selected and affirmed as leaders for the ministry.

Some months later, Sandra learned that two of the women were lesbians and were using their leadership roles in the women's ministry program to promote alternative lifestyle values and to encourage other women to explore their own sexual preferences openly. Sandra and another staff member of the church confronted the women involved, and they admitted that most of what Sandra had learned was true.

As a result, the two women in question were removed from their leadership roles in the group and also removed from the women's ministry program of the church. The two women secured an attorney and sued Sandra and her church for violation of their personal civil rights.

Churches and their professional and voluntary staff are not immune from lawsuits that may arise from alleged negligence in some aspect of their ministry. In both case studies cited, the churches and staff members involved as defendants in the lawsuits were found not liable in the actions that were filed. However, the lawsuits cost the two churches involved thousands of dollars and hours of time, not to mention the emotional strain placed upon the staff members who were sued. It is unlikely that either church will ever recover the costs of defending their staff in the two actions.

This chapter is not intended to be an exhaustive discussion of all the legal ramifications involved in the practice of ministry. The legal issues discussed in this chapter are the issues most likely to be faced by those working in the various Christian education functions of the church's ministry.

The federal government has, for the most part, steered clear of creating laws governing the practice of religion by churches or parachurch organizations, choosing rather to leave that to state and local government agencies. The laws that do exist vary greatly from one location to another. Five major areas of possible legal liability will be discussed: (1) the issue of liability insurance, (2) the use of medical release forms for participants in church activities, (3) the issues involved in international travel, (4) issues of privileged and confidential communication, and (5) issues involved in church discipline.

Liability Insurance

Whether or not your state requires it, it is a very wise church that chooses to protect itself with a comprehensive liability insurance policy. Basic liability coverage will protect the church in the event that someone is injured or suffers some other form of damage on church property. A variety of additional coverages can be added to the basic coverage in the form of what the insurance industry calls "riders."

Perhaps one of the most important riders on a liability policy related to the practice of Christian education ministry is protection against injury or damages suffered by a person or persons while participating in any kind of church-sponsored activity. Many churches provide a wide variety of activities, trips, and experiences for children, youth, and adults, and these churches need a comprehensive liability policy with appropriate riders that will protect the church and its workers in as many of these situations as possible.

Full Liability Coverage versus Coinsurance

The first significant issue to be dealt with by the church is whether it will purchase a full liability policy or a liability coinsurance policy. While the rules can vary somewhat from company to company, generally a full liability policy will pay a claim to an injured individual for any injury or damage suffered that is not specifically excluded from coverage in the policy. This type of policy will pay the claim regardless of whether the injured individual has other insurance that is equally liable or not. For example:

The youth pastor of First Church recently took a group of high school students roller-skating at a local skating rink. Earlier this year, First Church purchased a full-coverage liability insurance policy that guarantees coverage of all persons involved in church sponsored activities, whether these activities were held at the church or elsewhere. One of the boys in the group took a nasty fall at the skating rink and broke his arm, requiring immediate emergency medical care as well as follow-up care for several weeks following the injury. Because First Church has a full-coverage liability insurance policy, the insurance provider will reimburse the injured boy's family for the cost of medical treatment due to the injury, even though the skating rink also has an insurance policy and the boy's family has a health insurance policy, either of which would also have paid for all or part of the costs of treatment.

The cost of full-coverage liability insurance has become prohibitive for many churches, especially smaller ones. These churches have discovered that there is a way to protect themselves while at the same time greatly reducing the amount of their budgets that must be set aside for insurance coverage. This is called liability coinsurance. In many states, the annual premium cost for liability coinsurance is less than half that required for full-coverage liability insurance. There are several varieties of coinsurance, but the basic idea is that the coinsurance policy will pay for any injury or damage that is not covered by some other full coverage liability or health insurance policy. For example,

The youth pastor of Second Church took his youth group skating at the roller rink. Second Church is a new and small but growing church that needs to make sure it is getting maximum benefit from all money spent. So Second Church invested in a liability coinsurance policy. At the skating rink that night, a student from Second Church fell and was injured and needed immediate emergency attention as well as long-term medical treatment. When contacted about the medical claim, Second Church's insurance provider said, "We will gladly pay any claim arising from this injury that isn't also covered by some other type of insurance." In this case, the injured student's family has

a family health insurance policy that will pay for 80 percent of the cost of the medical care the student needs to recover from the injuries suffered. Therefore, the church's coinsurance policy will pay for the 20 percent of the cost that the family's health insurance does not cover.

If the church has selected liability coinsurance as its choice for insurance, church members and participants in church activities need to be fully informed of that choice. Parents of children and youth who participate in church activities will almost always assume that if their child is injured on a church activity, the church has full insurance coverage to pay for treatment or other costs related to the injury. If the church has coinsurance, that is not always the case, so some form of disclosure to parents and other church activity participants is the ethical thing to do. It will also help to keep injured parties from developing hard feelings about the church's coverage or even taking some form of legal action against the church because they were not informed.

Exclusionary Riders

The basic insurance policy your church purchases is a very simple document until additions called exclusionary riders are added. Each of these riders excludes something from the liability coverage. Churches opt for these riders to help reduce the cost of insurance premiums. The wise Christian education leader will carefully read the church's insurance policy (along with a board member who understands the legal language of the policy) to determine if exclusionary riders are in place.

There may be several of these riders. One common type excludes from coverage any injury that occurs during a church activity deemed excessively dangerous. Activities such as snow or waterskiing, rock climbing, white-water rafting, and others are examples that often show up in exclusionary riders.

A second type of exclusionary rider may limit or exclude coverage for injuries or illness on the part of a participant whose physical condition puts him or her at higher risk than normal while participating in the activity. Participants with chronic asthma, epilepsy, or certain physical handicaps, or who are mentally challenged in some way may be excluded from coverage by a rider.

A third exclusionary rider that may be part of your policy concerns insurance coverage for drivers on officially sponsored church outings. Many Christian education workers in churches that own buses know the minimum age of drivers who would be covered by the church's insurance policy. Few Christian education workers know whether the church liability policy contains a rider stating a minimum age for any drivers of other vehicles providing transportation for a church-sponsored outing. It is not uncommon for a church liability policy to contain a rider stating that coverage is extended only for drivers who are twenty-one years of age or older. Many riders even exclude adult drivers with less-than-exemplary driving records.

MEDICAL RELEASE FORMS

Every time a Christian education worker conducts a ministry activity with children or young people under the age of eighteen, he or she is taking a significant risk. The risk is that at any time or any place one of those children or young people could become injured or ill and need medical attention. In most, if not all states, obtaining professional medical care for a minor without the signed consent of his or her parents or legal guardians is extremely difficult and in some cases impossible. In some states, these forms must be signed and the signature notarized by a notary public to be legally binding. A sample medical release form that would be acceptable in the state of California appears at the end of this chapter. If you live in another state, consult with a hospital or doctor's office in your town and have them show you the form they use when parents bring children in for treatment at their facility. Under normal circumstances, if you model your form after the ones used by medical professionals in your community, you will be safe.

Since the parents or legal guardians will be signing this form, it is appropriate to put other necessary information on it as well in such a way that their signature indicates that they have read and understand the information on the form. This is also a good way to notify parents of the kind of liability insurance your church has and which kinds of activities are excluded from coverage.

Not only should you have a medical release form signed by parents or legal guardians for each trip or activity that your church sponsors for children and youth, but you should have medical release forms on file in your Sunday school or church office that give permission for medical treatment if needed during routine church and Sunday school activities. Your church may be one of many that has a number of children or youth attending whose parents do not come. Any one of those children or youth could become injured or ill during Sunday school, worship service, or another activity and be in need of emergency medical care. If you cannot reach the parents by phone or some other means, it will likely be difficult for you to get medical treatment quickly. However, if you have signed consent forms on file (usually updating them annually is sufficient), you don't have to worry if you cannot get in touch with the injured or ill child's parents right away.

Furthermore, it is also a good idea to have signed medical release forms with you for any adult who may become injured or ill on an activity. If one of your adult participants suffers an injury or illness that causes unconsciousness or loss of mental function, having a presigned medical release form for that person will facilitate getting medical attention quickly.

INTERNATIONAL TRAVEL

Mission trips to sites outside the United States have become an effective and popular ministry activity in many churches. It should be noted that in most cases your church's liability insurance will have a rider excluding coverage for travel outside the United States and Canada. Thus, your church could be found liable if a participant on an international trip or activity becomes ill or injured. Flight insurance, which can be obtained through a local travel agent or at the airport, usually covers such things as baggage loss, terrorism, or cancellation of flights, but it rarely covers the individual against liability claims while on the trip.

Christian education leaders who are planning mission activities outside the United States should do two things: (1) use a professional travel agent experienced in international travel to help plan the trip, and (2) consult with an attorney who specializes in international travel to get help in drawing up a specific liability waiver for participants in the international activity. While the cost of retaining such an attorney for about two hours of work may seem high, the waiver produced by the consulting attorney may well save the church thousands of dollars in liability costs later on.

CONFIDENTIALITY AND PRIVILEGED COMMUNICATION

Another legal and ethical issue that often arises for the Christian education worker has to do with situations when the worker is told things in confidence by another person, either in a counseling session or perhaps by a colleague in ministry. The question that arises is, "When am I allowed to keep a confidence, and when could I be required by law to reveal what I've been told?"

Generally speaking, there are two types of protection of the privilege of confidentiality: (1) the individual being counseled is protected from voluntary disclosure by the receiver of the information, and (2) the receiver of the information is protected from being compelled to disclose it by state law, a court of law, or a court of the church.[1] In other words, the parishioner in a counseling situation is protected against the counselor divulging what he or she (the parishioner) told the counselor in a counseling situation. Second, the ministry worker cannot be compelled to reveal something that was stated to him or her in confidence in most circumstances.

Communication is deemed confidential when one of the three following criteria is met: (1) confidentiality is a requirement or a tradition of the church, (2) confidentiality is an ethical or legal duty imposed by a license, or (3) confidentiality has been promised by formal or informal agreement between the person giving information and the person receiving it.[2] An example of the first criterion would be the Roman Catholic sacrament of confession. An example of the third criterion is a counseling situation where a Christian education worker has agreed to keep a confidence, and the parishioner involved has understood that the information given is to be kept in confidence.

There is currently no state that issues any kind of license for lay or professional ministry workers that would have anything to do with confidentiality. However, it would apply if the pastor is also a licensed marriage, child, and family counselor.

"So how does all this apply to me?" That question arises for the Christian education worker often. "In what context am I likely to hear information that may need to be kept in confidence?" There are at least six situations in which this kind of information may come up: confession of sin, spiritual counseling, emotional counseling, a comment in a small accountability or support group, a prayer request in a prayer meeting, and casual personal conversation.[3]

The next question that arises for the Christian education worker is, "How do I know if something I heard is something I could be required to voluntarily disclose?" In most states, the first consideration is whether or not the worker is ordained clergy, licensed clergy, or nonordained church staff. In most situations, ordained clergy enjoy rather sweeping and broad protections against being compelled to disclose confidential communications. Licensed clergy, on the other hand, enjoy protections related strictly to the limits of their license. Finally, in most states there are few protections against compelled disclosure on the part of volunteer workers.[4] It would be a good idea for Christian education workers to consult with persons in their churches who understand the local and state laws to become aware of the disclosure requirements in their state.

There are several situations in the state of California (and many other states) where a Christian education worker is required to report information to local authorities. The first of these is where the worker believes the person with whom he or she is dealing represents a potential harm to a third party and the potential victim is identifiable. In this case, the worker is required by law to warn the potential victim and involve the authorities that are necessary to protect the potential victim.[5]

The second case where disclosure is required by California law is in the case of suspected child abuse. California law defines child abuse as physical injury inflicted by other than accidental means—sexual abuse, unjustifiable punishment, willful cruelty, or neglect—and includes abuse in an out-of-home care facility.[6] In this case, the Christian education worker should consult immediately with his or her pastor and church board. If there is enough evidence to give rise to a reasonable suspicion of child abuse, a report must be filed in writing within thirty-six hours of the knowledge or reasonable suspicion.[7]

THE ISSUE OF CHURCH DISCIPLINE

The New Testament has much to say about discipline within the local church. Matthew 18 provides a procedure for the redress of a grievance between two members of the body. In 1 Corinthians 5 and 2 Corinthians 2, the apostle Paul addresses some of the disciplinary needs of the church in Corinth and basically tells them to discipline themselves or he will have to discipline them on his next visit there. In 1 Timothy 5, the apostle Paul gives instructions to a young pastor regarding the discipline of the members of his church. The fact is that God expects the church to be a disciplined body.

Secular government has historically realized that it is best to defer to church courts or councils when it comes to disciplinary issues within the church. However, in recent years there have been several cases where individual church members have sued churches and pastors in situations where the individual members were made subject to church discipline. How can a church protect itself and its workers from such a court action?

There is no way for a church or its workers to be guaranteed that they can't be sued for a disciplinary action against an individual member. However, there are some steps that the church and its workers can take to reduce the risk of losing a lawsuit following a disciplinary action.[8]

1. *Teach regularly and often about the disciplinary role of the church.* Christian education workers should make sure that students in their adult classes are clearly taught the disciplinary steps the church will take related to various infractions of the church covenant.
2. *Explain to potential new members the requirements of their commitment and the potential for discipline if they breach it.* Christian education workers should make sure potential new members clearly understand the require-

ments for membership and the penalties related to violation of those requirements.
3. *Ask new members to sign the vows of their commitment at the time of their membership.* Christian education workers should seek the affirmation of new members regarding the rights of the church to apply discipline.
4. *When discipline is necessary, carefully follow clearly defined procedures.* A Christian education worker should never carry out discipline on his or her own. Rather he or she should seek the support and involvement of the pastoral staff and the official church board, and all involved should follow the defined procedures carefully.
5. *Do not allow unsubstantiated charges to be publicly proclaimed by the church.* Christian education workers must be extra careful not to be the conduit of these unsubstantiated charges. It is both legally dangerous and ethically wrong to spread these charges to other people.
6. *Base disciplinary decisions on biblical grounds, and frame them that way.* Christian education workers should work with the pastoral staff and official church board to make sure that Scripture supports the disciplinary actions being proposed, and they should further be prepared to articulate that biblical position wherever necessary.
7. *Publish the disciplinary action, relating only the necessary information, and substantiate the whole action with scriptural support.* Christian education workers should support the disciplinary action taken by the church and refuse to participate in gossip or idle conversation about the one disciplined or the action itself.

Keep in mind that the main objective of spiritual discipline is the restoration of the individual. Too many churches get themselves into trouble by placing too much emphasis upon the judgment and conviction of the sinner, without enough concern being placed on the restoration process. When discipline must be done in the context of the local church, it must be done in love, with compassion for the sinner and with an eye toward the restoration of the individual if/once he or she has repented and taken appropriate actions.

CONCLUSION

We live in a time when people are anxious to cash in on a large settlement they think might be forthcoming from a civil lawsuit. In many cases, the church and its employees have not been at fault and are the innocent victims of harmful litigation. However, in some cases people have been seriously hurt and even killed because of the negligence of well-meaning church leaders. There is much that should be done to protect the lives and safety of those for whom the church is responsible. Vehicles and equipment must be properly maintained, volunteer staff must be adequately screened and trained, employees should receive guidance about church policies and procedures, and church boards must be educated about eliminating unnecessary risk.

There is virtually nothing a church can do to keep a determined litigant from suing for civil damages. However, there are many suggestions contained in this chapter that will enable a church to have some confidence that the plaintiff who files a lawsuit against them cannot win the suit in court. Due to the ever-changing nature of this subject, the wise church board periodically consults with an attorney who specializes in First Amendment or personal injury law for updates and advice. It is up to the church to prove beyond a doubt that it has done all that it could reasonably do to protect and serve those who participate in its ministries. Numerous publications are now available for churches on how to protect themselves from liability risks. Wise ministry leaders will avail themselves of this information on an annual basis.

NOTES

1. Jerry Mackey, "The Clergy and Legal Liability" (seminar, Fuller Theological Seminary, 6 February 1986).
2. R. R. Hammar, *Pastor, Church, and Law* (Springfield, Mo.: Gospel Publishing, 1983).
3. Ibid.
4. Mackey, "The Clergy and Legal Liability."
5. H. N. Maloney and T. L. Needham, *Clergy Malpractice* (Philadelphia: Westminster, 1986).
6. Mackey, "The Clergy and Legal Liability."
7. Ibid.
8. L. L. Gumper, *Legal Issues in the Practice of Ministry* (Franklin Village, Mich.: Psychological Studies and Consultation Program, 1981).

A sample medical release form
CENTRAL BAPTIST CHURCH MEDICAL PERMISSION SLIP

Name _____

Home phone _____ Work phone _____

Address _____

The person named above has an unusual medical need as stated below:

_____
_____
_____
_____
_____

___ I/we the undersigned do hereby give permission to Central Baptist Church and its representatives to obtain any necessary medical treatment for the person named above during the conduct of any program, ministry, or activity sponsored by Central Baptist Church.

___ I/we want the person named above to ride only with adult drivers approved for coverage on the church's liability insurance policy.

___ I/we will allow the person named above to ride with adult or teenage drivers not officially approved for coverage on the church's liability insurance policy, and

___ I/we have our own insurance coverage for this person in the event of injury.

Signature of parent(s) or legal guardian(s) _____ Date _____

NOTE TO PARENTS: Central Baptist carries only liability coinsurance. This means that should your child become injured or ill on a church-sponsored activity, your own family medical insurance will be billed first. If you have no insurance or if your insurance doesn't cover all necessary medical costs, our policy will make up the difference.

PART FIVE

Christian Education Applied to the Family

FAMILY LIFE EDUCATION

21

Judy Ten Elshof

amily life education should be centered in the home, supported by the church, and grounded in both biblical theology and strong intimate relationships with God and others. This means that guiding, training, and educating the next generation's spiritual lives is primarily the responsibility of parents in the home. When a couple is blessed by God with a child, their covenant task is to train that child to be in relationship with God in order to fulfill the purpose for which he or she was created. This is no easy task.

The values and virtues that knit together a healthy society begin to be formed in the everyday routines and choices of the family. "For better or for worse, the family remains the cornerstone of human development."[1] Family ministry is a central function of the church, for it provides the structures for healthy family life. The church needs to play a key role in society by modeling a healthy church family that is able to function and relate together regardless of the family and ethnic diversity in the makeup of the church. In order to accomplish this, our ministry programs must not be restricted to only the traditional family but be broad enough to include other family structures that are also evident in our communities. Therefore, a church that ministers to families recognizes this and elevates its service to meet the diverse needs of the contemporary family.

BIBLICAL FOUNDATIONS OF THE FAMILY

The best model for the development of a theology of the family is the relationship between God and the children of Israel. Myron Chartier has suggested that if God's actions toward Israel are taken as a model, parenting of children will be characterized by loving, caring, responding, disciplining, giving, respecting, knowing, and forgiving.[2] These characteristics are combined into four biblical themes by the Balswicks in their book *The Family*.[3]

Covenantal Commitment

The first theme is commitment, which is to be based upon a mature (i.e., unconditional and bilateral) covenant. The first covenant is found in Genesis 6:18, where God establishes a covenant with Noah. This covenant demonstrates unconditional love from God as parent to Noah. Later in Genesis 15:18, God extends a covenant to Abraham and his descendants. God's commitment was not based on Noah or Abraham's acceptance; rather, it was the same unconditional commitment that parents should have to their children. This unconditional love of God is demonstrated in the New Testament in 1 John 4:19: "We love because he first loved us." It is also beautifully articulated in Romans 5:8, which reminds us that God's love is lived out for us in the fact that "while we were still sinners, Christ died for us."

Parents are more equipped to make unconditional loving commitments to their children when God's covenant love first comes to them through the community of the body of Christ, the church. The church, through the grace of God, brings love, kindness, goodness, and discipline with gentleness to families so that their primary relationships (marital and children) are transformed by the mere experience of being exposed to healthy relating patterns. One needs to receive love in order to give love.

The paradigmatic passage is found in Hosea 2:16–20, which portrays the covenant and marriage between Yahweh and Israel as a mirror of the faithlessness of Israel and the faithfulness of Yahweh. This passage, according to R. S. Anderson, shows that covenant love is realistic, responsible, and resourceful.[4] Let's look at each of these characteristics in light of covenantal parenting.

A parents' covenant of love that is realistic is one that is not built on expectations of what the parents hope the child will become. Rather, parents become students of their children, discovering who each child was created to be by God. This ever-evolving picture needs to have at its foundation the two diverse parts of human nature: being created in the image of God and also possessing an inevitable sin nature brought on by the fall (Gen. 1:27; 3). Parents have the responsibility to recognize each child's giftedness, which is different from their own strengths and weaknesses, and not allow unresolved issues to create problems in these areas. Parents then need to choose to love the child as he or she is, with full knowledge that there is no ideal. This unconditional love includes a realistic acceptance of a child's unfaithfulness.

Second, the parent's covenantal love acts responsibly towards the child. This means that the parent is responsible to lay the foundational seeds that will help the child maintain the delicate balance of becoming an individual who is faithful to God and being faithful to the community to which he or she will someday be responsible. Although in our secular culture parental responsibility is not a contractual agreement, within the Christian community a covenantal promise should be made to the community that

cannot be broken. This means the Christian community will hold the parents accountable to their promise of responsibility to the child and the community.

Third, the parent's covenantal love is resourceful. The parent promises to empower the child to become the individual and community participant that God uniquely created him or her to be. This quality of parenting that reflects God's parental love goes beyond merely fulfilling parental responsibility—it actually initiates growth and addresses issues in the life of the family. It involves helping the child to heal from any experiences that would potentially take him or her away from the path God intended. This may be done through listening to and grieving with the child and then teaching confession, forgiveness, and reconciliation with God, self, and others in the community. In this process, parents empower by loving freely without strings of their own needs attached. Parents who are consistent and trustworthy in providing both grace and truth are like the refreshing dew that comes in the morning (Hos. 14:1–9).

The desire of God in each initiated covenant was that his unconditional commitment would be reciprocal and mutual just as the parents' desire is for their children to respond with unconditional love back to them. This can best be experienced when parents age and become dependent on their children, and love is returned.

Atmosphere of Grace

The second biblical theme is that family life is to be established and maintained within an atmosphere of unmerited favor, which embraces acceptance and forgiveness.[5] Unconditional love necessitates the grace to accept and forgive in light of one's flaws and shortcomings. God the Father models ideal parenting skills by graciously accepting us through his Son's incarnation, death, and resurrection. Christ's coming in human form makes our own forgiveness possible, which in turn gives us the ability to forgive others. Just as God does not expect us to trust him without first proving his immeasurable love, so parents cannot expect their children to follow their orders with blind obedience without first providing a loving context in which to understand that rules are intended for the good of the child. As parents are trustworthy in giving their children love and acceptance, children can trust them to love and direct them. Rules, just as the law, guide the way to God and should not be present to restrict or punish.

The church again needs to be actively modeling the redemptive process of forgiving the sins of its members. Hebrews 12 says loving discipline that includes forgiveness is good for everyone, parents and children alike. As the church creates an atmosphere of grace that includes acceptance and forgiveness, a model will be established for parents to raise their children within an atmosphere of grace.

Empowerment

The third biblical theme suggested by the Balswicks for family life is empowerment.[6] The resources of family members are to be used to empower rather than control one another. To empower means to be active and intentional in the process of enabling another person to acquire power. Jesus rejected the use of power to control others; rather, he demonstrated and affirmed the use of power to serve others, lift the fallen, forgive the guilty, and encourage growth and responsibility in the weak. God's work in people's lives is empowering. Jesus said, "I have come that they may have life, and have it to the full" (John 10:10). John 1:12–13 says that to those who believe in Jesus, he gave power to become children of God. Ephesians 4:13 and Galatians 5:22–23 say that this power to have the characteristics of God is unlimited. Members of a family applying this truth could give to each other out of their areas of strength—whether that is joy, kindness, self-control, peace, or patience—in an unlimited way. Successful parenting allows children to gain in personal power while the parents retain their power.

How can the church help parents empower their children? By empowering the use of parents' gifts in the body of Christ. If parents feel impotent, with no value in the body of Christ, they will feel powerless to empower their children. But if the church provides an empowering structure by equipping parents to ever-growing levels of impact at home and in the community, then parents will have an experiential model of how to empower their own children.

Intimacy

Finally, the fourth theme of biblical families is intimacy, which is based on a knowing that leads to caring, understanding, communication, and communion with others. In its perfect state, intimacy is the ability to stand completely open and transparent before God and other people, with nothing to hide. All of us long for a place like that, where there is acceptance and love just the way we are. Adam and Eve stood that way before God prior to the fall (Gen. 2:25). We, as members of the body of Christ, are encouraged to give our deepest feelings and thoughts to God in prayer, and God will understand us (Rom. 8:26–27). His forgiveness made this possible. Oh, how we long for this kind of intimacy within the community of the body of Christ!

Intimacy has to be expressed directly and indirectly and experienced objectively and subjectively. Only then will it bring comfort, adventure, negotiation, and stability to the relationship.[7] Anderson explains that comfort comes through nourishing the bond of attachment. Adventure is experienced through creative communication and interaction. Negotiation in conflict resolution reinforces the relationship. And finally, stability is established through loyalty to a covenantal commitment to the relationship. As Rodney Clapp proposes, covenantal fidelity is the necessary foundation for intimacy, because "intimacy is strengthened through complex commitment."[8]

If this kind of intimacy has never been experienced, parents may wonder if it is possible and more than likely will not have the resources to provide it to their own children. As we suggested earlier, members of a family are intimate when they are able to fully experience comfort, adventure, negotiation, and stability in their relationships with each other.

These four biblical themes of covenant, grace, empowerment, and intimacy are the elements of Christian family relationships that operate in a continual process. The Balswicks put it this way: "Intimacy can lead to deeper covenant love, commitment fortifies the atmosphere of freely offered grace, this climate of acceptance and forgiveness encourages serving and empowering others, and the resultant sense of esteem leads to the ability to be intimate without fear. The end product of this process is deep levels of communication and

Figure 21.1
A Theological Basis of Family Relationships

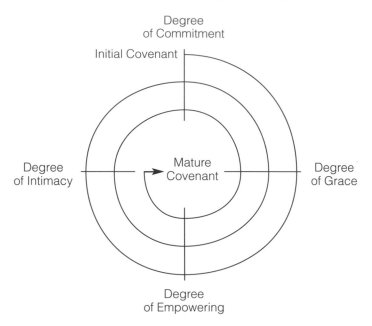

knowing."[9] This is demonstrated in figure 21.1, which was taken from the Balswicks' book. It depicts a spiraling inward in order to represent the potential for family relationships to grow into ever-deepening levels of mutual commitment, grace, empowering, and intimacy.

The church needs to make family life education a priority by developing a community that practices and models these four biblical themes of covenant, grace, empowerment, and intimacy within the body of Christ. James Houston suggests that the depth of intimacy in human relationships is what will bring depth to relationship with God.[10] "Children live what they learn and learn what they live."[11] This is particularly true today for parents who have come from broken homes and relationships. They have not experienced covenant love and trust because trust has been broken in their primary relationships. Often they are not able to trust God and experience love and intimacy with him. It is paramount, therefore, that family life education begins with the experience of these four biblical foundations within the church community that will empower parents to model with their children what the church has given them. In a sense, the body of Christ corrects or repairs unhealthy relating patterns that are inevitably transferred from generation to genera-

tion. Because "the church is the social agent that most significantly shapes and forms the character of Christians," the church must take seriously its redemptive role in shaping healthy families.[12]

This kind of covenantal understanding between the church and parents and parents and children would provide the family unit with the ability to fulfill the Great Commission, to go out into the world and preach the gospel. Second, there would be continuity of purpose between past generations and generations to come. This is what would give society stability, rather than Christian families standing isolated from society.[13] Third, such a covenantal understanding would provide the family unit with a sense of mission and destiny that exchanges ideas, resources, and productivity with the greater society. A biblical understanding of God's purposes for Christian life would drive this sense of mission and propel the family into effective outreach in the following areas: evangelism, teaching, healing, aid, and discipleship. "The Christian home is a mission base. It is where we strain and labor and sometimes weep in service of the kingdom. But it is also where we learn to 'do' mission as rest and play."[14] The Christian family then could deepen its relationship with the rich moral tradition of our faith and no longer be a safe haven separate from the world.

HISTORY OF FAMILY TRENDS

Historically, the family has had a powerful influence on society. Many of the major societal problems that are evident today reflect the values and quality of family life. Traditional values such as respect for authority, standards of moral conduct, teaching about right and wrong, not cheating or lying, and so on, are values that should be communicated to children from their parents in the context of the home.

Parents need to learn to teach what they believe, model Christian attitudes, and model values that they want their children to have when they are adults. So not only are biblical values to be articulated and spoken in the home, but they need to be integrated into all the areas of family life so that children are discipled in the ways of God by their experience of home life.

While espoused beliefs have not fundamentally changed within the evangelical tradition, societal factors have shaped the Christian worldview more than most Christians would like to admit.[15] As the modern family continually departs from biblical values that used to be engrained in secular mores, the cultural repercussions become increasingly evident. Unfortunately, the Christian family often reflects the trends and values of current culture or marginalizes itself against society, rather than being an agent of change in a wayward culture.

Figure 21.2 illustrates the types of changes that have taken place in our homes over the past few decades. These changes have influenced the values and trends in our society as a whole.[16]

Figure 21.2
1960s

I. Trends
- A. Cast off all restraints
  1. Social: dress, civil disobedience
  2. Academic: campus protests, cheating
  3. Emotional: "tune out" on drugs, postpone pain
  4. Sexual: the Pill facilitated a new revolution
- B. Vietnam War
- C. Civil rights movement
- D. Women's agenda

II. Values
- A. Lost respect for all forms of authority
- B. Guidance was primary role of school
- C. Musicians were the idols of the youth
- D. "Drop out" mentality and lifestyle of society
- E. Communes replaced the family and led to rise of cult leaders

III. Family:
- A. Mothers:
  1. Lost respect as caregivers
  2. Seen as authority figures
  3. Reject the role of authority
  4. Explore alternative roles
- B. Fathers
  1. Tried to "rule the roost"
  2. "Absent father" syndrome
  3. Role confusion leads to divorce
  4. Search for meaning

IV. Adolescent Rites of Passage:
- A. Boys
  1. Smoke marijuana
  2. Get a job
  3. Have sexual intercourse
- B. Girls
  1. Get a job
  2. Pursuit of dreams
  3. Have sexual intercourse

1970s

I. Trends
- A. Baby boomers entered the work force
- B. Wanted it all now!
- C. Personal debt skyrocketed
- D. Concern was for credentials and marketability
- E. Lost our urgency to solve the world's problems
- F. Focus now on self-gratification
- G. Egocentric materialism is national pastime

II. Values
- A. Material possessions in all markets
- B. Peers are the primary source of values
- C. Most popular TV shows reflect national values
  1. *Love Boat*
  2. *Fantasy Island*
  3. *Gilligan's Island*

III. Family
- A. Mothers
  1. Join women's movement
  2. Want equal jobs, pay, rights
  3. Go to college en masse
  4. Seeks divorce as escape
- B. Fathers
  1. Quest for self-identity
  2. Midlife crisis literature
  3. Self-absorption
  4. Recreational toys

IV. Adolescent Rites of Passage
- A. Boys
  1. High school sports
  2. Status (car, macho images)
  3. Drugs
- B. Girls
  1. High school sports
  2. Status (clothes, boyfriend)
  3. Drugs

Figure 21.2 (continued)
1980s

I. Trends
  A. Major demographic changes in our cities
  B. Mood: mixture of confidence and caution
    1. Confidence in business growth, economy, etc.
    2. Caution due to insecure future
  C. Patriotism strong once again
  D. Reliance on computer technology
II. Values
  A. Gender harassment no longer tolerated at work
  B. High reliance on litigation to solve problems
  C. Half of all college students work 20+ hours per week
  D. One in four admit to no use of the library in a week
  E. Most popular TV shows reflect national values
    1. *Dukes of Hazard*
    2. *Muppet Show*
    3. *M*A*S*H*
    4. *Sha Na Na*
    5. *Dance Fever*
    6. *Happy Days*
    7. *Mork and Mindy*
  F. "Anything goes" moral and ethical code: 43 percent of high school females and 47 percent of males had sex
III. Family
  A. The children run the home
  B. Creation of the first filiocentric family system
  C. New phenomenon: "latchkey" children
  D. U.S. level of child abuse is a national disgrace
  E. 1980 census report: 48 percent of those born in 1980 will be raised in a single-parent home
  F. Increased discipline problems in school, low achievement
IV. Adolescent Rites of Passage
  A. Boys: anabolic steroids, computer hacking
  B. Girls: "fitting in" is a major source of stress

1990s

I. Trends
  A. Communicating through technology (cell phones, pagers, E-mail, Internet)
  B. Distrust of and overdependence on government
  C. Distrust of school systems—shootings, homeschooling
  D. Economic optimism—stock market hits record highs
  E Lack of social control—random violence, carjackings, road rage, gangs
  F. Lack of integration between faith and life— compartmentalized view of skills and character
  G. Lack of time—busyness equals success, no reflection

II. Values
  A. Nonparticipatory entertainment—movies, TV
  B. Family protection—overprotection due to an amoral society
  C. Dependence on government—social security and Medicare need to be saved
  D. Individualism with need for community as seen in TV shows like *Friends* and *Seinfeld*
III. Family
  A. Crisis of authority and morality
  B. Dichotomy between private and public life
  C. Diverse backgrounds and linguistic styles
  D. Generation gap
  E. Isolated nuclear family
  F. Lack of community support and control
  G. Increased family dependence on mass institutions
  H. Equalization of power within the family
  I. Family as a unit of consumption instead of production
  J. Separation of work and family life
  K. Individual and family worth determined by economics
IV. Adolescent Issues
  A. Finding a place to connect and belong because this is so often missing from the family
  B. Negative attempts: gangs, sexual connections, Internet, pornography, addictions, anorexia/ bulimia, drugs, teenage pregnancy

As one can see, in forty years families have moved from conservative to liberal, from saving to spending, from respect to harassment, from family units to family disillusionment, and from parents heading the home to children being at the head. We have developed a new value system that tends to dominate Western youth.[17] A summary of these changes include:

- Personal relationships count; institutions don't.
- The process is more important than the product.
- Aggressively pursue diversity among people.
- Enjoying people and life opportunities is more important than productivity, profitability, or achievement.
- Change is good.
- The development of character is more crucial than achievement.
- You can't always count on your family to be there for you, but it is your best hope for emotional support.

- Each individual must assume responsibility for his or her own world.
- Whenever necessary, gain control—and use it wisely.
- Don't waste time searching for absolutes; there are none.
- One person can make a difference in the world—but not much.
- Life is hard and then we die; but because it's the only life we've got, we may as well endure it, enhance it, and enjoy it the best we can.
- Spiritual truth may take many forms.
- Express your rage.
- Technology is our natural ally.

In trying to deal with the stress of current trends in society that erode the stability of the family, people have reverted to solutions that have not always proven fruitful. These solutions have created a sense of false hope in people who are searching for real answers to family issues.[18]

In reaction to postmodern relativism and the separation of public and private life, Christians have sought refuge in traditionalism, expert advice, and the privatization of the family.[19] With the introduction of a new level of expectation for interpersonal communication, families tend to run to the newest technique, which reveals an overdependence on formulas.[20] These formulas promise success but often do not deliver the needed solutions that authentic relating offers. In trying to follow techniques as an end in themselves, communication gets separated from the reality of everyday life. "Communication will be greatly improved if it is embedded in the common experiences of developing family relationships."[21]

As the family gets redefined in modern society, the temptation is to become a self-contained unit, to turn to institutionalized help, or to just allow alternative lifestyles to have equal say. These, however, are the false hopes that non-Christians substitute in place of the need for authentic community.[22] The church as the family of God provides a better alternative to the false hopes that are being offered today.

Another problem families face today is their dependence on material possessions.[23] "A major effect of the dominance of commodities has been to change the family from the basic unit of production to the basic unit of consumption."[24] As society puts more and more value on acquiring and enjoying material goods, the value and dynamics of the family change to accommodate the achievement of these goals. The false solutions plaguing us are the desire for economic equality between spouses, community through consumption, and technology's ability to allow work to return to the home.[25]

Instead of buying into these false hopes and merely trying to "Christianize" them, the church needs to provide a biblically based response to the trends that affect the modern family. Figure 21.3 is helpful[26] when considering what the church's role can be to combat unbiblical values and offer real solutions to a world that is living out the consequences of relational brokenness.

Figure 21.3
Creating a Positive Family Environment

Challenges of Modernity	Christian Responses
Dominance of commodities	Release from bondage to commodities
	Employment programs that give priority to relationships
	Family takes precedence over socioeconomic goals
	Church support
	Mutual empowerment (rather than social exchanges) as the basis of family relations
Disintegration of community	Reconstruction of community
	Effective boundaries around the family
	Emphasis on the inclusiveness of the family
Complexity of communication	Revitalization of communication
	Family communication during shared activities
	Development of family rituals
Fragmentation of consciousness	Reintegration of consciousness
	Dependence on the beliefs and values provided by the church
	Openness to people who are different
	Service and witness to Christ

Ministry to families in the church is going to have to meet people where they are and move them toward biblical foundations of commitment based on unconditional love, grace embracing acceptance and forgiveness, empowering rather than controlling, and intimacy leading to caring, understanding, communication, and communion.

MINISTRY TO FAMILIES

It can be clearly demonstrated that dysfunctional families tend to produce more dysfunctional families. Therefore, it is imperative that the church ministers to families in a way that corrects their deficits.[27] This means that churches need to be assessing families on an ongoing basis to determine how they can provide corrective counseling, family enrichment, and other needed resources. The saying "an ounce of prevention is worth a pound of cure" certainly applies when used in the context of family ministry in the local church. Anything that the church can do to prepare its members for the next developmental stage they encounter will be energy well spent. Using the Balswicks' model of family ministry, let's look at what it means to minister to families in each of the essential areas: preparation, enrichment, and equipping.

Preparational Family Life Ministry

Preparational ministry seeks to prepare each individual in the family for the next developmental stage of life. There are physical, social, emotional, cognitive, spiritual, and family transitions that take place with each new developmental stage in the life cycle. These areas need to be examined, understood, and discussed before one reaches the next stage so as to be prepared to meet and live out each stage to the fullest capacity possible in ministry to others in the body. The developmental stages are birth, childhood (early, middle, and late), adolescence (early and late), adulthood (young, middle, and late), and death. Preparational family ministry is illustrated in figure 21.4:

Figure 21.4
Preparational Family Life Ministry

Goal	Rehearsal for upcoming issues
Nature	Educational, preventive, resource awareness
Focus	Large group, with small group experiences; age-graded with interstage testimonials
Process	Input and discussion oriented
Venue	Classroom, ongoing groups (i.e., Sunday school)
Criteria	Internalized educational objectives

Enrichment Family Life Ministry

There are several family life issues that spread over the range of developmental stages. Conse-

quently, individuals need more in-depth understanding and skill to experience them to their fullest potential. Such issues include marriage, parenting, career, and being single. Enrichment ministry is shown in figure 21.5.

The church has often neglected spending time and effort in training and enriching in the areas of marriage and parenting, so these will be discussed in greater detail below.

Figure 21.5
Enrichment Family Life Ministry

Goal	Better coping, new patterns and skills, exploration of alternatives, communality
Nature	Evaluative, experiential, multidirectional, fellowship-based, experimental
Focus	Small group, interest-based, open-ended
Process	Fellowship, communication, nonformal structure
Venue	Homes, interest-response initiated
Criteria	Feedback on intentional use of new skills, flow to redemptive, evangelistic ministries

Marriage. At the center of a family is a marriage. It has often been said that the best gift one can give to children is a good marriage. Yet today society has created confusion and chaos around the commitment and definition of marriage. Charles Sell describes dedicated and conscientious men and women who are caught between society's pressures and proclamations of the church. This dilemma causes sizable amounts of stress and guilt for them.[28] Too often couples in the church are pressured to keep any problems with their marriages under wraps; when the marriages fail, everyone is surprised.

For a church to have a marriage enrichment ministry, the assumption needs to be that most and probably all couples are struggling in some area of their marriages. It may be handling conflict, finances, intimacy, parenting, communication, growing spiritually together, dual careers, roles, relationships with others, distribution of power, trust, jealousy, and so on. The church should help people to take periodic assessments of their marriages. These assessments can help the church to see where resources should be directed. Assessment should be followed by pastoral counsel in choosing what method or action would best help any couple who needs to grow in an area of weakness. Couples today need help and encouragement in maintaining healthy marriages. Instead of feeling guilt over the pressure and failure of marriage, the church can be a safe place for couples to be fortified in the quality of their original commitment to one another.

Parenting. Because conception and birth happen in such a natural way, many believe that being a parent will also come naturally. Not true! One of the goals in parenting is to be able to answer the intergenerational question of how was the parent parented. Unless a person does something consciously significant about what was received through parenting, the same parenting style, habits, and negative effects of sin will be repeated and passed to the next generation.[29] The essential values will then continue to be passed down or overreacted upon. Separating the positive qualities you want to hold on to and repeat from the distortions you want to change and the negatives you want to let go of is difficult but primary.

Exploring these questions in the safe environment of a small group will help parents separate from the way they were parented to be more objective about their own parenting. The context of a small group that can be trusted is important because no one has been parented perfectly, and there is pain in looking at what was missing. Educators and counselors need to be willing to use the gifts God has given them to strengthen the parents in the community.

Equipping Family Life Ministry

Equipping needs to take on a twofold purpose. First, family members need to be equipped to carry out their individual roles in family life. This equipping is done mostly in the areas of preparation and enrichment. Second, equipping needs to be done to carry out the work of the body. This equipping is done by plugging people into areas of service in the greater community. The gifts and strengths of an individual need to be assessed and used to strengthen the body of Christ.

Figure 21.6
Equipping Family Life Ministry

Goal	Congregational leaders in effective ministries
Nature	Watching, listening, exploring, accompanying, interning, practicing, correcting, reproducing
Focus	Small group, supervised team, unleashed ministers
Process	A fellowship-learning group that becomes a ministry team
Venue	Homes, selected leaders, structured process; monthly review and reinforcement
Criteria	Congregational leaders doing effective ministries; redemptive, evangelistic

Remedial Family Life Ministry

Another family life ministry necessary for a local church body to be functioning as a healthy family is a remedial family life ministry. Figure 21.7 illustrates the components of such a program.

Figure 21.7
Remedial Family Life Ministry

Goal	To mainstream formerly dysfunctional people
Nature	Relationship, realization, responsibility
Focus	One-to-one, one-to-couple, families, groups
Process	Therapeutic, ministerial counseling
Venue	Office, as requested
Criteria	Refunctioning, mainstreaming

Figure 21.8[30] shows that parents' first choice for receiving help when they face problems is a member of the clergy. For this reason, a church must have a plan of intervention for assisting families that are struggling.

Families struggle over a wide variety of issues such as burdensome medical bills, physical stress, emotional turmoil, child care issues, and so on. As previously stated, dysfunctions of one generation are generally passed down to the next unless intervention takes place. As the church helps individuals and families evaluate their needs and strengths for ministry on a periodic basis, some people or families will be hurting and struggling too much to be prepared, enriched, or equipped by the mainstream church programs. Rather, they need to heal by being surrounded with love and acceptance from the body and counseled one-on-one until they are functioning and ready to be mainstreamed into the family of God.

CONCLUSION

The church needs to become a safe community if it wants to play a critical role in the reestablishment of the primacy of family. This will require discerning health from dysfunction, discovering strengths and weaknesses, and determining how families can best be met at their points of need and integrated into the church family. Commitment, grace, empowerment, and intimacy need to char-

Figure 21.8
Parents' Choices of Preferred Help on Problems*

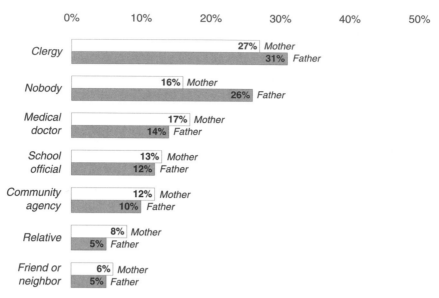

*Percentages reflect the responding parents' first choice for each category.

acterize our church communities so individual families will have a model to follow. Both the church family and individual families should be practicing preparation for new stages, pursuing enrichment in the stage they find themselves in, and equipping for ministry to others in areas of strength while getting remedial help in their areas of weakness. Only in an atmosphere of authentic love, acceptance, and forgiveness can this take place.

NOTES

1. George G. Barna, *The Second Coming of the Church* (Nashville: Word, 1998), p. 190.

2. M. Chartier, "Parenting: A Theological Model," *Journal of Psychology and Theology* 6 (1978): 54–61.

3. Jack O. Balswick and Judith K. Balswick, *The Family* (Grand Rapids: Baker, 1991), pp. 19–33.

4. R. S. Anderson, "Spiritual Formation as Family Therapy: A Social Ecology of the Family Revisited" (lecture, Seattle Pacific University, 1997).

5. Balswick and Balswick, *The Family,* pp. 26–27.

6. Ibid., pp. 27–30.

7. Anderson, "Spiritual Formation as Family Therapy."

8. Rodney Clapp, *Families at the Crossroads: Beyond Traditional and Modern Options* (Downers Grove, Ill.: InterVarsity, 1993), p. 130.

9. Balswick and Balswick, *The Family,* p. 21.

10. James Houston, *The Transforming Friendship* (Oxford: Lion, 1989).

11. Cameron Lee, "Family in Faith Community" (taped lecture series, Fuller School of Theology, 1996).

12. Clapp, *Families at the Crossroads,* p. 68.

13. Ibid., pp. 149–69.

14. Ibid., p. 169.

15. George Barna, *Generation Next* (Ventura, Calif.: Regal, 1995), p. 104.

16. Figures 21.2–21.5 are adapted from Balswick and Balswick, *The Family,* p. 285.

17. Barna, *Generation Next,* pp. 108–15.

18. Balswick and Balswick, *The Family*, pp. 286–87.

19. Ibid., pp. 285–87.

20. Ibid., pp. 287–88.

21. Ibid., p. 288.

22. Ibid., p. 289.

23. Ibid., p. 290.

24. Ibid.

25. Ibid., pp. 290–91.

26. Ibid., pp. 293–95.

27. Charles M. Sell, *Family Ministry,* 2d ed. (Grand Rapids: Zondervan, 1995), p. 46.

28. Ibid., p. 51

29. Cameron Lee, "Parenting Education" (lecture, Fuller School of Theology, 1995).

30. Merton P. Strommen and Irene A. Strommen, *Five Cries of Parents* (San Francisco: Harper and Row, 1985), p. 162.

CHILDHOOD EDUCATION 22

The mere mention of the word *children* elicits many feelings and emotions. To some it is a magical word of youth and freedom. To others it conveys the idea of annoying, loud nuisances. In our society we idolize the "idea" of childhood with romantic notions of carefree days at the baseball diamond or serene moments with a teddy bear and tea. We spend enormous amounts of money entertaining, feeding, and clothing children but rarely spend adequate time teaching and training them.

In almost every aspect of human life, we isolate ourselves from our children. We've created day care, baby-sitting, and nurseries to ensure that our time with them will be limited to the bare necessities. The effects of such a system separate our generations from one another. Children today know fewer and fewer adults and have less opportunities to relate with and learn from them than did their parents or grandparents.[1]

GOD'S PERSPECTIVE: A THEOLOGY OF CHILDREN'S MINISTRY

The Bible opens with a story of the first family. Adam and Eve were created to enjoy fellowship with each other and with their Creator. They were soon instructed to be fruitful and multiply (Gen. 1:28), thus enlarging their family structure. It was always God's intention that children would be part of his creative design. With this importance in mind, it stands to reason that God would provide us with guidance regarding the care and nurture of children. The Old and New Testaments specify clear teaching for parents concerning the physical, emotional, and spiritual care of children. Each adds an element of guidance toward the goal of raising healthy children. A look at the differences between Old and New Testament models will help us gain perspective on the development of biblical principles that can be applied to families today.

Old Testament

The most striking principle gleaned from the Old Testament regarding the upbringing of children is that the spiritual development of the child is done completely within, not separate from, the faith community. Children were included in the daily instruction provided by parents as they went about their chores. They were expected to play a part in the weekly Sabbath meal. In addition to the role parents played in the development of their own children, they also played a parenting role to children within the greater community. Parenting was viewed as a national priority; thus, children were viewed as an integral part of the community as a whole.

It was God's intention that the home would be the classroom for the most important life lessons. The commands that God gave would be passed on from one generation to the next through this means. In Deuteronomy 6:6–7, God says, "These commandments that I give you today are to be upon your hearts. Impress them on your children. Talk about them when you sit at home and when you walk along the road, when you lie down and when you get up." Religious instruction was to be a natural occurrence in Jewish family life. This instruction would guarantee the transference of important values and morals for personal and social conduct. In addition, such instruction would provide a continuance of the rituals associated with their annual festivals and memorials.

Each festival in Israel's year recapitulated significant events in their salvation history. For a child, these must have held the wonder equivalent to our Christmas celebrations today. As the family prepared the meal or sacrificed the lamb, the children were present and participating in reliving their nation's past, a past that shaped a national conscience and governed a new and distinctive way of living. These were times of teachable moments during days of Sabbath rest and play. In Exodus 12:25–27 God instructs the people, "When you enter the land that the Lord will give you as he promised, observe this ceremony. And when your children ask you, 'What does this ceremony mean to you?' then tell them, 'It is the Passover sacrifice to the LORD, who passed over the houses of the Israelites in Egypt and spared our homes when he struck down the Egyptians.'" It was always God's plan that the family home would be the greenhouse for the growth of faith.[2] Every event in a Hebrew child's life was a learning experience. "The camp, public assemblies, temples, religious and secular festivals supplemented the training given through tribal and family customs and occupations."[3]

Underscoring the importance with which Jewish parents viewed the religious instruction of their children, the Jewish historian Josephus writes, "Our chief ambition is for the education of our children. . . . We take most pains of all with the instruction of children, and esteem the observations of the laws, and the piety corresponding with them, the most important affair of our whole life."[4]

New Testament

Very little is mentioned in the New Testament regarding the teaching and training of children. From what is presented, we know that they are to obey their parents (Eph. 6:1); fathers are to bring them up in the "nurture and admonition of the Lord" (Eph. 6:4 KJV); bishops, deacons, and elders are to be faithful and successful in the rearing of their own children (Titus 1:6); and fathers are to be careful not to deal too harshly with their children (Col. 3:21).

Jesus was willing to interrupt his ministry for the urgent needs of a child. For example, while Jesus was busy teaching adults, Jairus came to him with an urgent request to attend to his ailing daughter. All three Gospel accounts indicate that

Jesus immediately stopped what he was doing and went to help her. Likewise, after Jesus came down from the Mount of Transfiguration, perhaps the greatest moment of glory he experienced while here on earth, he quickly laid aside any recollection of that glory to attend to a small epileptic boy in great need.[5]

It is clear that Jesus associated with children and saw them as a priority. Among his most severe warnings are those against causing children to stumble in their fragile faith or causing them to go astray (Matt. 18:5–6). With this short list, we can see the brevity of New Testament instruction regarding child rearing.[6]

Since home groups were the primary meeting place for early church gatherings, the children were most likely in close proximity to the teaching of God's Word. Whether they formally participated or scurried in and out among their parents, they were a vital part of the faith community, taking lessons from the modeling and instruction of their family members.[7]

During the early centuries that followed the formation of the church, there was little provision made for children to gain a formal education. Whether it was teaching basic literacy or instructing in the Christian faith, children were not viewed as an educational priority. It was not until the Reformation that tremendous focus on basic literacy and Bible study began. Martin Luther was dedicated to the educational development of children, but it was John Amos Comenius in the late sixteenth century who was committed to making broad Christian education available for all children.[8]

America was established as a result of the tremendous religious persecution that swept across Europe. Migrations of religious groups such as the Moravians and the Puritans came with the express desire of forming a society where the Bible could be studied and individual religious freedoms would be respected. In the New World the Bible was held in high esteem and used as the basis for laws, social conduct, and family governance. It was one of the primary textbooks in early colonial education. However, in time, an ever-growing secularization began to take its toll on religious priorities. There was soon a need for Christian education apart from formal educational efforts. Though parochial schools served to promote a moderate degree of religious instruction, it wasn't until England's Robert Raikes established the Sunday school movement in 1780 that a revival of Christian education would begin to spread across America.

Raikes placed a priority on teaching children the tenets of the Christian faith. After his initial success in England, he traveled across North America in an effort to form schools where children could learn to read and write by using the Bible as their text. This religious instruction was brought into the church and became the basis for the modern Sunday school.

CONTEMPORARY PERSPECTIVE: CHILDREN OF THE NEW MILLENNIUM

The twentieth century brought a new paradigm for understanding ministry and its application in modern society. In the early decades of the 1900s, there was a renewed emphasis given to foreign missions in both denominational and parachurch settings. Pastors spoke with passion about the urgency of reaching the world for Christ in the current generation. Two world wars made us acutely aware of the depravity of humankind and the need for bringing a spiritual solution to the many geopolitical problems facing the world. Mission agencies such as Samaritan's Purse, World Vision, Far East Broadcasting, radio station HCJB, and Wycliffe Bible Translators were formed with the purpose of spreading the gospel to the remotest parts of the earth. More than any previous era, this era would be known for its emphasis upon foreign missions.

Also, during this time there was an emphasis upon reaching the youth of America. Parachurch organizations such as Youth for Christ (founded in 1944), Young Life (founded in 1941), and Inter-Varsity Christian Fellowship (founded in 1928) provided churches with models for reaching this turbulent youth culture. Teenagers were facing unprecedented issues of sex, violence, war, divorce, and drug dependence. In the 1970s the church responded by adapting these parachurch models, which resulted in the creation of a professional staff member known as the youth pastor. Eventually, the youth pastor became an essential element in most churches.

As we enter the twenty-first century, America has turned its attention to a new group of individuals who seem to be at the highest margin of risk:

our children. With the divorce rate still hovering around 50 percent, 28 percent of children under the age of eighteen are being raised in single-parent homes, compared to 12 percent in 1970.[9] Children have lost the intimacy and security of the home. Those children whose parents remarry have the added adjustment of living in a blended family. This new family model includes more than 40 percent of all children in America. In 1996 there were 6.4 million children living with a never-married mother, as opposed to 500,000 in 1970.[10]

Beyond the obvious difficulties associated with growing up in a single-parent home, child abuse is another rising trend in our country. Take, for example, the following figures:

- Today in the United States, a child is abused every ten seconds.
- In 1996, an estimated 3,126,000 children were reported to Child Protective Services (CPS) agencies as alleged victims of child abuse. Reports have maintained a steady growth for the past ten years, with a total number of reports nationwide increasing 45 percent since 1987.[11]
- Three children die each day as a result of child abuse. Since 1985, the rate of child abuse fatalities has increased by 39 percent.[12]
- Child abuse occurs in all cultural, ethnic, occupational, and socioeconomic groups.
- Child abuse is largely a multigenerational problem. That is, hurtful patterns and behaviors are passed down to children and to their children's children, serving as the catalyst in the vicious cycle of abuse.[13]

This ill-treatment of children has left an ugly scar on the recent history of our nation, and an alarming number of parents have forgotten or ignored what their responsibilities are in the child-rearing process. Our families have strayed far from the biblical ideal for family life, and this gap between what is and what should be makes clear the need for children's ministry within the church.[14]

With children being abused, neglected, and overlooked in our nation, once again the church stepped in to be a resource to the family. In the 1960s and 1970s, the children's ministry was seen as little more than child care and Sunday school. The church usually recruited a volunteer Sunday school superintendent to oversee the volunteer teachers and curriculum ordering. Few churches did much else with children than one hour on Sunday mornings.

Because trust was a social norm, children were simply dropped off, bused, or walked to neighboring churches. Parents were not a necessary component of the structure. However, as the needs of society began to intensify, so did the needs of the church. In order to provide a sanctuary of help, the church needed to be able to track children, screen adult workers, and receive permission and assistance from parents.

During these decades, many churches took a step of faith to pay their superintendents to work part-time in their current positions or hired a director of Christian education to oversee the children's ministry along with youth and adult education. This trend continued throughout the early eighties, with the exception of the bigger churches who had already caught the vision to hire a full-time children's ministries director or children's pastor. As we move into the twenty-first century, we are seeing even smaller churches recruit and hire full-time ministry leaders for children. The job description of this individual includes essential items such as recruiting, screening, and training workers, selecting or writing curriculum, administrating a multidimensional budget, casting

vision, setting goals and objectives, empowering leaders, supervising additional staff, and in many cases, baptizing children and ministering to the diverse needs of the entire family. The role of the children's pastor has grown and expanded over time much like the role of the youth pastor during the latter half of the twentieth century.

SOCIOLOGICAL PERSPECTIVE: AGE-APPROPRIATE CHARACTERISTICS

Having a thorough understanding of any relevant biblical passages regarding children helps one form a theological perspective for children's ministry. In addition, knowing the historical development of the issues involved in developing a children's program puts it in ministry perspective. However, one cannot stop there. A comprehensive understanding of the Christian education of children must also take a serious look at the object of our ministry: the children themselves. Figure 22.1 illustrates what characteristics are appropriate at any given period of a child's physical, emotional, social, cognitive, and spiritual stage of development. Correlating with these various developmental issues are implications for ministry.[15]

Figure 22.1
Infancy (Birth–12 months)

Characteristics	Ministry Implications
• Physical needs predominate • Require adequate rest and nutrition • Need responsive adults to attend to their cries • Active sensory systems—learn through touch, taste; attracted to color and movement • Progress from rolling over to sitting up, crawling, and standing up	• Child care rooms need to be bright, cheerful, roomy, safe, and clean • Cribs, changing tables, and toys require weekly sanitation • Utilize quiet background music • Staffing should be sufficient to provide prompt attention to children's needs • Infants can sense care that is gentle, consistent, and loving and will feel the church to be a safe and welcoming environment • Ministry to infants is also potential ministry to new parents

Toddler (13–24 months)

Characteristics	Ministry Implications
Physical: • Rapid growth • Able to grasp and hold objects • Small-motor control not consistent • Beginning to walk	• Provide both cribs and adequate carpeted floor space • Large, colorful toys with rounded edges and no loose parts • Low shelf space for storage at a height toddlers can reach • Weekly sanitation of toys

Toddler (13–24 months) *(continued)*

Characteristics	Ministry Implications

Cognitivo:

- Language growth—imitation of adult sounds and words
- 5- to10-word vocabulary
- Able to understand simple commands
- Enjoy repetition
- Attentive to stimulation that is novel, surprising, puzzling, and curious
- Short attention span

- Address the child with simple statements
- Simple, one- or two-sentence Bible truth statements
- Use of Bible story pictures
- Clapping, finger movement, and simple songs about how Jesus and God love them and about creation
- Utilization of the "teachable moment," natural conversation about God and Jesus as part of their "play," as opposed to extended teaching time

Social/Emotional:

- Form attachment to primary caregivers
- Conscious of adult presence
- Display wide and unstable range of emotions
- Distinguish between "you" and "me"

- Gentle, calm, and patient teachers will calm the frustrated toddler
- Appreciate familiar routine, caregivers, and room environment
- Feel that church is a safe and happy place to visit

Spiritual:

- Parents and other caregivers are the toddlers' first impression and image of God

- Caregivers in the church who accept responsibility to minister to toddlers as an opportunity to do more than fulfill a "baby-sitting" request

Twos and Threes

Characteristics	Ministry Implications

Physical:

- Large muscle control—walking, climbing, running, and jumping
- Constant movement
- Fine motor skills developing, though not fully coordinated
- Limited endurance
- Working on toilet training

- Rooms with lots of open space
- Toys that encourage use of large muscles (blocks, slides, balls, etc.)
- Offer a choice of activities at any given time
- Craft supplies tailored to fit—jumbo crayons, large pieces of paper, puzzles with minimal pieces, long-handled paint brushes with wide bristles, paint smocks, paste rather than glue
- Utilize interest centers for most of the session's activities
- Provide opportunity for both active and quiet play
- Sufficient staff to be alert to the individual needs of the children
- Provide healthy, natural snacks in small amounts (fresh fruit, crackers, popcorn, juices, etc.)

Cognitive:

- Time-space world is expanding, though still limited
- Elementary reasoning ability
- Learn through the senses; love to explore; highly curious
- Short interest span—two to three minutes
- Elementary reasoning ability
- Vocabulary increasing at a rate beyond comprehension level—enjoy talking
- Love repetition
- Enjoy imitation

- Expect brief participation in activities
- Use simple words from the child's limited vocabulary rather than questions to communicate directions
- Give one direction at a time
- Provide much opportunity for hands-on learning and exploration
- Use objects, pictures, and other visual aids to tell simple Bible stories
- Children need to actively participate in the Bible stories being told: use movement, songs, rhymes, play-acting

Social/Emotional:

- Parallel play—playing alongside the other children, but little interaction with them
- Like to do things without the help of others
- Sense of self and their uniqueness
- Sensitive to adult feelings and attitudes
- Desire close physical contact from caregivers in their environment

- Provide opportunities for the children to play alongside and with each other; encourage and demonstrate "taking turns"
- Learn and use the children's names
- Attend to each child when they are attempting to share personal information
- Avoid shaming any child

Christian Education Applied to the Family

Twos and Threes (continued)

Characteristics	Ministry Implications

Social/Emotional:

- Provide materials and experiences in which each child can find success
- Allow children to work at their own pace
- Demonstrate appropriate love and affection: hugs, cuddling, holding on lap while reading

Spiritual:

- "God loves me, takes care of me, and is with me at all times"
- "God made me, my family, the world, and all that I can see and touch"
- "Jesus is my friend and God's Son"
- "Jesus was born as a baby and grew up to be a man who did good and kind things"
- "The Bible is a special book that tells me stories about God and Jesus"
- "Prayer means that I am talking to God"
- Twos and threes are beginning to distinguish between right and wrong

- Twos and threes enjoy hearing Bible stories and learning simple Bible words
- Lead them in simple prayers to God where they tell him they love him
- Teach and sing happy songs about and to Jesus
- Help these children practice simple ways to obey what they hear read from God's Book

Kindergarten (4–5 Years)

Characteristics	Ministry Implications

Physical:

- Rapid growth with constant physical activity
- Developing muscles require exercise
- Beginning to gain control over small muscle movement
- Great variation in rate of growth among children
- Play is becoming more purposeful and directed

- Chairs and tables should fit the body size of the four and five-year-old
- Provide room to move about
- Offer activities that utilize both large and small muscles
- Gaining in ability to use more sophisticated toys and art materials (however, do not expect neatness and perfection)

Cognitive:

- Eager to learn and curious
- Ask many questions
- Vocabulary far exceeds their comprehension
- Symbolic function appears—able to put thoughts and ideas into words
- Thinking is concrete and not logical
- Egocentric
- Think from particular to particular; unable to generalize
- Enjoy using imaginative and imitative play

- Primary learning mode is through personal exploration; provide many opportunities for firsthand taste, touch, sight, and smell
- Fours and fives love to hear Bible stories
- Constantly review and check for accurate understanding of verses and Bible stories being used
- Make simple, concrete application points
- Avoid using symbolism and figures of speech; words and phrases should mean exactly what the words say
- Provide concrete pictures and objects of subjects discussed
- Rule learning, for classroom management purposes, is difficult, but can be encouraged with consistency and patience

Social/Emotional:

- Tend to be loving and expressive
- Enjoy opportunity to initiate activity on their own
- Beginning to play in groups with other children
- Fears become more prominent
- Self-centered
- Testing limits
- Gender role socialization is occurring

- Praise the child's efforts
- The child needs opportunities to play and learn in groups; watch for teachable moments to aid the child in learning to share and work with others
- Allow the child to express fears; do not deny their validity
- Children need the security of consistent discipline and behavior guidelines; look for chances to reinforce and praise the desirable behaviors
- Staff with both men and women

Kindergarten (4–5 Years)

Characteristics   **Ministry Implications**

Spiritual:

- "God created the world and me"
- "God is good, powerful, loving, and always with me"
- "God cares for me and helps me to do right things"
- "God loves me even when I do wrong things; he will forgive me"
- "Jesus is God's Son"
- "Jesus is my friend"
- "Jesus died on the cross, arose from the dead, and now lives in heaven with God"
- "I can learn about God and Jesus in God's Word— the Bible"

- Help children in choosing and doing simple activities that show their love for God
- Practice being kind, sharing, taking turns, saying "please/thank you" during class
- Provide planned and spontaneous simple worship experiences
- Talk to God in short prayers of thanks and about matters of concern to children
- Sing songs that tell about Jesus and God
- Encourage children to bring friends to church with them
- Encourage children to repeat the Bible stories to others
- Information should be accurate and truthful

Primary (6–7 Years)

Characteristics   **Ministry Implications**

Physical:

- Increased small muscle coordination, though clumsy at times
- Slower growth period; girls tend to be ahead of boys
- Constant movement—need to wiggle
- Like to make things

- Provide activities using such skills as printing and cutting
- Provide opportunity to change activities and pace often
- Provide for physical movement about the room and from activity to activity
- Enact Bible stories
- Create projects relevant to concrete aspects of Bible stories

Cognitive:

- Eager to learn
- Ask a lot of questions
- Still limited in time-space concepts
- Much variation in reading skills
- Tend to focus on only one or two details of a story or experience at a time
- Attention span limited—seven to ten minutes
- Literal thought processes
- Able to use simple categories

- Listen and respond to their questions
- Avoid symbolism in telling Bible stories and Bible concepts
- Avoid object lessons
- Use visual illustrations to support the Bible story
- Plan for active Bible learning involvement
- Do not overly depend on a child's ability to read in utilizing printed curriculum materials
- Emphasize one main point or idea at a time
- Teach the Bible as a book of true stories, not as a story that might be mistaken for one more fairy tale or fantasy adventure

Social/Emotional:

- Need for adult approval
- Sensitive to criticism
- Testing ability to be independent
- Awkward in knowing how to get along with others
- Beginning to pair up with "best friends"
- Competitive with siblings
- Positive attitudes toward school and church
- Moodiness

- Communicate care to each individual child
- Help children in accepting each other and practicing acts of kindness
- Facilitate group activities
- Give time for solitary activities

Spiritual:

- Creation story
- Stories of Bible people and how they obeyed God and so should we
- How to worship God
- "Jesus is God's Son and my friend, and he teaches me how I should live"
- Expand on the events in Jesus' life and ministry

- First and second graders are now able to begin to use their Bibles in simple fashion—looking up a Bible verse and reading it
- Emphasize the truth of the Bible stories
- Provide opportunity for them to experience as much of the Bible story as possible
- Lead them in worship and celebrative experiences

Christian Education Applied to the Family

Primary (6–7 Years) *(continued)*

Characteristics	Ministry Implications

Spiritual:

• The Bible has two main divisions; it also has different books and chapters and verses.	• Encourage children to pray to God with others
• "I can respond in love, worship, and obedience to God"	
• Desire to live like Jesus did	
• Beginning to understand the emotions in Scripture	

Middler (8–9 Years)

Characteristics	Ministry Implications

Physical:

• Active use of developing large and small muscle coordination	• Provide opportunity for children to work at tasks with little assistance
• Increasing in strength	• Focus on participation and trying one's best rather than on winning
• Attempt mastery of basic skills	• Praise children for their efforts at attempting new skills
• Enjoy team sports and other athletic activities	• Design out-of-class experiences for children to play together
• Impulsive in their active pursuits	• Facilitate activities that require following game rules
	• Help children learn to appropriately handle the property of others
	• Challenge children to create projects on their own that illustrate Bible stories and personalities being studied

Cognitive:

• Continued eagerness to learn	• Greater use of the Bible in learning activities—able to locate Scripture passages
• Growing in ability to understand the viewpoint of others	• Beginning to grasp some of the chronological sequencing of Bible events and simple Bible geography—use concrete means to discuss these time-space concepts (maps, timelines, etc.)
• Concerned with the "why" of events	• Enjoy discussing Bible topics, Bible personalities, and Bible stories
• Time-space concept expanding beyond the here and now	• Able to memorize books of the Bible and Bible verses/passages; comprehension should be checked as memory skills exceed ability to understand all of the words and concepts; help children to verbalize and practice practical application of biblical truth
• Continued development of writing and language skills	• Able to learn new games and songs at an increased pace
• Academic achievement becoming important	• Provide for a variety of Bible learning activities that utilize writing, crafts, drama, and music
• Able to comprehend more of the "whole" picture	
• Highly creative and inventive	
• Highly curious	
• Memorization comes easily	
• Refinement of right/wrong concepts	

Social/Emotional:

• Primary involvement with peer group of same-sex friends	• Allow children to work in same sex groups if desired
• Group influence is strong	• Facilitate social activities
• More critical in choice of friends	• Provide opportunities to assume responsibilities within the learning environment
• Sensitive to criticism and ridicule	• Create options from which children can choose learning activities
• Generally outgoing and self-confident	• Provide a wide assortment of varied and unique learning experiences
• Competitive attitudes developing	• Workers with this age-group will become models for the children of what acceptable and Christlike behavior looks like
• Sensitive to fair play	• Capitalize on stories of Bible heroes and strong personalities
• Attentive to adult actions and behaviors	
• Growing in awareness of sex-appropriate behaviors	
• Beginning to separate from family; able to participate in activities apart from the family	
• Developing a sense of humor	
• Experiencing range of emotions—fear, guilt, anger, etc.	
• Enjoy camping and "club-type" activities	

Middler (8–9 Years) *(continued)*

Characteristics	Ministry Implications

Social/Emotional:

- Awareness of current social issues, though not emotionally mature enough to handle all the implications

- Introduce children to more recent Christian "heroes"
- Be transparent with children concerning personal experience of normal human feelings
- Turn current events and social issues into possible curriculum emphases; explore what the Bible says about related topics; avoid abstract discussions

Spiritual:

- Continued expansion into greater detail of basic concepts studied earlier
- "God is all-wise, all-powerful, all-knowing, and always loving"
- "God hears my prayers and answers them"
- "Sin is when I am disrespectful and disobedient"
- "Jesus died for my sin. When I ask for forgiveness, God will forgive me"
- Awareness and understanding of need for salvation
- Awareness of need for God's daily care and help

- Plan activities to demonstrate God's love and kindness to others
- Facilitate participation in mission involvement and support activities
- Provide opportunity to interact with people of other races, nationalities, and social statuses
- Design means for children to become more active members of their local church and its ministries
- Encourage and help children to begin reading the Bible and praying on their own at home
- Provide opportunity for children to give financially to needy projects; include visual aids of how their money will help
- Be prepared to talk with interested children on an individual basis about their need for salvation

Junior (10–11 Years)

Characteristics	Ministry Implications

Physical:

- Rapid physical growth
- Becoming increasingly well-adapted to their bodies
- Fine motor coordination developed
- Boys moving ahead of girls in strength and endurance
- Girls often taller and heavier than the boys
- Tremendous energy and activity
- Increased appetite
- Increasing concern and curiosity about sex (especially among girls)

- Structure active learning activities
- Challenge this age-group with projects requiring greater concentration, inventiveness, and fine motor skills
- Be sensitive to the child who is feeling awkward about his/her appearance
- Discuss with parents the possibility of designing a unit on sexuality and the preadolescent from a biblical perspective

Cognitive:

- Becoming rational, logical, and reasonable
- Development of classification, conservation, and reversibility in thought
- Thinking and fantasizing about the future—considering vocational options
- Curious, questioning, and challenging
- Prefer material that can be learned easily
- Concrete in understanding, though may "parrot" concepts that sound abstract

- Require tasks suitable to their ability level; they fear failure and despise tasks that seem "childish" to them
- Beginning to understand the person and work of the Holy Spirit as someone who helps and guides the Christian
- Able to understand the basics about baptism and the Lord's Supper
- "God's Word is inspired, true, and available for personal advice about daily living"
- Lay foundation for teaching evidence of biblical creation
- Teach children how to use Bible aids like concordances, encyclopedias, and dictionaries
- Encourage memorization of Scripture, but continue to check for concrete understanding and practical application
- Provide opportunity for children to write and create their own responses to application of Bible stories and concepts

Junior (10–11 Years) *(continued)*

Characteristic	Ministry Implications

Social/Emotional:

- Powerful peer group influence replaces adult influence
- Eager to "fit in" with peers
- Fairly stable emotionally; occasional outbursts—become increasingly irritable as approaches puberty
- Enjoy organized group activities
- Working at self-identification and demanding independence
- Desirous of making own choices
- Challenged by basic moral questions
- May demonstrate the beginnings of conflicts with parents
- Beginning to challenge authority and becoming critical of adults
- Hero worship is strong—often choosing heroes from the entertainment and sports industry
- Enjoy competition

- Continue to provide group learning activities
- Facilitate time to be with same-sex peers—perhaps in out-of-class settings
- Be alert for opportunities to engage in conversations with children as communication with adults decreases
- Avoid judgmental attitudes in interacting with this age-group
- Become familiar with their social culture. Discover what TV programs, games, etc. are of value to them
- Adult guidance should be of the low profile variety
- Involve fifth and sixth graders in developing creative service projects
- Utilize Bible stories of people "on the move"
- Bring current topics and issues into the curriculum at a level they can deal with—drugs, alcohol, sex, divorce, abuse, violence, war, etc.
- Facilitate development of their own group identity within the church—their own club, their own room, etc.

Spiritual:

- Share naturally about God with friends
- Increased sense of responsibility toward involvement in church activities and feeling of belonging to the local church
- Deepening feelings of love for God
- Acceptance of Jesus as personal Savior
- Able to seek God's guidance in decision making
- Critical of lifestyle discrepancies they may notice in the lives of family members and/or other Christians in the church

- Able to read and study Bible at home
- Pray regularly
- Encourage them to bring friends to "fun" activities
- Offer Christian reading material appealing to their interests
- Facilitate opportunity to plan and lead both social and Bible learning activities for the rest of the group
- Recruit couples and singles to work with this age-group
- Discipleship and relational emphasis

Though these particular age-appropriate characteristics provide helpful information for the concerned ministry professional, it is also very important to stay informed regarding the various cultural and sociological trends that may have implications for ministry. What worked once may no longer be effective today. Traditional methods need to be evaluated as to their effectiveness. The next section will give the reader an overview of the various ministry models being employed today across North America.

Ministry Perspective: Reaching Children for Christ

Highlighting the need for a relevant paradigm of children's ministry in the twenty-first century, Robert Choun states, "At present, children's ministry suffers from an unfortunate combination of vital importance and low status. The pressures of life today make the need for a ministry to children greater than ever before. Millions are in danger of imminent starvation—emotionally, spiritually, or physically. The pressing question for us is, What should the role of the church be in a society that considers children disposable?"[16]

For many churches, the traditional children's ministry format serves the needs of the local body well. The entire program is propelled by the Sunday school in its standard Sunday morning time slot. There is a nursery staffed by caring mothers who volunteer their time to serve. The children's classes usually cover preschool through grade six. In addition to Sunday school, there may be additional programming such as VBS during one week in the summer, midweek clubs sponsored by CEF, Pioneer Ministries, or AWANA, and summer camp opportunities.

As a church experiences growth, the student-teacher ratio may exceed ideals and the class may be further divided into closely graded groups for age-appropriate learning. If the church experiences growth and decides to expand to two or more worship services, this action will pose a dilemma for the children's workers. They will have to decide if they will offer the same program twice (e.g., during each service) or design an alternative program for the children during the second worship service. Often, churches have opted for a children's church model during the second hour, as this program element requires fewer adult leaders.

As many churches across North America respond to the ever-changing needs of our society, they are discovering that the way church has been presented and experienced in the past is woefully inadequate today. Church has become revitalized as it renews its vision for attracting the disenfranchised members of our community. This changing church paradigm has also impacted the way children's ministry has been practiced.

Figure 22.2 helps summarize some of the changes that have and are taking place in churches across North America in the area of ministry to children.[17]

Figure 22.2
Changing Paradigms of Children's Ministry

Characteristics of the Traditional Model	Characteristics of the Contemporary Model
Staffed by volunteer workers	Staffed by paid professionals
High teacher:student ratio (e.g., 1:15+)	Low teacher:student ratio (e.g., 1:5)
Little, if any, worker screening	Significant worker screening
Voluntary participation in teacher training	Mandatory participation in teacher training
Large group assemblies, few small groups	Few large assemblies, many small groups
Low enthusiasm and creativity	High energy, active learning, very creative
Heavily dependent on lecture method	Oriented toward all learning styles
Curriculum purchased from publisher	Curriculum custom-written or adapted
Low level of accountability	High level of accountability
Program planned by volunteers	Program planned by professionals
Primarily women volunteers	Men and women volunteers
Centralized structure	Decentralized structure
Sunday morning time slot only	Sunday A.M. and Friday P.M. or Saturday P.M.
Program name: Sunday school	Program names are catchy and trendy
Children worship in sanctuary	Children's church

A church with an emphasis on outreach may use a variety of options to encourage neighboring children to attend. These options may include buses, concerts, midweek activities, and a variety of social programs. Some churches that are restricted for space utilize parks, apartment buildings, and school buildings to be able to house more children. An example of a radical departure from the traditional children's Sunday school model has been developed by Metro Ministries in New York. This program takes Sunday school out of the church and into the ghettos. The Sidewalk Sunday School, as it has come to be known, now ministers to tens of thousands of children each week, most of whom have never attended a local church prior to attending the Sidewalk Sunday School.

Changes are being made to the manner in which curriculum is being designed and written as well. Publishing companies are moving away from the traditional lecture method of instruction and incorporating more experiential and kinesthetic oriented methods. Group Publishers began this trend with their *Active Bible Curriculum* line for junior high and senior high learners. This instructional methodology has now also been incorporated into their children's materials, *Hands On Bible Curriculum*. Group's trailblazing efforts have resulted in other publishing companies following suit. Bright colors and updated logos and lingo replace outdated graphics and black-and-white pages. The market for children's Bibles alone has surged, with over forty styles available from nursery to preteen.

A rapidly growing influence in children's ministry in the last decade has been the model of children's church used by Willow Creek Church. This model borrows ideas and formats from the secular world such as professionalism, security, creativity, and fun-centered learning. Professionally trained staff and highly trained volunteers "intentionally shepherd" children in small groups. Learning is done in the context of the small groups through peer discipleship and accountability. Children experience both large and small group opportunities and are challenged by drama, art, music, game centers, colorful signs, banners, and cheerful greeters.

But which method of children's ministry is best? The best model for children's ministry is one that meets the needs of your church, your community, and the children entrusted to your body of believers. Obviously, no single model can be applied to every church due to the many differences that exist in culture, geography, denomination, and so on. However, the model you choose to implement must be biblically based, educationally appropriate, and easily adapted to the particular needs of your church.

CONCLUSION

When Jesus spoke about his imminent return to earth, he asked, "When the Son of Man comes, will He find faith on the earth?" (Luke 18:8 NASB). Jesus could have asked to find anything when he returned, but he chose faith. This then is our mission as believers: We will work as the body of Christ to instill faith in the next generation, thus ensuring their ability to skillfully pass down the spiritual values and beliefs to the following generation in our absence.

In light of such a sobering challenge, our teaching methods must be clear and defined, led by the power of the Holy Spirit. At best, we can teach the Christian faith using traditional instructional methodologies. However, it is impossible to teach faith in the context of a classroom. Faith must be modeled in the life of a caring teacher. The only way to instill faith in another is to carefully and purposefully model it on a daily basis, tenderly and with admonition. What children's ministry needs most in this next generation is not religious educators but faith modelers and disciplers. It is not our goal to raise a generation of religious minds but rather faithful hearts.

NOTES

1. Robert E. Clark, Joanne Brubaker, and Roy B. Zuck, *Childhood Education in the Church* (Chicago: Moody, 1986), p. 4.

2. Lawrence O. Richards, *A Theology of Christian Education* (Chicago: Moody, 1983), pp. 194–95.

3. Fletcher Swift, *Education in Ancient Israel from Earliest Times to 70 A.D.* (Chicago: Open Court, 1919), p. 21.

4. Josephus, *Against Apion 1.12,* cited in William Barclay, *Educational Ideals in the Ancient World* (Grand Rapids: Baker, 1974), p. 12.

5. Miriam J. Hall, *New Directions for Children's Ministries* (Kansas City, Mo.: Beacon Hill, 1980), p. 23.

6. Clark et al., *Childhood Education in the Church,* p. 8.

7. Richards, *Theology of Christian Education,* p. 193.

8. Clark et al., *Childhood Education in the Church,* p. 10.

9. Bureau of the Census, *Current Population Reports, 1997,* Special Studies, Bureau of the Census (Washington, D.C., 1998, P23–194), p. 4.

10. Ibid.

11. National Committee for the Prevention of Child Abuse (NCPCA). 1996 Annual Fifty State Survey, 1996, n.p. This source can be accessed at http://www.yesican.org/statistics.html.

12. Ibid.

13. Bureau of the Census, *Current Population Reports, 1997,* Special Studies, Bureau of the Census (Washington, D.C., 1998, P23–194), p. 4.

14. Robert Choun and Michael S. Lawson, *The Christian Educator's Handbook on Children's Ministry* (Grand Rapids: Baker, 1998), p. 15.

15. Adapted from Shelly Cunningham, "The Christian Education of Children" in *Foundations of Ministry: An Introduction to Christian Education for a New Generation,* ed. Michael J. Anthony (Grand Rapids: Baker, 1992), pp. 138–48.

16. Choun and Lawson, *Christian Educator's Handbook on Children's Ministry,* p. 46.

17. This content was based on a class lecture presented by Instructor Jane Carr at Talbot School of Theology, 21 October 1999.

MINISTRY TO YOUTH   23

Dave Rahn

Youth ministry is undergoing growing pains. Its theological root system is being discussed vigorously and with good cause, since youth ministry's identity springs primarily from its theological lineage.

Embedded as it is within the relatively recent phenomenon of adolescence, youth ministry targets some of the most confused and complex members of modern society. Youth ministry's effectiveness depends upon our ability to relate to the most "hip" audience in our contemporary world.

Youth ministry is also intertwined with the volatility of teenage development. The scope and severity of change we experience as adolescents is among the most significant in our lives. There is evidence to suggest that even these patterns may be on the move, like giant tectonic plates shifting under the surface of the earth. Youth ministry's transformational potential is linked to how well we monitor life's natural growth processes.

Finally, the landscape of youth ministry is cluttered with abandoned programs, time-tested methods, and professionalism under construction. Like investors considering e-commerce options, there's a certain amount of speculation involved in determining ministry strategies. Youth ministry's future will be determined largely by the choices and timing of decisions that we make today.

This chapter will explore youth ministry by getting insights on these growing pains from theological, contemporary, sociological, and practical perspectives.

GOD'S PERSPECTIVE: A THEOLOGY OF YOUTH MINISTRY

Youth ministry isn't easy to identify in the Bible. A single verse in the gospel of Luke sweeps through Jesus' developmental years: "And Jesus grew in wisdom and stature, and in favor with God and men" (Luke 2:52). Youth for Christ used this text to formulate their "balanced life philosophy" in the 1960s,[1] but it hardly seems that a theology of youth ministry can be built on one verse.

Churches all around the country practice occasional youth Sundays, where the teens take over the leadership. References are made to Timothy's youthful but competent leadership. Paul admonishes him not to "let anyone look down on you because you are young, but set an example for the believers in speech, in life, in love, in faith and in purity" (1 Tim. 4:12). If anyone follows Paul's counsel, he or she will likely be a significant contributor to the church, regardless of age. Paul's advice to young Timothy really challenges him to pattern himself after Jesus' leadership model. That's good advice for all of us.

————— 217

Since there is little chance to develop a theology of youth ministry from the same sort of primary biblical material that informs a theology of salvation, those of us committed to youth ministry must do the next best thing. We need to build theological parameters to frame the practice of youth ministry. In doing so, we will do well if we pay attention to God's perspective on the church and culture. Both of these contexts are crucial in defining the scope and nature of youth ministry.

It also makes sense to explore the theological mandate of disciple making. When disciple making as mission, assimilation, and nurture is allowed to intersect with both church and culture, we can begin to appreciate theological foundations that are critical for youth ministry (see figure 23.1). We will also understand what's at stake in the distinctions made about youth ministry's theological identity.

Figure 23.1
Theological Foundations for Youth Ministry

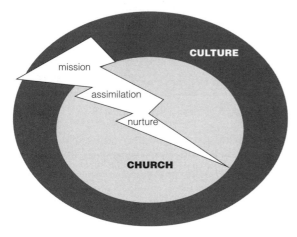

God's Perspective on the Church

Howard Snyder's succinct definition of the church as "the community of the King"[2] helps us consider God's viewpoint. Though God's people have historically expressed themselves in institutional forms, the church is not primarily an institution. While there are considerable programs that intertwine with the activities of God's people in local fellowships, the church must not essentially be defined by its clusters of programs. Neither is the church a building or a denomination. Heart and soul, the church is God's people, gathered together under his lordship.

There are logical consequences to this declaration that have much to do with youth ministry.

First, teenagers are normally present among the people of God called together in a particular place. When people put their trust in Jesus Christ as Savior and Lord, they enter into a bond with all others who have done the same. This group of people includes teens. Any age distinctions merely add to the multigenerational beauty of the church. In fact, just because every local expression of the church might not bear witness to its heterogeneous nature doesn't mean that it is not fundamentally a diverse body. Its intergenerational properties are part of its diversity. "If Jesus were doing a 'file-sort' of the master database for his church he could arrange his great cosmic list according to current age. There are plenty of adolescents on the list."[3]

When one realizes that Mary was very likely a teenage mom,[4] it is difficult to exclude teens from full participation as members of God's church. Neither should they be exempt from the obligations of belonging to the body of Christ because of their age. A theology of youth ministry asserts that teens are included in God's plans for his church.

Too often, in our hurry to develop a specific youth ministry theology, we rush past the penetrating implications of what it must mean for teens to be identified with the church of Jesus Christ. By faith we must place a higher priority on their identity as Christians than on their status as adolescents. This suggests that any agenda related to the health of the church is an agenda to which youth ministry must adjust. For example, since every believer has been given gifts to be used on behalf of the church (Rom. 14; 1 Cor. 12–14; Eph. 4), teens must explore their giftedness. "The Bible does *not* teach that such gifts and expected service are hidden like time-release capsules in the lives of Christians, inoperable until they reach the age of twenty."[5]

Therefore, the first building block of a youth ministry theology is ecclesiological inclusiveness. Whatever is important for the church in God's eyes is a priority for teenage believers, too.

God's Perspective on Culture

Why does a theological response to culture need to be explored for youth ministry? Perhaps it's because of the prominent role that culture plays in influencing adolescents. Consider the tremendous amount of economic activity that is generated by the adolescent segment of our population. As a result, teens are the focus of demographic studies, marketing campaigns, and trend watchers.[6] They infuse modern culture with energy and innovation. Many of us in the church shudder at the culture-shaping outcomes that have been generated, convinced that an MTV world must be resisted rather than accommodated.

Jesus' prayer on behalf of believers in John 17 reveals his intentions with regard to our involvement in the world. First, as believers we are to remain within the world, set apart by God's truth for the task of revealing him to lost people. In so doing, we will contribute to God's overall desire to reconcile the world to himself (Eph. 1:9–10; Col. 1:19–20). Second, we are to assume that we are never going to be comfortable with the world's values. This point is reinforced in John's letter to believers when he details why it's impossible to love both the world and the Father (1 John 2:15–17).

It's apparent that most youth ministers have embraced this transformational agenda as a part of their theological purpose. While it is natural to want to protect our young people from what may harm them, we must take our cues from Jesus, who understood that the only guarantee of safety comes because of the loving vigilance of God and his Word (John 17:11, 12, 15, 17).

The second critical building block of a youth ministry theology is cultural engagement. Young people, immersed within the culture as they typically are, must not be taught to run and hide for Jesus' sake. Rather, following his example, they must seek to transform their world (John 17:18). This is not just change for the sake of change but intentional activism that seeks to reconcile the fallen world to Christ.

God's Prime Directive

It's no surprise that the mandate of disciple making should emerge at the intersection of ecclesiological inclusiveness and cultural engagement. If the Great Commission (Matt. 28:19–20) is a central task for the church, then teenagers ought to be both the target of and contributors to this focus. In other words, disciples ought to be won from among the ranks of teens. As their faith is developed, these same teens must be encouraged to reach their friends for Christ and help them grow in Christ.

This process parallels the grammatical construction of the disciple-making mandate. A mission mind-set is rooted in the "going" dimension of the verse. Once won to faith in Christ through the initiatives of evangelism, converts need to be assimilated into the body of Christ, a value caught by the word "baptizing" in the Great Commission. Disciples are made as they are nurtured in the faith. This nurturing is best described by the phrase "teaching them to obey." And so disciple making includes mission, assimilation, and nurture. Each of these three elements presents unique challenges to youth ministry. Nonetheless, they also represent a biblically derived mandate that must not be dodged.

Pete Ward makes a compelling case for an entirely different approach to youth ministry, one he labels *Outside-in*. This approach begins with a mission mind-set. Among the beliefs fueling this model is the assumption that Christian teens within churches experience a typical limitation on the range of their outreach, necessitating other strategies to carry the gospel to unchurched young people. As this approach has been practiced in England, its natural consequence has been to plant youth churches within subcultures that were not being reached with the gospel.[7]

Parachurch organizations such as Young Life and Youth for Christ have long targeted their efforts toward reaching unchurched teens, initiating relationships with non-Christians and establishing clubs that allow them to proclaim the gospel in a variety of ways. Recent thinking and writing by a number of influential youth ministry educators contribute a credible depth of theological insight that makes the Outside-in model something to be reckoned with. In 1999, an entire issue of *Christian Education Journal* was devoted to articles that promoted the theme of "youth ministry as mission."[8]

While Inside-out and Outside-in youth ministry strategies place a starting emphasis within either the nurture or mission components of the Great Commission, neither one suggests that the remaining elements of Jesus' disciple-making mandate can afford to be ignored. In fact, one of the richest contributions of Ward's book is his acknowledgement of the vast difference between assimilation strategies, depending on one's ministry model starting point.[9] The concern among many youth ministers over the noninvolvement of post-graduates in church life is a further testimony to the importance of assimilation to youth ministry's theological mandate.

CONTEMPORARY PERSPECTIVE: YOUTH OF THE NEW MILLENNIUM

The demographics of world population growth cry out for ministry strategies targeted toward young people. More than one-third of all persons in the world are either teenagers or younger. Our world population reached the six billion mark on October 12, 1999, and it will grow by another billion in just twelve years. At the turn of this century, over two billion persons were under twenty years of age.[10] How will the church make disciples for Jesus Christ from this huge population?

First, who are these kids? They resist convenient categories. Wanting to see a composite picture of today's young people, we instead find a hologram staring back at us, defying us to offer a title that describes completely what we see.

Those familiar with the characteristics of postmodernity ought not be surprised by this description. "Both a plague and a feature of postmodernity is its fluidity and viscosity. It takes different shape under many eyes and in many hands."[11] Vocational choices are unimaginably rich for postmodern teens. Neat designations of time have given way to the postmodern influence, and boundaries are blurred. The same can be said of the undifferentiated physical spaces of postmodern life, as evidenced in neighborhood shopping malls. Art, national identities, and electronic media are all affected. Of particular importance to those of us who practice youth ministry, truth is seen as a personal option, always relative, never transcendent.[12] Are the youth of the new millennium an "autonomous generation,"[13] sailing on a self-referential sea without the inclination to trust stars, maps, compasses, or adults for where they want to go? That may be part of the picture. "A new youth culture has emerged based on the adolescent experience."[14]

What do we know about this experience? Kenda Creasy Dean and Ron Foster pull together a wide variety of research in painting the following picture of the American teens:

> If today is an average day, more than one-third of American teenagers will spend their free time this evening visiting with their friends. In a town with 1,000 girls between the ages of eleven and seventeen, 830 will call their friends on the telephone. If this town has 1,000 boys of the same age, 400 of them will have a computer at home and about half will communicate by going on-line.
>
> If today is an average day, the vast majority (96 percent) of teenagers—despite what we might think—will say they get along well with their parents (although they will intimate that this is not true for their best friends). Twice as many teens will admit they get along better with mom than with dad. At dinner tonight, three-fourths of them will talk about school with their parents and about half will discuss family matters or current events. If a visitor at the table were to ask, "What is the biggest problem facing your generation?" they would probably say drugs, followed by peer pressure and AIDS. Yet if asked about the biggest problem facing them personally, most would reply, "Grades at school." Slightly more than half of these teenagers will say they attended worship this week. Most of them because they wanted to. Ninety-five percent of them believe in God. Nearly all of them recycle.[15]

An accurate portrait of youth in the new millennium won't be an oil painting, a theme-park caricature, or a still photograph. And if someone tries to sell you such a picture, be sure to check the date. Major change is happening, and it's happening with incredible speed.

SOCIOLOGICAL PERSPECTIVE: AGE-LEVEL CHARACTERISTICS

After reviewing the volatility of the contemporary adolescent scene, it's nice to focus on a more dependable sort of change. The common characteristics of teenagers offer us enough insights that we should feel safe asking the question,

"How should age-related developmental characteristics impact youth ministry practices?" The short answer is, "Probably more than they commonly do." Here's why.

Understanding youth experience is an essential prerequisite to gaining influence with them, and the disciple-making task at the heart of youth ministry is a task of influence. There are three developmentally powerful experiences that take place during the teenage years. When youth ministers take into account these experiences, they take advantage of some of the natural forces shaping the formation of a teenager. Physical changes, mental changes, and psychosocial changes are all part of the tumultuous process of development taking place during adolescence.

The Physical Changes Accompanying Puberty

Hormonal activity brings about changes in a young person that are as significant as any they have experienced since birth.

The average age for the onset of puberty for females (as measured by the beginning of breast development) is 10.5 years. Breast development takes approximately 4.5 years and spans most of the pubertal process for girls. For boys, the first pubertal indicator (initial growth of the testes) occurs somewhere between 11 and 11.5 years of age, on average.[16] The difficulty in measuring puberty is connected to the fact that it is not "a singular process, but a series of linked physical changes."[17] There is also the likelihood of great variation between individuals in their physical development. Added to this complication is research that suggests that puberty is starting earlier,[18] with at least one theory used to explain pubertal timing in relation to better nutrition and other environmental factors.[19] Nonetheless, though there is considerable difference between teens in the pace of change, there are dependable similarities in the nature of the changes taking place during puberty.

- Teens will get bigger. There is a dramatic growth spurt affecting both height and weight. More particularly, females naturally get fatter. This growth spurt is commonly uneven, with hands and feet growing faster and earlier. It's natural to expect awkwardness as a result of this growth.

- Teens will get sexier (developmentally speaking). This is the period of time when reproductive features of gonads and secondary sex characteristics are activated like time-release capsules. As is generally true during puberty, these characteristics may also develop unevenly; for instance, one breast may be bigger than the other during this development. Further evidence of this unstable growth is reflected in the fact that when menstruation begins for females, it may be a full year or more before the cycle becomes steady.

- Teens will get stronger. Their circulatory and respiratory systems enlarge during puberty, making it possible for them to exercise harder and longer.

- Teens will get brainier (at least by physical standards). During puberty the nervous system is enlarged and the brain mass gets heavier.

- Teens will get oilier. One irritating developmental consequence of this time of life is the appearance of the sebaceous (oily) glands. These are the glands that form acne when clogged.

- Teens will get sweatier. The apocrine (sweat) glands also develop during puberty. Their unpleasant contribution to a teen's life results in body odor, which sometimes can be difficult to manage.

- Teens will get hairier. Pubic, underarm, and facial hair are among the most recognized indicators of the onset of puberty.

It's hard for teens to avoid comparing their development to that of their peers, but the tremendous variation in growth during puberty makes this an unreasonable activity. Their body image will change as they move through puberty, and the challenge for adolescents is to see their bodies as much more than a never-ending construction zone.

Mental Changes Accompanying Formal Operational Thinking

Piaget's inquiry into the stages of mental development alerts us to the fact that adolescence is marked by a transition from concrete operational thinking to formal operational thinking.[20]

Teens whose thinking is confined to the concrete (what is) make the significant leap to possibility thinking. They can now think in hypothetical (what if) terms. This increased mental capacity has implications for prior commitments and understanding in all kinds of areas, including matters of faith. It is developmentally predictable that teens who are testing out their new brain style will begin to question matters they had previously accepted at face value. What we sometimes perceive as rebelliousness may actually be expressions of unsatisfied curiosity by teens who can now imagine alternative explanations.

They can also imagine other things. As a matter of fact, David Elkind coined the term "imaginary audience" to explain how adolescent egocentrism works.[21] His explanation helps us understand that in the self-absorbed world of teens, they imagine that their peers are vigilant and alert to their every move. So, for example, the small pimple barely visible behind a shock of hair can be traumatic because "everyone will see it."

One additional observation about the sort of mental changes that take place during adolescence also derives from the adolescent's capacity to think hypothetically. In fact, teens now cultivate the ability to see things from other persons' perspectives. As this role-taking ability progresses, a more objective stance is assumed, allowing teens to evaluate their own actions and attitudes with a certain amount of distance and dispassion. This most generalized posture is attained when a young person can move from the perspective of a neutral third person and assume the hypothetical consensus of multiple third-person vantage points.[22]

When summarizing the impact of mental changes upon adolescents, it may be helpful to consider what happens when a young person who has only traveled via bicycle is suddenly given the keys to an automobile. There's a lot more power and a lot more potential to be explored. This new mental capacity is a tremendous factor in adolescent formation.

Psychosocial Changes Accompanying Identity Formation

The primary developmental task of adolescents is their search for identity, according to Erik Erikson.[23] He theorized that this is one of eight developmental challenges distributed throughout life that must be dealt with. If adolescents reckoning with this fourth stage do not successfully navigate their way toward a healthy sense of personal identity, they will move into the next period of their lives encumbered by a sense of identity confusion. Similarly, if they have not moved through the three earlier developmental tasks effectively, they will be hindered in their identity formation.

This process is complicated by the confusion of adolescence in modern society. It is easy enough to assert that adolescence begins in biology and ends in society. It is quite another thing to agree upon the societal benchmarks that confirm the passage of a young man or woman into adulthood. As Chap Clark has observed, there is a lengthening adolescent time span that matters because "what used to be a relatively short-lived transitional process now takes up to three times as long to complete. . . . The problem is that what has always been a tricky and often painful time of relational and identity experimentation now takes a person so much longer."[24]

James Marcia helped to explain this process by describing three options that persons may encounter on the way to identity achievement.[25] Many teens have not yet formulated personal identity-defining commitments, values, or standards. They are not yet ready to say, "This is who I want to be." This delay may be due to the fact that people must experience an active personal struggle (crisis) of searching, testing, and trying on different sets of commitments. People's identity is "diffused" when they have yet to work through any of these formation-building crises so as to arrive at their own identity-defining personal commitments. On the other hand, there are those teens who have made identity choices and commitments without experiencing a crisis of personal evaluation. Marcia labels them "foreclosed" in their identity formation. That is, they chose their identity commitments before adequately exploring their options. The ultimate goal—identity achievement—is not possible without going through some period of moratorium, whereby commitments are suspended until the crisis of alternatives can be genuinely investigated.

The matter of family membership and adolescent identity calls to mind the process of individuation,[26] illustrated by the imagery of birds who are finally learning to fly. This picture captures perfectly how the adolescent task of identity formation interacts with family membership. Individuation takes place when teens break free of the role of the child within the family and become ultimately responsible as interdependent persons within society. This psychosocial experience serves as the ultimate achievement of healthy adolescent development.

Stretching the bonds of family group membership does not, however, mean that group affiliation is unimportant to a teen's psychosocial development. In fact, it may be valuable to explore the particular group of friends that teens have cultivated when trying to understand where the influence of their identity formation is headed. Berndt summarizes the research on peer influence by stating that "on all behaviors, the best friends' influence seemed greater than that of other friends, and other friends' influence seemed greater than that of peers in general."[27] Cohen offers support for this conclusion by asserting that most peer influence is reciprocal between close friends.[28]

"How can we know if the expressions of identity seen by teens today are part of the 'exploration' phase of their formation or part of the 'commitment' phase of their development? We don't. In fact, we should hope for the best, assume the worst, and plan our ministry strategies accordingly."[29] What we do know is that these psy-chosocial experiences are powerful factors to consider as youth ministers seek to make disciples.

MINISTRY PERSPECTIVE: REACHING YOUTH FOR CHRIST

Developmental differences among teens highlight the need for person-centered approaches to youth ministry. Attention to the dynamics of peer influence can help youth ministers steer courses toward effectiveness. Sociological methods can help youth ministers to track the needs and movements among the youth population in their communities, but in the end personal ministry is required. As the youth culture fragments into increasingly diverse interest groups, one-size-fits-all approaches to youth ministry are simply untenable. But we don't want to form our youth ministry strategies on the basis of "what works." Fundamentally, we want to be faithful. We want to make disciples because Jesus commanded us to do so. Our interest is in how to best accomplish this task with young people. We'll find the answer by pursuing a focused, disciple-making inquiry in the middle of the adolescent world.

Young People Are Lost

Youth ministry takes up the mission of helping young people discover life in Jesus Christ.

Figure 23.2

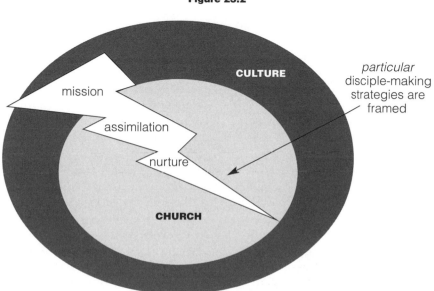

Some youth ministry efforts never quite get on target here. They try to mobilize programs that will effectively reach lost teens. They've bought into a flawed assumption. They believe they can attract non-Christian young people with the right strategies.[30] While that may be true for a segment of unchurched kids, it will not reach the masses. It is essentially a "come and see" strategy, one that is fundamentally different from our Lord's incarnational initiative taking. In fact, incarnational ministry will compel us to adopt "going" strategies if we are serious about communicating the gospel to lost young people. And one of the essential truths of "incarnational ministry is that the Person is the program."[31]

So rather than spending valuable energy creating attractive programs, youth ministries must commit themselves to finding, equipping, and mobilizing attractive (Christlike) people who will go wherever there are teens. When youth missionaries—and some of them will be teens themselves—build relationships with teenagers who don't know Jesus, they will establish an essential bridge across which the gospel message can travel and be understood. It's not that programs can't be useful in this process. But unless youth ministers and their ministry partners practice two key "going disciplines," programs will eventually become ingrown, victims of their own spiritual centrifugal force.

Initiating contact with teens is the first discipline. To be sure, there's plenty of homework that could be done before striking out, but this fact-finding can actually serve a useful purpose while moving among kids. Youth ministers who seek to move into the teens' world humbly, hungry to learn, and eager to serve will find that they can build new relationships while discovering fresh insights about those they want to reach.

Building nonjudgmental relationships is the second discipline, one that takes time and availability. Sometimes a conversation will help a youth minister progress from making contact to building a relationship. Often it will require a more significant investment in the lives of teens. Common experiences and shared confidences help build relationships of mutual trust. This incarnational bond helps add clarification, context, and meaning to the words of the gospel.

Without such disciplines, youth ministers will be ivory tower missionaries. Their knowledge of the lost teens in their communities will be sanitized by distance. Missionary passion is born from proximity and intimacy; when we move close to non-Christians, we'll find the Lord fires our hearts with his own passion for the lost.

Youth ministers need to be aware of a particular snare. As young people come to know Christ and a degree of evangelistic fruitfulness is realized, the sheer numbers from a growing youth ministry can demand constant attention. That's why these are not so much going "strategies" as they are "disciplines." Vigilant to the mission of the disciple-making strategy, we must always be pushing ourselves into meaningful relationships with those who do not know Christ.

Young People Won't Naturally Connect to the Church

Youth ministry takes up the task of trying to assimilate young people into the life that Jesus' people share in a particular community. Those who have been won and wooed to Christ through our going initiatives must now learn to come and see what it means to belong to the family of God. This assimilation effort has culture shock written all over it. As Paul Borthwick has noted, this is some of the bridge building that's necessary when the gospel takes root among new believers.[32]

In truth, this youth ministry effort may only begin to take place during the teenage years. It may take a considerable amount of time, and it will certainly take intentional focus for new believers to truly become a part of the life of the church. When Doug Fields maintains that youth ministry benefits from identifying students' level of commitment, he is actually setting the stage for assimilation strategies.[33]

Many youth ministries have used worship services to draw kids deeper into the purposes of the church. In fact, teen-friendly worship models have led to youth-targeted congregational worship, youth cell groups, and youth churches in many places. The effectiveness of these strategies no doubt has been connected to the fact that they "use the stuff of youth culture in worship."[34]

Many of the common methods of youth ministry might be usefully employed for assimilation purposes. Large group meetings can be places where familiar faces and comfortable surroundings make it easier to discover previously unknown biblical realities. Small groups can help kids learn about Jesus' way of relating to one another. Prayer can be practiced, and answered prayers can be experienced in such settings. Retreats offer a chance to immerse kids in life together centered around the life of Jesus. Mission and service trips help them experience the power of God.

Young People Won't Naturally Learn to Be Christlike

Youth ministry does what it takes to nurture young people in their faith, helping them grow into the fullness of life in Christ Jesus. Spiritual disciplines such as personal prayer time, Bible study, fasting, meditation, and service have long been considered to be a part of the formation process of students. Research studies have shown those students who pray and read their Bibles most frequently are also more likely to engage in evangelistic behaviors with their friends[35] and avoid immoral behaviors.[36] Certainly these practices, both personal and communal, are part of nurturing the faith of teens. But we dare not neglect the powerful force of experience in student formation. Our experiences have tremendous formative influence on us. Why can't they be used more naturally and deliberately in the nurture of students?

If we want our youth ministries to help bring about the real transformation of students so that they become increasingly like Jesus Christ in their actions, attitudes, and thoughts, we must adapt our ministry strategies. Significant life change takes place when we are engaged by that which is most important to us and integrate what we've learned into the natural patterns of our lives.[37]

So rather than insisting that young people immediately shift their priorities to reflect those of Jesus, we would do well to plan around that which is already important to teens. By acknowledging this, we can harness the natural motivations that are so critical to real change. For example, one youth minister launched a very effective small group Bible study among cheerleaders, in part because it tapped into the established importance the girls had already placed on becoming a tight squad. This example also illustrates the second predictor of transformation. Because this group takes place within the natural rhythms of these girls' lives, it has the advantage of making integration easier. The bridge from what is learned in the group study to what will be practiced in life is a relatively short span, and there are plenty of accountability partners to keep tabs on their progress.

We should expect that as the Holy Spirit works in young people's lives their priorities will shift, giving us a greater foothold for influence. Frequent patterns of applying God's truth to their lives will also make it possible to help students think more naturally about integration, easing that element of transformation.

Those students who have emerged as mature, faithful leaders among their peers have a tremendous natural advantage over adults when it comes to tapping into the potential of nonformal learning. The majority of their time with friends is largely of this variety. If they "make the most of every opportunity" (Col. 4:5), they will raise the importance of following Christ while demonstrating his relevance throughout their lives. When students emerge as models chasing after Christlikeness among their peers, they take advantage of powerful dynamics to have a heightened impact on their friends.[38]

At this point it's important to realize that student leadership strategies have taken us full circle. Student leaders not only represent those youth ministry teens who demonstrate the most progress toward Christlikeness, but they then become some of those people (not programs) who can assume the responsibility of going to their lost friends with the gospel message. As good examples of disciples, they are living illustrations of youth ministry's primary task.

CONCLUSION

There is a complexity and breadth to biblical disciple making that can't be adequately addressed in a chapter dealing with youth ministry. By exploring God's perspectives on youth ministry, we know that we must embrace the task and understand our role in the church and the world. By exploring contemporary perspectives on youth ministry, we appreciate the challenge of the task. By surveying sociological perspectives on youth ministry, we gain some clues into the shape that youth ministry ought to take. And by sketching principles for a ministry perspective, we can focus our energies on what God has called us to do. May the

Lord continue to sharpen our insights as we discover how to best intersect our culture for Christ.

NOTES

1. James Hefley, *God Goes to High School* (Waco, Tex.: Word, 1970).

2. Howard Snyder, *The Community of the King* (Downers Grove, Ill.: InterVarsity, 1977).

3. Dave Rahn, "Focusing Youth Ministry through Student Leadership," in *Starting Right: Thinking Theologically about Youth Ministry,* ed. Chap Clark, Kenda Creasy Dean, and Dave Rahn (Grand Rapids: Zondervan/Youth Specialties, forthcoming).

4. Charles Laymon, ed., *The Interpreter's One-Volume Commentary on the Bible* (Nashville: Abingdon, 1971), p. 674. Also see Lawrence O. Richards, *The Teacher's Commentary* (Wheaton, Ill.: Scripture Press, 1987), p. 644.

5. Rahn, "Focusing Youth Ministry through Student Leadership."

6. See, for example, Janine Lopiano-Misdom and Joanne De Luca, *Street Trends* (New York: HarperBusiness, 1998).

7. Pete Ward, *God at the Mall* (Peabody, Mass.: Hendrickson, 1999), pp. 134–35.

8. *Christian Education Journal* n.s. 3, no. 2 (fall 1999).

9. Ward, *God at the Mall,* pp. 131–35.

10. United Nations Population Fund, *World Population Prospects: The 1998 Revision,* www.unfpa.org.

11. Martin Marty, "Youth between Late Modernity and Postmodernity," in *The 1998 Princeton Lectures on Youth, Church, and Culture* (Princeton, N.J.: Princeton Theological Seminary, 1999), p. 31.

12. Ibid., pp. 31–33.

13. Sharon Daloz Parks, "Home and Pilgrimage: Deep Rhythms in the Adolescent Soul," in *The 1998 Princeton Lectures on Youth, Church, and Culture* (Princeton, N.J.: Princeton Theological Seminary, 1999), pp. 53–54.

14. Paul Borthwick, "Cross-Cultural Outreach: A Missiological Perspective on Youth Ministry," *Christian Education Journal* n.s. 3, no. 2 (fall 1999): 64–65.

15. Kenda Creasy Dean and Ron Foster, *The Godbearing Life: The Art of Soul-Tending for Youth Ministry* (Nashville: Upper Room, 1999), pp. 13–14.

16. Julia A. Graber, Anne C. Petersen, and Jeanne Brooks-Dunn, "Pubertal Processes: Methods, Measures, and Models," in *Transitions through Adolescence: Interpersonal Domains and Context,* ed. Julie A. Graber, Jeanne Brooks-Dunn, and Anne C. Petersen (Mahwah, N.J.: Erlbaum, 1996), p. 26.

17. Ibid., p. 25.

18. Chap Clark, "Creating a Place for a New Generation: An Ecclesiological Perspective on Youth Ministry," *Christian Education Journal* n.s. 3, no. 2 (fall 1999): 96.

19. Graber et al., "Pubertal Processes," p. 46.

20. Rolf E. Muss, "Jean Piaget's Cognitive Theory of Adolescence," in *Theories of Adolescence,* 5th ed. (New York: Random House, 1988), pp. 176–89.

21. David Elkind, *All Grown Up and No Place to Go* (Reading, Mass.: Addison-Wesley, 1984), pp. 33–36.

22. Rolf E. Muss, "Social Cognition, Part 1: Robert Selman's Theory of Role-Taking," in *Theories of Adolescence,* pp. 245–61.

23. Erik H. Erikson, *Identity: Youth and Crisis* (New York: Norton, 1968).

24. Clark, "Creating a Place for a New Generation," p. 97.

25. James Marcia, "Identity in Adolescence," in *Handbook of Adolescent Psychology,* ed. J. Adelson (New York: Wiley, 1980).

26. Ronald M. Sabatelli and Aviva Mazor, "Differentiation, Individuation, and Identity Formation: The Integration of Family System and Individual Developmental Perspectives," *Adolescence* 20, no. 79 (1985): 620–21.

27. Thomas J. Berndt, "Transitions in Friendship and Friends' Influence," in *Transitions through Adolescence,* p. 60.

28. Ibid.

29. Dave Rahn, "Reckoning with Adolescent Influence: A Sociological Perspective on Youth Ministry," *Christian Education Journal* n.s. 3, no. 2 (fall 1999): 83.

30. Jim Petersen, *Church without Walls* (Colorado Springs: NavPress, 1992), p. 177.

31. Dean and Foster, *The Godbearing Life,* p. 29.

32. Borthwick, "Cross-Cultural Outreach," pp. 69–70.

33. Doug Fields, *Purpose-Driven Youth Ministry* (Grand Rapids: Zondervan/Youth Specialties, 1998), pp. 83–97.

34. Pete Ward, "The Worship Explosion," *Group* (May/June 2000): 28.

35. The program effectiveness studies conducted by Link Institute on behalf of DC/LA '94 (1995) and DC/LA '97 (1998) both support this contention.

36. A program effectiveness study conducted by Link Institute on behalf of Youthfest (1999) supports this contention with regard to the following behaviors: illicit sexual activity (including premarital intercourse), alcohol use, and drug use.

37. Dave Rahn, "Marketplace Youth Ministry," *Group* (Sept./Oct. 1996): 41–44.

38. An example of this was found in research related to student leaders' evangelism behaviors as reported in Dave Rahn and Terry Linhart, *Contagious Faith: Empowering Student Leadership in Youth Evangelism* (Loveland, Colo.: Group, 2000).

ADULT MINISTRIES

24

James A. Davies

The demographics of North America are making a dramatic shift. The graying of the adult population is slowly but methodically becoming a reality. With life expectancy growing from just 68.3 years in 1950 to a projected 78.1 years in 2020, we will soon have nearly a quarter of our population as adults over the age of sixty-five. If individuals become adults around the age of eighteen, and if they live until the age of seventy-eight, then they will have spent sixty years of their lives as adults. The facts confirm that almost all of us spend the majority of our lives as adults.

America became alarmed in the early 1900s about how little we knew about childhood. Since that time, studies and research projects were initiated that specify what is normative development along almost every week of childhood development. Likewise, in the 1950s America became infatuated with trying to understand its adolescent population. Again, research studies were authored, and soon a myriad of books and articles chronicled the lives of those between the ages of eleven and eighteen. Consequently, America knew little about what was normative in the lives of its adult citizens, even though we spent the vast majority of our time in this stage.

Things have changed now, and researchers have begun a major emphasis in understanding adult stages of development. The result is that we now have a better handle on the issues and needs facing people throughout the various seasons of adult development: young adulthood, middle adulthood, and later adulthood. Each era has its own unique and distinguishing characteristics that allow us to look down the road of life to see where each of us is headed.

This knowledge has proven beneficial to those of us in church leadership as well. Pastors of adult ministries have examined this research information and have learned how to more appropriately plan for the spiritual needs of the adult population. Adults are concerned about what lies ahead in their lives. They want to know what physical, emotional, and relational changes will take place in the future. Along with these concerns, adults also seek to gain some satisfaction and meaning from their lives to date. Many also want their remaining years to count for something beneficial for the next generation. They want to leave legacies behind that will have a positive effect on future generations. Integrating our understanding of social science literature regarding human development with biblical truth is at the heart of adult Christian education ministries.

GOD'S PERSPECTIVE: A THEOLOGY OF ADULT MINISTRY

The Bible is predominately an adult-oriented book written by adults for an adult audience.

While many passages provide information about youth and children's ministry, almost all of them take place in the context of a congregation or family in which adults carry out that ministry. Adult ministries aim at transforming both the minds and lives of those involved (Rom. 12:1–2). Once a person becomes a believer, God desires growth so that Christ may be "formed in you" (Gal. 4:19). The goal is to lead adults to spiritual maturity.

Spiritual growth is most effectively accomplished when linked to two important theological truths. The first theological truth that forms a foundation for adult Christian education is a recognition of the centrality of the Bible as the authoritative Word of God. This is a major foundation for adult Christian education and sets it apart from religious indoctrination. God's Word is living, powerful, and eternal (Isa. 40:8). It has transforming power (Heb. 4:12–13; 2 Tim. 3:16–17) to renew the mind, fashion new character, and influence behavior regardless of age or cultural heritage. When we allow Christian education to focus primarily on the transmission of truth without regard for a transformed life, we create what German theologian Dietrich Bonhoeffer referred to as "cheap grace." True grace demands involvement with the total person.[1] Biblical truth that is separated from life produces a contemporary Pharisee. The product is a fruitless life devoid of God's power.[2] Indeed, the Book of James teaches that knowledge isolated from character and behavior is of little value. Holistic adult ministry involves the physical, emotional, mental, social, and spiritual dimensions of our beings (Luke 2:52).

The second theological truth that forms the foundation of adult Christian education is a partnership with the work and role of the Holy Spirit. It is here that the information-oriented culture of the North American educational system can be countered.[3] The Spirit is the One who instructs (John 14:26), reminds (John 14:26), guides (John 16:13), declares (John 16:13–15), reveals (1 Cor. 2:9–10), and empowers for change (Col. 1:11). Edward Hayes describes this process well when he states,

Discovering the relationship between the inner work of the Spirit and the educative process is one of the great tasks of the evangelical Christian educator. A basic principle of evangelical Christian education is that the inner change and modification of behavior in the learner is dependent on the Spirit of God working in and through the Word of God.[4]

The ancient Hebrews believed the heart to be the all-important component in one's relationship to God. Jesus responded that this involved more than just the emotions and mind. Christ said the greatest commandment was to "love the Lord your God with all your heart [emotional] and with your soul [spiritual] and with all your mind [intellectual] and with all your strength [physical]" (Mark 12:30). God wants adults who are full of functional competency. He desires people who both know and practice the Word.

The local church places a high priority on its ministry to adults when it recognizes the theological truths of the primacy of God's Word and its partnership with the Holy Spirit.

CONTEMPORARY PERSPECTIVE: THE AGING OF NORTH AMERICA

The adult population of North America is astounding. At the start of the new millennium, there were nearly 208 million adults over the age of eighteen living in the United States.[5] It has been estimated that the adult population in the U.S. will grow to over 301 million in the next thirty years. In Canada there are currently 18 million adults out of a population base of 25 million.[6] In Mexico, which has a population of 91 million people, approximately 57 million are adults over the age of fifteen.[7] Adults comprise by far the largest demographic segment in North America, since they represent three-fourths of its population.

Diversity is a one-word synopsis of this adult demographic. As adults age they do not become more uniform. Indeed, they become more assorted and varied. Authors of adult development literature have used a variety of metaphors and motifs to describe adulthood. The concept of adult stages conveys the image of a capacity to map fixed passages. Literature is replete with examples of adult development through the stages of life. Examples including Shakespeare's "Seven Stages of Man,"[8] Ruth Harriet Jacobs's "Don't Call Me a Young Woman,"[9] Lin Yutang's "Human Life a Poem,"[10] and the family wellness literature of Nick Stinnett[11] and Dolores Curran[12] all indicate there are broadly defined periods in adult life. These stages of life have been referred to as "life-events."[13]

The second motif, that of adult aging as a *journey*, is also well represented in literature. It focuses on adult life as a voyage and a sacred pilgrimage. Examples of this approach to describing adult development include Dante's *Divine Comedy* and Sterling Brown's "Sister Lou."[14] The journey metaphor emphasizes individual selection, experience, and growth.[15] Choices of marriage, divorce, remarriage, career options, interests, participation (or lack thereof), challenges, accomplishments, personality styles, and culture all create a kaleidoscope of possibilities as one moves through the grand journey of adult life. Issues of doing and being, transcendence and purpose, meaning and legacy are addressed in this metaphor.

The analogies of stage and journey, while historical and nostalgic, remind us that no two people have the same life experiences. Those ministering to adults in the local church must take this reality into consideration during programmatic design. They must also consider important issues such as gender, age, marital status, the presence of children in the home, denominational affiliation (if any), and cultural heritage. It is this diversity that has given birth to such a wide variety of models for adult ministry. Each of them will be explored in the following section.

MINISTRY PERSPECTIVE: MODELS OF ADULT MINISTRY

Different models are used by churches when structuring adult ministries. No one style has been empirically shown to be more effective than another. Each type has its own advantages and disadvantages. Therefore, each model is useful for a particular type of adult and needs to be affirmed for what it does best. Simply stated, the question is not which model is best but which is most appropriate given the unique needs represented among the adults in attendance. Each model will be described briefly.

Permanent Grouping

Permanent grouping is one of the most traditional models of adult ministry in North America. This adult class or small group expects to remain together indefinitely. It is generally made up of adults who are approximately the same age. Adult ministries using this fixed approach focus on the people of the group. They desire to see deeper levels of community and service develop between the members. It is important to remember that permanent groupings have life cycles. They age as their members age. They will eventually cease to exist or be combined with the next younger adult grouping. When this occurs, the wise adult minister will help participants realize that this is normal and will celebrate the legacy of changed lives that the older generation accomplished with its resources.

In smaller churches, the permanent adult groups often revolve around two or three prominent family units. Moderate-sized churches may follow three broad chronological clusters for their base units: maiden adults (18–35 years), middle adults (35–55 years), and mature adults (55 plus). Multiple mini-congregations of adults, selected by either geographic area or age, are patterns frequently used by large churches and megachurches.

Temporary Grouping

Some adult ministries intentionally structure their groups for a limited period of time. The emphasis is usually on a topic to be studied or a ministry task to be accomplished rather than on the participants themselves. Such groups are not usually structured according to age, gender, or marital status. In these short-term groups, participants have limited opportunities for developing intimate friendships. Limited ministry service is done unless it is a short-term task force group. Still, this subject-focused adult learning often speaks directly, instructively, and powerfully to an immediate felt need or crisis.

The use of curricular electives is the strongest example of temporary groups for adults. *Straight Elective Systems* have the total adult program designed around ancillary groups of short duration. *Modified Elective Systems* attempt to keep a permanent group structure as the base while providing elective options within. A recent variation is *Hot Button Topics*. These short duration experiences appeal to middle-aged adults and fit well into their busy suburban lifestyles.

Segregated Grouping

Gender forms the basis of adult groups in some Christian education programs today. Prior to the twentieth century, almost all adult Christian education was done on a gender-segregated basis. We see a renewal of this pattern in today's men's ministry and women's ministry. In undeveloped countries around the world, the delivery system through which adult nurture occurs most frequently is the matriarchal or patriarchal system. Kenneth Gangel reminds us of a fascinating passage in Titus 3 where five adult target groups are identified: older men, older women, younger men, younger women, and slaves. Each group is given specific kinds of educational experiences they need in light of their age, status, role in the church, and cultural surroundings.[16]

In addition, some churches in North America group their adult education based on racial origin. For example, one church in San Francisco is made up of four "congregations" grouped according to national heritage. The first represents people born and raised in Hong Kong. Its services are done in Chinese only. This is followed by a second service for those who function equally well in Chinese or American culture (referred to as the 1.5 generation). The third congregation is for American-born Chinese (second generation), and the service is in English only. The fourth congregational group is for Vietnamese. All four congregations share the same church board, but each has its own set of programs and ministries designed to meet the particular needs of their adults.

A third approach to a segmented model is to organize around marital status: married or single adults. Churches using this format see the life needs and interests of singles being so different from couples that they demand specialization.

Special Interest/Task Force Grouping

What do hunters, prayer intercessors, parents of teens, adult choir members, and a junior high ministry team have in common? They are all part of the adult module groups from one church. The goal is to have every adult in a unit. The cluster becomes the first line of pastoral care for its members. Groups are added as God raises up several people with similar interests. They are disbanded when attendance falls below a minimum number.

In this structure the cell becomes the base from which service, evangelism, and ministry are done. Advantages to this style include great structural flexibility (can add or subtract a group quickly) and an extremely high degree of passion that members have for their group. Some churches using this model have found it difficult to staff for traditional ministries such as Sunday school and children's church. However, this has not been the case in every situation.

Life Stage Grouping

Probably the most contemporary model for adult ministry today is the life stage grouping. The educational basis for this is the work of Robert J. Havighurst. He discovered the critical importance that adult roles and responsibilities play in learning. Havighurst indicates there are "teachable moments" when an adult is more open for special impact learning. This occurs when a combination of factors intersect. These factors include:

1. A pressing or new need, condition, or situation
2. Resources with which to deal with it
3. The support of cooperation expertise
4. A willingness to work with the situation[17]

Warren Wilbert discusses the integration of this educational theory to adult ministries when he says,

> At every developmental stage new elements which will have an effect on learning come into play. Although some of the items (for example, parenthood) are repeated several times, each developmental stage brings a fresh, unique set of circumstances. These unique circumstances should be taken into account in the selection, arrangement, and conduct of the adult's learning projects.[18]

In many ways, organizing around the life cycle is similar to permanent grouping. The difference is that of intentionality and specific developmental specialization. Further, life stage groupings are only semipermanent. Membership is constantly changing.

An example of the life cycle approach is Rolling Hills Covenant Church in Rolling Hills Estates,

California. Their primary structure for adult ministry is built around these stages:

Life Stage 1: Single Adults   20s and 30s

Life Stage 2: Married Adults   20s and 30s; parents of children birth–grade 6

Life Stage 3: All Adults   40s

Life Stage 4: All Adults   50s and early 60s

Life Stage 5: All Adults   65 and above

With increased emphasis on intentional spiritual formation, some churches are organizing their adult ministries around the spiritual maturity level of the adult. These churches recognize that sanctification is both a product and a process. The progression has nothing to do with chronological aging. It is based on an individual's level of spiritual maturity. Figure 24.1 shows a schemata around which courses and ministry can be built.

Another example of a different adult ministry format is presented by Saddleback Valley Community Church in Mission Viejo, California. Their CLASS (Christian Life And Service Seminars) model is an example of building around an intentional progression toward spiritual maturity (see figure 24.2).

The model you choose to implement at your church will vary depending on a host of variables. These may include denominational affiliation, numbers of years your church has been in existence, church size, social and demographic patterns of the congregation, vision and goals for ministry, philosophy of ministry, facilities, staffing capabilities, established traditions, and cultural expectations.

Figure 24.2
Saddleback's CLASS Strategy

Level 101—Knowing Christ	Goal: Lead to Christ and membership
Level 201—Growing in Christ	Goal: Grow to maturity/covenant
Level 301—Committed to ministry	Goal: Equip people with skills
Level 401—Committed to missions	Goal: Enlist people in worldwide mission of sharing Christ

PRINCIPLES OF ADULT MINISTRY

A comprehensive program of adult Christian education should provide multiple opportunities to facilitate the spiritual formation of those involved. This may be done in both formal and informal ways. Adult ministry programs that have proven to be effective and lasting are developed around the following seven principles of ministry.

Principle #1: View Adults as Lifelong Learners

The contemporary term that describes the ongoing nature of learning throughout adulthood is *lifelong learning*. This concept helps us understand that learning may begin in childhood, but it does not cease to exist there. All through youth and adulthood people acquire and use new knowledge. In essence, all of life is a learning process. The only people who don't learn are dead or suffer from a severe pathological condition that prevents learn-

Figure 24.1
Spiritual Audience Groups in a Healthy Church

	Description	Role	(Theirs)	Tasks	(Ours)	Program	Need
5	Adult 1 John 2:13	Partnering	Multiplier Self-starter	10 9	Support Encourage	401	Honoring God
4	Teen 1 John 2:14b	Leading	Responsibility Ability	8 7	Stewardship Facilitator	301	Seeking independence
3	Child 1 John 2:13b	Training	Learning Fundamentals	6 5	Mentorship Cultivate	201	Habits
2	Newborn 1 John 2:12	Investing	Assurance, Assimilation	4 3	Parent Relationship	101	Hunger
1	Unbeliever 1 John 14:6	Gospelizing	Conversion Contact	2 1	Witness Friendship	Discovery groups	Savior

ing.[19] "Lifelong learning is an all-encompassing experience and quite in keeping with the biblical concept of education. It is exciting today to consider the renewed interest in learning on the part of adults."[20]

A great deal of research has been done this century regarding the growth and/or decline that takes place during adulthood. Researchers have sought to answer important questions regarding the possible link between physical decline and mental reasoning. It has long been assumed that there is a general intellectual decline during the later adult stage of life.[21] The first studies that were conducted, especially cross-sectional studies, generally found that intellectual reasoning peaked around age twenty-four and then had a marked decline after age thirty. However, many of these early studies, such as Thorndike's classic curve, emphasized rate of learning rather than ability to learn. His findings showed adult learning dropping off at 1 percent or more per year after age forty-five.[22] More recent studies do not show the severe declines reported in earlier studies.[23] Those studies which revealed a straight-line decline after age thirty appear to be more in motor skills rather than in mental capacity or creative capabilities.[24] The research of Baltes and Schaie found that the upper limits of adult learning ability were significantly higher (even into the mid-eighties) than those reported in earlier studies.[25]

Adults continue to learn and grow throughout all of life. The catch phrase "lifelong learning" accurately describes this reality. It is possible however, that when we talk about adults growing old, too often we put the emphasis on "old" rather than "growing." Indeed, many adults live highly successful and productive lives long into their senior adult years. For example, Michelangelo completed the dome of St. Peter's Cathedral at age seventy, and Handel, Haydn, and Verdi created their most acclaimed works after age seventy. Goethe completed *Faust* after age eighty, while Thomas Hobbes was quite prolific up until the age of ninety-one. Tennyson continued to write poetry even after he turned eighty. The great British statesman and politician Winston Churchill became prime minister at age seventy-seven. The American inventors Benjamin Franklin and Thomas Jefferson made some of their greatest contributions to the world after the age of eighty.[26]

Wise teachers of adults promote lifelong learning by following the above guidelines. Adult educational ministries desire to help people not only go through life but also to grow through it.

Principle #2: Integrate Evangelism into Every Ministry and Program

The message of salvation is like a scarlet thread to be woven throughout the tapestry of all adult ministries. This emphasis reminds us that all individuals are sinners and separated from God's love and forgiveness (John 3:17–18; Rom. 3:9–20). The good news is that God has provided a means of bridging the gap between himself and humankind through his Son Jesus Christ (Acts 2:29–36).

Clearly, the Scriptures place primary evangelistic emphasis on adults as heads of their households.[27] The degree to which evangelism will be emphasized in each activity may be different, depending on the objectives of the activity. It may take the form of a devotional talk, personal testimony, or shared answers to prayer, but periodically there needs to be an opportunity for participants to respond to the gospel message. This may be done in a formal, corporate setting or an informal, private one.

Concerns have been raised about the lasting effects of programmed evangelistic programs such as Evangelism Explosion[28] or large-scale crusades such as the Harvest Crusades or Promise Keepers. The criticisms center on the use of allegedly manipulative techniques or the failure to plan for long-term follow-up of converts.[29] Current research suggests that decisions made via lifestyle or friendship evangelism have greater potential for lasting impact.

Principle #3: Emphasize the Relational Benefits of Involvement

Almost all adults have strong desires for belonging and acceptance. They look for friendships to provide encouragement and affirmation. The church is a natural place for this relationship need to be met. That is why a crucial concern for many adult ministries is the assimilation of new people. In America, programs attract people, but relationships keep them. It is critical to cement people together relationally in the first six to eight weeks after their initial visit. Barna and McKay describe the contemporary attitude well:

> Many Christians are desperate for friendships with spiritual kinfolk. Many people interviewed in our opinion surveys indicated their willingness to sacrifice first-rate preaching and Sunday school teaching for the opportunity to develop deep and lasting bonds with other Christians.[30]

An effective adult ministry is concerned about assimilation and incorporation. It will build bridges through existing friendships and relationships, monitor involvement and respond when needed, work at creating an "incorporation consciousness," and encourage subgroupings as a basis for deeper fellowship.[31]

Adults want to know that some individual or group of people cares for them, prays for them, and loves them in spite of their shortcomings. This is why the small-group movement has had such far-reaching success in recent decades.[32] Since 1984 more adults have participated in a weekly small group experience for religious purposes than those who attend Sunday school.[33] Solid theological foundation for the importance of Christian community in small groups has been articulated in separate works by Davies, Gorman, and Icenagle.[34]

Principle #4: Challenge Adults to Serve Their Church and Community

According to Ephesians 4:11–16, the essence of the church is active engagement in the lives of people. God gave his church gifts for the purpose of reaching out to the lost and for serving the needs of the local body of believers. Both are essential activities. Robert Pazmiño sees this active engagement as one of the five primary functions of the church. He believes this includes actual deeds of service to both Christians and non-Christians.[35] Adults should be reminded that the word *ministry* literally means "to serve." As such, we are called to be servant-ministers to the world on God's behalf. God himself set the example when he revealed to us his servant nature by searching for Adam and Eve after their sin (Gen. 3) and by sending the Messiah as a servant (Isa. 42–53). He commissioned his people to be a servant nation (Gen. 12). Further, we see this servant-minister theme clearly in both

Jesus Christ (Matt. 16:24–26) and the Holy Spirit (Gal. 2:20).[36] Adult ministries must foster people who serve both individually and corporately.

Adult ministries will teach and promote that all grown-ups—not just the clergy—are ministers to voluntarily serve God. They will promote structures and organizational climates that encourage service and leadership development. They will recognize the uniqueness of recruiting, training, placing, caring for, retaining, and managing volunteers.[37] They will understand the changing motivations for service.[38] Finally, they will focus on supporting adults as they exercise their personal spiritual gifts and passions. Adult ministries promote the conviction that ordinary people can accomplish the extraordinary when they rely on the Holy Spirit.

The breadth of adult ministry is impressive. Each year millions of volunteer service hours are donated in nonprofit organizations. Most obvious is service within the local church. This may take the form of being an elder, deacon, deaconess, Sunday school teacher, children's club worker, youth sponsor, home Bible study leader, cell group or recovery group leader, usher, or nursery worker. Each plays a critical role in serving Christ and local believers.

Beyond these internal means of service are numerous opportunities for community assistance and service. Proscriptive adult ministries should encourage and structure activities that get people involved in setting larger boundaries to express their God given giftedness and creativity.[39] Adult believers are to minister beyond the doors of the local church and in their local community. This might include delivering Meals on Wheels, coaching a little league team, volunteering to help at the adult day care center or a home for unwed mothers, serving as a city councilor or on a local school and library board, working with the poor or single parents, helping in soup kitchens, or serving as an advocate for a special-interest group such as Habitat for Humanity.

Increasing attention to social, political, and economic concerns will enable the church to effectively care for the needy and those who are hurting. Integrating radical social action with evangelism is the only true hope for restoring at-risk communities.[40] Adult ministries have often been slow in responding to these latter concerns, and the church is long overdue in its efforts to activate church members for community involvement.

Principle #5: Leave a Legacy for the Next Generation

The notion of mentoring dates back to classical Greek mythology, from which the term *mentor* is derived. Odysseus entrusted his house as well as his son Telemachus to an older, wiser, and more experienced individual named Mentor. Mentor had the responsibility for the total development of Telemachus. This encompassed every facet of his life, including the spiritual, physical, social, educational, and moral aspects. Classical mentors provided experiences that allowed for the complete development of a younger protégé. It was done in "a series of interactions that were sometimes strong and emotional, in which the mentor was viewed as a trusted and loved person."[41]

In the Bible, there are numerous examples of mentoring relationships. Most prominent is the mentoring relationship that Jesus Christ had with his twelve disciples. In addition, Barnabas mentored Paul in his early days at Antioch, and Paul carried on this tradition by mentoring Timothy.

Some adult ministries have formal mentoring programs. They may last for as much as three years or as little as a few months. They may have designated beginning and ending points or be ongoing and continuous. The African-American community has done a masterful job incorporating a mentoring program into its churches through the "rites of passage" program. (Specific details on this program, along with additional links to other mentoring organizations, may be accessed at www.ritesofpassage.org.) In this light Robert Hargrove reminds us that effective mentors are like masterful coaches.[42] They have six characteristics:

1. The ability to inspire
2. Higher standards
3. Honesty and integrity
4. Disciplined intensity
5. Forwarding action
6. A passion to help others learn, grow, and perform

Characteristics of Christian mentors (or spiritual guides) include wisdom, unselfishness, modesty, a hiddenness of life, confident self-giving to God, sensitivity to the Spirit, and a desire to live rather than talk about the Christian life.[43] Thankfully, most adult ministries have chosen to utilize informal mentoring. This occurs with a "significant other" during a conversation.[44] Counsel and "seed thoughts" are shared. Godly wisdom is passed on.[45] Houston reminds us that it is primarily a love relationship freely given and unsolicited. He sees Christian mentors being resolute spirits.[46]

An old-time logger, after winning a grueling all-day competition, was asked by the younger, defeated competitor what his secret was. The man replied, "To perform at a consistently high level, you must stop every once in a while and sharpen your axe." Good mentors help sharpen one's axe.

Principle #6: Focus on Genuine Spiritual Formation

At the center of contemporary adult ministries is a renewed attention to spiritual formation. The revival of interest in local church spiritual formation is in part a rediscovery of biblical and historical roots. It also represents a sociological shift in our culture: from scientific, objective rationalism to intuitive sensing, concern for wholeness, and inner being.[47] Many Christian adults feel a gnawing hunger for a deeper spiritual walk. They long for a lifestyle of spiritual vitality and personal fulfillment. They want to grow more fully into the image of Christ and know God intimately. They sense something is missing in their busy, overly committed, and often draining Christianity. One of the greatest movements of the last quarter century has been the resurgence of literature that helps support a more mature walk with Christ. These materials draw our attention back to the essential spiritual disciplines of our faith. Disciplines such as fasting, journaling, guided meditation, rituals, meditative prayer, and use of the Jesus Prayer have seemingly been rediscovered. Mulholland has written persuasively on how to use the Bible for spiritual formation rather than information.[48] These methods, and others, are returning people to biblical practices found within the Word of God. These techniques are soul-shaping tools that help to condition our souls.[49] They are deliberately chosen and intentionally cultivated in order to focus on God and grow in the Christian life. Practicing these spiritual disciplines is not the means by which one earns grace; rather, they put us in a place where we are more receptive to God's grace and goodness.

Each of these programmatic principles should be used to guide the leader of adults toward an intentional ministry that contributes to the personal and corporate spiritual maturity of the church.

CONCLUSION

Shaping a pastoral strategy that offers spiritual nourishment to the whole congregation and also empowers individual spiritual development is one of the most fulfilling areas of adult education ministry. This needs to be the focus of adult ministry as we make long-range strategic plans. It has been estimated that approximately 20 percent of our North American population will be over the age of sixty-five in the next millennium. The church must look ahead to the future and project where the needs of the world will be and proactively plan for these needs. A well-designed and comprehensive ministry to adults must be at the forefront of our long-term planning.

NOTES

1. Dietrich Bonhoeffer, *Life Together* (New York: Harper and Row, 1954), p. 37.

2. M. Robert Mulholland, *Shaped by the Word: The Power of Scripture in Spiritual Formation* (Nashville: Upper Room, 1985), p. 41.

3. Robert N. Bellah et al., *Habits of the Heart* (Berkeley, Calif.: University of California Press, 1985).

4. Edward L. Hayes, "Theological Foundations of Adult Christian Education," in *Adult Education in the Church,* ed. R. B. Zuck and G. A. Getz (Chicago: Moody, 1970), pp. 30–31.

5. Bureau of the Census, *U.S. Census Facts,* Bureau of the Census (Washington D.C., 1994), p. 56.

6. Bureau of Statistics, *Statistics Canada,* Canadian Bureau of Statistics, (Ottawa, Ont., 1994), p. 11.

7. http://lcweb2.loc.gov/frd/cs/mxtoc.html

8. William Shakespeare, *As You Like It* 2.7.139–66.

9. In Ruth Jacobs, *Don't Call Me an Old Woman,* rev. ed. (n.p.: KIT, Inc., 1994).

10. Cited in *The Oxford Book of Aging,* ed. Thomas R. Cole and Mary G. Winkler (New York: Oxford University Press, 1994), pp. 39–40.

11. Nick Stinnett and John DeFrain, *Secrets of Strong Families* (New York: Berkley, 1986).

12. Dolores Curran, *Traits of a Healthy Family* (San Francisco: Harper and Row, 1993).

13. Ronald Habermas and Klaus Issler, *Teaching for Reconciliation* (Grand Rapids: Baker, 1992), p. 163.

14. Sterling A. Brown, "Sister Lou," in *The Collected Poems of Sterling A. Brown*, ed. Michael S. Harper (New York: Harper-Collins, 1980).

15. Habermas and Issler, *Teaching for Reconciliation,* p. 163.

16. Kenneth O. Gangel and James C. Wilhoit, eds., *The Christian Educator's Handbook of Adult Education* (Wheaton, Ill.: Victor, 1993), p. 16.

17. Robert W. Havighurst, *Developmental Tasks and Education,* 3d ed. (New York: McKay, 1972), p. 78.

18. Warren W. Wilbert, *Teaching Christian Adults* (Grand Rapids: Baker, 1980), p. 87.

19. Huey B. Long and Curtis Ulmer, *Are They Ever Too Old to Learn?* (Englewood Cliffs, N.J.: Prentice-Hall, 1971). Also see Huey B. Long, Kay McCrary, and S. Ackerman, "Adult Cognition: Piagetian-Based Research Findings," *Adult Education* 30, no. 1 (1980): 3–18.

20. Gilbert A. Peterson, *The Christian Education of Adults* (Chicago: Moody, 1984), p. 25.

21. Ibid., p. 186.

22. Huey B. Long, *Adult Learning: Research and Practice* (New York: Cambridge University Press, 1983).

23. Alan B. Knox, *Helping Adults Learn* (San Francisco: Jossey-Bass, 1986).

24. Peterson, *Christian Education of Adults,* p. 186.

25. Paul B. Baltes and K. Warner Schaie, "Aging and I.Q.: The Myth of the Twilight Years," *Psychology Today* (March 1974): 35–40.

26. Peterson, *Christian Education of Adults,* p. 186.

27. Gene A. Getz, *Sharpening the Focus of the Church* (Chicago: Moody, 1974), pp. 43–46.

28. D. James Kennedy, *Evangelism Explosion,* 4th ed. (Carol Stream, Ill.: Tyndale, 1996).

29. Juan Ortiz, *Disciple* (Carol Stream, Ill.: Creation House, 1975).

30. George Barna and William McKay, *Vital Signs: Emerging Social Trends and the Future of American Christianity* (Westchester, Ill.: Crossway, 1984), p. 184.

31. Win Arn and Charles Arn, *Catch the Age Wave* (Grand Rapids: Baker, 1993).

32. Kenneth Gangel, *Ministering to Today's Adults* (Nashville: Word, 1999), p. 74.

33. George C. Gallup, "Religion in America," Gallup Poll Research, 1984.

34. See James A. Davies, "New Testament Principles of Relationships," *Christian Education Journal* 12, no. 3 (spring 1992): 131–46; Julie A. Gorman, *Community That Is Christian* (Wheaton, Ill.: Bridgepoint, 1993); and Gareth Weldon Icenagle, *Biblical Foundations for Small Group Ministry* (Downers Grove, Ill.: InterVarsity, 1994).

35. Robert W. Pazmiño, *Foundational Issues in Christian Education* (Grand Rapids: Baker, 1997), p. 11.

36. I am indebted to a faculty colleague, Dr. Lennard W. Wallmark, for his thinking in this regard. Personal conversation with the author, 16 September 1998.

37. See Dennis E. Williams and Kenneth O. Gangel, *Volunteers for Today's Church* (Grand Rapids: Baker, 1993); Donald Ratcliff and Blake J. Neff, *The Complete Guide to Religious Education Volunteers* (Birmingham, Ala.: Religious Education Press, 1993); and Marlene Wilson, *The Effective Management of Volunteer Programs* (Boulder, Colo.: Johnson, 1976).

38. Mark Senter III, *Recruiting Volunteers in the Church* (Wheaton, Ill.: Victor, 1990).

39. Thomas G. Bandy, *Christian Chaos: Revolutionizing the Congregation* (Nashville: Abingdon, 1999).

40. See Ronald J. Sider, *Cup of Water, Bread of Life* (Grand Rapids: Zondervan, 1994); and John M. Perkins, *Restoring At-Risk Communities* (Grand Rapids: Baker, 1995).

41. T. Thomas, "Mentoring in the Career Development of Illinois Community College Presidents" (Ed.D. diss., Northern Illinois University, 1985).

42. Robert J. Hargrove, *Masterful Coaching* (San Francisco: Jossey-Bass, 1995), pp. 42–51.

43. See Kenneth Leech, *Soul Friend* (San Francisco: Harper and Row, 1980); James A. Davies, "Patterns of Spiritual Direction," in *Christian Education Journal* 13, no. 3 (spring 1993): 49–65; and James Houston, "Why the Contemporary Interest in Mentoring?" *Christian Education Journal* n.s. 3, no. 1 (spring 1999): 81–89.

44. Laurent A. Daloz, *Effective Teaching and Mentoring* (San Francisco: Jossey-Bass, 1986).

45. Ted W. Engstrom, *The Fine Art of Mentoring* (Brentwood, Tenn.: Wolgemuth and Hyatt, 1989); and Houston, "Why the Contemporary Interest in Mentoring?" pp. 88–89.

46. Houston, "Why the Contemporary Interest in Mentoring?" pp. 81–89.

47. See Mulholland, *Shaped by the Word* and Bellah et al., *Habits of the Heart.*

48. M. Robert Mulholland, *Shaped by the Word;* and idem., *Invitation to a Journey: A Road Map for Spiritual Formation* (Downers Grove, Ill.: InterVarsity, 1993).

49. Douglas J. Rumford, *Soul Shaping: Taking Care of Your Spiritual Life* (Wheaton, Ill.: Tyndale, 1996), p. 87.

GENERATIONAL PERSPECTIVES: MINISTERING TO BUILDERS, BOOMERS, BUSTERS, AND BRIDGERS

25

Wesley Black

While there are many ways to describe people, none has caught the attention of Christian educators in recent years like the generational categories. Developmentalists, sociologists, psychologists, and even futurists have all contributed to our efforts of understanding people and effective ways of teaching and ministering to them. Generational theorists offer a fresh perspective in describing and understanding those who make up the audiences for Christian education.

DEFINITION OF GENERATIONS

In telling the story of Adam, the writer of Genesis says, "This is the book of the generations of Adam. In the day when God created man, He made him in the likeness of God" (Genesis 5:1 NASB). The concept of generations in biblical accounts is understood in two distinct ways. There is a larger, more general perspective and also a more narrowly defined approach.

Taking the broader perspective, a generation is understood as a "specific period of time and its significant events making up the life span of a group of people."[1] History is often recounted in this way. A specific time frame is described, and all the people who lived during this time are treated equally in the historical setting. An example of this would be Psalm 24:3–6:

Who may ascend the hill of the LORD? Who may stand in his holy place? He who has clean hands and a pure heart, who does not lift up his soul to an idol or swear by what is false. He will receive blessing from the LORD and vindication from God his Savior. Such is the generation of those who seek him, who seek your face, O God of Jacob.

However, another biblical description of a generation can be seen in a "more indefinite time span, referring to an individual time span or to a group of people living at a particular time."[2] This usage focuses more on the people who experience similar events during a span of time. An example of this would be seen in Deuteronomy 1:34–36, where Moses speaks to the people who have left Egypt and are journeying to the Promised Land:

When the LORD heard what you said, he was angry and solemnly swore: "Not a man of this evil generation shall see the good land I swore to give your forefathers, except Caleb son of Jephunneh. He will see it, and I will give him and his descendants the land he set his feet on, because he followed the Lord wholeheartedly."

Thinking in generational terms provides a different approach in understanding people. Developmental approaches provide understanding of the various stages of a person's life span. Socio-logical perspectives provide understanding of the various social groups to which people may belong. Psychological perspectives provide understanding of the various personality and attitudinal cate-gories of people. But generational perspectives provide a picture of the "why" behind the actions, values, and beliefs of segments of society.[3]

A generation can best be defined as a group of people born within a span of about twenty-two years (about the length of time from a mother's birth until she also gives birth). People born within a generation are placed there invol-untarily and permanently.[4] This provides a stronger basis for generalizing about people other than by social categories such as gender, race, region, or age.[5] Their common treasure of memories and experiences flavor the entire body of values, beliefs, and attitudes of a generation of people. "What makes the cohort group truly unique is that all its members—from birth on—always encounter the same national events, moods, and trends at similar ages. They retain, in other words, a *common age location in history* throughout their lives. Since history affects people differently according to their age, a com-mon age location is what gives each cohort-group a distinct biography and a distinct lifecycle."[6]

GENERATIONAL CATEGORIES

There have been many attempts over the years to categorize generations. If one uses the com-monly held definition of twenty years as the di-viding point for marking a generation, then in the past one hundred years there have been five dis-tinct generations—each marked by some signifi-cant group life event such as war, economic crisis, or social turmoil. Some sociologists differ on the twenty-year marker and therefore reduce the number of generations in the twentieth century to four.

Strauss and Howe label the categories and cor-responding years as follows:[7]

G. I. Generation	1901–1924
Silent Generation	1925–1942
Boom Generation	1943–1960
Thirteenth Generation	1961–1981
Millennial Generation	1982–present

Hanks applies different labels to the genera-tions and places them as follows:[8]

PowerBuilders	1901–1925
PeaceMakers	1926–1944
PathFinders	1945–1963
PaceSetters	1964–1981

Rainer, who classifies generational periods by birth rates, places the generational categories in slightly different years:[9]

Builders	1910–1946	approx. 76 million births
Boomers	1946–1964	approx. 77 million births
Busters	1965–1976	approx. 44 million births
Bridgers	1977–1994	approx. 72 million births

Though there may not be any agreed-upon for-mula for defining a generation or generational la-bels, the important thing to remember for our pur-poses is that there clearly are four to five different generations within the twentieth century. Each is marked by different social circumstances and co-hort life events. A brief description of each gen-eration and a strategy for ministering to those within each generational category will follow.

DESCRIPTIONS AND IMPLICATIONS OF THE GENERATIONS

The Builder Generation

The generation born during the first quarter of the twentieth century is known as the Builder Generation.[10] Born between 1900 and 1925, this generation is sometimes referred to as the G. I. Generation because they were alive during both world wars. In addition to these wars, this gener-ation also experienced the Great Depression in America. The size of this group is approximately thirty-seven million people.[11]

This generation exhibits a strong community spirit, and the family unit is very important to them. They tend to be organized, well-disciplined, highly structured, left-brained, friendly, and opti-mistic. They are achievers, leading the world in number of recipients of Nobel Prizes, landing a man on the moon, and creating the "American Dream." President John F. Kennedy was a stereo-typical member of this generation.[12]

In spite of their great strengths, they also have some weaknesses. With their intense focus on science and technology, naturalism tends to lead them away from God. Also, their pursuit of success brings a focus on the masses rather than a regard for individuals. They have been content to provide economic rather than emotional support for their children. Environmental concerns such as conservation, renewable resources, and saving the rain forest were set aside for what are seen as more important economic and entitlement issues. This is the generation in which the nuclear bomb and the cold war were created.[13]

The Builders provide a stable model for marriage. Exhibiting a can-do spirit, they have been the most mission-minded generation in the twentieth century.[14] These characteristics provide models for younger generations that have lacked such patterns in both home and church families.

The teaching/learning effort with Builders should center on inductive methodologies as the primary approach to learning. They recognize the value of lecture, memorization, and drill as learning tools. This generation generally is made up of rational pragmatists who rely on reason rather than sense perceptions as their major source of information.[15] They are not known as being "touchy feely" in the classroom or in life.

Churches will need to recognize that Builders still value the King James Version of the Bible and enjoy reinforcing their theology through the singing of Christian hymns accompanied by the organ. For the most part, they are self-motivated learners, preferring active learning or kinesthetic activities as the dominant learning style.[16]

The Silent Generation

Born between 1925 and 1942, the Silent Generation is also referred to by some sociologists as the PeaceMaker generation.[17] Born shortly after World War I, they lived through both the Great Depression and World War II. The size of this group is approximately thirty million.[18]

The Silent Generation tends to be recessive and conformist. They avoid risks but show concern for others and their trials in life. They generally excel in human relations skills and are compassionate and empathetic with others. They are polite and have a strong collective social conscience. Raised during the Great Depression, they exhibit strong people skills, with many choosing careers in the helping fields—teachers, doctors, and ministers. It is interesting to note that this generation has never produced a president of the United States.[19]

This generation also has some tendencies that may cause concern. Their low-risk approach and pluralistic attitudes may lead to tolerance for lifestyles and worldviews that are antithetical to biblical Christianity. Others simply adopt a values-neutral attitude. This generation has exhibited weaker family values, high numbers of abortions, and the highest divorce rate of any generation. The concept of latchkey kids came from this generation. With ambivalent political views and a tendency to find therapists and psychoanalysis as the answer to life's problems, this generation gave rise to the term *midlife crisis*.[20]

Members of the Silent Generation provide a good pool of volunteers for Sunday school and other church ministries. They are outer-directed, compassionate, and people-oriented. They are good at meeting the needs of a broad spectrum of people. As strong supporters of the church, they are committed to tithing and view the deacon as a servant-leader. Intergenerational skills are a real plus for this generation.

PeaceMakers, with strong relational skills, enjoy intergenerational Bible studies. They sense the need for inclusion, pluralism, and tolerance. They are open to discussing new ideas and value social action as a means of improving society. Inductive logic and discovery learning are their primary means of gaining knowledge. They are excellent facilitators of learning groups. An auditory style of learning, including discussions and debates, is preferred. They tend to be creative, artistic, and musically oriented.[21]

The Baby Boom Generation

The generation born immediately following World War II, known as the Boomer generation, gains its name from being the largest number of babies born in this century. The population of this generation is approximately seventy-six million.[22] Raised by stay-at-home mothers who were younger than later generation mothers, they lived through the Vietnam War and Woodstock. Growing up during the countercultural and antiauthoritarian days of the 1960s, they developed a self-centered and independent spirit. They contributed to New Age spiritualism and self-help movements.[23]

Boomers are characterized as idealists. Disillusioned by civil, state, and federal corruption, they were going to secure world peace, purge the world of poverty and pollution, create a new utopian society—and have it all accomplished by tomorrow. With high spiritual sensitivity and a desire for spiritual awakening, they concentrated on cultural and moral issues. Growing up as indulged youth, this generation fragmented into narcissistic young adults and moralistic midlifers. They triggered cultural creativity and challenged existing values.[24] Even though the decades of sexual enlightenment and social freedoms left their imprint on this generation, they tend to challenge sex, profanity, and violence in the media. They want to give more to their children than they felt they received from their parents. They champion causes with vision, principles, and moral correctness.[25]

Boomers possess a strong work ethic and find satisfaction in their careers. They work long hours and are willing to sacrifice family for their professional advancement. Their public voice has called for protection of children from dangers such as sexual abuse, violence, drugs, and so on. They increasingly watch over youth activities and seek to punish criminals for transgressions.[26]

The Boomer generation emphasizes individuality, thus leading to problems in reaching consensus and mobilizing the masses. Choosing to reject many of the values held in esteem by their parents, the Boomer generation contributed to the highest divorce rate ever experienced in this country. As a result, families are fragmented, and the result has been an entirely new definition of what constitutes a family. As a result of their divorce and remarriage patterns, we now have blended families, stepfamilies, and multigenerational families. Their actions can sometimes be ruthless, selfish, arrogant, and judgmental.[27]

Due to their individualistic natures, Boomers do not generally relate well to members of other generational categories. There seems to be a real generational gap between those born before and those born after 1945. Tension may grow between those who are traditional church members and those from the Boomer generation.[28]

Those who serve as teachers for the Boomer generation will do well to remember the idealistic bent of this generation. They value the world of ideas, vision, and principles. They still desire to shape the cultural and moral issues of society. There is an inclination for deductive logic over inductive experimentation, with a tendency to accept biblical truth, but they are slower to apply it to real life.

Boomers enjoy a visual approach to learning, having grown up in the world of television. They are motivated by learning techniques that are visual, creative, and appealing to the eye. As champions of individualism, they demand a high level of personal choice in learning methods, topics, and materials. They expect high quality in Christian education for their young and make excellent teachers.[29]

The Buster Generation

Following the Boomer generation during the years 1961–1981, there was a sharp decline, or "bust," in the number of births. This gave rise to one of the names for the next generation, the Busters. There are approximately forty-four million Busters.[30]

Busters have been called by several names, including Generation X,[31] the Thirteenth Generation,[32] PaceSetters,[33] and also Bridgers.[34] At times they have been called the particularly derogatory name Slackers, especially by those of the Boomer generation, and stereotyped as pessimistic, possibly because of poor involvement in the job market.[35] One possible reason for the nondescript label "Generation X" is that they do not easily fall into categories.

Busters are seen as being reactive in character. That is, they are recessive, growing up as underprotected and criticized youth and moving into young adulthood as risk-taking, alienated people. They will mellow into pragmatic midlife leaders and reclusive elders. Members of this generation cherish individualism and have a declining view of institutions.[36]

Busters have a realistic view of life, with a streetwise, practical approach to problems. They lean away from idealistic views and prefer practical fields of study and careers. They value personal relationships with family and friends. Busters are survivors, having demonstrated courage, bravery, and resilience on the battlefield and the streets. This generation has slowed the rates of divorce and abortion and seems to believe in marriage.[37]

Along with these strengths, however, are some weaknesses. Perceived by older generations as dysfunctional, many Busters are skeptical and cynical. They have grown up emotionally weakened and stressed-out, with low self-esteem and a cautious attitude about life. Many in this generation exhibit an amoral lifestyle with a high level of sexual activity and other at-risk behaviors. They have a low level of economic security, often not faring as well as their parents, whereas others have unrealistic expectations, hoping to match their parents' achievements at a far earlier age.[38]

Busters are ravenous consumers, especially of technological gadgets. Raised in a technologically rich environment, they tend to have short attention spans and a preference for eye-catching, fast-moving forms of information and entertainment. They are not avid readers since they prefer movies to literature. Many are pleasure-seekers and passive learners, often preferring "edutainment" in their learning experiences. Corporate managers often have to provide skill training to overcome deficiencies and have to act as parents to them.[39]

Busters relate best to experiences and stories. They may prefer their learning to come from real-life biblical stories and characters rather than abstract theological principles. They are biblically illiterate compared to previous generations. They are more responsive to apologetics than a comparative religions approach. Leaders must be transparent, vulnerable, and real.[40]

Some Busters may treat the Bible study leader as a parent, desiring personal attention, love, and direction in life decisions. They attend Bible studies and small groups in order to find practical and relevant answers to real-life experiences. They are most interested in action-oriented ministry. This generation is racially diverse, quite accepting and comfortable in experiences with multicultural groups. They have shown erratic Bible study attendance patterns. Their learning style blends the auditory, visual, and kinesthetic. There is a high preference for a multimedia approach to Bible learning.[41]

Tim Celek and Dieter Zander, two ministers with experience in teaching Busters, offer some insights into effective educational approaches for this generation. They contend that the gospel is attractive, relevant, and true since these are terms that catch the attention of the Buster generation and draw them into the learning experiences.[42]

They state, "The first thing we have to do is start with the attractiveness of what we're trying to communicate. We don't just start by saying, 'This is true because it's true.' We start by saying, 'This is attractive. Wouldn't you like to take a closer look?' We seek to draw their attention to the attractiveness of the message."[43]

Part of the attractiveness of the gospel is the peace that it brings to life. This relates to the biblical concepts of redemption and reconciliation. Redemption can be compared to the contemporary concern with recycling. As Celek and Zander state, "Redemption is taking something that should be thrown away and making it useful again. And that's where busters are at."[44] Celek should know. Over the years he has developed a nationally acclaimed ministry to Busters at Calvary Church Newport Mesa, located in Southern California.

There are a number of terms that seem to strike a nerve with this generation. Among them is *reconciliation,* which is about bringing peace into life and relationships. Peace is often missing in the lives of Busters. "What brings about so much anguish within Busters' lives? The lack of reconciliation—with their family and with their society. That is what the gospel is all about, when it gets right down to it."[45]

A second term that ranks high in teaching Busters is *relevance*. In order to effectively communicate the gospel to a postmodern mind, it has to be seen as relevant. Not only are the truths of the gospel attractive, "but they're [also] practical and pertinent: You can experience them and they will make a definite difference in your life."[46]

Truth is the third term that connects with Busters. But truth must be communicated in a style different from that used with previous generations. Older generations wanted answers in logical, linear forms of reasoning. They deferred to traditional forms of authority such as the church and the Scriptures. Builders and Boomers wanted sermons and lessons that had several logical points and could be readily applied to life. But the most effective way to communicate the gospel to the Buster generation is through stories. "Busters are storytellers and story listeners."[47] This does not imply that Busters do not want answers. They just might not want those answers in the form of an outline or a well-reasoned argument. They want their answers "couched in the context of life.

That's why they like the Gospels and the Old Testament stories more than the Epistles."[48]

An important ministry consideration for reaching and teaching the Buster generation is authenticity. This can be seen in such things as clothing, attitudes, and preaching styles. University Baptist Church, a Generation X church in Waco, Texas, appeals to large numbers of Busters by stressing authenticity in worship styles, music, and leadership. Pastor Chris Seay often wears drab shirts, sneakers, and baggy jeans in leading a worship service that seems thrown together. They may start late and follow no obvious script or schedule. This differs greatly from the worship styles at Willow Creek, where the services start promptly, follow a tight script, and feature actors and musicians with color-coordinated clothing. "Authenticity is an important concept for Seay and members of his flock because they see the lack of authenticity as a huge problem for some churches and their leaders. Seay believes that unless Christians are truly open and honest about their own shortcomings, unchurched Gen Xers will view believers as hypocritical and self-righteous."[49]

Flexibility is another important consideration in ministering with Busters. Their culture is fluid, shifting, and ever-changing. As the authors of *Twentysomething* have observed, "How adaptable you are to shifting conditions, how responsive you are to bend to the situation—these capabilities will be the keys to your success."[50]

The Millennial Generation

Those born in the last generation of the twentieth century (1982–2000) are known as the Millennials.[51] Those who study characteristics of generational groups believe this generation reflects the values of the Builder generation. "This generation parallels the attributes associated with their grandparents and great-grandparents—the Power-Builder generation born in the first decades of this century."[52] Obviously, it is too soon to tell, but if this is a correct characterization, they will grow up as overprotected youth, move into a powerful midlife group of adults, and emerge as busy elders.[53]

The birth years and total population of this last category differs according to various authors and perceptions of what makes up a generation. Strauss and Howe indicate the birth years from 1982 to just past the year 2000, with a total population of approximately 76 million.[54] Rainer defines the birth years between 1977 and 1994, with a population of approximately 72 million.[55] In either case, this is a very large group, rivaling the Boomer generation's 76 to 77 million births.

Millennials are growing up in an increasingly multiracial and multicultural world. Less than two-thirds of them are Anglos (non-Hispanic white), while the Boomers were three-fourths non-Hispanic white. Nearly two million of these births were to multiracial parents. This multicultural environment opens up the possibility of interest in non-Western religions. While this generation is eager to learn about religion, their interest includes almost any expression of a higher power. Islam, for example, is one of the fastest-growing influences among this generation.[56]

The Millennial generation's pulse runs fast. Bombarded by frequent images, they are in need of continual "hits." The remote control symbolizes their reality: change is constant; focus is fragmented. They have eaten from the tree of knowledge and have developed a sense of enlightenment. They live for now, since they have little connection to events in the twentieth century. They are jaded, having a "been-there-done-that" attitude. As a result, nothing shocks them. Movies and television keep pushing the envelope on what is socially acceptable and receive few complaints.[57]

Millennials take consumerism for granted. They are into shopping on the Internet, where comparisons are quick and easy to make. They want to test and experiment with their purchases before making them. They want demos and sound bites of everything that interests them. They are a cyber-suckled community that has grown up on the Internet. They've had virtually everything handed to them, so they value little.

Churches that have developed a ministry emphasis to Millennials describe several key concerns. Topping their list is unconditional love. Youth workers need to make an intentional decision to love these kids unconditionally. This is demonstrated in overall attitudes of members of the congregation as well as in specific programming. Millennials also need to have clear boundaries. Though they may not be receiving clear boundaries at home, they seem to respond well to guidelines offered in love. In addition, they have high expectations about life and want to be challenged and given opportunities to respond. Finally, Millennials are culturally sensitive. Churches must understand the generational perspectives and maintain a proper tension between cultural sensitivity and biblical faithfulness.[58]

While some Christian educators from older generations fear technology, especially the forms related to virtual reality, E-mail, Internet, chat rooms, and media applications, those of the Millennial generation see technology as a unifying tool. E-mail, chat rooms, and personal Web pages, for example, serve as important means of communication. Internet music channels, streaming music and video, and other Internet resources provide a common language of culture. "They increasingly view technology as a community force rather than a tool to promote individuality."[59]

Since the popular culture of this generation centers around rampant consumerism and the influences of media, the Millennials are being shaped into consumers before they have had a chance to shape values and morals to make ethical decisions. Consuming products is one of their favorite pastimes. Much of this consumption is related to media. Television and movie screens project images of anorexic-looking models that define beauty. Computers and recorded music provide messages about relationships and values. "What is indecent at school?" teens write in a student newspaper. "Not much. Not even mooning. . . . Indecency is no longer deemed vulgar. It is now looked upon as typical day-to-day living. . . . Peer pressure pushes you into being all-out hateful. . . . Society has made so many things that shouldn't be [normative] *normal,* it's hard to know what is *really* right."[60]

As a result, churches must become authentic in their desire to cross the great divide between church and the "youth group ghetto" to keep these young people in church and to develop them into courageous, disciplined leaders. Several current models serve as examples of ways churches are doing that. One of these, the peer ministry model, is an innovative new strategy for churches hiring youth ministers. Churches hire them as church planters with the objective of developing a team of spiritually mature young adults who will eventually start a new church. The youth minister and selected adult leaders mentor the youth as the core leaders of the new church. Youth sense an immediate responsibility for the success or failure of carrying out the Great Commission. This new approach is still in its infancy and questions still linger, such as how the newly converted teens will be integrated into the larger believing community. Intergenerational relationships are also a major concern.

Churches tend to be bound by traditions, and making significant changes in youth ministry strategy might be a difficult transition for some. The younger generation is often considered to be a subplot in the larger church narrative, despite all the evidence that the majority of faith commitments are made during teen years and that the likelihood of coming to faith declines considerably as people get older. Christian educators will be wise to consider the characteristics of the Millennials and strive to make appropriate adjustments in ministry approaches and strategies.

CAUTION: UNCHARTED ROAD AHEAD

While there is much to appreciate about a generational approach to ministry, there are some other considerations that must be kept in mind while defining and describing people. Much of the generational theory, for example, seems to be based on speculation rather than empirical research. Important events and popular culture are chosen as anecdotal evidence and often used to build generational theories. Grouping sometimes seems arbitrary. For example, some theorists select birth years along lines of life stages, while others select generational boundaries along population sizes. People born near the borders of generational categories are arbitrarily placed in one or the other with little consideration of family, cultural, or developmental influences. Much of generational theory seems to have a North American perspective.

Generational theory categorizes people into groups with little consideration for other descriptive categories such as gender, race, economic status, ethnicity, regional influences, or intergenerational influence. Despite abounding evidence of family and parental influence, most generational theory ignores this important facet. Strauss and Howe concede that, "Even though generational membership does not depend at all on family lineage (brothers and sisters or husbands and wives may fall anywhere with respect to cohort-group boundaries), the special bonds—emotional, biological, social, economic—connecting parents to their own children clearly matter."[61]

Finally, the conclusions and descriptions of persons in the various generations are not drawn from quantified data or empirical research but from theoretical frameworks in the parameters of the generations as defined by the authors. There is little quantitative data to back up the generational approaches and conclusions.[62] Christian educators should wisely consider the valuable insights that grow out of generational perspectives but should also keep in mind the limitations of this approach.

Conclusion

In spite of the limitations cited above, there are significant reasons why we should investigate the generational distinctives of the twentieth century. The church is called to be a student of culture, with an emphasis upon making the Bible culturally relevant. The only way to do that is to research demographic differences and prayerfully consider ways to integrate unchanging biblical truth with an ever-changing society. Since it is clear from the Book of Acts that the pattern of one church (e.g., the Jerusalem church) did not become the established pattern of worship and ministry practice for those churches that were planted later (e.g., Antioch, Ephesus, Corinth), then it should not come as a surprise that a "one size fits all" attitude does not work for us either. The Holy Spirit was given, in part, to give us wisdom in the application of his Word to a fallen and lost generation. May God give us this wisdom as we bring the gospel to current and successive generations.

Notes

1. Louis B. Hanks, *Vision, Variety, and Vitality* (Nashville: LifeWay, 1996), p. 43.
2. Ibid.
3. Ibid., p. 44.
4. William Strauss and Neil Howe, *Generations* (New York: William Morrow, 1991), p. 9.
5. Ibid., p. 63.
6. Ibid., p. 48.
7. Ibid., pp. 261–335.
8. Hanks, *Vision, Variety, and Vitality*, p. 49.
9. Thom S. Rainer, *The Bridger Generation* (Nashville: Broadman and Holman, 1997), pp. 1–7.
10. Strauss and Howe, *Generations*, p. 261.
11. Rainer, *Bridger Generation*, p. 7.
12. Hanks, *Vision, Variety, and Vitality*, p. 58.
13. Ibid.
14. Ibid., p. 59.
15. Ibid.
16. Ibid.
17. Strauss and Howe, *Generations*, p. 279.
18. Rainer, *Bridger Generation*, p. 7.
19. Hanks, *Vision, Variety, and Vitality*, p. 68.
20. Ibid.
21. Ibid., p. 69.
22. Rainer, *Bridger Generation*, p. 5.
23. Ibid.
24. Strauss and Howe, *Generations*, p. 299.
25. Hanks, *Vision, Variety, and Vitality*, pp. 83–85.
26. Ibid.
27. Ibid.
28. Ibid., p. 85.
29. Ibid.
30. Rainer, *Bridger Generation*, p. 7.
31. This term was made popular in Douglas Coupland, *Generation X: Tales of an Accelerated Culture* (New York: St. Martin's, 1991).
32. Strauss and Howe, *Generations*, p. 317.
33. Hanks, *Vision, Variety, and Vitality*, p. 49.
34. Rainer, *Bridger Generation*, pp. 1–7.
35. Ibid., p. 6.
36. Strauss and Howe, *Generations*, p. 74.
37. Hanks, *Vision, Variety, and Vitality*, p. 96.
38. Ibid., pp. 96–97.
39. Ibid.
40. Ibid., p. 99.
41. Ibid., pp. 99–100.
42. Tim Celek and Dieter Zander, *Inside the Soul of a New Generation* (Grand Rapids: Zondervan, 1996), pp. 122–26.
43. Ibid., p. 122.
44. Ibid.
45. Ibid., pp. 122–23.
46. Ibid., p. 123.
47. Ibid., p. 125.
48. Ibid., p. 126.
49. Steve Rabey, "Church in Action: Pastor X," *Christianity Today* 40 (11 November 1996): 40.
50. Lawrence J. Bradford and Claire Raines, *Twentysomething* (New York: MasterMedia, 1992), p. 124.
51. Strauss and Howe, *Generations*, p. 335.
52. Hanks, *Vision, Variety, and Vitality*, p. 101.
53. Strauss and Howe, *Generations*, p. 74.
54. Ibid., p. 336.
55. Rainer, *Bridger Generation*, p. 1.
56. Ibid., p. 13.
57. Wendy Murray Zoba, "The Class of 00," *Christianity Today* 41 (3 February 1997): 18.
58. Ibid.
59. Hanks, *Vision, Variety, and Vitality*, p. 107.
60. Quoted in Zoba, "Class of 00," p. 18. (Zoba's italics.)
61. Strauss and Howe, *Generations*, p. 62.
62. Ibid., p. 49.

PART SIX

Specialized Ministries

COUNSELING MINISTRY IN THE CHURCH

26

Donald W. Welch

There has never been a greater need in the history of Christendom for pastors, theologians, Christian educators, evangelists, and counselors to work hand in hand than the present time. As people express unprecedented pain due to the modern-day complexities of life, Christian counseling has become a vital tool for mending fractured lives and nurturing spiritual health. There exists an unparalleled openness for Christian educators and Christian counselors to work hand in hand to serve the hurting masses.

We have more information and proven ways in which to organize and cope with life; yet people seem less able to manage life's complex issues. Pastors today increasingly share their frustrations about the onslaught of needy and disconnected people knocking on their office doors asking for direction and guidance. As one pastor put it, "I have so many hurting people that I'm not sure where and how to begin; the life issues people are facing today are overwhelming."

Although *The Barna Report* suggests that "marriage remains the most popular voluntary institution in our society, with about 85 percent of the population marrying at least once,"[1] the rate of divorce in the church is outpacing the secular world. *The Barna Report* further suggests that "born again Christians are slightly more likely than non-Christians to go through a divorce. Twenty-seven per-

cent of Christians have seen their marriage break up, compared to 23 percent of non-Christians."[2] Add to that an increasing number of children living in blended families and single-parent homes, and it's easy to see why our society is experiencing unparalleled stress, pain, and confusion. One study reports that in divorced families, "approximately 16 percent [of fathers] manage to see their children as often as once a week."[3] With the growing number of latchkey children and our increasingly mobile society, the extended family plays less of a role than once experienced by the family. Our society's children are expressing this deterioration of connectedness by turning on each other in anger, often with guns. Others choose to end their own lives.

Encouraging people to enhance both their individual relationships with God and their collective life relationships must be at the forefront of Christian ministry during the twenty-first century. There has never been a more demanding time in the history of the world to unite a counseling ministry with the ministry of the church. Working together to help the troubled and hurting in God's church strengthens the entire body. Not only do people need to experience and relish God's grace, but they also need to hone the relational skills necessary to navigate the treacherous waters of life.

BIBLICAL FOUNDATIONS OF COUNSELING

Christian counseling, more than any other field of study, focuses on the very core of who we are as God's creation. This helping ministry first attempts to assist people in their understanding of who they are in relationship to God their Creator. Second, Christian counseling assists those who are committed in applying their relationship with God to forming healthy relationships with those around them. Essentially, it applies God-ordained principles to relationships, recognizing "that the Scriptures are more than a description of human nature, a listing of moral principles, or a guidebook for behavior. The Bible calls for commitment and obedience."[4]

The Bible contains numerous references to the importance of good counsel. From the very first days in the Garden of Eden when God counseled Adam and Eve, there was a need for objective counsel that would help people rise above their subjective outlook on life. Throughout its pages, the Bible continues to espouse the importance of wise counsel for abundant living. During the wilderness years, Moses sought God's counsel and utilized this counsel as he led the children of Israel. Isaiah presented counsel through his prophetic announcements. Jesus, our supreme role model, frequently sought counsel from his heavenly Father throughout his earthly ministry (Luke 3:21; 6:12; 9:29). From the forty days in the wilderness to his grueling moments in Gethsemane, Jesus continued to seek his Father's counsel. Jesus also prayed for his counselees; in John 17:21, Jesus prayed that his disciples would be one, as he was one with the Father. The apostle Paul provided counsel on a number of occasions. For example, he encouraged and admonished the young pastor Timothy.

THE DISTINCTIVES OF CHRISTIAN COUNSELING

Although there are numerous counseling theories available to the counselor, Christian counseling begins with specific biblical principles rather than secular theories (cf. 2 Tim. 3:16). First, it is important to consider that theories can be ex-

tremely useful and that many are based on sound principles; yet not all theories begin with the same philosophical foundation. Although it goes without saying that a competent counselor will understand and be prepared to implement a particular counseling theory useful at an appropriate counseling moment, the Christian counselor analyzes all theories through one lens—the Bible.

Second, since we are created in the image of God, Christian counseling will provide an environment by which the counselee can become more open and responsive to God's healing touch.[5] Giving respect without condemnation or unsolicited advice toward the counselee's choices throughout the sessions is crucial. Whether or not the counselee is open and willing to change and/or willing to further develop necessary spiritual and relational skills, it is imperative to give ultimate respect to the person seeking counseling, always striving for a friendly, open, and respectful counseling environment.

Certainly one of God's most foundational principles is that he has given humanity the ability to make choices. He never forces his way into our lives, even though he never wavers in his pursuit of us. God is the gentleman above gentlemen; he provides the space and opportunity for each person to make a choice to obey or disobey him. Counselors must do everything within their power to encourage a counselee to make biblical choices and to assist each person to take the necessary steps toward personal and relational healing and holistic change. "It is movement, not just insight, that produces change."[6] Christian counseling is not advice giving; rather, it provides an atmosphere whereby the counselee may develop his or her abilities to successfully maneuver through painful life challenges.

A third distinctive area of Christian counseling is the recognition of the power of the Holy Spirit. Romans 8:26 speaks of the Holy Spirit praying for us in ways that we are unable to conceive or understand. Without invoking the Holy Spirit to intercede within our sessions, counselors will be attempting to counsel from a purely knowledge-based approach without God's personal wisdom leading the session. Divine revelations discovered during a counseling session and insights and ways in which to make application of these revelations are directly from the Holy Spirit. Jesus said in John 14:16–17, "And I will ask the Father, and he will give you another Counselor to be with you forever—the Spirit of truth." Perhaps this is why the apostle Paul suggests in 1 Thessalonians 5:17 that we "pray continually."

A fourth area that is unique to Christian counseling is the Bible's teaching that God is able to free us from our past. Hebrews 8:12 tells us that our sins are not only forgiven, but they are no longer remembered: "For I will forgive their wickedness and will remember their sins no more." The Bible clearly teaches that Jesus paid the price for our sins once and for all: "So if the Son sets you free, you will be free indeed" (John 8:36). Observing that biblical truth can enable one to sing the old hymn with vigor, "Glorious freedom! Wonderful freedom! No more in chains of sin I repine! Jesus, the glorious Emancipator—Now and forever He shall be mine." This freedom experienced in and through Jesus Christ enables a person to journey onward, looking to the future rather than the past.

In several instances, Jesus would continue to ask a person who was in great turmoil what he or she needed from him before providing healing. The invalid in John 5:1–15 was asked, "Do you want to get well?" Jesus looked past the invalid's obvious physical handicap and peered into the condition of his heart. Jesus demonstrated that often there are hidden issues that may need to be dealt with before forgiveness and healing can be fully assimilated. If a minister or counselor is ineffective in getting at the core of the issue, a person may superficially experience the freedom of forgiveness. Only the symptoms are dealt with, rather than the core issues.

Christian counseling sessions illuminate the gift of forgiveness. But if the Christian is unable to accept this gift, then forgiveness serves only as cognitive calisthenics. Until the counselee understands and accepts God's forgiveness, he or she cannot truly offer forgiveness to others. One can only know God fully when God's complete pardon is accepted. Unfortunately, many pastors and Christian counselors can regretfully name individuals who later walked away from their relationship with God because they were never able to assimilate God's grace into their lives. They only experienced cognitive knowledge of God without receiving and enjoying the heartfelt freedom expressed in Romans 8:1–2: "Therefore, there is now no condemnation for those who are in

Christ Jesus, because through Christ Jesus the law of the Spirit of life set me free from the law of sin and death."

THE INTEGRATION OF THEOLOGY AND PSYCHOLOGY

Many well-meaning evangelical leaders have an underlying suspicion regarding the place of psychology in the church. They believe that Scripture alone should be sufficient to unlock all of the troubles within an individual. However, once they have exhausted all their efforts and the individual is no better off, they reluctantly begin to consider the limited role of psychology. What is needed is a well-informed analysis of how a sound biblical hermeneutic can help utilize what for many years was an untapped resource for pastors.

In the twenty-first century, there is an increasing awareness that theology and psychology can complement one other, so a growing number of pastors and professionals are welcoming a synergistic relationship between these two fields of study. Simply stated, theology is our understanding of who God is and "the methodical explanation of the contents of the Christian faith."[7] An understanding of God is derived through the revealed Word of God and through God's actions by the Holy Spirit. Therefore, a healthy understanding of the human experience can only be understood by articulating clearly who God is and who we are in him. Psychology, on the other hand, is a scientific approach to understanding humankind. It seeks to understand what makes people feel, think, and behave in certain ways. Answers to psychological questions are found through the five senses or empirical evidence and are analyzed using rational thought. "Thus the scientific method is a marriage of Platonic rationality and Aristotelian empirical observation."[8]

Theology has existed for thousands of years. By comparison, psychology has only been an academic discipline for a little over a century. When God conversed with Adam and Eve in the Garden of Eden, human nature was expressing itself to God through words and actions. As the Designer, God knew all about human nature and permitted Adam and Eve to remain free moral agents grappling with their decisions and consequences. It was as if God were coupling their attempts to understand and relate to him (theology) with their attempts to understand and relate to each other and to their world (psychology).

Throughout history, theologians have attempted to define who God is and how we are to appropriately relate to him and to each other. They have paved the way in answering one of the primary philosophical questions asked by all humans: "What is my reason and purpose for existing?" Too often we have mistaken theology for psychology, or vice versa. It is true that correct theology will lead us in the direction of correct and vital living. It is also true that a correct understanding of how people behave psychologically will better equip us to assist persons struggling to navigate life. Utilizing only theology or psychology is bound to limit our ability to assist hurting persons who are seeking spiritual and emotional guidance. It is best to consider the mutual benefits of these two fields of study when attempting to minister God's grace in the life of a challenged individual or family. Pastor Richard Exley has communicated this clearly: "There's nothing in life more meaningful than working with God in the reconstruction of a shattered life. Some call it *counseling.* I call it *ministry,* and it's always been a team effort among the three of us—God, the person and myself."[9] The more fully counselors understand God, the other person, and themselves, the better able they will be in assisting the discouraged. "In Christian education, learning is measured by life change. This is more than just the mere soaking up of facts! Learning is a vibrant process that involves a change of mind and heart evidenced by one's behavior."[10] Truly the consummating beauty of ministry is to experience counseling and Christian education (the process of understanding theology) as marriage partners that serve as a conduit through which God works his atoning grace and victory.

Since the Bible is very clear that we are made in the image of God (Gen. 1:27), there is no way to come to an understanding of God without attempting to understand the plight of humanity. This understanding must begin with the history of God's relationship with his people throughout the pages of both the Old and New Testaments. Furthermore, it would be unwise to attempt to understand humanity by beginning with psychology at the expense of theology. Therefore, it is necessary to begin with God and an understanding of him before embarking on a true understanding of what it means to be a human being.

THE COUNSELING PROCESS

Christian counseling is a reconciliation process: a person seeking healing needs to be fully reconciled to God and others. Gary Collins describes it as "a long-term, in-depth helping process that attempts to bring fundamental changes in the counselee's personality, spiritual values, and ways of thinking."[11] Although there are a myriad of areas important to the counseling process, there are three areas essential to successful Christian counseling: establishing confidentiality, building relationship, and creating awareness.

The first area is confidentiality. The exchange of information shared during the counseling session must remain confidential, or the counselee may never feel secure enough to openly work through the presenting issues. Confidentiality produces confidence towards the minister or counselor. Confidentiality also serves to turn the counseling area into a secure and safe haven; the dark secrets will remain inside the walls. Unless the information is life threatening to the counselee or to someone else, the counselor must maintain a strict code of confidentiality.

One method to assist in the area of confidentiality is to provide an intake form describing the counselor's mode of operation. On this form, the counselor would describe his or her counseling expertise, including degrees, ordination, licensure (including the state in which he or she received it), and years of counseling. Also included on this form would be the scope of the counselor's limitations, meaning that the work with the counselee will need to operate within the counselor's skill-level and area of expertise. For instance, if a person in the congregation with schizophrenia seeks out the pastor's counsel, it would be well for the pastor to advise the person that his skill-level precludes him from assisting with the disorder; however, he could assist the person with spiritual issues related to the disorder. A referral would take place depending upon the severity of the counselee's problem. Assisting the person(s) under your care to know your skill-level limits will help him or her know the specific ways in which you may assist. The intake form should also include a description of the counselee's understanding of the counselor's role as a mandated reporter, meaning that a report to the local authorities would occur if the counselee is believed to be harmful to self or others or to have committed certain crimes. The counselee's signature on this form, giving the counselor the privilege to provide counseling, is essential for establishing clear boundaries.

A second area essential to the counseling process is relationship. Those in counseling need to know that they are not being judged or condemned. The counselee needs to sense early on that the counselor is an unbiased therapeutic listener. This is necessary to a healthy relationship. Michael Nichols says, "The real issue in listening isn't whether we do or don't give advice but whether or not our response is focused on reading and responding to the other person's feelings or is simply a way of dealing with our own."[12] Focused listening has been referred to as "mirroring" or "attending." Deciphering eye contact, hand gestures, and the differences between a closed or open stance on the part of the counselee may reveal nonverbal communication. This interpretation skill is a continual process as the counselor seeks to understand the developmental, social, environmental, economic, and overall functioning of the counselee.

Ideally, the counselor should not attempt to counsel someone when he or she is also dealing with personal issues similar to those of the counselee(s). A professor of pastoral counseling illustrated this by saying, "If you are moving through some difficult times in your marriage, it is important to remember that you should not be attempting to help those who are also moving through a similar and difficult time in their marriage."[13] It would be impossible to differentiate between the difficulties in your own marriage and those in the counselee's marriage. This can produce "countertransference," where the listener becomes the subject rather than the objective listener.[14]

Although listening is essential to providing an atmosphere whereby the counselee can feel safe and is able to work through life challenges, building rapport is also very critical. A person experiencing trauma is tentative and prone to withdraw. Determining the types of questions that probe the sensitive areas without being threatening will usually begin to soften the clenched heart. Permitting God's compassion to flow through counseling is a tremendous gift to the person searching for health and wholeness. Martin Buber expressed this best by saying, "Relation is reciprocity."[15]

If a person believes the counselor is sincerely interested, reciprocity will occur. And if a person feels cared for, hope may open the way for healing. As one put it, "The greatest gift I ever received was another person who believed in me." Viktor Frankl learned a prevailing truth that revealed itself through his experiences in the Nazi death camps of Auschwitz and Dachau: "The truth—that love is the ultimate and the highest goal to which man can aspire."[16] Since love is God's greatest command, a Christian counselor will only be effective as his or her love relationship with God is extended to others in need.

Awareness is a third area essential to Christian counseling. It is a catalyst for the healing process to begin. Viktor Frankl quotes Spinoza as saying: "Emotion, which is suffering, ceases to be suffering as soon as we form a clear and precise picture of it."[17] Another way to look at this is to consider that we cannot change something of which we are not aware. In Mark 10:51 Jesus looked past the blind man's eyes and into the man's heart when he asked, "What do you want me to do for you?" This question revealed that there was more than just a physical need—there was a spiritual need as well. Until this question was asked, the blind man may have been unaware of the great chasm inside his heart. Jesus was giving him the opportunity for this realization.

An ultimate concern for the counselor is helping people recognize the source of their personal pain. Once a counselee recognizes and embraces the pain, Christian counseling provides a safe place where the counselee can discover and implement more useful ways for confronting and dealing with the source of the pain. Defenses can often disable a person from facing threatening challenges. Henry Cloud suggests, "If people can't admit their faults, they can't bring their real self into a confessional relationship with God and others. They can never resolve their critical conscience, and they can never emotionally reach the state of 'no condemnation.'"[18]

THE CHRISTIAN COUNSELOR—
A SKILLED HELPER

A minister is perhaps one of the more likely and best qualified persons a Christian will visit in order to discuss life's challenges. Therefore, there is a tremendous amount of responsibility in Christian counseling. Unfortunately, many ministers graduating from Bible college, university, or seminary may have had only one or two courses in Christian counseling. Consequently, some ministers may feel insecure about their lack of formal skill and methodological development for dealing with complex human issues. Although exposure to formal counseling methodologies may be minimal for many, if not most, ministers, the experience of pastoring does provide opportunities and relationships valuable to a helping counselor. For all in the field of counseling, there are four basic components that can greatly enhance effective counseling.

First, the minister or counselor must have a daily relationship with God and a love for Scripture. Nurturing this personal relationship with God through Christ on a daily basis is the most important and significant skill for counseling. Living in a constant prayer life with the Master Counselor is essential for cultivating the skills and wisdom necessary to care for people at their deepest needs.

Second, the Christian counselor must commit to counsel others only when his or her life is both biblically and emotionally sound. As mentioned earlier in this chapter, the effectiveness of the counselor is greatly hindered when the counselor is attempting to counsel someone about an issue that the counselor is also facing in his or her personal or professional life. It is a difficult task to help someone else when one is facing a similar challenge. Confusion and pain only increase the trauma that one is attempting to manage. Referring people to support groups can be helpful to those struggling with life's challenges.

Third, it is essential for the Christian counselor to learn early on where his or her expertise begins and ends. Since the health field contains many varied and uniquely qualified health professionals in the area of counseling, it is pivotal to learn the art of referring. One very successful minister who has a Ph.D. in an area other than counseling has said,

"I am a spiritual counselor only. I am definitely aware of where my abilities begin and end."[19] Wherever ministry leads one, there will be health professionals who may assist in counseling ministry:

- Psychiatrists are trained medical physicians who diagnose and treat mental disorders. These doctors have completed a residency in counseling; they diagnose the health condition of persons by utilizing the *Diagnostic and Statistical Manual of Mental Disorders* (DSM-IV), a tool of the American Psychiatric Association. They are board-certified in psychiatry for specific areas such as adult, adolescents, geriatrics, or in all three. The psychiatrist may also prescribe appropriate medication for behavioral stabilization.

- Another clinician who may be of assistance is the clinical psychologist, a person with a Ph.D. or Psy.D. in clinical psychology and holding licensure in his or her respective state. These professionals study the science of emotions, behavior, and the mind and will typically specialize in certain psychological treatments for depression and personality disorders. They are able to perform tests such as the Minnesota Multiphasic Personality Inventory (MMPI), which "is the most widely used objective personality test,"[20] the Taylor-Johnson Temperament Analysis Profile (T-JTA), the Myers-Briggs Temperament Indicator (MBTI), the Weschler Adult Intelligence Scale-Revised (WAIS-R), and the Weschler Intelligence Scale (WISC) for children. They are also capable of interviewing and analyzing for Attention-Deficit Hyperactivity Disorder (ADHD).[21] They apply diagnostic treatment from the DSM-IV and typically do not prescribe medications.

- Many states license marriage and family therapists (LMFT) and licensed professional counselors (LPC) who are masters-level counselors. The LMFT is skilled in assessing individual and family issues, whereas the LPC typically focuses on treatment to individuals. Both the LMFT and LPC utilize the DSM-IV in order to prescribe treatment. They are skilled in working collaboratively with other medical professionals but are not able to prescribe medications.

- The licensed social worker is another health-field professional who works with families and assists in improving the overall social condition of the family. Their expertise includes skills related to working as a liaison between the counselee(s) and local and state health facilities.

Finally, the Christian counselor should not work in isolation. Each person is uniquely different in the image of God; consequently, there are no set techniques that work in all circumstances. Ideally, the Christian counselor should work in collaboration with other counseling professionals, perhaps even placing himself or herself under the care of a licensed supervisor for advice and perspective on challenging issues. Consultation is key to giving the best care possible to a troubled and traumatized human being. In Hebrews 10:24–25, Scripture is clear that Christians are to encourage each other and support each other as they face the challenges of life.

CONCLUSION

As we move into this new millennium, the complexity of life has never been greater. God's church should be a place where people find healing and wholeness. A Christian counselor's duty is to facilitate a nurturing environment whereby hurting individuals and families may receive and express God's grace. Christian counseling is a way to help people become transformed into God's image.

It would behoove Christian counselors to learn more about Christian education (which includes methods for coming to an understanding of who God is and how to nurture a relationship with God) and about psychology (knowing and understanding the human spirit). The union of these two very important fields of study will greatly aid in discipleship enhancement. The new millennium presents grave challenges unparalleled in previous centuries. Pastors, theologians, Christian educators, evangelists, and Christian counselors, working together, can make a difference.

NOTES

1. Cited in David Olsen and John DeFrain, *Marriage and Family* (Mountain View, Calif.: Mayfield, 2000), p. 6.
2. George Barna, "The Sad Truth about Christians and Marriage," *The Barna Report* (September-October 1996), p. 6.
3. Don Martin, Maggie Martin, and Pat Jeffers, *Stepfamilies in Therapy* (San Francisco: Jossey-Bass, 1992), p. 9.
4. Gary R. Collins, *Excellence and Ethics in Counseling* (Dallas: Word, 1991), p. 24.
5. Saint Augustine, *The City of God,* trans. Marcus Dods, Modern Library (New York: Random House, 1950), p. 407.
6. David B. Waters and Edith C. Lawrence, *Competence, Courage, and Change* (New York: Norton, 1993), p. 40.
7. Richard S. Taylor, ed., *Beacon Dictionary of Theology* (Kansas City, Mo.: Beacon Hill, 1983), p. 520.
8. Wesley R. Burr, Randal D. Day, and Kathleen S. Bahr, *Family Science* (Pacific Grove, Calif.: Brooks/Cole, 1993), p. 8.
9. Richard Exley, *The Rhythm of Life* (Tulsa, Okla.: Harrison House, 1987), p. 41, cited in Gary R. Collins, *Christian Counseling* (Dallas: Word, 1988), p. 589. (Collins's italics.)
10. La Verne Tolbert, *A Practical Guide to Christian Education in Your Church* (Grand Rapids: Zondervan, 2000), p. 23.
11. Collins, *Excellence and Ethics in Counseling,* p. 17.
12. Michael P. Nichols, *The Lost Art of Listening* (New York: Guilford, 1995), p. 73.
13. Donald W. Welch, "Minister as Counselor," (lecture, MidAmerica Nazarene University, Olathe, Kans., 8 September 1999).
14. Jeffrey J. Magnavita, *Relational Therapy for Personality Disorders* (New York: John Wiley and Sons, 2000), p. 233.
15. Martin Buber, *I and Thou* (New York: Charles Scribner's Sons, 1970), p. 67.
16. Viktor E. Frankl, *Man's Search for Meaning* (New York: Simon and Schuster, 1984), p. 49.
17. Ibid., p. 82.
18. Henry Cloud, *Changes That Heal* (Grand Rapids: Zondervan, 1992), p. 189.
19. Jacob Blankenship, telephone interview with author, 7 May 2000.
20. Jerrold S. Maxmen and Nicholas G. Ward, *Essential Psychopathology and Its Treatment* (New York: Norton, 1995), p. 41.
21. Ibid.

Michael J. Anthony

The single adult phenomena is here, and it is apparent that the trend toward the singles lifestyle will not be reversing itself in the near future. Millions of unmarried adults are creating a new lifestyle that is affecting every corner of North America. This singles phenomenon is by no means restricted to just the Americas. All across Europe, Asia, and other vast reaches of this planet, adults are choosing to postpone marriage to complete personal goals. The singles phenomenon is global in its scope and influence. This trend has far-reaching effects on business, government, and society as a whole. Single adults are setting the tone for much of what this country watches, wears, eats, and enjoys in its leisure time. Our nation's sexual mores have been heavily influenced by this new wave, translating into new laws, policies, ethics, traditions, and values. As a result, sociologists are hesitant to predict what the future holds.[1]

The Bible calls us to be discerning in our ability to relate our faith to the world around us. We must exegete our culture in order to understand how to effectively present the gospel to a lost and needy world. Understanding the world of the single adult requires a good deal of effort. It is far more complex and dynamic than most people realize. Stereotypical television commercials that depict the singles lifestyle as a carefree pursuit of eternal happiness couldn't be further from the truth. The reality is that most single adults are concerned about the same things that their married peers are concerned about: secure employment, housing stability, parenting issues (for those with children), continuing education, finances, health issues, and retirement. Ministry directed toward the single adult requires a thorough understanding of just who the single adult is and what his or her needs are. This chapter has a fourfold purpose: (1) to provide the reader with a biblical perspective on the single adult; (2) to help the reader understand the historical perspective of single adults living in North America; (3) to discuss some trends among single adults today; and (4) to provide some principles to guide those who seek to develop a single adult ministry.

Did You Know?

- There are currently 274 million people living in the United States; of those, 79.5 million are single adults.

- The average single adult professional has 8.2 first dates per year.

- It takes the average single adult woman an hour to decide if she is interested in a first date. Single adult men, however, make that decision in just fifteen minutes.

- The average twenty-seven-year-old has eleven single adult friends. The average thirty-four-year-old has eight single adult friends. The average forty-one-year-old has only six single adult friends.

- The average chance of liking a date set up by a friend is only 12 percent. The average chance of liking a date set up by a family member is 17 percent.[2]

SINGLE ADULTS IN BIBLICAL PERSPECTIVE

God has a long-standing and abiding love for all people regardless of race, gender, age, ethnicity, and marital status. Genesis helps us understand God's initial perspective on single adult living. Although God had provided Adam with all that was needed for his physical needs (e.g., food, shelter, security), he lacked companionship. Even though God had created every beast of the field and the birds of the sky, apparently this was not enough to fulfill Adam's need for social, emotional, and physical bonding, so God created Eve to become his helpmate (Gen. 2:18–25). The pronouncement, "It is not good for the man to be alone" (Gen. 2:18) confirms the basic human need for interaction with others of our own kind. This passage helps us confirm our need for interpersonal relations, companionship, and intimacy with others.

Many of the individuals who were used by God in significant ways were single adults. They were unencumbered by the needs of a family and were therefore able to be used by God in dramatic ways. Certainly the young Joseph, Ruth, Daniel and his three friends, Elijah, and many of the other prophets reveal the desire of God to use individuals to fulfill his kingdom goals regardless of the individual's marital status.

In the New Testament, God provides us with clear teaching regarding the value of remaining single for those who desire a life in ministry. Jesus serves as a primary example of one who chose to remain single so that he could fulfill the greater purposes of his heavenly Father. Jesus clearly taught in Matthew 22:30 that marriage was a temporary state of human experience and that it will not be part of our condition when we enter eternity. Jesus went on to teach us about the spiritual gift of celibacy. He tells us that there are three classifications of celibates, only one of which is seen as God's gift: (1) those who were born with a desire to remain single from birth; (2) those who were made that way as a result of a condition placed on them by others; and (3) those who specifically chose the gift in order to build up the kingdom of God (Matt. 19:11–12).

The apostle Paul builds upon this teaching in his letter to the church at Corinth. Evidently they had written him a letter asking for clarification about the nature of celibacy. Paul stated that one of the purposes of marriage was to avoid sexual immorality. Recognizing the freedom for ministry that was available for those who remained single, Paul desired that all people might have the gift of celibacy as he did in order that they may be more free from the pressures of this life. Paul acknowledged the tension that exists between trying to please God and one's mate (1 Cor. 7:28–35). Paul clearly taught that the unmarried adult has greater freedom to develop his or her relationship with God and be of greater benefit to the kingdom of God in that he or she is less distracted in service.

A commitment to celibacy is first of all a voluntary decision (though, admittedly, few are seeking to make it). Nowhere in Scripture is it taught as a punishment. Those who are the recipients of this gift will receive greater freedom. This freedom is seen in a number of ways:[3]

1. *Freedom from restraints on your time.* Those with the gift of celibacy have the freedom to come and go as they choose, to set their own priorities, and to establish their own patterns regarding the use of their time.
2. *Freedom to live a simplistic lifestyle.* Those who are married must concern themselves with providing for the diverse needs of an entire family. Issues such as what type of car to buy, house to own, community to live in, schools in that community, insurance, and retirement concerns all increase in importance when you're married. Being single allows you to live a simpler lifestyle without having to live up to the expectations of a mate, in-laws, or children. Trying to "keep up with the Joneses" is not as big an issue when you're single.
3. *Freedom to be more efficient in what you do.* Without the demands of a family, you can focus on the contribution you feel is your calling in life. You are free to work more hours, pursue your dreams without being sidetracked, and make a more extended

commitment of your life in some areas, especially avenues of ministry.

4. *Freedom to develop deeper friendships.* It simply isn't possible to maintain the quality of friendships in marriage that you enjoyed before such a commitment. Quality relationships take time to develop and nurture. Time that was once given to developing relationships with many friends has become restricted by the need to contribute to a young marriage bond. This is especially true when dealing with friends of the opposite sex. Marriage does not mean you can't have them, but a wise spouse will restrict the time involvement of such friendships to minimal amounts.

5. *Freedom to serve God.* Paul spoke of his desire for others to be single, as he himself was, because he experienced the benefits of single living every day. It simply would not have been possible for Paul to have accomplished all that he did if he were married. The proof of such a claim is seen in a comparison of the ministries of Peter and Paul. Peter traveled very little after his ministry began—presumably because he had a wife and family to maintain (Mark 1:30–31). Paul was not encumbered by a family; therefore, God was able to use him in such a unique traveling ministry such as church planting.

It should be abundantly clear that God loves the single adult and desires to use him or her to help reach the world for Christ regardless of marital status. There was a time when many Bible colleges taught that you had to be married to serve God in ministry. Such a faulty perspective is clearly not based upon biblical teaching. Though there are many circumstances in ministry where being married would be advantageous, it is clearly not the social requirement that it once was in many local churches and mission boards.

Every child transitions into adolescence as a single. Some choose to get married young, but most prefer to postpone marriage. Some remain single for a longer period of time than others, and the trend in America these days is to postpone marriage longer than in any previous generation. Statistics reveal that half of those who do opt for marriage will return to their single adult life after experiencing a divorce. These are referred to in the popular literature as "single again" adults. For this reason it may be helpful to view single adult living much like the seasons of a year. One begins adulthood as a single adult, at least half of us return to it (via divorce or widowhood) at some point after marriage, and many will return once again as a result of the death of a spouse. Consequently, the average person may be a single adult several times after reaching the age of eighteen. This concept of the "seasons of singleness" helps us understand the dynamic nature of single adult living and sets the stage for our understanding of how to program single adult ministries in the local church.

SINGLE ADULTS IN HISTORICAL PERSPECTIVE

Though the percentage of single adults living in North America is close to 50 percent, it was not always that way. Historically, the single adult population often was far less than 10 percent. In fact, in the 1800s the single adult population hovered around just 3 percent. This was due to a number of important sociological factors. First, it was undesirable and impractical to be single since large families were needed to tend to the many chores on the farm. Second, in some instances it was considered unlawful to remain single, and women who were widowed had the men of the town planning their remarriage before the funeral was over. After all, this was long before the days of welfare and social security. Third, there was simply no practical way for a single woman to endure life alone in a rural community. Therefore, women in particular did not stay single long. There were fewer women than men, and a great deal of attention was paid to having women marry soon. Men and women were married in their early teens and were encouraged to have children quickly so they could endure the rigors of farm life.

As the Industrial Revolution swept across America, factories sprang up in the big cities. This created a need for a large labor pool, so men began to slowly migrate off the farm and into the city. As these men, and eventually women, began this migration pattern, they chose to remain single a little longer now that parents were no longer around to enforce preestablished courtship practices.

Two major events contributed to the reshaping of America's demographics at the turn of the twentieth century. During World War I, men and women were forced to delay marriage while the men were fighting the war in Europe. During the Great Depression, families were put under such an economic strain that parents needed all of their children to work to support the basic needs of family. Leaving your family and no longer contributing financially was viewed as selfish. During the 1930s, the single adult population grew to approximately 30 percent of the United States population.

World War II brought a further escalation to the single adult population because men were once again gone from the scene. However, a big change was about to take place in the lives of many women across America. Women were needed to join the factory workforce in order to supply the armed forces with the heavy equipment and machinery needed to fight the war. Women were employed in the factories in occupations never before imagined. They were employed as welders, assemblers, equipment operators, and pilots. The image of Rosie the Riveter portrayed a woman who stood for long hours on the assembly line dedicated to supporting the war effort. But once the war was over, many of these women no longer wanted to return to life as dependent housewives. They had been given education, training, and a working wage. They had learned how to survive on their own and enjoyed the perks of independent living.

After World War II, most young single women chose to marry and start a family, resulting in the baby boom. The single adult population dipped drastically to only 3 percent of all adults in the U.S. But as career opportunities for women increased, some women now considered divorce as an option for ending destructive or unsatisfying marriages. They no longer needed men for protection and provision and were willing to strike out on their own if needed. Surviving in the working world during the '50s gave them confidence to face the uncertainties of single adult living in the '60s.

During the 1960s, life in America was anything but stable. Hippies preferred to experiment with drugs, sex without commitment, and social anarchy. All forms of civic and social authority, including marriage, were viewed with suspicion. The invention and easy accessibility of the birth control pill allowed men and women to experience sex without the restrictions formerly associated with it. Marriage was no longer viewed as a prerequisite for sex.

In the '70s and '80s, women enjoyed continued freedom to pursue their dreams. They increased in political power, which in turn opened doors of opportunity in education, employment, and government. In 1977 the single adult population living in America grew to an astounding 33 percent of all adults. The trend toward postponing marriage, increasing divorce, a public acceptance of cohabitation, and single parenting contributed to a further escalation of the single adult population. In the mid-1980s, the single adult population hovered around 47 percent until it plateaued in the early 1990s. At this point the tide of our nation's divorce rate began to subside. According to the 1998 Census Bureau statistics (the latest figures available at the time of this writing), the single adult population living in the United States is 40.3 percent.

There is no denying that the number of single adults has increased dramatically during this past century. It is highly unlikely that the percentages will ever go back to what they were during the early nineteenth century. These changes are here to stay and will probably shift only slightly in the next millennium. The important issue for the church today is to recognize who these single adults are and then determine how to minister to this large segment of our population.

NOT ALL SINGLE ADULTS ARE CREATED EQUAL

There was a time when the church viewed all single adults alike. Sunday school was grouped according to those who were married and those who were not married. Those who were not married ranged from age thirteen to sixty. Imagine sharing a classroom as a forty year-old single adult with a teenager just because you weren't married! Needless to say, single adults didn't feel very welcome in the church and left in droves. It was not until we began to examine more closely the types of single adults who were in our communities that we began to understand their unique needs. Not all single adults are single for the same reasons. Each approaches his or her single experience from a different perspective. In essence, we have four categories of single adults: never-married, divorced, separated, and widowed. Each is distinct and unique.

Beyond the obvious differences that exist between these types of single adults, there are also gender and age differences. Men and women experience their single adult years from very different perspectives. For example, a young man may not be overly concerned about finding a mate because he is busy enjoying his independence and freedom. The young woman may feel the same way until she reaches her mid-twenties. At this point her anxiety about remaining single will grow as she sees the window closing on her ideal childbearing years.

Once they approach their forties, however, role reversal will take place. The man will become increasingly anxious about finding a mate who can provide for his needs. The woman, already having learned how to provide for her own needs, finds her anxiety subsiding. She no longer feels the urgency to find a man to protect and provide for her. She has become established in her career and has probably already purchased a house and established a retirement plan.

As these two single adults leave their mid-fifties, another emotional transition takes place. The mathematics of the single adult population living in their retirement years reveals a startling observation. There are far fewer single men available than single women. The single adult male approaching his sixties finds himself being invited over for dinner and out for dancing quite frequently. "Where is the hurry to find a spouse now?" he wonders. The single adult female approaching her sixties is growing anxious about facing life alone with faltering health and uncertain financial demands.

Life as a single adult is anything but static. Just because an individual is a never-married single adult doesn't mean he or she has anything in common with a widowed single adult. Imagine the differences that exist between a single man in his twenties living in a college dorm and a divorced mother of three in her late fifties. They may both be single adults, but they are worlds apart in terms of their single adult experience. That's why it is so important for those who desire to minister to single adults to understand the complexity of single adults living in the United States and Canada

today. No one program will minister to all single adult needs.[4]

The Needs of Single Adults

Single adults are by nature not as religious as their married peers. Surveys reveal they are less inclined to practice traditional forms of spirituality (e.g., prayer, Scripture reading). The following chart illustrates what single adults say best describes their personal beliefs about God (by percent), compared to their married peers:[5]

	Single Adults	Married Adults
God is the all-powerful, all-knowing, perfect Creator of the universe who rules the world today.	65.0	71.9
God represents a state of higher consciousness that a person may reach.	12.3	11.2
God refers to the total realization of personal, human potential.	6.5	5.9
There is no such thing as God.	4.7	2.3
Everyone is God.	3.4	2.5
There are different gods, each with different power and authority.	2.6	1.6
I consider myself to be spiritual.	80.5	81.9
I personally have a satisfying spiritual life.	78.9	86.1
I believe that having a satisfying spiritual life is either a high priority or top priority.	57.3	62.9
I believe that what happens in life is largely a matter of chance.	36.8	25.7

It is apparent from this data that single adults have a long way to go in terms of their understanding about God. What remains is for the church to develop creative and effective avenues for reaching this lost and needy segment of our population.

Since there is such diversity in the types of single adults, it only stands to reason that no one program will meet all needs. A program designed to meet the unique needs of divorced single adults will have little appeal among never-married college singles. Designing a single adult ministry in the local church starts with a survey to assess needs.[6] The key to effective ministry is balance. Few programs will be large enough to meet the diverse needs among all single adults. Try to determine what kinds of singles you have in your community, and then design a focused ministry to meet the needs represented among that cross section of your single adult population.

REALITIES OF SINGLE ADULT MINISTRY

Reality #1: Singles Are Mobile

Single adults are highly mobile and rarely stay at any one church for long. One of the primary reasons why they are single is because they love their freedom and independence. For this reason, don't be discouraged if your singles ministry seems like a revolving door. That is simply the nature of singles ministry. The challenge lies in keeping your regular attenders interested and spiritually fed while at the same time trying to be creative enough to attract new singles.

Reality #2: You Can't Be All Things to All Singles

Look at the kind of single adults you have in your community and target them. If your church is located near a large college or university, focus your ministry toward those needs. Likewise, if you have a large apartment complex nearby, chances are high that you will have numerous divorced and single parents living there. If you are near a retirement community, gear your efforts toward meeting their needs. Don't waste limited resources trying to develop ministries to all segments of the single adult population unless you are a megachurch with vast financial and human resources.

Reality #3: Single Adults Are Sexually Active

A recent survey revealed 75 percent of single adults have had sex with someone in the past twelve months.[7] You may be tempted to assume that just because a large number of your single adults attend church regularly, read their Bibles regularly, pray as often as a monk, and participate in short-term missions projects, they aren't sexually active. Indeed, every survey that has ever been conducted among Christian single adults reveals that they are involved in sexual activities that they know are wrong but in which they are still actively engaged. Since this is a reality of single adult ministry, you will need to gear your program toward several things: clear biblical teaching regarding sexual abstinence, forgiveness, grace, and restoration. If your ministry is not characterized by grace and unconditional love, it will be small and limited in number.

Reality #4: Singles Need Community

Surveys and interviews of single adults reveal the number one disadvantage of being single is loneliness. It takes a lot of time, energy, and effort to establish relationships with people outside of work. If they are making the effort to come to church, do everything in your power to help them assimilate and find a place to belong. Develop small groups where they can develop interpersonal relationships that get beyond superficial issues in their lives. Structure the group so as to provide them with opportunities to serve. Another way to do this is to get them involved in a variety of committees (e.g., social, special events, service projects, sports), as this can help establish a sense of connection and community for many. It will give them a sense of ownership in the group, which is also healthy.[8]

Reality #5: Emphasize Reconciliation and Redemption

Many single adults struggle with feelings of inferiority, guilt over past decisions, fear of what the future may bring, and a host of other issues. They need to see themselves through God's lens of unconditional love and acceptance. Single adult leaders need to remind singles that God cares for them and offers countless opportunities for restoration. Though at times many singles feel unworthy and unwanted, God never turns away from someone who genuinely desires to live a life of holiness. He is there to strengthen and support them in their time of trial.

Reality #6: Market the Ministry

A church that sponsors a single adult ministry will need to let singles know where and when meetings occur. If the target of the ministry is the young college-aged single adult, then advertisements should be placed in the local college newspapers. Different marketing strategies are needed for ministries targeting older singles: flyers and handouts posted on local community center bulletin boards, advertisements run on local radio public service announcements, notices on the Internet via the church home page, posters in community rooms at a local condominium complex, and so on. Look for creative ways to advertise your ministry. One important note: Use printed materials of high quality. Anything less will communicate a lack of interest and concern on your part.

Reality #7: Dating among Single Adults Will Occur

Don't be surprised if single adults in your group begin dating each other. After all, that is part of the reason why single adults come to a singles group. They want to meet and associate with other singles. Many will also be looking for a potential mate, and dating is one means of exploring that option. Most single adult leaders play down this aspect of their ministry, since broken dating relationships can often have a dampening effect on the group unless it is quite large.

Reality #8: Maintaining Christian Standards Will Be a Challenge

Since many of the individuals who are attracted to a singles group are not Christians, it is important that you have standards of acceptable behavior for your events. Consult your church policies regarding whether things like dancing, smoking, or drinking are allowed. You may not be able to control what the single adults do when they are not at a church function, but remember that as long as they are at a church event, you and your church are liable for the actions that occur at and after the event.

The issue of cohabitation is common among single adults. There was a time when society looked down on single adults living together. The term "shacking up" once referred to such a living arrangement. This dimension of the singles lifestyle has grown increasingly common—even among those who attend church on a regular basis. A 1989 study revealed that almost half of all adults under the age of thirty-five had cohabited at some time in their lives.[9] A 1999 U.S. Census Bureau report revealed that there were 4,236,000 unmarried couple households. That is up significantly from only 523,000 in 1970.[10]

Cohabitation presents a difficult dilemma for the single adult ministry leader. Does the leader condemn the couple's action and require them to separate as a prerequisite for coming to church? If so, will the leader lose the opportunity to influence the couple since, in most cases, the couple will leave the church altogether? Or, does the single adult leader ignore the action and take the attitude that private conduct between two consenting adults is none of his or her business? This approach ignores the biblical teaching and gives the impression that the church is condoning their behavior. There may be no ideal answer, but one popular recommendation among many single adult leaders is to ask the unmarried couple living together to attend the couples class instead of the singles group since, for all practical purposes, they are a couple. They should be lovingly counseled to reexamine the appropriateness of their behavior and encouraged to separate or get married.[11]

Reality #9: There Will Be Misunderstandings

Because of the nature of single adult ministry and its unique focus, count on having at least one major misunderstanding every so often. This may be between the single adult leadership and the senior pastor, the church board, or perhaps even the congregation as a whole. Since most church congregations are made up of married adults, they may be suspicious of nontraditional methods or forget how challenging it was for them to be single. The unique and creative methods of reaching single adults may lead to misunderstanding.

Conclusion

Ministry to single adults is both a rewarding and challenging venture. It is not for the faint of heart. However, with the challenge comes the reward of impacting the lives of individuals who have the potential for changing the world. If ever there was a cross section of our society that had the freedom and mobility to radically change the culture in which we live, it is single adults. With reckless abandon, single adults are able to throw themselves into a concerted effort of reaching the world for Christ. More single adults visit the local and foreign mission field each year than any other segment of our population.[12] With skills, passion, and a heart for Christ, they are well on their way to fulfilling the Great Commission. Those who seek to minister alongside these wonderfully chosen vessels of God will have the privilege and opportunity of seeing God move in powerful and at times miraculous ways.

NOTES

1. Carolyn Koons and Michael J. Anthony, *Single Adult Passages: Uncharted Territories* (Grand Rapids: Baker, 1991), p. 15.

2. *Orange County Metro,* 13 January 2000, 33.

3. Ibid., pp. 74–75.

4. For an excellent discussion of this, consult the article, "Generations: Can One SAM Reach Them All?" *Single Adult Ministries Journal* 127 (May/June 1998): 10.

5. "God and Single Adults," *Single Adult Ministries Journal* 130 (November/December 1998): 16.

6. Two excellent articles pertaining to single adult needs assessment can be found in the *Single Adult Ministries Journal* 124 (September/October 1997): 18–19.

7. "Sex and Single Adults," *Single Adult Ministries Journal* 130 (November/December 1998): 17.

8. An excellent resource for building community among your single adults is found in the *Single Adult Ministries Journal* 125 (January/February 1998): 8–15.

9. Bureau of the Census, *Cohabitation and the Measurement of Child Poverty* (Washington, D.C., 1998).

10. Bureau of the Census, *Fertility and Family Statistics Branch* (Washington, D.C., 1999).

11. Susan Bautista and Iglesia Bautista, "Raising the 'Lifestyle' Question," *Single Adult Ministries Journal* 131 (January/February 1999): 14–15.

12. Two helpful resources to help single adults get involved in short-term missions are Paul Clough and Phyllis Ellsworth, "Short-Term Missions with Long-Term Benefits," *Single Adult Ministries Journal* 126 (March/April 1998): 17–18. Also see Michael J. Anthony, *The Short-Term Missions Boom* (Grand Rapids: Baker, 1994).

The Ministry of Christian Camping   28

Richard Leyda

Americans love the outdoors. This has been woven into the fabric of our nation since its founding. We view ourselves as a nation of pioneers and adventurers and have incorporated nature and camping into our heritage and culture. A wide variety of organizations have recognized the value of a camp setting to provide renewing recreation, an educational environment, and socialization of the individual through experiences of group living. Some camps even profess a spiritual dimension for the growth of campers. Christian camps share many of the same purposes with secular camps but are unique in this added spiritual dimension. The central purpose of a Christian camp is to "use as fully as possible the camp experience as an opportunity for discipling individuals toward maturity in Christ."[1]

Considering the camp as an extension of the complete educational ministry of the local church or ministry group has two distinct advantages. First, the camping experience is planned well in advance and within the context of a comprehensive program that has overall goals and direction. The camp educational program actually begins several months prior to the outing, starting with the active involvement of campers themselves in prayer, team building, planning, promotion, and preparatory biblical learning. After camp, the results of the experience can be conserved and extended through continued relationship building, follow-up on life decisions, discipleship training, and guided reflection.

The second advantage of viewing camping as a part of the total ministry of the local church is that the group can utilize the particular strengths of the camp setting to meet objectives that can best be accomplished there. For example, team sports can be played in the city, but developing skills in nature study or wilderness sports might only be possible at camp. Speaker-led Bible teaching times may be effective in either environment; yet individual study in Scripture followed by spirited interaction with cabin mates seldom happens in the city. When choosing the type of camp and its programming, church leaders should consider the unique contributions of camping and select the program that best meets their ministry needs.

Christian camping, like many other ministry areas, is undergoing a great deal of change. Bob Cagle's book titled *Youth Ministry Camping* identifies a trend toward "camping without boundaries." Camp directors and especially youth leaders have felt increasing freedom to go beyond the bounds of what has traditionally been done before. Options for Christian camping ministry are limited only by the vision and creativity of its leaders.[2] New concepts of creative camping might include "designing and implementing a specialty camp for a particular target audience, such as children of divorced parents, a particular ethnic group, or physically or mentally handicapped individuals."[3] Such new designs also include "service camps" where campers are challenged to go beyond serving their own needs to reaching out in Christian service and caring.[4]

A Philosophy of Christian Camping

Camps have been categorized by a number of different criteria. The first and probably most important division relates to a camp's philosophy or underlying emphasis. This approach affects almost all other elements of the camp, including programming, staff selection, training, and facility development and utilization. The two major philosophical approaches are the *centralized* and the *decentralized,* with a third, the *eclectic,* being a blending of the other two.[5] A detailed contrast between the characteristics of the two major philosophies is found in figure 28.1.

The centralized approach corresponds to what traditionally has been called the "Bible conference."[6] The Bible conference, a permanent site camp which experienced its beginning development in the 1920s and '30s, in turn grew out of the "old-time camp meeting" held in the 1800s by many evangelical churches.[7] In many ways, the conference approach simply transferred the standard church service to a camp setting. The focus of the centralized approach, as the name implies, would be on large group participation in standardized activities involving all campers or major segments of the camp population at one time. Programs would tend to focus on professional speakers, musical performances, or other forms of mass communication to the large group. Other elements in the program, such as the cabin group or recreational activities, are usually not seen as central to the spiritual purposes of the camp. These camps are often geared toward evangelistic pre-

Figure 28.1
Comparing General Characteristics:
Camping Philosophies

Centralized	Decentralized
Large group/all-camp meetings and activities	Small group meetings and activities
Program focuses on a few trained professionals	Program focuses on counselor
Bible taught by platform speaker	Bible taught by cabin counselor
Campers receive Bible content by listening	Campers study Bible content on their own
Mass evangelism	Personal, one-to-one evangelism
Life-decision/commitment-making orientation	Discipleship/spiritual growth orientation
Counselor is in a support role to staff and tends to be primarily a disciplinarian	Counselor teaches and conducts activities
Counselors tend to receive little training	Counselors usually receive extensive training
Dormitory-type arrangements	Individual cabin/group arrangements including eating by cabin in dining hall
Central planning of all elements, including programming, by administration	Cooperative, democratic planning of some elements including programming by counselors and campers
Large-scale program elements	Small-scale program elements
Highly structured programs and scheduling	Flexibly structured programs and scheduling allow some spontaneity
Fast-paced programming	Leisurely paced programming
Campers are either spectators of exciting entertainment or participants in all-camp events	Campers are involved as active participants
Recreation focuses on team sports and individual sports and activities under program specialists	Recreation focuses on crafts, nature study, and outdoor skills
Competition to encourage camp spirit is promoted	Individual competes only with self in personal achievement and performance
Site usage tends toward large buildings and playing fields grouped closely together	Site usage tends toward smaller buildings and activity areas that are well-separated and that fit into the natural lay of the land

Note: In actuality, few camps follow either philosophy exclusively but blend them to some degree.

sentations or general calls for deep, life-changing commitment to Christ. Often the recreational programs of these camps will be geared toward such activities as competitive team sports.

The decentralized approach, on the other hand, corresponds to what traditionally was called the "church camp."[8] Organizational camping, which embodied this approach, did not begin until 1885 with the first YMCA camp, which at the time had a strong evangelical emphasis.[9] The camp that follows the decentralized approach emphasizes the small group as the central unit for fulfilling its spiritual purpose. The cabin counselor becomes the focus of ministry; the capabilities of this staff person are crucial in the success of the program. Most of the program, including Bible study and recreation, is accomplished within the dynamic of the small group. Discipleship and accountability, along with the building of relationships, are emphasized. Recreation often emphasizes nature study or skills that are appropriate to the natural environment, and camps often make the attempt to integrate such activities with the biblical teaching.

The eclectic approach attempts to take some of the best elements from each of the two distinct approaches and bring them together in one camp setting.[10] For example, the morning Bible study may be led by the cabin counselor, while the evening may be reserved for an all-camp rally with a speaker and special music. Most Christian camps are tending toward this middle position, an increasingly popular compromise due to the obvious advantages and disadvantages in each of the two extremes. As Todd and Todd note, the majority of evangelical camps probably fall somewhere between the approaches of the centralized conference and the decentralized camp, "endeavoring to inject as much 'real camping' as possible in their program while retaining the aspects of conference programming considered essential."[11]

USING AN EXISTING FACILITY OR CHOOSING THE SELF-DIRECTED CAMP

One final option in camping is of vital interest to most camp leaders in the church and other ministries at one time or another. This involves the choice of whether to use the services of an established camping program or running the program by yourself without the aid of such resources. For some, this may not be a choice at all. Traditional church ties or camp ownership by the denomination may dictate a particular camp facility. Lack of proximity to or availability of a suitable established camp may preclude the option as well. If the leader or leadership team has an option, a number of factors must be considered.

Utilizing the Established Camp

The advantages of using an existing camp are many. They include the availability of trained professional staff, the provision of a wide variety of services and resources, and a consistent degree of quality. Because these elements are provided, church leaders have the freedom to spend time ministering to their campers rather than being concerned with camp details. The presence of trained camp professionals becomes especially important while participating in elements of wilderness camping such as a ropes course, rock climbing, or white-water rafting. During such program elements, health and safety issues become more critical than in camp activities that involve less risk. Trained camp professionals are also more experienced in how to utilize the camp situation for maximum spiritual impact.

It has been estimated that there are over two thousand Christian camps operating in North America.[12] If an existing camp program would be best for a church group, then it is essential to follow the process for selecting the proper camp. First, get recommendations on camps that will fulfill your ministry goals. Ask other pastors about their experiences with various camps. Membership in a national accrediting organization for camps, the American Camping Association or Christian Camping International/USA, is a positive recommendation since each has recognized standards for excellence in camp operation. Each has published lists of member organizations; the *CCI/USA Membership Directory,* for example, gives detailed information on approximately one thousand member facilities.

Spending time with the camp representative is vital, since he or she can help you know whether the camp will be a good match for your needs. Ask questions about anything—observations, concerns, or potential problems. Find out about the camp's history, provisions for the safety and health of campers, and food and lodging arrangements. Discuss programming and ministry options. Find out exactly what services the camp is providing and what the group must supply. For example, often the camping group is required to supply one counselor for a given number of campers.

You should be clear on contractual arrangements, such as the amount of deposit required, to determine if a group can adhere to these standards. Ask whether there is a minimum number of campers you must provide. What happens if your group falls below that minimum? Christian education leaders should look for camp personnel with a genuine desire to serve their group and meet their needs, not those only interested in booking the camp. The Christian camp must see itself as a supportive extension and servant of the church or ministry group, not an autonomous ministry of its own.

After finalizing arrangements and booking the camp, periodic contact should continue with the camp representative to coordinate any further details. This person can be a valuable resource for ideas and materials on promoting the camp to a group and aiding them in camp preparation. After the camp, follow-up contact and evaluation should be conducted with the camp for feedback on the services provided and the degree of effectiveness in reaching the planned objectives. A long-lasting relationship between the camp and the group may emerge from a positive camping experience.

Choosing the Self-Directed Camp

The group that elects to run a camp using its own resources may do so for a number of reasons. The most immediate may be the cost of the program. Rental of the facility alone, without using the program personnel of a camp, will result in substantial savings. A church group will also have the added advantage of program flexibility, which many established camps lack. The group can tailor the camp and the program specifically to meet its own ministry goals. One final benefit that may be overlooked is the advantage of having the campers themselves involved in planning the camp. They may achieve a sense of camp "ownership" and a spirit of teamwork with one another that is not possible when a complete package is provided for them.

If a church or organization decides to run its own camp, a whole new set of considerations and responsibilities becomes important. The biggest single consideration in deciding to run your own camp is the presence of trained, capable staff or volunteers. In fact, lack of skilled small-group counselors is a major deterrent to using the decentralized camp approach. Look for spiritually mature and clear-thinking people to serve as solid Christian models for the campers. The proven Christian character of the individual is primary. While camp skills can be taught fairly quickly to motivated staff, development of solid character takes a lifetime. Wright and Anthony list a number of additional qualifications for the camp counselor, including knowledge of the Scriptures, positive attitude, love, reliability, flexibility, physical health, and a servant attitude.[13]

Pre-camp training sessions will need to be conducted in a number of areas. These will vary according to the type of camp you use and the quality of volunteers you bring. Training sessions should include instruction in Bible study methods, health and safety rules and procedures, small group leadership, and sports or recreation skills. An important focus must be the age-level needs and abilities of the group to be counseled so that all teaching and programming can be geared to that developmental level. Staff should be trained for individual counseling in such situations as leading a camper to Christ or helping a young person who is homesick. Simulations, role play, and case studies can be particularly helpful in these sessions. A training program can provide the additional benefit of team building among the staff, a vital element for a successful camp.

Counseling staff should be trained in emergency procedures, how to deal with sensitive issues, and when to make referrals. In addition, a trend toward more stringent government regulation means camp leaders must be aware of any regulations that will affect a camp's operation. Acquisition of permits and observation of guidelines for use of public lands for wilderness camps are one case in point. Camps involving remote travel place an additional burden of risk on the camp leadership. The camp leader is judged by the "current peer practices" of outdoor professional guides and may be held legally liable in the event of a lawsuit over a camper accident or injury.[14] Unless the camp leader is well-qualified and experienced, a professional guide or wilderness camping leader is highly recommended for the margin of safety provided.

A consideration crucial to the success of any camp is the leadership team. In most cases professional staff, lay leaders, and campers should all be included on this planning team. Among this group's many activities will be surveying the campers regarding their needs and interests, selecting a camp director, choosing a site and major program elements, deciding on a theme, determining a budget, and ensuring that all camp responsibilities are delegated and covered adequately. The planning team should begin meeting well in advance of the event, since popular facilities and speakers often must be contacted many months before the event. After the camp, its job is not done until a thorough post-camp evaluation has been completed.

Also, the more variety in the methods used, the greater the likelihood that all campers will be affected to some degree, since campers vary in individual interests and learning styles.

While many events can be scheduled, others occur unexpectedly. Teachable moments have wonderful potential for learning. Staff should be aware of the educational benefit of spontaneous and unplanned events that transpire in and around the scheduled program. A sudden downpour, a mistake in meal planning, a confrontation between two campers—all serve as opportunities for memorable teaching and learning. Mattson views these teachable moments as one of camping's most powerful forces because they point campers toward personal spiritual discovery.[16] "At camp, every moment holds spiritual potential. The setting, the staff, the program become sources of spiritual input—curriculum."[17]

CREATIVE CAMP PROGRAMMING

A few general considerations should be noted for those responsible for camp programming. The actual camp planning process must begin with goals for the educational ministry based on biblical imperatives and the needs of the campers. Specific objectives should be chosen for a particular camp experience based on these general goals. The philosophy of the camp (centralized or decentralized) and the type of camp should be selected based on the probability that the objectives could be achieved best in that setting.

When planning the actual activities of the camper's day, a number of important concerns emerge. One must first "attempt to re-think camp experiences, going back to the drawing board and asking: Will that activity *really* meet the desired objective in the lives of the campers?"[15] In a thoroughly integrated program, almost every activity, if selected and planned carefully, can support the theme and contribute to one or more of the objectives. Balance and variety are other key concepts to keep in mind. For example, a time for individual reflection, journaling, and prayer can be balanced by providing group time for sharing and worship. The combination of these two learning environments can be more valuable to the spiritual formation process than either one separately.

OPPORTUNITIES IN CHRISTIAN CAMPING

A wide range of opportunities exist for those desiring to minister through camping. The vast majority are short-term positions, usually those of counselor or seasonal program specialist. The importance of short-term staff ministry must never be underestimated. In large measure "camping success rests primarily in the hands of the short term staff."[18] These individuals are on the frontline of ministry. They are able to make the most enduring impact on the campers because they spend the most time with them. Summer or weekend opportunities may be an initial proving ground for leadership development as a young person takes on a role of responsible ministry service, possibly for the first time.[19] This may also be a wonderful opportunity to begin to explore the possibility of full-time camp ministry. The desire to be a servant to children and youth for Jesus' sake is a necessary qualification if camp counselor is the role one seeks. A ready smile, a listening ear, and a caring heart are also essential. This ministry is challenging and sacrificial; the counselor must continually put the needs of the campers ahead of his or her own needs. Yet it is also intensely rewarding as God makes a life-transforming impact through friendship and the counselor's life model.[20]

The pursuit of Christian camping ministry as a full-time vocation begins with honest self-assessment regarding spiritual gifts, character qualities, education, experience in related job skills, and personal desires. Camp professionals have identified such spiritual gifts as hospitality, administration, leadership, and faith as common ones among full-time staff. Interpersonal warmth, transparency, perseverance, and self-discipline are essential personal qualities for this setting. While a college degree is not essential in some camp roles, certified training in camping, Christian education, business, or physical education and recreation can be helpful. While full-time positions in administration and programming are not abundant, opportunities also exist for those with hands-on skills.[21] One must be willing to take an entry-level position and stay at a camp for an extended period of time, since loyalty and commitment are highly valued among staff.

Investigate particular camps and positions that appear to be a good match. Talk to camping professionals and, if possible, serve a long-term internship role at a camp to get a realistic view of day-to-day work. This strategy is particularly important if you want to develop a new camp ministry; find people who are running the desired type of camp, talk with them, and even work with them in an on-the-job training role. Christian Camping International/USA sponsors national and regional conferences that can aid in job networking. This organization also has a number of resources that will assist in the job hunt. These include a directory of member organizations, a computer-based job service for full-time as well as for short-term positions, and ads in the CCI/USA journal.[22] Prayer and seeking the Lord for his direction support the whole process. Camp directors "recruit people who are committed to personal transformation and believe that others can be transformed through positive camping experiences."[23]

THE FUTURE OF CHRISTIAN CAMPING

A number of recent trends present opportunities and challenges as Christian camps enter this new century. Broken individuals and families are the evidence of an ever-increasing need for Christ and the new life he brings in the midst of an increasingly complex society with much information but few answers. The camp's potential to minister to those who need healing and renewal will continue to be more strategic and critical in a world with fewer moral absolutes and little hope. Demand for an ever-broadening range of camp models and programs will grow as children and youth seek new camping options and the church ministers to diverse groups with specialized needs.

A major challenge to quality short-term staffing will be competition from an increasingly wide range of options—such as summer internships—that are available to young adults. Growing environmental consciousness, government regulation, and demand for scarce natural resources such as land and water will make development of new camps and operation of existing ones increasingly difficult. Finally, these challenges and opportunities, as well as increasing demands for quality, will call for professional staff who have training that is more highly specialized than ever.

CONCLUSION

More than any other parachurch agency, the Christian camp occupies a unique position to support the ongoing Christian education ministry of the church. The camp continues a rich heritage of bringing many to salvation, nurturing them in the faith, and developing trained leadership. Those in educational ministry need to recognize the strengths of the camp to provide new environments, programming, and community, and utilize these to accomplish the goals and objectives that both institutions share in common.

FOR FURTHER INFORMATION

Christian Camping International/USA
P.O. Box 62189
Colorado Springs, CO 80962-2189
(719) 260-9400
www.cciusa.org

American Camping Association, Inc.
5000 State Road 76 North
Martinsville, IN 46151-7902
ACA Bookstore: (800) 428-CAMP
www.acacamps.org

NOTES

1. Werner Graendorf and Lloyd Mattson, eds., *An Introduction to Christian Camping* (Duluth, Minn.: Camping Guideposts, 1984), p. 25.

2. Bob Cagle, *Youth Ministry Camping* (Loveland, Colo.: Group, 1989), pp. 20–21.

3. Stephen Venable and Donald Joy, *How to Use Camping Experiences in Religious Education* (Birmingham, Ala.: Religious Education Press, 1998), p. 118.

4. Ibid., p. 71.

5. Graendorf and Mattson, *Introduction to Christian Camping,* pp. 49–61.

6. Floyd Todd and Pauline Todd, *Camping for Christian Youth,* rev. ed. (Grand Rapids: Baker, 1969), p. 30.

7. Ibid., pp. 8–12.

8. Ibid., p. 30.

9. Ibid., p. 5.

10. Graendorf and Mattson, *Introduction to Christian Camping,* p. 57.

11. Todd and Todd, *Camping for Christian Youth,* p. 32.

12. H. Norman Wright and Michael J. Anthony, *Help, I'm a Camp Counselor,* rev. ed. (Ventura, Calif.: Regal, 1986), p. 11.

13. Ibid., pp. 21–30.

14. Tim Sanford, "Caution . . . ," *Group* (June–August 1987): 17.

15. Venable and Joy, *How to Use Camping Experiences,* p. 118 (Venable and Joy's emphasis).

16. Lloyd Mattson, *Christian Camping Today* (Wheaton, Ill.: Shaw, 1998), p. 15.

17. Mattson, "Camp Curriculum," *Journal of Christian Camping* (May-June 1996): 7.

18. Mattson, *Christian Camping Today,* p. 15.

19. Ibid., p. 133.

20. Jim Badke, *The Christian Camp Counselor* (Crofton, BC: Qwanoes, 1998), pp. 12–19.

21. Rebecca Cowan Johnson and Robert Frembling, "How to Get a Job in Christian Camping," Focus Series (Colorado Springs: Christian Camping International/USA, 1999), p. 1.

22. Ibid., p. 4.

23. Venable and Joy, *How to Use Camping Experiences,* p. 119.

James E. Gaffney

Recovery ministry is a new phenomenon impacting churches in the twenty-first century. The young adults who grew up during the turbulent '60s and '70s produced a generation of people who looked for peace and contentment in all the wrong places. Their search took many of them on a long road of drugs, alcohol abuse, and illicit sex. Many of these young people grew into adults with troubled pasts, their lives torn apart and in need of healing.

Unfortunately, the church failed to answer their search as young adults and has also turned its back on them as adults. When these people do enter the church, they fail to find the answers they so desperately need. A few churches have learned lessons from the missed opportunities in the '60s and are now trying to find creative solutions. One of those solutions is the development of a recovery-based ministry designed to provide real answers to their guilt, shame, and addictions.

Recovery ministry is a specialized ministry dedicated to the healing of individuals who have encountered issues in their lives that have become life controlling. These can include compulsive behaviors, addictions, significant family dysfunctions, and a myriad of other painful losses. Recovery is not an easy concept to explain; yet by the end of this chapter, my prayer is that readers will have their ministry worldview broadened. It is also my prayer that readers might be challenged to ex-plore ways in which they can get involved in this growing ministry trend.

BIBLICAL BASIS OF RECOVERY MINISTRIES

The biblical basis for reaching out to broken and hurting people should be obvious to anyone with even a superficial understanding of the Bible. Reaching out to the outcast strikes at the very heart of who God is and the message taught throughout the pages of the Old and New Testaments. The issue, then, is not whether God calls us to love and reach out to hurting people; rather, it concerns the appropriate method of ministering to them.

In Numbers 35 God directed his people to set up six "cities of refuge" to serve as safe zones for people who had inadvertently injured or killed another person. These were to be places of safety where they would be protected from vengeful family members. These are the forerunners of Christian rehabilitation programs whose purpose is to provide hurting individuals with a safe environment where they can process both their sins and the sins done to them. Out of this context can come biblically based healing and proper restitution.

In Luke 4, Jesus begins his public ministry by reading from the scroll of Isaiah. He read a portion of chapter 61 that declares the Messiah's purpose is to bring good news to the poor, proclaim freedom for the prisoners, recovery of sight for the blind, and release for the oppressed. It is obvious from an examination of Jesus' life that he spent time with prostitutes, tax collectors, and the sinners of his day. In essence, he spent time with people needing recovery. In a very real sense, his disciples formed a type of support group.

In 2 Corinthians 1:3–4, Paul encourages us to serve "the God of all comfort, who comforts us in all of our troubles, so that we can comfort those in any trouble with the comfort we ourselves have received from God." In a recovery support group, this is what happens; comfort is passed from God to another through the conduit of recovery experiences.

In Ephesians 4:11–16, Paul tells us that it is the responsibility of gifted church leaders to "equip" God's people to do the work of the ministry. The original Greek word usually translated "equips" or "trains" could also be translated "repair." The common uses of this phrase in Paul's day were for either the medical healing of a broken bone or the mending of ripped fishing nets. Therefore, it could be said that church leadership is called to "repair the saints" so that they can effectively perform the work of the ministry. This clearly explains the focus of what happens in recovery ministries. The people of God undergo repair so that they in turn can repair others in the body of Christ. This takes place in part by sharing their own experiences with Christ (evangelism) and pointing others to the same source of life-giving transformation (teaching, counseling, etc.).

James tells us that our trials come to make us "mature and complete, not lacking anything" (1:2–4). Jesus promised us trials and tribulation in this world. He never promised that we would not experience pain and hardship, but he did promise not to leave us alone (Heb. 13:5) and encouraged us to be of good cheer, for he had "overcome the world" (John 16:33). Jesus walked with people as he walked on this earth. He told us to do likewise. He commanded us to follow his example (1 Pet. 2:21). Recovery ministries are those specialized ministries with the goal of being the incarnational hands and feet of the risen Christ.

No one questions whether the church should visit sick individuals in the hospital, yet we question loving a person who is depressed. Will we wait until a mentally ill person attempts suicide or harm to others before we act? Jesus called his followers to visit those in prison (Matt. 25:36) and bring them the good news of God's love. Are those on a direct path toward incarceration being ignored until *after* they have been arrested, tried, and put in prison?

The issue is not whether Christian recovery ministry is biblical. The issue is how to facilitate Christian recovery in a church that so often turns its back on those in need. Many mainline churches (United Methodist, Presbyterian, Episcopalian, etc.) in North America have such programs, but they often neglect a bold proclamation of the gospel message. Conservative churches, which boast of their evangelistic zeal, often fail to include a heart of grace and mercy in their efforts to reach out to the downcast of society. Both of these traditions miss the point. What is needed is a blending of the two priorities in order to achieve a biblical foundation for recovery ministries.

Who Needs Recovery?

The following is a partial list of the issues that people involved with recovery ministries present for healing:

- ADD and ADHD
- Adult child issues
- Alcoholism
- Anger management
- Anxiety disorders
- Authority struggles
- Bereavement
- Bipolar disorder, manic depression
- Borderline personality
- Chemical dependency
- Codependency
- Counseling referrals
- Depression
- Divorce recovery
- Domestic violence
- Eating disorders
- Exercise addiction
- Family dysfunctions
- Incest
- Inner healing

- Learning disabilities
- Multiple personality disorder
- Parenting and reparenting
- Pastoral misconduct
- Pornography addiction
- Post-abortion trauma
- Post-traumatic stress
- Reconciliation
- Relationship, love addiction
- Safe dating
- Satanic ritualistic abuse (SRA)
- Setting healthy boundaries
- Sexual abuse
- Sexual addictions
- Substance abuse
- Suicidal tendencies
- Verbal abuse

It should be noted that most people come with multiple issues. A pastor of recovery or any other leader in Christian recovery is not expected to have expertise in all of these areas. Instead, a leader in Christian recovery should be familiar with the struggles that are typical within each issue. All healing comes from God, but God often expresses his love and acceptance through knowledgeable individuals who have learned how to care.

A balanced recovery ministry will help individuals view their issues as having multiple components, for example, spiritual, emotional, behavioral, and physical. Dividing issues into separate components does little to speed healing. Often this method confuses already disoriented people. God made us to be multidimensional, so it stands to reason that failure to acknowledge any one element may slow the entire process down considerably. That's why so many secular recovery programs fail to bring about long-term healing. How can they when they fail to consider the spiritual dimension of our lives?

CONTEMPORARY MODELS OF RECOVERY MINISTRIES

Many recovery programs exist outside the church as secular nonprofit organizations dedi-

cated to helping people in need. Some programs (such as Alcoholics Anonymous) started in the church and now enjoy thriving popularity outside the church. Many of these programs are supported by local, state, and federal taxes. They provide people with resources to counter the effects of their dysfunctional lives. They do good work and are worthy of our community support.

Although such secular programs do a great job bringing help to people in need, they are limited in what they can offer. It is my conviction that long-term healing and Christ-centered recovery occur best within the context of the local church. Complex issues are at the heart of many people who come to the church looking for answers from a troubled past. No matter how complex their problems may be, in almost every case the root problem can be traced to sin. Only the church has the answer to this need. It is found in a relationship with Christ and in the unconditional love of a community of believers committed to the restoration and growth of God's prodigal children.

Many churches have recently begun to offer limited resources of recovery ministry to their hurting people. Some of these programs have done amazingly well and serve as models for other churches to follow. Others are in the process of building this "back door" into the church and are looking for further resources.

Counseling programs have proliferated in many conservative Christian churches. These are biblically based, with pastors who have learned to effectively use *only* God's Word as an instrument of healing for hurting people. Thousands have received care and counsel in these types of ministries. Such well-intentioned programs are not without criticism, however, as some participants have felt misunderstood and at times spiritually abused. Some hurting people are just not prepared for this approach and unfortunately feel that God's Word is used to shame rather than heal.

The most common model for an integrated church-based recovery ministry is a Christ-centered Twelve Step program. This approach reaches people through the integration of Scripture and a time-tested curriculum. Some find the standard reading of the preamble, the recitation of the twelve steps aloud, and the praying of the Serenity Prayer to be somewhat liturgical in nature. Nonmainline churches should feel the freedom to make minor modifications in order to more accurately reflect their doctrinal preferences.

Some prominent Christian therapists have sought to integrate solid theological teachings with widely accepted psychological principles. This "Christian psychology" has resulted in a significant stream of books and workbooks that are invaluable resources in the hands of recovery pastors. Larry Crabb, Dan Allender, John Townsend, and Henry Cloud are proponents of this integrated solution. Thousands have gleaned unique insights from their writings, and nationwide seminars have been instrumental in deep, long-lasting healing. Some people struggle with the validity of psychology and reject these approaches. As an alternative, they gravitate toward programs that are more exclusive in their biblical perspective.

The model I currently use reflects the values of this last model. We offer Twelve Step groups dealing with primary addictions, as well as specialized support groups designed to meet unique needs, such as grief support for those who have experienced the death of a loved one. We have developed a peer counseling program where Christian therapists indirectly lead volunteer caregivers in ten sessions of nonprofessional lay counseling. We maintain professional standards for programs, including psychological screening exams. Most of our recovery ministry revolves around a two-year program of small groups and weekly teaching from volunteer Christian therapists. We supplement these meetings with readings from four primary books: *Changes That Heal* (Henry Cloud), *Hiding from Love* (John Townsend), *Boundaries* (Henry Cloud and John Townsend), and *Safe People* (Henry Cloud and John Townsend). The resulting life change of this combined teaching and small group format coupled with the availability of issue-specific groups and peer counseling has been outstanding.

STAGES OF CARE IN RECOVERY MINISTRY

People coming to a church for healing desire a ministry that is specifically created to meet their needs. This isn't unique just to hurting individuals, but it is more pronounced in their cases. Hurting people usually desire one of four types of care:

1. *Support.* Those desiring support want unconditional love and acceptance. They may have heard through the grapevine about your program and arrive in person to check it out. Their "burn victim" antennae are up for any signs of rejection, shame, or spiritual abuse. Your ministry can only pass their tests if they can attend virtually unnoticed for some period of time. They want a strange combination of feeling welcomed and ignored at the same time. They want to proceed at their own pace, and they're testing you to see if you demonstrate a nonjudgmental attitude. These support-minded hurting people will eventually get in the water and swim but only if they don't feel rushed.

2. *Growth.* This stage is for individuals who desire growth more than just support. They are looking for more challenge, committed small group participants who complete assigned homework, and an increased degree of spiritual vitality. They tend to frown on those who are not at their level of growth or on the same pathway of healing. These people know just enough about God's healing and the process of recovery to be dangerous. This group is often not very accepting of others who are slower or further back in the recovery process than themselves. They were once members of the stage-one crowd but have since moved to a higher level of functioning. They are still in the process of healing, but often they are not as far along as they think they are.

3. *Recovery.* These hurting people have often progressed through the two previous stages and learned that they may be in the process of recovery for the rest of their lives. People in this stage understand that they have a choice of either being on the healing side of recovery or in relapse. Their experience has taught them how easy it is to return to their old dysfunctional ways of behavior. They devour any book recommended to them and often buy three or more copies to give to their friends. They are committed to Jesus, recovery, living their program, and maturing no matter what obstacle is put in their way. Unfortunately, they don't understand why everyone else isn't as dedicated to their recovery process as they are. With some

softening over time, these recovery-minded people develop into very caring servant leaders who will embrace other hurting people at all levels.

4. *Servant Leaders.* Those who arrive at the fourth and final stage do so as a result of slowly moving through the initial three stages. These are the individuals who have resumed a healthy lifestyle and desire to reach back to others who are still in process with answers from his or her own experience. They understand that everyone has his or her own road to walk down and are willing to lend a helping hand as needed. They are patient and tempered. They are not naive and have little patience for those who are trying to make excuses for their dysfunctional living. They have developed a firm foundation in God's Word and have learned the accurate interpretation of relevant passages, which they offer with grace and truth, usually in the context of a small group meeting.

PRINCIPLES FOR STARTING RECOVERY MINISTRIES

Recovery ministries exist for people struggling with very difficult issues and for people with troubled lives. I rarely need to advertise for people to attend a recovery group meeting. In fact, if the program is designed properly, advertising is seldom needed. When a church offers a place of unconditional love and acceptance, hurting people will respond. Whether they stay and go through a program of recovery depends on the leaders of the program and the quality of the help they receive.

Here are a number of important considerations for a church that is pondering the formation of a recovery ministry program. These are not presented in any particular order of priority.

1. *Give people the freedom to respond.* Opportunities can be presented to individuals, but ultimately they must choose to respond. Any strategies that even hint of manipulation will be discovered and rejected by hurting people. A recovery ministry should present opportunities for spiritual growth in a safe, nurturing, yet challenging environment.

2. *Don't neglect an emphasis on spiritual growth.* Your program may offer a variety of different program elements, but each one of them should emphasize the importance of a relationship with God. Needy people are searching for ways to connect with God, and they know deep in themselves that they are not right with God. They need no reminders. They need assistance in repairing their spiritual relationships.

3. *Safety is paramount for a recovery ministry.* Appropriate guidelines for support groups and constant reminders of confidentiality are vital for individuals to feel comfortable sharing their deepest and darkest secrets. (See the next section, "Guidelines for Support Groups," for further discussion of this important consideration.)

4. *Be people-centered, not program-centered.* Remember that you are in the business of repairing broken lives. Ministry is not just about applying neatly packaged programs to people's needs. It goes far deeper than that. When you lose sight of people and rely more heavily on program attendance, you have crossed over from an emphasis on people to an emphasis on programs.

5. *Don't be afraid to challenge people.* Challenge is not only desired; it is mandatory. Appropriate challenge is difficult to achieve with hurting individuals and must be approached with caution. However, God's Word provides us with the answers to mankind's greatest needs. We do not need to be ashamed of proclaiming truth. We do, however, need diplomacy to speak the truth with love and grace as Jesus did (John 1:17).

6. *Prepare the church for recovery ministries.* Ministries to the outcasts of society are not always welcome at all churches. Although they should be a component of all churches, recovery ministries are actually only found in a few. Most churches cannot handle the social stigma of having so many broken people as part of their congregations. Too many years of tradition and social standing have influenced their decision making. Having divorced persons and recovering substance abusers in the church will no doubt have an effect on your congregation's personality.

7. *Provide well-trained leadership for the program.* A common mistake is believing that recovery ministry can be led by a "good volunteer with the right heart." The complexity of a recovery ministry requires a designated staff person, full- or part-time depending on the environment. Any church that has tried to do otherwise has usually failed to sustain the program for any length of time. This person will require the assistance of several caring volunteers. However, one responsible, well-recovered individual is mandatory for a successful program. The gender of the leader will not determine success or failure. However, most female-led programs do not draw large groups of men desiring healing. If a woman is designated the key leader, she should seek several male volunteers for visible positions within the ministry to attract men. The leaders need not be members of the church's pastoral staff. However, when they are, it sends a clear message of the importance and priority of this program to the surrounding community.

Because there are so many variables that influence the formation of recovery ministry in the local church, it is difficult, if not impossible, to establish a "one size fits all" approach to designing such a program. There are many resources available to the Christian leader who is seeking guidance in this regard, including books, tape series (audio and video), material on the Internet, and regional and national training conferences.

GUIDELINES FOR SUPPORT GROUPS

The following are suggested guidelines, rules, and boundaries that, when enforced with grace and love, significantly increase the safety that is so vitally important to hurting people. It is recommended that the titles of the seven rules be read at the start of each group meeting to remind people that when these guidelines are bent or broken, the facilitator will hold members accountable. The facilitators' responsibility for keeping their small groups safe and caring is much like a referee blowing a whistle to call a foul in a basketball game. Once they blow the whistle, they explain the foul and quickly get play resumed. The whistle should never be used with a heavy hand.

1. *Anonymity.* This is defined as "keeping my identity secret, confidential, and private from everyone." Traditional Twelve Step groups have accomplished this for years by members only being known by their first names and their last initials. This is important to new members who desire to keep their identities totally secret, and it should always be respected. In our recovery meetings, name tags are left on the front table as people enter, and individuals may choose if they want to wear them. Some put their full name on it, while others use only their first name. Some prefer not to wear them at all. The choice is theirs.

2. *Build trust through confidentiality.* In keeping with Christian integrity, there should be no violation or breach of confidentiality. Refrain from gossip, both inside and outside the group meeting. Gossip is defined here as "any discussion of or about any other group members, without their being present, that is positive or negative, no matter what the intended purpose. What you hear and whom you see here should not be discussed anywhere."

3. *Respect others' boundaries.* This includes boundaries in the spiritual, emotional, and physical realms. We respect each other's needs by not assuming what expression of care they feel comfortable receiving. Some people need a hug to remind them of God's care. Others associate that same hug with painful reminders of abuse. It is important to use discretion and express affection in a manner appropriate to the individual. Persons in the group meeting are to be respected and accepted as they are. The purpose of the support group is not to bring about change but rather to allow change to happen by the hand of God and by choice. Acceptance always comes before change.

4. *Give and receive support and encouragement.* When we come together as a group, we can comfort each other as God has comforted us. This may occur when we share something about our own pilgrimage at just the right

time for someone who needs to hear it. Supporting other persons is *not* the same as giving them advice or trying to rescue them. If we are struggling with a problem, we usually can find at least one other person who has worked through a similar struggle. That person is often the one best-equipped to minister without giving advice. Encouraging one another or affirming one another is excellent and always provides more support than telling people what they should or should not do.

5. *When sharing, focus on your feelings.* We seek to avoid intellectualizing and spiritualizing problems. We refrain from trying to "explain" situations when sharing, and we do our best to clearly identify and share our feelings. Feelings do not require analysis; they require proper response. As we progress in this feeling work, appropriate labels for feelings will develop (e.g., joy, fear, peace, sadness, depression, anger, love, resentment, guilt, loneliness, and fulfillment). Most of us have the opportunity to exercise our minds during the week. The support group time is designed to exercise our hearts.

6. *Remember that the Holy Spirit is in charge.* We realize that the leader is simply facilitating the support/small group. God is ultimately in charge. We ask that all would prayerfully seek the guidance and direction of the Holy Spirit, asking him to be present within each member.

7. *Limit your own talking and allow others to share.* We allow everyone in the group to have an equal opportunity to share. No one is required to speak; however, it is encouraged. When sharing, we will talk about our own experience, strength, and hope without giving a full-length autobiography. We will take turns talking and not interrupt each other.

CONCLUSION

Recovery ministries are used by God to minister to and care for hurting people, although they are certainly not the only methods that God uses. Being involved with recovery ministry changes one's life. Over time you will see dramatic life change and divine healing. You will also see and hear a tremendous amount of pain, sorrow, and hardship. At times I have felt very privileged to serve hurting human beings as a vessel of God's therapeutic touch. At other times, I have wondered why God isn't intervening in this situation in the way I desire him to work. In such times, I have learned to wait patiently on God's sovereignty and rely on prayer as a means of bringing peace.

In my short-lived career as a hospital pharmacist, I witnessed an event in an emergency room one evening that correlates to recovery ministry. An infant child was rushed to the hospital, and a number of the nurses had unsuccessfully tried to give the child an intravenous. The child's small blood vessels were difficult to locate due to severe dehydration.

After many attempts, they contacted a friend of mine who was a pediatric physician and a strong follower of Jesus Christ. He too was unsuccessful in his attempts to locate a viable vein. The life of the child was slipping away. Finally, in desperation this unassuming doctor knelt down in the emergency room, surrounded by about fifteen hospital personnel, and verbalized a simple prayer. The doctor cried out, "Lord, you are the Great Physician. I have tried with everything that you have taught me, and I am failing. Please guide my hands and save this child's life." He stood up and placed the surgical needle directly into a viable blood vessel. He then spoke a simple "thank you" and turned the patient over to the team of caring (and amazed) emergency room personnel. I often benefit from this reminder that without God, I can do nothing.

PUBLIC EDUCATION, CHRISTIAN SCHOOLS, AND HOMESCHOOLING

30

Mary Letterman

A balanced foundation for children to learn and grow is created in an environment where the home, school, and church each present the same messages of biblically based character, values, and purpose. In the early years of American education, all three institutions provided a united foundation. For the most part, a family's values were consistent with the lessons taught at school and at church. Currently, the messages a student receives vary depending upon the type of school environment he or she attends. There are profound implications that exist for those who serve in Christian education ministries. The increased pressure for separation of church and state, a pluralistic approach to education, and the eroding emphasis in society of Judeo-Christian values all contribute to the growing need of effective ministry to church families.

The purpose of this chapter is to present the reader with an overview of the history and foundations of education, to discuss the three approaches to the education of our youth, and to present practical ways in which those involved in Christian education ministry can support and encourage both the students and parents in their churches and local schools.

THE CONDITION OF THE AMERICAN EDUCATIONAL SYSTEM

Many parents find that their local public schools provide adequate academic education, employ teachers who are caring and capable, and fund adequate programs and supplies. Others are openly critical. In a recent Gallup poll, 29 percent of Americans are concerned about violence and poor discipline as the leading problems in public schools.[1]

There have been many changes in public school curriculum over the past few decades. Some parents have been alarmed by the steady secularization of values that these changes have caused. Commenting on the changes, Kidder points out, "We once had a healthy educational system that fostered and trained business and political leaders, plumbers, builders, and electricians whose word was as good as a contract; doctors, lawyers, teachers, and judges with faith and values, who put people before privilege, fearlessly discerned right from wrong, and focused on the well being and the good of others."[2] A morally strong and very different educational system once accomplished just that.

Children learned to read using stories and primers based clearly on biblical truth. Not only did copies of the Ten Commandments and the Constitution hang in the classroom, but teachers upheld them, taught them, and sought to practice them. Communities held teachers accountable for their example to their children.[3] Our major colleges and universities, including Harvard, Princeton, and Yale, were founded on Christian principles. New entrants were required to sign statements of faith in Christ and attend prayer meetings or chapel. These students received an education that was moral and spiritual.

76 ——

David Noebel, author of *Understanding the Times,* says that Christianity has been "deliberately, some would say brilliantly, erased from America's educational system. The direction of America's education can be seen as a descent from Jonathan Edwards (1750) and the Christian influence, through Horace Mann (1842) and the Unitarian influence, to John Dewey (1933) and the Humanist influence."[4] Whether it is humanism in the public school curriculum or the influential New Age movement, both worldviews are in direct conflict with biblical Christianity because they remove God from his place as Creator and Sovereign Ruler over all of creation.[5]

In establishing and maintaining public schools, the government has a compelling interest in providing education to the masses. At its most basic, the purpose is for people to attain competency in reading, writing, and math and to pursue self-supporting employment and/or a profession. In addition, the goal of public education is to produce responsible citizens capable of not only voting but also understanding the issues when they cast their votes. Education should also produce individuals who desire to serve their country by becoming involved in the government of that country at some level.

Through the years, however, public schools have become the avenue for addressing a myriad of social issues including naturalism, alternative sexual orientation, pluralism, AIDS education, and teen pregnancy. Through the inclusion of social curriculum and the push for outcome-based education rather than standards-based education, the achievement levels of students in public schools have continued to fall well below the academic levels of private and Christian school students worldwide. Agenda 2000 articulates the government's goals for measuring improvement in the performance of U.S. students compared to those in other countries. Goal five of that agenda states that our students will be first worldwide in math and reading by the year 2000; yet as of this writing, U.S. twelfth graders still rank near the bottom compared to their peers in the thirty-five ranked countries.[6]

IMPLICATIONS FOR THOSE IN CHRISTIAN EDUCATION MINISTRY

It is important for those in ministry to be aware of the sociopolitical limitations on public school curriculum and the influence that various groups have on the curriculum content. Eighty percent of the students in the various ministries of the church will attend public schools. In addition to the demise of moral and ethical curriculum in public schools, there is in American society and in the media a deterioration of traditional values and institutions such as marriage, family, discerning right from wrong, sanctity of life, and education of children emanating first from parents.

Whether the parents in your ministry have chosen to educate their children at home, in a Christian school, or in a public school, there is an overarching mandate for the church to offer support to all parents as they train their children to be adults who are confident in their relationship with Jesus Christ and in their pursuit of a life pleasing to him.

It is important for us to realize that the home and the church may be the only places where biblical foundations are taught and modeled. Even those parents who choose to educate their children in a Christian school or in a homeschool setting will need support in expressing love to their children, being godly role models, and giving their children a sense of hope and a vision for the future in Christ.

PARENTAL CHOICE: PUBLIC, PRIVATE CHRISTIAN, OR HOMESCHOOL

How then should one approach the decision of where to send your child to school? The primary question that a parent must answer is simply this: Do you want your child educated from a Christian worldview in every area of the curriculum and by teachers who are themselves Christians? If yes, then homeschooling is one option. The second is to seek out an independent Christian school or church-based Christian school that will provide such a setting. These two options will be discussed later. The vast majority of parents will choose to send their children to a public school either because they are unaware of the extent to which Christian values and morals have been eliminated from the curriculum or because they are aware but choose to supplement the school curriculum with the teaching of godly values, character development, and other Christian foundations through home study, parenting, and involvement at a local church. Let us look first at the public school setting and the support needed through the church.

Choosing a Local Public School

In choosing public education for their children, Christian parents need to evaluate the quality of the local public schools and determine which elementary, middle, and/or high school will match the family's requirements. Simply because a school is located in your neighborhood does not mean that it offers the quality of education that you desire for your children. Here are several factors to explore before making your choice:

- What are your child's specific educational needs? (Small class size? Provision for a learning or physical disability?)
- What are the school's expectations for student achievement, including mastery goals? What are the results of student achievement tests of this school compared to other students in the state or nation? What is the dropout rate?
- What behavior standards and student conduct were displayed during your visits?
- Is the school well-run and efficient?
- Is there parent involvement at the school—serving on school improvement committees, as volunteers in the classroom and activities, or in a parent-teacher organization?
- Is there a values or character education program in place? What is it based on? Have you personally reviewed it?
- What provision is made for learning and physical differences?
- What is the quality and turnover rate of the faculty?
- What unique educational opportunities exist for your child?

While advocating ways to make your child's public school education successful, Steven and Virelle Kidder, in their book *Getting the Best out of Public Schools,* illuminate the severe problems associated with public schools. For example, there is a rise in the number of students who exhibit sexual promiscuity, drug and alcohol abuse, smoking, and declining academic achievement.[7] It is im-

portant to discern whether students in your local school are at risk. If your local school exhibits some or many of the indicators below, you may want to transfer to a better school or choose a private school or homeschool as an alternative. To assist in your evaluation, the Kidders have provided some indicators of ineffective schools:[8]

- Attendance rates below 90 percent
- Low reading scores as measured by nationwide standardized tests
- "Safe sex" education and condom distribution (abstinence not presented as an effective choice)
- Gay and lesbian agenda promoted
- Drift from the foundational truths of American history
- Unsafe school climate (poor disciplinary systems)
- Pupil-to-teacher ratio higher than 30:1
- High dropout and suspension rate
- Increasing costs/decreasing student achievement
- High teacher turnover, frequent union problems
- Lack of communication with parents
- Buildings in poor repair

If your school appears to be effective and well-run, parents may choose to stay involved in the public school system. They need to be armed with correct information, possess a willingness to be proactive rather than reactive, and demonstrate a respectful attitude toward others even in the midst of conflict. Christians are needed to influence an environment in which 80 percent of the nation's children will be educated. The decline of American schools and American society will not stop without Christian influence. We need to be salt and light, to offer a distinctly moral and ethical perspective to the development, implementation, and reformation of school policies and curriculum choices.[9]

How can you as a Christian education minister be salt and light in the public school arena? Apart from your efforts within your own church ministry, schools need Christians to serve on school boards and parent-teacher associations, to speak at assemblies, to be present as youth sponsors modeling godly character, and to contribute articles that reflect a moral and ethical foundation to local papers and school publications. In addition, you can continue to present students with scriptural principles and instruction concerning marriage and family. You can help them learn truth through study of the Word. You can model a faith that is active in your relationships and daily decisions.

Support the parents who have chosen public school, but remember that it is critical that Christians continue their efforts to reform the public school system and their own local schools to once again provide an educational system that supports high educational goals and godly values. A graduate from such a school is not only personally committed to a moral life but also "understands and is committed to the moral foundations of democracy: respect for the rights of individuals, regard for law, voluntary participation in public life, and concern for the common good."[10]

Homeschooling

In the last decade, there has been a dramatic rise nationwide in the number of students who are being homeschooled. In 1994, over a million children were being educated at home. This number accounts for about 2 percent of the nation's children.[11] The vast majority of these home educators are Christian couples who see homeschooling as an opportunity to integrate spiritual, intellectual, and character development in a positive, nurturing setting. Debra Bell, in *The Ultimate Guide to Homeschooling,* relates that "it is a proactive stand against a disintegrating culture that splinters families apart and exalts self-absorbed individualism."[12] Homeschooling is increasing in popularity as more couples become disillusioned with public schools.

While most parents first consider homeschooling as a means to withdraw from a public school system that they view as unacceptable, they often proceed with homeschooling because they recognize the positive impact that it will have on their entire family. A dedicated couple who can devote the time to educate in a home setting will receive many advantages. Transference of family and spiritual values is the number one result of the close connection between parent and child in this environment. It maximizes the parental influence

by allowing the parents to spend more quality time with their children. A home that has been changed by the gospel of Christ has a greater opportunity to foster the development of Christlike character in their children.

> **Did You Know?**
> - The number of children being homeschooled in the United States has doubled every three to four years over the past decade.
> - During the 2000 school year, between 1.3 million and 1.7 million children in grades K–12 will be homeschooled.
> - A survey of 5,204 homeschooled students by the National Home Education Research Institute found that 87 percent scored above average in reading, 80 percent in language, and 82 percent in math. (In conventional schools, which are the standard, 50 percent of students scored above average.)
> - Homeschooling is legal in all fifty states. Several states revised their laws restricting homeschooling as the practice became more common over the past ten years.[13]

In addition to the transference of family values, spiritual faith, and the development of Christlike character, homeschooling allows for the individualization of the curriculum. It allows for pacing and presentation suited to the needs of each child in the family unit. It also allows time to delve deeper into a subject and to hold students accountable for mastery learning before proceeding on to the next level or to other subjects. In addition, the parent can expand the exploration of the subject to include tailor-made field trips, time with experts in the field, library and Internet research, and more.

Perhaps the greatest gift that parents give their at-home students is nurturing and the affirmation that they are loved and possess a God-given potential to be successful at what they attempt. Not only is a healthy self-image fostered through this nurturing but also a sense of purpose and worth. More time with parents also builds a bond of communication and interaction that will be foundational to strong relationships with others in later years.

With homeschooling usually comes more time and encouragement from parents for children to play, spend time with friends, read a good book, and build time machines or secret hideaways. In *The Hurried Child,* David Elkind stresses the advantages of giving children time to be children instead of pushing them into adult situations and expectations prior to being developmentally ready.[14] More time for age-appropriate play gives them the gift of growing up unhurried.

Successful homeschool families also recognize the pitfalls that can occur when children are homeschooled. Debra Bell discusses these concerns in depth.[15] The first is the requirement of the teacher to know his or her subject. While most states have affirmed that a parent who teaches his own children at home is not required to hold a teaching certificate, it is true that students are limited by the knowledge and capabilities of their teacher. Those parents who do not seek out support groups or research and do not obtain quality curriculum will hinder the quality of education that their child receives.

To succeed in homeschooling, parents must carefully plan and organize the lessons. While many parents approach the organization and planning for homeschooling in a very commendable manner, following through on daily lessons requires considerable self-discipline. It is also important for parents to hold children accountable for content mastery, study habits, and attitudes.

Other pitfalls that are inherent in homeschooling are the lack of outside recognition for a student's achievements and the lack of competition as a motivating factor that some students need. Becoming involved in various support groups may be the most comprehensive solution to most of these disadvantages. Socializing with other students, whether through Scouts or on the soccer field, helps homeschooled students interact. Some Christian colleges and universities have developed cooperative arrangements with local homeschooling associations in order to provide resources for homeschooled children that would not otherwise be possible. For example, Biola University has developed Biola Youth Arts. This program provides music (band, choir, etc.) and drama performances specifically designed for homeschooled children. These programs allow children to socialize with other homeschooled kids for activities that require a large number of students. Check with a Christian college in your area to see if something similar is available.

The decision to homeschool is a family decision because of the time and energy required by both parents. Meeting the special learning requirements of a gifted child or of a child with learning disabilities may be feasible in a home setting or may preclude homeschooling because of their difficulty. Also factored into the decision must be the financial commitment made when only one parent works to support the family.

One last concern that must be addressed is the legality of homeschooling. Homeschooling is legal in all states as of this writing, although it is subject to some regulation that varies from state to state. A teaching certificate is not required to homeschool in any state as of this writing. In a 1993 ruling, the Michigan Supreme Court found that "families whose religious convictions prohibit the use of certified instructors" are exempt from needing a teacher's certificate to teach one's own children in a home setting.[16] This decision is a reaffirmation of previous state court decisions. Interested parents may research the regulations in their own state regarding homeschooling by contacting the state's department of education.

Christian Schools

The verse that is the primary mandate for parents to educate their children in the nurture of the Lord is Proverbs 22:6: "Train a child in the way he should go, and when he is old he will not turn from it." While parents have the primary responsibility for their children's education, most will delegate the daily curriculum studies to a school. In choosing a Christian school, parents bring the greatest strength to their children's education by partnering with a Christian institution that has special expertise in curriculum and spiritual teaching.

According to Ken Smitherman, president of the Association of Christian Schools International, parents can expect five critical elements to be provided through the Christian school.[17]

1. *Truth.* The revealed Word of God in Scripture is taught as truth. Students learn that they are wonderfully and individually created in the image of God. This truth helps them to understand their own worth and to value and respect the worth of others. They will hear the truth of the gospel and be encouraged to accept Jesus Christ as their personal Savior. They will be led to a deeper knowledge of God through Bible study and chapel programs and through the godly role models of their teachers.

2. *Biblical Integration.* Because all curriculum adheres to some value system, no neutral curriculum exists. Combining faith and learning was evident in ancient civilizations. The Jews took on the early teaching of subjects and religion at home and later turned over the instruction to the local rabbis. Curriculum alone is insufficient to build an adult who has a sense of purpose, is a contributing member of society with excellent character and values, and possesses an ability to stand against the overt and covert enemies of a democratic society. Christian psychologist Clyde Narramore once said, "A tree that is planted in poor soil doesn't have the advantages that one planted in good earth has. Contrary to some beliefs, we do not grow through resistance. Children do not develop because they resist their food. Their growth comes as a result of good food and care."[18] However, proponents of the "salting principle" would argue that children should be put into public schools to act as salt and light in a setting that is weak in many areas and even dangerous in others.

3. *Christian Staff.* The teachers, administrators, and staff in a Christian school are committed Christians who not only know Jesus Christ but model Christlike behavior in their lives, classroom, and leadership. Students see that the teachers' faith is essential to who they are and how they do their jobs. When students begin to emulate their teachers, they move from being self-absorbed to becoming concerned, active Christians.

Many years ago, Yale University president Timothy Dwight said, "Education ought everywhere to be religious education. . . . Parents are bound to employ no instructors who will not educate their children religiously. To commit our children to the care of irreligious persons is to commit lambs to the superintendency of wolves."[19] The New Testament presents a similar principle, "A student . . . who is fully trained will be like his teacher" (Luke 6:40), attesting to the impact that the early years of education have on our children.

4. *Potential in Christ.* The major objective of any school is to help a child reach his or her full potential and be prepared for the next level of learning. Unlike public schools, the Christian school brings every aspect of the learning experience and the child's performance into focus through an eternal view of life in Christ. "In addition to emphasizing how to live in this world . . . the school aims beyond the inward focus of serving self to the outward focus of a life that honors God now and will live and reign with Christ in eternity.[20] Students desire on a deep level to know that their lives will have meaning and purpose. The Christian school is able to openly help the students learn of God's love for them and his desire for an abiding relationship with them in this life and into eternity.

5. *Organizational Practice.* Parents should expect all the school's business and operational practices to be biblically based, including those of policy development and implementation. A strong partnership with parents exists at most Christian schools, and parents should expect clear and open communication, opportunities for volunteers to serve, and involvement by parents in activities and committees. Serving on the school board offers parents the opportunity to provide quality oversight and lend support to the faculty and administration while providing for the needs of their own children and the student body.

During the late 1960s, many small church-sponsored Christian schools were established to meet the demands of parents who wanted their children educated in a Christian worldview. In the '90s, regional accreditation agencies (e.g., Western Association of Schools and Colleges [WASC], Southern Association of Schools and Colleges [SASC], and Association of Christian Schools International [ACSI]) have promoted the improvement of church-sponsored Christian schools and private, independent Christian schools through the accreditation process. A prospective parent should investigate the accreditation status of a school to determine if it meets the standards of a regional accreditation agency or ACSI in regards to teacher requirements, health and safety standards, curriculum quality and teaching effectiveness, and financial stability. One should be cautious if there is no accreditation process pursued at the school. In addition, a parent should evaluate the variety and quality of cocurricular offerings such as music, art, computer, foreign language, and physical education, all of which are crucial to a well-rounded education.

IMPLICATIONS OF CHRISTIAN SCHOOLS AND HOMESCHOOLS FOR CHRISTIAN EDUCATION MINISTRY

There are several ministry implications in meeting the needs of both Christian school and homeschool parents and students. While a Christian school teaches Bible, has chapel services, and educates through a distinctly Christian curriculum, the church is still a critical element. The church provides support through holding the child accountable or encouraging him or her to put head knowledge into practice in friendships, in relationships to parents, in choices made in daily life, and in his or her personal relationship with Christ as exemplified by character. Unfortunately, some Christian school parents leave the bulk of Bible study, prayer, and character education to the school and the church. Through classes, seminars, and support groups offered by the church, the role of the parent can be emphasized and supported as one that is critical to the spiritual development of the child. Attendance at a Christian school or homeschool does not prevent some children from going through an adolescence that requires intervention. Such intervention is often begun or supported through the caring, involved youth workers in the child's local church.

It must also be acknowledged that even private Christian schools have their pitfalls. It can be challenging to motivate Christian students in Bible-related subjects if they are also actively involved in their local church activities such as Sunday school, VBS, children's church, or AWANA. When these children also receive daily doses of Bible stories and chapel services at their Christian school, there is the danger of reaching a saturation point. When this occurs, well-meaning Christian students may find it difficult to remain motivated and excited about their Bible curriculum.

In addition, it must also be acknowledged that there is no such campus as "Utopia Christian Academy." No school, including church-based and private Christian institutions, is perfect. There will be drugs, alcohol, and other illicit activities present. As long as the old nature is battling with the new spiritual nature, there will be manifestations of sin at Christian schools as well. The percentage and degree to which these activities are present will be significantly less than in the public school setting. However, it is best for all parents, Christian educators, and students to have a realistic perspective on church-based and private Christian schools.

Conclusion

The best environment for the maturing of an individual who will grow to be a fully devoted follower of Christ capable of flourishing in whatever career or profession God calls him or her to exists in a partnership between home, school, and church. With the dramatic changes in the last four decades, the burden of providing a quality foundation increasingly rests with the home and the church. We need to be aware of the profound impact our involvement and efforts in Christian education ministries will make on our children in the coming years. The church is always just one or two generations away from extinction. The current generation of Christian students who are in public, Christian, and homeschool settings will be the ministry leaders of our future. What we do in our homes, churches, and schools will determine the strength and vitality of our church in the years to come.

Notes

1. L. C. Rose and A. Gallup, "Phi Delta Gallup Poll," *Phi Delta Kappa* 32 (September 2000): 41–57.

2. Steven Kidder and Virelle Kidder, *Getting the Best out of Public Schools* (Nashville: Broadman and Holman, 1998), p. 6.

3. Ibid., p. 7.

4. David Noebel, *Understanding the Times* (Eugene, Oreg.: Harvest House, 1991), p. 13.

5. Kidder and Kidder, *Getting the Best out of Public Schools,* p. 15.

6. Kevin Bushweller, "Education Vital Signs 1999," *American School Board Journal* (December 1999), 7.

7. Kidder and Kidder, *Getting the Best out of Public Schools,* p. 6.

8. Ibid.

9. Ibid., pp. 13–19.

10. Thomas Lickona, *Educating for Character* (New York: Bantam, 1991), pp. 6–7.

11. Christine Field, *A Field Guide to Home Schooling* (Grand Rapids: Revell, 1998), p. 16.

12. Debra Bell, *The Ultimate Guide to Homeschooling* (Nashville: Nelson, 1997), pp. 34–36.

13. Information collected by the National Home Education Research Institute, P.O. Box 13939, Salem, Oregon 97309. (www.nheri.org).

14. David Elkind, *The Hurried Child* (Reading, Mass.: Addison-Wesley, 1981).

15. Bell, *Ultimate Guide to Homeschooling,* pp. 29–38.

16. Field, *Field Guide to Home Schooling,* p. 19.

17. Ken Smitherman, *Christian School Comment* 31, no. 7 (Colorado Springs: ACSI, 1999), p. 1.

18. Quoted in Paul Kienel, *Christian School Comment* 25, no. 7 (Colorado Springs: ACSI, 1998), p. 1.

19. Ibid.

20. Smitherman, *Christian School Comment,* p. 1.

Jonathan N. Thigpen

The parachurch movement is a major force in evangelical Christianity, particularly in North America. Researchers estimate that there may be anywhere from ten thousand to as many as one hundred thousand parachurch organizations in the United States and Canada.[1] Not only are parachurch organizations growing in number, but some studies suggest they are receiving almost half of the total dollars given to religion, money that in the past might have gone to local churches and denominations.[2] Some of the larger parachurch organizations are well-known, including Focus on the Family, the Billy Graham Evangelistic Association, and Campus Crusade for Christ. They have multimillion dollar budgets, large staffs, and a high media profile. Many other parachurch organizations are less well-known, have modest budgets, and often operate below the radar of the media. And yet parachurch organizations—large, medium, and small—are making unique contributions to the Christian community and to the expansion and edification of the kingdom of God throughout the world.

DEFINITION OF PARACHURCH

Exactly what does the term *parachurch* mean? A proper definition involves breaking the word into its component parts and then viewing the word within its current context. The word *church* is a translation of the Greek word *ekklesia,* which means "assembly" or "called out ones." *Ekklesia* was not a word introduced into Greek by the writers of the New Testament but was a commonly used word they adopted for a specific meaning within their writings.

The term *church* has at least two distinct uses in the New Testament. First, it refers to the "community of all true believers," also called the universal or invisible church.[3] This clearly seems to be the meaning of passages such as Matthew 16:18, Ephesians 1:22, and Ephesians 5:25. Second, *church* is used to refer to a local group of believers who gather together for worship, instruction, fellowship, and ministry, also called the local or visible church. This usage is seen in 1 Corinthians 1:2, 1 Thessalonians 1:1, and Philemon 2. This use of *church* is also clearly evident in Jesus' letters to the seven churches of Asia Minor in Revelation 2–3.

There are two additional meanings of the word *church*. The word is often used to refer to the building in which a group of believers meet on a regular basis (e.g., "Let's go to the church over on Elm Street."). This usage is colloquial, not scriptural. *Church* has also come to mean the denomination of which a local church is a part (e.g., the United Methodist Church or the Roman Catholic Church). But even denominations disagree on whether they are a collection of local churches or one church manifested in many locations.

The prefix *para* is transliterated from the Greek and means "alongside of" (e.g., parallel). Thus, the literal meaning of the word *parachurch* is an organization which is alongside of the church. It is a word that was coined in the 1960s to describe organizations that were clearly religious in purpose but were not local churches or part of denominational structures. Although the term itself is of relatively recent origin, the roots of such organizations reach back to the 1700s.

The most significant work on the parachurch to date is *The Prospering Parachurch* by Willmer, Schmidt, and Smith. They compare the word *parachurch* to two other words that came into common usage about the same time: *paramedic* and *paralegal*. The paramedic is not a medical doctor but is someone trained in emergency medical procedures that can be performed until the patient is transported to an appropriate medical facility. The paralegal is not a member of the bar but has received specialized training so as to be able to assist lawyers in a variety of ways. In both cases, these people work to support and enhance the work of the doctors or lawyers with whom they serve, not to replace them.[4] Thus, we could say the purpose of the parachurch is to support and enhance the work of the local church, not to replace it.

THE RELATIONSHIP OF THE PARACHURCH TO THE LOCAL CHURCH

The parachurch organization as defined above is an important component to the overall work of the kingdom of God around the world. However, a tenuous balance exists between the local church and the parachurch. Jerry White suggests four key areas of controversy in this relationship: the biblical legitimacy of parachurch ministries, the related issue of conflicts in spiritual authority for people in these ministries, the competition for spiritual leaders, and the competition for the same financial support.[5]

White discusses the scope of options regarding the biblical legitimacy of parachurch organizations. These positions range from the belief that the local church is the only God-ordained mode of ministry to the view that every parachurch ministry is on equal footing with the local church because both are part of the universal church. A mediating position would be that parachurch organizations are but temporary structures to meet the needs of churches that do not have resources or trained people able to meet those needs. Regardless of one's position on this specific issue, the parachurch is present, and many in church leadership consider the parachurch movement a good thing.

White's second issue is directly connected to his first: Who has the spiritual authority over parachurch ministries? This issue was brought to the forefront in the 1970s and '80s during a series of scandals and improprieties primarily involving the raising and spending of funds given to parachurch organizations. As a result, all parachurch organizations were lumped together in the public's mind. Donors had nowhere to turn for an objective appraisal of a ministry's fiscal integrity. One of the outcomes of these concerns was the formation of the Evangelical Council for Financial Accountability (ECFA) in 1979.

ECFA was established to assist evangelical parachurch organizations to earn the public's trust through their ethical practices and financial accountability.[6] ECFA helps its members to make appropriate public disclosures of their financial achievements and policies in order to protect their credibility and encourage support from present and prospective donors. Today, it has a membership of over nine hundred charitable, religious, missionary, social, and educational parachurch organizations, all of which are nonprofit and tax-exempt.[7]

ECFA has adopted a set of seven standards with which its members must comply annually in order to stay ECFA-approved. These seven standards require each member to have:

1. A written doctrinal statement affirming the basic tenets of the evangelical theological position.
2. A board of at least five directors (a majority of whom are not employees nor related to employees) that meets at least twice a year and has an audit committee responsible for hiring an outside audit firm.
3. An annual audit of all financial records by an outside firm.
4. Adequate internal controls to ensure funds go to the purpose for which they were raised.

5. Annual audited financial reports available to anyone who requests them.
6. A conflicts-of-interest policy that is designed to avoid them altogether or publicly disclose them when they exist.
7. Compliance with twelve ECFA fundraising standards, which include: honesty in all fundraising appeals, full disclosure of the use of all funds, premium and incentive guidelines, and acting in the interest of the donor.[8]

While not addressing all of White's concerns, ECFA has certainly been a step in the right direction in providing some oversight of parachurch organizations.

White's last two concerns are related to the competition between the local church and parachurch organizations for scarce resources of both people and finances. First, the church and parachurch are not just competing against each other for leaders; they are also competing against the secular world. Since it is God who through the Spirit gives gifts to believers and gifted individuals to the church universal (Eph. 4), there are biblical grounds to believe God will provide the leadership needed for both local church and parachurch ministries. The competition for finances may be more reflective of an ongoing shift in giving patterns away from specific institutions to specific projects, whether in the local church or parachurch.

There are several practical steps leaders in both the local church and parachurch can take to ensure harmonious relationships between each sphere of ministry. Local church leaders should consider these steps:

1. *Get to know the parachurch ministries your church is already supporting.* Call or write for information regarding their governance, doctrinal position, financial controls, and availability of financial reports to the public. Keep a file on each organization, and make the information available to the congregation.
2. *Invite a representative of the organization for a visit to establish lines of communication.* Use the time to express any concerns you have about the organization.
3. *Seek an opportunity to meet with the top leadership of the organization when available.* If you live near an organization's offices, set up a tour of their facility.

4. *Identify the members of your congregation who work for parachurch organizations.* Encourage their involvement in the various ministries in your local church. You may discover that these men and women have specific gifts that can be a tremendous asset to your local church.
5. *Pray regularly for the parachurch ministries your church supports.* Ask them to supply specific items for which your congregation can pray.

Leaders of parachurch organizations can take several steps to bridge the gap between their ministries and the local churches that support them.

1. *Encourage your employees to be active participants in their local churches.* The temptation for employees of parachurch ministries is to view their employment as the only ministry in which they should be involved. Often parachurch ministries receive criticism because their employees are not more than church attenders.
2. *Parachurch leaders should seek counsel from local church leaders among their constituency.* Too often parachurch ministries unintentionally give the impression that local churches exist to fund their ministries, when the opposite should be true. Parachurch leaders must listen to those on the frontlines of ministry.
3. *Parachurch ministries should seek to work with local churches in their geographical area to fill positions in their organizations.* Parachurch leaders should take every opportunity to honor local church pastors and provide programs that are of direct help to them.
4. *Parachurch organizations that are not members of ECFA should consider membership or seek to uphold the same fiscal standards.*
5. *Parachurch leaders should seek to establish lines of communication between parachurch organizations, especially those with similar ministries.* There may be aspects of ministry that are duplicated that could be combined. This would not only help the organizations but local churches as well. Willmer, Schmidt, and Smith write:

The key to role clarity is dialogue. Leaders from the church and the parachurch need to be in contact with each other. The expectations of both sides must be frankly stated and discussed. Financial issues must be touched on, so that each side can come to understand the other side's financial concerns and needs. As talk proceeds, church and parachurch will begin to see that those they consider their competitors actually are fellow workers.[9]

A BRIEF HISTORY OF THE PARACHURCH MOVEMENT

Correct analysis of the modern parachurch movement is possible only in light of the historical development of such organizations. Although the parachurch movement today is far broader than Christian education, its roots go deep into the foundations of modern Christian education. The following historical survey will view the development of parachurch organizations primarily related to the field of Christian education.

The beginning of the modern parachurch movement could be traced to the beginnings of the Sunday school. The Sunday school was started in London in 1780 by Robert Raikes, a newspaper publisher. Although the Sunday school would ultimately become an integral part of the vast majority of churches in North America, the movement also spawned a plethora of parachurch organizations to support its growth and development. (See chapter 1 for a review of the Sunday school movement.)

The rapid growth and popularity of the Sunday school movement spurred the development of Sunday school conventions that began meeting in various parts of the United States and throughout the world on a regular basis. These conventions were attended by thousands of Sunday school teachers looking for training, inspiration, curriculum materials, and help with organizational issues. The ultimate outgrowth of a national Sunday school convention held in Philadelphia in 1824 was the formation of the American Sunday School Union (ASSU), which is today known as the American Missions Fellowship (AMF).[10] The mission of the ASSU was ambitious. Clarence Benson writes, "[It was] to concentrate the efforts of Sabbath School societies in different portions of our country; to disseminate useful information; to circulate moral and religious publications in every

part of the land; and to endeavor to plant Sunday Schools wherever there is a population."[11] The ASSU was perhaps the first parachurch ministry of the modern era in the United States.

With the expansion of the Sunday school movement came the beginnings of Christian publishing houses that were producing curriculum materials to be utilized in the schools. Although denominations led the way, there arose the need for materials that were nondenominational in nature. David C. Cook, a teacher in one of Dwight L. Moody's Sunday schools in Chicago, worked in his father's print shop during the week. In 1875 Cook began producing Sunday school curriculum materials and started what would become David C. Cook Publishing Company. Although at first a for-profit company, the nonprofit David C. Cook Foundation was incorporated in 1942 as the owner of the publishing house. Today known as Cook Communications Ministries International, it continues as a nonprofit foundation that owns the for-profit Cook Communications Ministries, the largest nondenominational producer of Sunday school and other Christian education curriculum.[12]

In addition to Sunday school publishers and conventions, a new breed of highly educated religious educators saw a continual need of reform in the Sunday school movement and looked for ways to exert their leadership. George Albert Coe and William Rainey Harper were at the forefront of this movement. Harper was frustrated with the leadership of the Sunday school movement; they were primarily laypeople who for the most part had no formal training in education. Harper sensed that these untrained Sunday school teachers and leaders had a limited vision for what the Sunday school could become.[13]

In 1903 the Religious Education Association (REA) was created as an interdenominational organization promoting religious education. From its beginning, the organization took an ecumenical approach to religious education. Philip Lotz writes, "The R.E.A. has sought the answer to the question of how to improve the cooperation of orthodox and liberal Christians, orthodox and liberal Jews, and unchurched idealists."[14] At its first meeting Harper, now considered the founder of the organization, urged that the REA be universal, cooperative, scientific, and pioneering in spirit.[15] From its beginning, the organization opened its membership to individuals.[16]

While the REA was working primarily with leaders in the academic world, the International Sunday School Association (ISSA) and the Sunday School Council of Evangelical Denominations (SSCED) were focused on working with denominations, denominational publishing houses, and local churches. The ISSA was founded in 1908 as the outgrowth of the national Sunday school convention movement, and the SSCED was founded in 1910 with the hope of providing standardization of Sunday school curriculum and teacher training. In 1922, the International Council of Religious Education (ICRE) was created by the merger of the ISSA and the SSCED, with forty denominations in the United States and Canada becoming charter members.

The Bible institute movement in America began with A. B. Simpson in 1882 in New York City. D. L. Moody started what was to become the Moody Bible Institute in 1889. Simpson's and Moody's efforts were the beginnings of an avalanche of over thirty Bible institutes that were started from 1886 to 1915. The original focus of the institutes was the training of laypeople for ministry in the local church. However, by 1950, the emphasis had been expanded to include the professional preparation of pastors and missionaries for full-time ministry. This happened in large part because the fundamentalists believed theological liberalism was infiltrating the major American theological seminaries of the day.[17]

In 1933 Henrietta Mears, director of Christian education at Hollywood Presbyterian Church, started Gospel Light Publications as a publisher of Sunday school curriculum. Gospel Light continues today as a leading independent publisher for evangelical churches. In 1934 Clarence Benson of Moody and the Evangelical Teacher Training Association (ETTA) teamed with Victor Cory to begin Scripture Press Publications in Chicago. Benson and his Christian education students wrote the curriculum, while Cory printed and distributed it. Scripture Press became part of Cook Communications Ministries in 1996.

Christian Service Brigade was started in 1937 as a church-based boys club organization. Young Life was started that same year as a ministry to high school students through Bible clubs during the school year and camping programs in the summer. In 1939 Pioneer Girls began as a club program for girls.

In 1942 the National Association of Evangelicals (NAE) was founded to provide evangelical denominations and churches an alternative organization to the liberal-controlled Federal Council of Churches (now the National Council of Churches). The mission of the NAE is "to extend the kingdom of God through a fellowship of member denominations, churches, organizations, and individuals, demonstrating the unity of the body of Christ by standing for Biblical truth, speaking with a representative voice, and serving the evangelical community through united action, cooperative ministry, and strategic planning." From its first convention attended by 147 delegates, the NAE has grown to approximately 50 denominations (totaling 43,000 congregations), local churches from an additional 27 denominations, several hundred independent churches, and about 250 parachurch ministries and educational institutions. The NAE has started several dynamic subsidiaries over the years, the best known being the National Religious Broadcasters and World Relief.[18]

Near the end of World War II, large meeting rallies designed to minister to servicemen in major cities of the United States led to the beginning of Youth for Christ (YFC). In addition to its rally ministry, local YFC clubs were started in high schools. The ministry has continued to grow into an international organization.

In 1950 AWANA (the name taken from an acrostic of 2 Timothy 2:15, "Approved workmen are not ashamed") was started in Chicago as a club ministry to boys and girls. Featuring fast-paced games and an emphasis on Bible memorization, AWANA has grown to be international in scope.

Youth with a Mission (YWAM) began in 1960 by providing teenagers evangelism training and sponsoring mission trips with those teens to places around the world. The 1960s saw a growth in Christian camping throughout North America, which led to the organization of Christian Camping International (CCI) in 1961.

The 1970s saw a renewal in youth ministry and creative forms of Christian education. In that decade, Youth Specialties (1970), Group Publishing (1974), and Walk Thru the Bible Ministries (1976) all began and have continued to grow in their influence into the present. The 1970s also saw the growth of parachurch ministries focused on television broadcasting and cable networks, such as the *700 Club* and the Trinity Broadcasting Network (TBN).

In the 1980s and 1990s, there was explosive growth in what has come to be known as contemporary Christian music (CCM). Parachurch organizations relating to the writing, publishing, recording, distribution, performance, and broadcast of CCM sprang up across the continent. There was an increase in the number of Christian bookstores. Specialized age-group ministries such as the International Network of Children's Ministry (1980) and Teen Mania Ministries (1986) found receptive constituencies for their ministry niches.

CATEGORIES OF PARACHURCH ORGANIZATIONS

The growth of the parachurch movement has had its fastest growth during the last fifty years of the twentieth century. While many parachurch organizations are directly or indirectly involved in Christian education, the scope of these organizations is as wide as the needs of humankind. In recent years there have been attempts to classify parachurch organizations as an aid to local churches looking for help in specific areas and Christians looking for employment within the parachurch world.

Richard Leyda has suggested seven broad categories of parachurch ministries:

1. Missions
2. Evangelism and discipleship
3. Childhood and adolescent ministries
4. Camping and recreation
5. Schools and educational institutions
6. Media and technology
7. Special interest[19]

For a number of years, the National Association of Evangelicals (NAE) has biennially published a *National Evangelical Directory,* listing about 3,900 parachurch organizations. Because this directory also includes ministries not directly affiliated with NAE, it is perhaps the most exhaustive list of parachurch organizations that consider themselves evangelical in theology.[20]

ISSUES FACING PARACHURCH MINISTRIES IN THE TWENTY-FIRST CENTURY

The amazing growth of the parachurch ministry movement, due in large part to its unique fit with the mind-set and context of the contemporary Western church, is certain to continue into the twenty-first century. However, this optimistic view of the future of the parachurch is not without its challenges. At least five major challenges confront the parachurch movement today.

First is the challenge of leadership. Many parachurch ministries that were founded by strong charismatic leaders are now facing the question of who will take over their leadership in the near future. For example, the Billy Graham Evangelistic Association (started in 1950 by Billy Graham) and Campus Crusade for Christ (started in 1951 by Bill Bright) are already seeking the next generation of leaders to follow in the footsteps of the founders. Many lesser-known parachurch ministries face a similar challenge. The World War II generation is making way for the Baby Boomers, who will ultimately turn over the reins of leadership to members of Generation X. The parachurch organizations that prioritize the preparation of younger leaders are those that will survive the transfer of leadership.

Second is the challenge of funding. George Barna has found that although slightly more than half of all adults in the United States give money to a church in an average month (54 percent), Baby Busters (ages 17 to 34) are less likely to give (35 percent) than are adults 35 and older (61 percent).[21] Thus, both churches and parachurch organizations are faced with devising new strategies for educating givers and raising funds to maintain the growth rates of the last twenty years.

Third is the challenge of the growth and influence of the megachurch. Barna considers a megachurch to be a congregation of one thousand or more in average attendance.[22] As these large churches grow, there is an increase in the resources at their disposal. Thus, the size and resources of the megachurch are allowing some congregations to take back ministries often passed off to parachurch organizations by small to middle-size churches. For example, a megachurch may have the staff, equipment, and capital to produce customized curriculum materials for their various educational ministries. This trend has in part been fueled by the availability and affordability of desktop publishing programs, clip-art software, and high-speed networkable laser printers. Such a megachurch may not need the parachurch publishing house; it may actually be the other way around. Another example is of the megachurch that has it own camping facility. In this case, it has not only replaced their need to use other camp facilities in the area, but they are in some cases competing with them for rental groups.

Fourth is the challenge of emerging technologies. Some have likened the development of the Internet and World Wide Web in the 1990s to be as significant a technological leap as the invention of the printing press by Gutenberg in 1452. The ability of the parachurch to harness these and other newly developed technologies for the growth of the kingdom of God and serve as a resource for local churches to do the same is critical. Already Christian education programs offering everything from certificate programs through Ph.D.s are available online.[23] An important question is whether the parachurch will be ready for the next technological wave that is sure to come.

Fifth is the challenge of the relationship of parachurch ministries to the government. In many locations there is an uneasy truce between nonprofit organizations and local, state, and federal governments. The latter sees lost revenue rather than positive contributions to society. To this point, the Supreme Court of the United States has upheld the tax-exempt status of nonprofit organizations, but it is an issue that is likely to surface again, especially if the parachurch movement continues to expand.

CONCLUSION

The parachurch movement in North America, which started with the Sunday school over two hundred years ago, continues to grow and expand in helping local churches fulfill the Great Commission. Though the relationship between the local church and parachurch has been a tenuous one, organizations like the ECFA have provided a standard of integrity that local churches can trust. A key factor in improving relationships between the local church and parachurch is for each side to build bridges of communication to the other.

Three parachurch organizations particularly helpful to Christian educators are the Professional Association of Christian Educators (PACE), North American Professors of Christian Education (NAPCE), and the Evangelical Training Association (ETA). There are many opportunities for involvement in parachurch organizations in both paid and volunteer positions. The parachurch movement faces some serious challenges ahead, but there is also a multiplicity of exciting avenues of life-changing ministries around the world.

NOTES

1. See Richard J. Leyda, "Parachurch Ministries," in *Foundations of Ministry,* ed. Michael J. Anthony (Wheaton, Ill.: Victor, 1992), p. 310; and Wesley K. Willmer, J. David Schmidt, and Martyn Smith, *The Prospering Parachurch* (San Francisco: Jossey-Bass, 1998), p. xii.

2. Willmer, Schmidt, and Smith, *Prospering Parachurch,* p. xi.

3. Wayne Grudem, *Systematic Theology* (Grand Rapids: Zondervan, 1994), p. 853.

4. Willmer, Schmidt, and Smith, *Prospering Parachurch,* pp. 12–13.

5. Jerry White, *The Church and the Parachurch: An Uneasy Marriage* (Portland, Oreg.: Multnomah, 1983), pp. 31–32.

6. For the complete text of ECFA's mission statement and statement of faith, see their Web site: www.ecfa.org.

7. For detailed information about ECFA members, refer to www.ecfa.org.

8. "Seven Standards of Responsible Stewardship," www.ecfa.org/7standards.asp.

9. Willmer, Schmidt, and Smith, *Prospering Parachurch,* p. 184.

10. C. B. Eavey, *History of Christian Education* (Chicago: Moody, 1964), p. 253.

11. Clarence H. Benson, *The Sunday School in Action* (Chicago: Moody, 1941), p. 19.

12. From Cook Communications Ministries Web site: www.cookministries.com.

13. Stephen A. Schmidt, *A History of the Religious Education Association* (Birmingham, Ala.: Religious Education Press, 1983), pp. 29–30.

14. Philip Henry Lotz, ed., *Orientation in Religious Education* (Nashville: Abingdon, 1950), p. 450.

15. Marvin J. Taylor, ed., *Religious Education: A Comprehensive Survey* (Nashville: Abingdon, 1960), pp. 360–61.

16. Schmidt, *History of the Religious Education Association,* p. 35.

17. Gene A. Getz, *MBI: The Story of Moody Bible Institute* (Chicago, Ill.: Moody, 1969), p. 69.

18. From NAE Web site: www.nae.net.

19. Richard J. Leyda, *Foundations of Christian Ministry* (Wheaton, Ill.: Victor, 1992), pp. 314–19.

20. From NAE Web site: www.nae.net.

21. From Barna Web site: www.barna.org.

22. Ibid.

23. From Association of Christian Continuing Education Schools and Seminaries (ACCESS) Web site: www.access web.org.

INDEX

Index

Index

Index

ITHACA

ITHA<A

A NOVEL BASED ON HOMER'S *ODYSSEY*

PATRICK DILLON

PEGASUS BOOKS

NEW YORK LONDON

ITHACA

Pegasus Books Ltd.
148 W 37th Street, 13th Floor
New York, NY 10018

First Pegasus Books edition July 2016

Interior design by Maria Fernandez

Library of Congress Cataloging-in-Publication Data is available.

ISBN: 978-1-68177-155-7

10 9 8 7 6 5 4 3 2 1

Printed in the United States of America
Distributed by W. W. Norton & Company